To ANDY—

WONDERFUL INTRO—

JAMES RIELY GORDON

James Riely Gordon. *Portrait ca. 1909, photographer unknown, courtesy Lucy Virginia Gordon Ralston.*

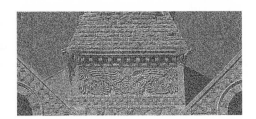

James Riely Gordon

HIS COURTHOUSES AND OTHER PUBLIC ARCHITECTURE

Chris Meister

TEXAS TECH UNIVERSITY PRESS

This book is typeset in Monotype Albertina. The paper used in this book meets the minimum
requirements of ANSI/NISO Z39.48-1992 (R1997). ∞

Design, composition, and project management by Books By Design, Inc.

Library of Congress Cataloging-in-Publication Data
Meister, Chris, 1957–
    James Riely Gordon : his courthouses and other public architecture / Chris Meister.
        p. cm.
    Includes bibliographical references and index.
    Summary: "Describes, analyzes, and contextualizes the courthouses and other public build-
ings of James Riely Gordon, an architect working in Texas in the late nineteenth century who
went on to establish his reputation at a national level. Includes photographs and illustrations"—
Provided by publisher.
    ISBN 978-0-89672-691-8 (hardcover : alk. paper) 1. Gordon, James Riely, 1863-1937—
Criticism and interpretation. 2. Public architecture—United States—History—20th century.
I. Gordon, James Riely, 1863-1937. II. Title.
    NA737.G627M45 2011
    720.92—dc23
                                                                          2011026596

Printed in the United States of America
11 12 13 14 15 16 17 18 19 / 9 8 7 6 5 4 3 2 1

Publication of this work was made possible by a generous grant from The Summerlee
Foundation.

Texas Tech University Press
Box 41037
Lubbock, Texas 79409-1037 USA
800.832.4042

ttup@ttu.edu
www.ttupress.org

TO KATHRYN AND EDWARD,
FOR PROVIDING MY FOUNDATION,
AND KATIE, FOR MY STRUCTURE.

A courthouse, more than any other structure, is expected to elevate and educate public judgment to discriminate and appreciate an architectural masterpiece.

JAMES RIELY GORDON

~~

Contents

~~ɔ

Illustrations

COLOR SECTION, FOLLOWING PAGE 128

Preface

James Riely Gordon (1863–1937) may well be the country's most prolific designer of county courthouses. Although essentially self-educated, he rose to the top echelon of talented architects working in Texas in the late nineteenth century. From there he went on to New York City, where he cemented his reputation among public building designers on a national level.

He is perhaps best remembered for his Texas courthouses, which include some of the finest regional expressions of the Richardsonian Romanesque style. Noteworthy as it is, this work represents only half of a career that touched upon many of the issues and events shaping American architecture, including the effort to organize as a profession, the controversial Office of the Supervising Architect of the United States Treasury, the "golden age" of Texas courthouse construction, the 1893 World's Columbian Exposition, and the City Beautiful Movement. In the East, Gordon demonstrated that he was equally adroit working within Beaux-Arts classicism as he was in the Richardsonian style.

Gordon's career was long, prolific, and spread over a wide geographic area. It would require a volume much larger than this to capture every significant aspect in detail. While such a chronicle would be unwieldy, the study of Gordon's area of specialization, his courthouses, provides a suitable perspective for an initial consideration of the man and his art. This approach also allows for discussion of the politics and scandals that sometimes accompanied these commissions and provides insight into the overlooked business side of public architecture. However, Gordon designed many fine buildings in both the public and private sectors that still await further study.

While constructing this narrative, a problematic issue arose in addressing the various terms given to county-level governmental offices in different states. For example, Louisiana's Police Juries fulfill roughly the equivalent function as New Jersey's Boards of Chosen Freeholders and Texas's Commissioners' Courts—that of an elected executive board. There seemed to be no satisfactory way to discuss the governmental offices other than to use the legal, local terms (awkward as that can sometimes be) with a brief explanation at the point of their first use. Adding to the potential for confusion are group titles such as grand juries and building commissions, but every effort has been made to draw distinctions within the text.

What follows is the first major monograph on J. Riely Gordon. It is hoped it will encourage further scholarship on this worthy architect.

JAMES RIELY GORDON

CHAPTER ONE

Catching on Nicely

James Riely Gordon's success as an architect is a bit of an anomaly. His background is devoid of the benefits enjoyed by the prominent designers of his day: he had no formal education in his art, he had no association with a well-known architect, and he established himself far away from the urban areas where the profession garnered the most critical attention. He compensated for these shortfalls with talent, ambition, hard work, and a dogged pursuit of opportunities. Ultimately, he was rewarded with a very successful architectural career in which he specialized in the design of public buildings, primarily county courthouses. Perhaps the most conspicuous recognition of his achievement was an invitation extended to him to participate in the 1912 New York County Courthouse competition. Restricted to a select few, the invitation reveals that his contemporaries placed Gordon's courthouse work on par with such architectural luminaries as the firms of McKim, Mead & White and Carrère and Hastings.

This accolade came thirty years into a long career that stretched across much of the United States. That Gordon achieved such success is all the more remarkable given his limited schooling and upbringing near the frontier.

James Riely Gordon was born August 2, 1863, in Winchester, Virginia, the son of George Muir Gordon and Sarah Virginia (Riely) Gordon. He typically used his middle name, which was pronounced "Riley." His father had been a civil engineer with the US Army and later rose to the rank of major in the Confederate army. Often referred to as Major Gordon, after the Civil War he worked as a surveyor in Washington, DC, during the years the city was governed as a territory (1871–74). Much-needed public improvements were implemented during this period, and engineers were in particularly high demand. The work bankrupted the city/territory, however, and Congress resumed direct control under a cloud of scandal. Major Gordon moved with his wife and son to San Antonio, Texas, in 1873 or 1874 as the Federal City's brief experiment in territorial governance drew to an end.[1]

One of the earliest Spanish colonial towns in the Southwest, San Antonio follows a design dictated by ordinances set down in 1573. Implementing Renaissance-era ideals in town planning, the "Law of the Indies" governed Spain's settlements in the New

World. Among other details, it directed that towns be built around a main plaza left open as a public space with the principal church, the local council house, and commercial structures around its periphery. Additional plazas were mandated throughout the municipality as well.[2] In observation of this decree, San Antonio's Main Plaza was marked off on July 2, 1731. Establishing the town was the third of Spain's three-part colonization process; the other components were the religious conversion of the indigenous population and a military presence. Toward these ends, missions were established in the area as early as 1718, and an outpost garrison occupied a site later known as Military Plaza beginning in 1721. Work began in the 1730s on permanent structures for the five famous missions in the vicinity, including Mission San Antonio de Valero, which is more familiar now as the Alamo. This work stretched on for decades. Construction on the church (now cathedral) of San Fernando began in 1738.[3] Situated on the block between Main and Military Plazas, San Fernando's original design reflected the Moorish impact on the colonists' heritage (fig. 1.1).

In 1873 the town was described in *Scribner's Magazine* as having "a thoroughly European aspect" where, in one of the Mexican sections, "the life of the seventeenth century prevails, without any taint of modernisms." The ever-present ruins of the missions were still very much an attraction, providing "here and there hints of the Moorish spirit." Yet, the city was enjoying many of the advantages of post–Civil War urbanism. Streets bustled with wagons filled with goods bound for frontier communities, military outposts, and Mexico. Numerous shops offered as wide a variety of goods as could be had just about anywhere at the time. Local limestone was the favored building material for a nascent building boom that saw two- and occasionally three-story business houses going up on the principal streets such as Commerce.[4]

In San Antonio, Major Gordon set himself up as a land agent and Virginia operated a boardinghouse in the family's home.[5] Young Riely attended public school, and his formal education ended in 1878 with his graduation at age fourteen. He then entered the civil engineer corps of the International-Great Northern Railroad. At the time, positions such as this provided the typical basis for a career in civil engineering, and Gordon cited his work there as valuable experience in the construction arts.[6]

Late in 1881 Gordon began a brief period of employment under architect William K. Dobson. The door of Dobson's office at 10 Yturri Street proved to be a portal to Gordon's lifelong career. It was also an entry into a vocation that in the early 1880s had few serious practitioners in San Antonio. Indeed, there were few in the state. This decade would develop into the seminal years of architecture as an organized profession in Texas. Designers cautiously joined together to build respect for their art while competing against each other for coveted commissions. Some of these founding architects would, along with Gordon, leave their personal marks upon the Texas landscape. The careers of these architects, very briefly introduced here, intertwine with that of Gordon.

1.1.
Military Plaza, San Antonio, Texas. Stereoview ca. 1875 showing the Moorish-influenced rear section of San Fernando Cathedral on the left. *Courtesy Prints & Photographs Division, Library of Congress.*

Any discussion of San Antonio's architecture during this period must recognize the prominent role of Alfred Giles (1853–1920), acclaimed by the *San Antonio Express* as "one of the pioneer promoters of correct architecture in Texas." Born and educated in England, Giles came from a wealthy family that supported his studies. After a brief period of employment with an architectural firm, he left for the United States and settled in San Antonio. Finding employment with a contractor, he provided designs while gaining familiarity with regional building materials and skill levels. Giles opened an independent architectural practice in 1876. In the following decade he authored many impressive commercial and residential structures in San Antonio and the region. He also designed a number of county courthouses, including nine built in Central and West Texas during the early 1880s.[7]

Giles's first courthouse work came in 1881, the year the state legislature passed an act enabling counties to finance courthouse construction by selling bonds. The legislation was expanded to include county jail construction in 1884.[8] Texas counties were now able to incur debt to finance their public buildings, marking the start of a "golden age" in courthouse construction that continued during Gordon's practice.

Additional factors contributed to this boom. The increasing state population engendered the creation of new counties needing new courthouses. At the same time, growth in older counties rendered their facilities inadequate. Advances in building construction, such as fireproofing, sanitation, and electrical service, also caused many to consider older courthouses obsolete. Fireproofing (or more accurately, fire-resistant construction) was particularly crucial since courthouses held vital paper records at a time when flames commonly ravaged communities large and small.

The 1881 legislation allowed county officials to consider larger, more elaborate buildings than they otherwise may have. Citizens often enthusiastically supported such projects even though it increased their tax burden. There were powerful incentives for this, particularly the promotional value that a courthouse offered counties encouraging immigration and commerce. Both were thought necessary to fuel growth and wider prosperity. County promoters sought immigrants, asking them to leave familiar surroundings for places not far removed from the frontier and where Indian depredations and banditry were real concerns. Those considering business transactions in a county sought assurance that legal remedies were available should those transactions go awry. For both groups, a substantial courthouse was seen as tangible evidence of local commitment to the Rule of Law. Indeed, the then commonly used phrase *temple of justice* was synonymous with *courthouse*. Of course, such perceptions could be misleading, but a fine courthouse was an effective draw nonetheless.

Communities serving as the seat of county government had an added interest in ambitious courthouse construction. These towns prospered by being the center of local government, and a costly structure tended to anchor the seat where it was built: taxpayers were not inclined to abandon such an investment on a whim. Conversely, a small or poorly built courthouse undermined the security of a county seat since any need for replacement created an opportunity to move. Courthouses, therefore, were usually intended to last longer than other contemporary structures. (Later in life, Gordon stated that a courthouse should serve for a hundred years.)[9] Such considerations justified incurring public debt through bond sales as an investment in future prosperity. For an architect, a courthouse project was attractive for its relatively large commission and the promotional boost it could give a career. Furthermore, it was an opportunity to create a monument and a legacy for its author.

Today, as in Gordon's era, responsibility for a county's physical improvements rests upon its board of directors, called the "Commissioners' Court" in Texas. This body is composed of four members, titled "commissioners," who are elected by districts and one member, titled "county judge," who is elected by the entire county. All five enjoy an equal vote and have the power, as a group, to levy taxes and determine how they are spent. This is their source of authority in raising funds, choosing designs, and letting contracts for courthouse construction. Despite the terms *Commissioners' Court* and *county judge*, this board's role is administrative and should not be confused with regular courts of law, such as the state's district courts, which are also held in county courthouses. (There was, in Gordon's time, a narrowly defined exception to this that becomes relevant in Chapter 5.)

These somewhat cumbersome terms reflect the Mexican antecedents of Texas government. Prior to Texas Independence, a local magistrate governed regional areas with the assistance of a judicial council. Smaller districts within the region were represented by an elected *comisario*. Briefly stated, the judiciary eventually became separate from county administration, but the latter's executive board retained the titles "judge" and "court" while absorbing the "commissioners."[10]

Because courthouse construction was often the most costly single project a county undertook, decisions related to it were often the subject of controversy. Debate often became heated, as opposition politicians were quick to exploit the fears of citizens wary of their liability for public debt. (While a majority may have voted for the project, support was rarely universal or unqualified.) As a result, many courthouse projects were surrounded by accusations, founded and unfounded, against officials or those they hired. Of course, occasionally such projects were indeed used to defraud taxpayers, but jealousy and greed may have been the more common motivations for criticism by those missing out on the spoils. Guilty or not, elected officials were rarely penalized beyond being voted out of office. Architects and contractors, however, were attractive targets for prosecution. They could easily find themselves "taking the fall" for collaborating politicians or, if innocent, scapegoats in a real or fabricated scandal. Alfred Giles was caught up in one such local imbroglio over the El Paso County Courthouse, as noted below.

Another San Antonio architect, James Murphy, came to the city around 1876—the year Giles hung out his shingle. Little is known about Murphy's origins and it is difficult to determine his exact role on a number of structures he is associated with. In addition to his design work he was often employed as a superintendent. It was not unusual for architects of the time to provide this service for their own projects or those designed by others. Superintendence involved approving the work of the contractor and verifying that the plans (architectural drawings) and specifications (written instructions) were followed. To affirm superintendents' authority, their approval of work vouchers was usually required before a contractor was paid. (For clarity, this volume distinguishes between *superintendence* and *supervision*, the latter of which is defined herein as the contractor's management of his own workforce. The terms were often used interchangeably in the past.)

Unfortunately, contemporary sources rarely differentiate between Murphy's design projects and his superintendence work. We do know that by the end of 1886 Murphy had been involved in the Southern Hotel, the Adams and Wickes Building, the McDermott Building, and the Joske Brothers' Store Building (not to be confused with the later structure designed by Giles). Newspaper accounts establish his authorship of the Dullnig Block, the Smith Block, and San Antonio's five ward public schools, as well as the homes of many local notables.[11]

Irish-born architect William K. Dobson (ca. 1839–?) came to San Antonio by way of Nashville, Tennessee, where he enjoyed previous success as an architect. One of his more prominent designs there was the Vine Street Temple, an exuberant example of Victorian exoticism (fig. 1.2). Dobson drew upon Middle Eastern motifs in recognition of Judaism's geographic origins. As the temple neared its 1876 completion, one commentator found himself "inadequate to describe the exact style of architecture. Mr. W. K. Dobson, the architect who in his ever ready and versatile genius, succeeded

1.2.
Vine Street Temple,
Nashville, Tennessee (1876,
demolished). William K.
Dobson, architect. *Courtesy
Tennessee State Library &
Archives.*

in combining the oriental with many other styles, producing thereby a most majestic
and happy effect." A prominent feature of the façade was an imposing onion dome of
galvanized iron, surrounded by eight smaller ones, looming 145 feet above the street.
Inside, the concave ceiling was deemed "perfectly adapted to acoustics, which was held
in paramount consideration during its erection. The finest modulations of the voice
can be heard in the most remote part of the building."[12]

Dobson left Nashville for unknown reasons and was practicing architecture in San
Antonio by 1879. Within three years he built a practice second in local prominence
only to that of Alfred Giles. Among Dobson's public designs is an unsuccessful entry
in the Texas State Capitol competition early in 1881. Although there is no detailed
description of it, the *San Antonio Daily Express* recognized his submission's "novelty
and originality" while noting that it was not as "gaudily polished" as other entries. The
newspaper also considered it a leading contender, but this may reflect a bias toward the
sole competitor from San Antonio.[13]

Gordon entered Dobson's employ a few months later. At the time, the senior architect was advertising "plans and specifications for public and private buildings in the
city or country." In the realm of public architecture, we know the Dobson-designed
San Antonio Central High School was constructed during Gordon's employ (fig. 1.3).

1.3.
Central High School, San
Antonio, Texas (1882). William
K. Dobson, architect. *From the
San Antonio Daily Express,
February 20, 1888.*

The styling of this three-story, limestone structure shares much with the classic reserve of Giles's designs. This may have been intentional imitation on the part of Dobson or simply a demonstration of how local materials and craftsmanship influenced the architecture of San Antonio. Nonetheless, Dobson did assert his Victorian proclivities through the school's spirited observatory and clock tower.[14]

Gordon often cited his time with Dobson as being very instructional, and it is likely he learned valuable lessons about acoustics from the author of the Vine Street Temple. Stylistically, it seems Dobson's Victorian exuberance was passed on to his apprentice, seen most directly in the Aransas County Courthouse (see Chapter 3). However beneficial Gordon's apprenticeship with Dobson may have been, it only lasted about a year. Dobson entered into partnership with James Wahrenberger (1855–1929) in the fall of 1882, and Gordon left the office about the same time. The reason for his departure is unknown, but perhaps young Gordon felt it was he who should have been made partner or he simply did not get along with Wahrenberger.[15]

Dobson left the city at the end of the year, reportedly bound for the Hawaiian Islands to superintend construction of public buildings.[16] Inquiries made to Hawaiian historical organizations for this volume uncovered no documentation to establish that he ever arrived at this destination, however. The post–San Antonio fate of the man credited by Gordon for his training is currently a mystery. Wahrenberger continued to practice from the office on Yturri Street, taking on Albert F. Beckmann as a partner.

Gordon then worked as a draftsman for J. N. Preston & Son. A native of New York State, Jasper N. Preston (1832–1922) had been a draftsman himself in Lansing, Michigan, in the early 1870s, possibly working for Elijah E. Myers, whose Michigan Capitol was then under construction. Preston began his own practice in Austin in 1875 and was appointed superintendent of construction for the new Texas Capitol project in 1879. Although he assisted the capitol commissioners on much of the preliminary work for the design competition, he resigned from the position in April 1881 (just before the prize was awarded to Elijah Myers). Shortly thereafter, Preston's son, Samuel A. J. Preston (1858–89), joined the practice. Jasper maintained his Austin office and residence while Samuel, who studied at the Massachusetts Institute of Technology, ran a newly opened San Antonio branch where Gordon worked. Its offices were above the Groos National Bank at 45 West Commerce. Samuel Preston boarded at the Gordon house at 272 East Commerce Street.[17]

The *Austin Statesman* reported that the Prestons had been involved with every public building in that city. While the senior architect authored a number of public designs, the courthouse and jail for Bell County (constructed in Belton between 1883 and 1885) is one of the few credited to the firm of J. N. Preston & Son (fig. 1.4). Commissioners' Court records indicate the county contracted with the Austin office, but it is possible that Gordon was involved with some of the work during his employment.[18] Bell County's courthouse is an elaborate Renaissance revival structure built of limestone quarried in the Belton vicinity. Grand porticos surmount entrance loggias on all four façades and lightweight sheet metal was employed in the construction of the center tower and the cornices. The structure also features the corner pavilions that are typical of many Texas courthouses of the era. Such a commission would have been an ideal educational experience for Gordon.

J. N. Preston & Son closed its San Antonio office before the fall of 1884. Perhaps the Prestons had been disappointed in their attempt to make a significant inroad into the city's building boom. Samuel returned to Austin to continue the architectural practice he shared with his father. Two years later they moved the firm to Los Angeles, California.[19]

As the years passed, Gordon placed great importance on his experience with Dobson. Given its short duration, this seems overstated.[20] Meanwhile, he curiously ignored his work with Jasper Preston—who may have more public buildings to his credit than Dobson—and his MIT-schooled son Samuel. Gordon's failure to acknowledge this experience may be an indication that it was not a happy time for the young draftsman. Another possible explanation is that the Prestons were in competition with Gordon while they were still in Texas. Dobson, in contrast, was likely no longer in the state

(whether or not as far away as the Hawaiian Islands). Gordon could boast about his employment with Dobson, perhaps even embellish the details, without risk of losing business to him. Another motive for Gordon to elevate his tenure with Dobson was to hide the fact that he was, in reality, mostly self-trained. One may look back on Gordon's accomplishments and marvel at this fact, but he surely saw this as a liability as he competed against designers with formal education in architecture.

When the Prestons closed their San Antonio office, Gordon opened his own and shortly thereafter, near the end of 1884, entered into a partnership with Frederick B. Shelton. Touting his graduation from a London school, Shelton was much older and had experience in New York, Chicago, and other large cities. In San Antonio, he previously partnered with James Murphy. Gordon and Shelton billed themselves as "architects and superintendents," officing in the space vacated by J. N. Preston & Son in the Groos National Bank Building.[21] The office had a telephone, which was rather novel. Information on this period in Gordon's career is sparse, and Shelton's responsibilities in the partnership are unknown. Gordon seems to have been the primary salesman and maintained a higher profile in the press. Equipped with an outgoing personality, well-developed sense of humor, and a penchant for storytelling, Gordon worked as an itinerant architect traveling to other communities to find work for the firm. On these trips he carried generic plans for a variety of structures that he adapted to the specific needs of anyone he could interest.[22] While some of this travel was undoubtedly horse-drawn, Gordon appears to have relied heavily on the rapidly developing railroad system for business. A study of the architect's known work finds most of his early structures in communities along rail lines connecting with San Antonio.

His first commission in the public realm was a jail for a newly organized West

Texas county. On March 1, 1885, Val Verde was created from sections of Crockett, Kinney, and Pecos Counties. Its business was conducted in a rented store in the county seat of Del Rio beginning in May. Over the next several months, the Commissioners' Court selected a site for future county buildings and on December 14 voted to advertise for plans and specifications for a jail. Interested parties were apparently anticipating the vote since, within a mere five days, the officials had considered several proposals and chose the plans offered by the construction firm of Martin, Byrnes & Johnston of Colorado City. Later records identify J. R. Gordon as the architect.[23] In the absence of evidence to the contrary, it appears that the Val Verde Commissioners' Court solicited submissions only from building contractors and not architects. This was not unusual at the time. While some contractors surely prepared their own plans, Martin, Byrnes & Johnston apparently recognized that Gordon's talent could give them a competitive advantage. This arrangement also provided the young architect with an opportunity that may not have been otherwise open to him.

The firm of Gordon & Shelton was chosen by county officials to superintend the jail's construction in January 1886 and Gordon personally oversaw the work. Within a month he had made a name for himself in Del Rio, drawing the attention of a local newspaper, the *Dot*, and its proprietor, the engaging Miss Lottie Lyons. With tongue in cheek, the *San Antonio Express* remarked that

> Riley [sic] Gordon, a San Antonio favorite, has "caught on" nicely at Del Rio. The *Dot* calls him the "handsome and brilliant young architect." If he can stand that from the prettiest young lady in the west and survive, there is no salvation for him....[24]

Val Verde's jail was completed in the fall of the same year (fig. 1.5). It is a rectangular, two-story building not unlike many built in the West during the 1880s. Although it has virtually no ornamentation, its sound composition and subdued detailing exhibit the presence of a capable, if neophyte, architect. Local limestone is used for the entire exterior with walls random coursed and quarry-faced while such details as lintels are dressed smooth. Rugged walls above a slightly battered base convey solidity while the proportion and rhythm of the window and door openings suggest security but not oppression. The jail is severe, utilitarian, and was appropriate for a new, frontier county's first building. Reports from Del Rio boasted of the jail as being "a very beautiful, as well as a very strong and durable structure." It was equipped with four double-deck steel cages from the Pauly Jail Building and Manufacturing Company of St. Louis, a nationally renowned supplier of jail equipment, for the containment of prisoners.[25]

This $20,000 structure was also used to hold court until the county could fund and build a more suitable temple of justice. This dual use allowed Gordon to be essentially accurate when he elevated the structure to the status of courthouse in some

1.5.
Val Verde County Jail, Del Rio, Texas (1886). Gordon & Shelton, architects. *2008 photograph.*

accounts of his achievements at the time.[26] The county began building its permanent courthouse in 1887 to a design by Jacob Larmour and Arthur O. Watson of Austin. After its completion, Gordon's building continued on with the sole function as a jail. A three-story annex was added onto the rear sometime later, and it was remodeled for offices around 1956. Gordon & Shelton's jail for Val Verde County still occupies the southeast corner of the courthouse square in Del Rio, and it is likely the earliest extant example of Gordon's work. Although the jail is a competent design, it does not reveal the Victorian flair that characterizes his later work.

Back in San Antonio, Gordon & Shelton had built a practice that was respectable but not exceptional. The city itself continued to grow, demanding new buildings. According to the *City Directory*, the field had increased to six architects and firms operating in 1885. Of these, five principals—Beckmann, Giles, Gordon, Murphy, and Wahrenberger—would play a significant role in San Antonio's building boom over the following years.[27]

Their profession was beginning to mature on the state level, as witnessed by the January 1886 formation of the Texas State Association of Architects (TSAA). The association's charter objectives were to "unite in one common fellowship the architects of Texas; to combine their efforts, so as to promote the artistic, scientific and practical efficiency of the profession; and to cultivate and encourage the kindred arts and to correct unprofessional practices." This appeal for unity was key at a time when one of the obstacles to establishing their art as a profession nationwide was the penchant of architects to defame each other. In the words of an early TSAA president, Wesley

Clark Dodson of Waco (not to be confused with Gordon's mentor), "We cannot expect success if each is trying to work the injury of others by deprecating all merit, and, by innuendoes and evil speaking, seeking to pull others down so that we may rear ourselves upon their ruins." Such backbiting, along with politically motivated accusations as discussed earlier in this chapter, would dog Gordon's courthouse work.[28]

The Texans were part of a wave of professionalism that moved west through the United States as architects tried to differentiate themselves from builders and amateur designers. The American Institute of Architects (AIA) formed as a national organization in 1857 but operated as a rather exclusive gentlemen's club dominated by northeastern designers. Outsiders complained it had an elitist internal hierarchy and admission was restricted to members' friends. Although dominated by Chicagoans, the Western Association of Architects was far more egalitarian in its organization. Established in 1884, it formed associations with local organizations like the TSAA and soon rivaled the AIA in influence.[29] While differing in their composition, these groups and various state and local organizations shared the same goal of securing respect for their work.

One of the TSAA's charter members was Alfred Giles, who had dominated San Antonio's architectural scene with over $2,250,000 in buildings to his credit by 1886. He was suffering a professional setback in that year, however, due to groundless, politically motivated attacks related to his El Paso County Courthouse work. This assault led to a farcical trial that culminated in Giles being jailed briefly for perjury. After a three-year battle the architect cleared his name in court, but for a while his practice was reduced to clients with personal knowledge of his true character. During this lull in his career, and probably in part because of it, Giles left with his family for an extended trip abroad. They returned to the San Antonio area in March 1887, whereupon the architect drew from an inheritance to begin acquiring land for Hillingdon, his beloved ranch near Comfort. For a while the requirements of a gentleman rancher appear to have occupied his attention at the expense of his architectural practice. It was not until January 1888 that Giles returned in earnest to the San Antonio architectural scene. As he took control of the design for the Joske Brothers' new mercantile emporium, it was announced that the esteemed architect was ready "to enter business again as vigorously as ever."[30]

This interruption of Giles's career may have been a factor aiding two talented interlopers, the novice Gordon and newcomer Wahrenberger, in their establishment of successful San Antonio practices. Gordon, with his public school education and on-the-job training, lacked the impressive credentials Giles and Wahrenberger possessed. Gordon's growing portfolio of work was still relatively modest when a major professional opportunity presented itself. This was the long-anticipated building of the United States Courthouse and Post Office in San Antonio.

CHAPTER TWO

The Federal Building

The role of the United States government grew in the two decades following the Civil War, giving rise to a federal building boom as new structures were needed to house expanding services and bureaucracy. Fueling the movement were lobbying efforts by communities across the country hoping to host government offices. This civil building program reached San Antonio in 1886 and played a pivotal role in Gordon's career.

The Office of the Supervising Architect of the United States Treasury was established in 1852 to oversee the design and construction of nonmilitary buildings for the United States government. A system developed in which the Supervising Architect, appointed by the secretary of the Treasury, and his staff drew up the plans and specifications for federal buildings and contracted their construction to local firms. Builders worked under a superintendent representing the government's interests, often a local architect appointed by the Supervising Architect. This system, designed to regulate the appearance of federal buildings while preventing shoddy workmanship and overpricing, was not without critics. Among the most vocal were the nation's top architects and the AIA, who felt wrongly shut out from these prestigious commissions.[1]

Nevertheless, civic leaders pressured their congressmen to secure appropriations for these projects. Even more than a county courthouse, a large federal edifice was a landmark signifying a city's success. It also furnished construction employment and raised surrounding property values. Federal politics, however, often outweighed need and qualifications in the distribution and staffing of such projects.

In 1882 the House of Representatives' Committee on Public Buildings and Grounds acknowledged the need for a federal courthouse and post office building in San Antonio. Government agencies were operating from leased facilities scattered about the city where federal documents and other property were insecure and vulnerable to fire. Although the city's growth generated enough increased tax and postal revenue to easily justify new, more fitting quarters, nothing came of the committee's recommendation. A similar proposal two years later, which had the support of the US attorney general and the postmaster general, also languished. Perturbed San Antonians believed that partisan politics played a role in Congress's denial of their Federal Building.[2]

Democrats enjoyed virtual one-party control of Texas, like other former Confederate states, since the end of Reconstruction. Nationally, Democrats gained majority control of the House in 1893, but Republicans held the Senate and the presidency (which appointed the secretary of the Treasury).

On April 15, 1886, with Democrat Grover Cleveland newly installed as president, an appropriation for $200,000 for San Antonio's courthouse and post office was finally approved.[3] While this was but the first step in a long bureaucratic process, Gordon and others began lobbying to secure the superintendency. In addition to his credentials, Gordon was a lifelong Democrat (as the son of a Confederate veteran, his political affiliation was all but preordained). Within days he wrote to the Supervising Architect and the new Treasury secretary applying for the position. Meanwhile, supporters sent numerous letters and a petition recommending Gordon's appointment to San Antonio's representatives in the US Congress. Signed by prominent San Antonio citizens, the letters extolled his accomplishments and qualifications. Many also made note of his sobriety. (Family tradition holds that Gordon feared alcoholism, which ruined a relative, and therefore remained temperate his whole life.) Val Verde and Medina County officials also sent testimonials of his work on their jails.[4]

With the appropriation of funds, the Supervising Architect could move forward with the site selection process. Mifflin E. Bell held the position at the time. Appointed during the previous administration, Bell often complained of the office's excessive workload and low pay. He was anxious to leave as soon as his replacement could be installed. Adding to his misery were attacks on his talent by private sector architects wishing the office abolished and blame for a backlog due more to congressional meddling.[5] Despite the backlog, San Antonio's project proceeded quickly, suggesting Bell was under great pressure to make it a priority.

Julius C. Holmes, a Treasury representative, traversed the country in the 1870s and 1880s as "the eyes of the Supervising Architect." He arrived in San Antonio early in June 1886 charged with identifying the most acceptable and cost-effective site for the future federal building. Holmes inspected potential sites accompanied by the local federal tax collector, San Antonio's postmaster, and Gordon. Afterward, Holmes wrote Bell of meeting Gordon, whom he "cheerfully and fully" endorsed as the future superintendent.[6]

Gordon's participation in Holmes's site inspections was another demonstration of community support for his appointment. In addition to this support, his qualifications, and his political affiliation, social connections in Washington may have contributed to his getting the job. Many members of the closely knit engineering community of the territorial days had risen to positions of authority in the city by the mid-1880s. Major Gordon and his wife, Virginia, who had been part of this community, maintained social ties with Washington. So, too, had James Riely Gordon: three years later he married "one of Washington's fairest belles" (and a daughter of an engineer).[7]

Of course, others sought the prized superintendency, and some had vied for the position long before appropriations made the project official. Like Gordon, James Wahrenberger sent an application accompanied by letters of recommendation.[8] Although obviously qualified, he may not have had the volume of support and other advantages that Gordon enjoyed. Although his official employment as superintendent did not come for some time, Gordon seems to have had a lock on the position early on.

The wheels of the bureaucracy turned slowly and it would be another year before Bell's office produced plans for the Federal Building. In the meantime, Frederick Shelton's participation in the firm of Gordon & Shelton waned, leaving Gordon to run things alone for some time. During this period he supervised the remodeling of the Medina County Jail, provided plans for the Wilson County Jail, and worked on a number of commercial and residential jobs. After straightening out its financial affairs, Gordon announced in January 1887 that the partnership was formally dissolved.[9]

In February Gordon traveled to Washington to receive instructions and information regarding his duties as superintendent. He was gone nearly a month and reported seeing progress on the plans while consulting with a variety of federal authorities about the project. Gordon may have called upon the Supervising Architect's office again in late May when, as a member of the San Antonio Rifles drill team, he traveled to Washington for a national competition.[10]

Plans, specifications, and other documents for the Federal Building were finally sent to Gordon on June 2, 1887. Ten days later, eager citizens of San Antonio saw a rendering of the projected building published in the *San Antonio Daily Express*. The paper boasted the design as "declared by experts at Washington to be the handsomest of a building ever constructed within the cost named."[11] A site on the north side of Alamo Plaza was selected. Nearby stood the Grand Opera House, Sam Maverick's bank, and the Alamo itself.

Gordon was now finally able to start work on his portion of this prestigious project. Typically, the responsibility of a superintendent of construction for a federal building was limited to overseeing construction, resolving disputes, and furnishing monthly progress reports. His staff usually consisted of a clerk and a disbursing agent. The scope of Gordon's job, however, was substantially larger due to the public pressure placed on the Supervising Architect's office. Bogged down with a workload that included projects that had been authorized a year before San Antonio's Federal Building, Bell could hardly refuse an opportunity to delegate some of the burden. Gordon, willing to shoulder additional responsibility, was therefore charged to hire draftsmen and create detail drawings. For his efforts, the young architect received six dollars per day, Sundays included. Such compensation was the norm for the Supervising Architect's office, as opposed to a set percentage of the construction cost, which was typical in the private sector.[12]

Upon reviewing the plans in relationship to the site, Gordon had serious reservations about room and window arrangements. The Federal Building in Austin (1878, James G. Hill, Supervising Architect) was a notorious "hot box" for want of ventilation, and Gordon feared the same problem with the San Antonio design. He was also concerned that Bell oriented the building with its back toward the Alamo—that revered landmark from the Texas War for Independence. Proper respect was due, even though a store and warehouse complex stood between the Federal Building site and the Alamo chapel at the time.[13]

At his own expense Gordon drew up a set of revised plans and traveled to Washington twice to discuss his concerns. It was a brazen act for an aspiring, twenty-three-year-old, local designer to second-guess the Supervising Architect. It was particularly daring when any revisions could cause delays in the face of political pressure to proceed as quickly as possible. Nevertheless, Bell recognized merit in the changes. On July 20 he telegraphed his total approval to Gordon with instructions to implement the changes immediately. The young architect was allowed twelve months to complete revised plans. He finished them in three.[14]

Necessity may have compelled Bell's acceptance of the revisions, but surely he would not leave them in Gordon's hands had the San Antonian not proved himself capable. In his swift execution of this honor, Gordon also demonstrated his industry and integrity by delivering the work in a quarter of the time expected. This must have shocked those back at the Treasury, who were more used to local superintendents dragging out their work to milk the per diem rate.[15]

In a newspaper interview Gordon explains his revisions to the Federal Building, revealing his brilliance in maximizing site aesthetics in tandem with natural lighting and ventilation needs:

> The tower as it exists in the original is on the east side; it will now be on the west side. This brings the stairway on the end nearest to the heart of the city, on the corner opposite Maverick's bank. Then it brings the United States court room, which was originally on the northwest corner of the building, on the southeast corner with 11 east and 6 south windows, giving the room an uninterrupted southeast breeze. In the United States commissioner's court room there are two windows on the east and three additional windows on the southeast so as to make it cool. All the breeze that comes in from the corridors and tower has to pass through these windows, as they are the only outlet and as it will be largely condensed in its passage, it will make it so much the stronger.
>
> The office of the collector of the internal revenue is now on the 2nd story, the southeast end of the building instead of the northwest, and it will have 12 windows in the south and east. The best looking end of the building, fronting on Alamo

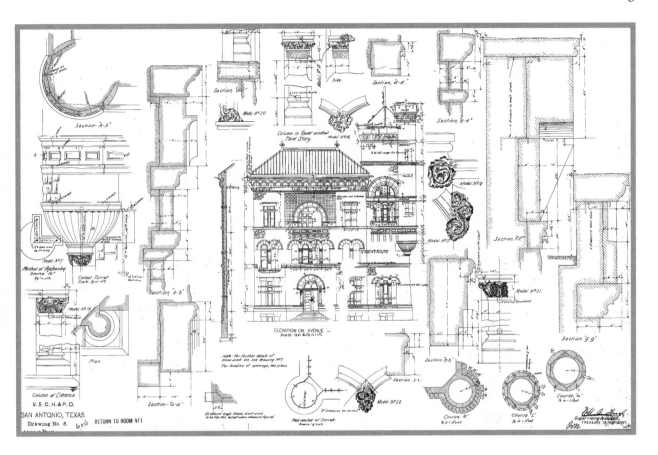

2.1.
United States Courthouse
and Post Office, San Antonio,
Texas, *detail drawing, Office of the
Supervising Architect of the United
States Treasury, courtesy of the
National Archives.*

Plaza, will now be on avenue D instead of avenue E. The stairway will be in the tower in the corner near Sam Maverick's, making it much more convenient for people approaching it to go upstairs, without having to go through all the offices.

You will see by examining the new plans that all the windows are now arranged so that the breeze plays right through all of them, and every room in the building gets southern and eastern exposure.[16]

Shortly after approving Gordon's revisions to the San Antonio Federal Building, Mifflin Bell was finally released from his position. His successor was William A. Freret, an accomplished architect and native of New Orleans who, like Gordon's father, had served as a Confederate engineer. He was pleased with the Texas architect's work and made only slight alterations to the revised design for the sake of economy.[17]

Despite Gordon's best efforts, the work slowed to a snail's pace while he waited for necessary approvals from Washington. With four draftsmen employed on the project, he dutifully sent pencil drawings off to the Treasury as soon as they were completed only to have them languish there. Acknowledgment that "your specifications received and filed, and will be taken up in their regular order," was little comfort. Once the preliminary work was complete (fig. 2.1), all Gordon could do was wait and suffer questions from reporters and citizens alike as to when they could expect to see any progress. Finally, in October 1887, Gordon received the order to commence construction.[18]

Excavation began in December and workers soon uncovered human remains presumed to be of the Alamo's defenders during the famous thirteen-day battle in 1836. The remains were set aside and work continued. In March 1888 the supervising architect awarded the construction contract to William Braden and D. C. Anderson of San Antonio for $97,000.[19] Shortly thereafter, San Antonians watched the walls go up for their long-awaited Federal Building.

While Gordon rearranged elements of the plan, the styling was unchanged from the original design, which is credited to the Supervising Architect. For the San Antonio Federal Building, Bell adopted the Richardsonian Romanesque style that was being used with increasing frequency across the country. This style, which would be a fundamental aspect of Gordon's courthouse work in the next decade, was made popular by the recently deceased Boston architect, Henry Hobson Richardson. The Romanesque revival and Richardson's influence will be discussed further in Chapter 4, but it is worth noting that Gordon had firsthand experience with the style on this project.

Referred to at the time of completion as "modernized Romanesque," the styling enhanced the monumental quality of the San Antonio US Courthouse and Post Office Building (fig. 2.2).[20] The exterior was sheathed in random-coursed, quarry-faced stone, with granite, terra-cotta, and stone detailing. On the south façade an arcade of five massive arches, each 10 feet wide and 15 feet high, welcomed patrons to an open corridor leading to the Post Office workroom. This mighty entrance visually expressed the strength of the US government and a national commitment to San Antonio. Granite steps led to the entrances on Alamo Plaza and Avenues D (now North Alamo Street) and E. Access to the rear of the building was from an alley protected by iron gates at the avenues that were closed while mail wagons were loaded and unloaded. Such security was important when negotiable notes were commonly sent through the mail, but, had the building not been reoriented according to Gordon's suggestion, wagons would have stood on the open Alamo Plaza, requiring more armed guards.

The tower had its own monumental nature, lending a flavor of a medieval fortress to the rest of the building (fig. 2.3). From its slightly battered base, the tower rose 94½ feet above the sidewalk with a turret projecting from the southwest corner that rose another 9 feet 9 inches. The tower served as a station for the US Army Signal Corps, whose duties included gathering meteorological information. An 8-foot-tall band of stone near the top of the tower was left unfinished so that a heroic sculptural frieze could be carved later. (Gordon provided its design, which glorified San Antonio's past, and it was to be sculpted by European craftsmen, but it was never executed.)[21] The building's length prevented the tower from completely dominating the structure.

Ornamental details made popular by Richardson enhanced the composition. Some surfaces were enriched with checkerboard patterns of alternating dressed (smooth) and quarry-faced stone squares. Capitals carved with varied Romanesque

2.2.
United States Courthouse and
Post Office, San Antonio, Texas
(1887–89, demolished). M. E.
Bell, supervising architect of the
United States Treasury, architect.
*Photograph ca. 1890, photographer
unknown.*

2.3.
United States Courthouse
and Post Office, San Antonio,
Texas. *1892 photograph, The
Albertype Company.*

floral designs topped columns. This program of foliation was carried through to other details, enlivening the surface of the building. Human faces stared out from the floral corbel stops between the first-floor arches. Gordon would employ similar decoration in his courthouse work.

During this period, the work of the Supervising Architect's office was at the forefront of engineering innovation. Charged with the task of designing buildings that were among the largest of their day, the office continually challenged construction norms and materials.[22] While leading architects still groused that they could do better, Gordon's exposure to the office's methods was an invaluable primer for his subsequent courthouse work. Structurally, the San Antonio Federal Building employed brick walls and structural iron. (At this time the term *iron* could refer to wrought iron, cast iron, or steel.) Iron girders and columns spanned the large, relatively open spaces of the courtrooms and the postal work area. At least some of the flooring employed fire-resistant technology patented by Joseph Gilbert, a Philadelphia builder, in 1867. Later used by Gordon, Gilbert's system employed shallow vaults of corrugated iron to span open spaces, with wood flooring leveling the surface above. While the space between the corrugated iron and the wood floor could be left empty, greater fire resistance and strength was achieved by filling the void with cement. The underside of the corrugated plating could be left exposed to provide the ceiling for the room below, or it could be hidden behind plaster or some other material.[23]

The federal courtroom was about 50 x 35 feet with a 25-foot ceiling. A newspaper-man who toured the building shortly after its completion described the courtroom as "handsomely finished in oak, the wainscoting, door jambs and window frames being exceptionally massive and artistic. The floor is highly polished, and the panels at the head of the door are beautifully carved with national designs." Every room in the building featured mantled fireplaces, which were augmented by a system of steam heating. Other modern apparatus with which the building was equipped included electric lights, sanitary plumbing, and an elevator. Cast iron details enhanced the interior columns while oak finishing and checkered floors of white marble and dark slate contributed to the decorative scheme of the public areas. A Spanish tile roof topped the structure, masking skylights for the third story.[24]

As superintendent, Gordon was responsible for making sure that all construction was executed with strict adherence to prescribed construction methods. He had latitude with some of the building materials, perhaps explaining the substitution of Spanish tile in place of the standing seam metal roof illustrated in the plans. While this substitution could have been made for practical reasons, it also increased the Federal Building's visual compatibility with its surroundings, particularly the Alamo. Such local sensitivity was sometimes a goal of the supervising architects, but it was also a hallmark of Gordon's Texas work.

Gordon made other recommendations as the work progressed. He believed the courtroom floor was not sufficiently supported and therefore suggested that two iron beams be set into a strategic wall to distribute the weight from above. The supervising architect approved the additional expense of this alteration. The San Antonian's recommendations were overruled on at least one occasion, however. Gordon advised using red granite cut from the Burnet quarries thirty-five miles northwest of Austin for at least some of the columns. The supervising architect opted for limestone from beds along Balcones Creek near Van Raub, over Gordon's objections. This Balcones stone is considered soft, but its price was likely more attractive to government budget officers. Later problems seem to vindicate Gordon's position in this particular matter.[25]

While Gordon was involved with the Federal Building he entered into a brief partnership with James Murphy, the industrious, established San Antonio architect and superintendent. According to the *Daily Express*, the partnership was

> one of the strongest combinations in the architectural line that can be mentioned
> in the state. The shadow of Mr. Murphy's work is cast upon all our principal streets
> as well as throughout the southwest, and all his public and private buildings
> command admiration. . . . What we say of the senior member is equally true of its
> junior member [Gordon]. A young man of recognized ability, he has carved his
> way successfully through, and his work stands forth as a lasting endorsement of
> his faithfulness. So highly has he climbed the rounds step by step that Uncle Sam,
> the most exacting of builders, has made Mr. Gordon superintendent of the new
> federal court house and postoffice at this place.[26]

This partnership began in early July 1887 with Gordon moving his practice to join Murphy in rooms 9, 11, and 13 of the new Smith Block, at the corner of Soledad Street and Main Plaza.[27] The firm of Murphy & Gordon was likely a partnership of convenience in which the architects pooled their talents and resources while attending large projects. Gordon was working on the Federal Building and Murphy expected to be busy with the detail plans and superintendence of a new Bexar County Courthouse in San Antonio.

Just prior to his partnership with Gordon, Murphy had been invited by the county judge to submit plans for a courthouse, and his design was approved on July 12. Murphy received $150 for the plans and was looking forward to additional compensation as the superintendent of construction, but the project stalled as officials contemplated sites. In September San Antonio's mayor, Bryan Callaghan II, suggested the building of a joint county courthouse and city hall. The Bexar County Commissioners' Court voted a provisional agreement with the city and Murphy's plans were abandoned.[28] Perhaps the loss of the Bexar courthouse job rendered Murphy's association with

Gordon unnecessary, for the partnership was dissolved by mutual consent in January 1888, a mere six months after its optimistic formation. They both remained in the Smith Block, but Murphy moved to room 5. Gordon, enjoying a larger practice, retained the firm's suite of offices.[29]

The fate of the joint city-county building project was the genesis for a series of events that eventually had a profound impact on Gordon's career. Among the results was the award of one of his most significant, if problematic, commissions: the 1891 Bexar County Courthouse (Chapter 5). Because of the importance of this award to Gordon's career, the city-county project and some persons connected with it warrant further notice here.

A key figure in the city-county project was Mayor Callaghan, whose political life was nothing if not controversial, and his city-county scheme was true to his form. Callaghan's plan called for the building to be erected on Military Plaza, one of the open spaces specified by the Spanish decree establishing the city. Long abandoned by the military, the plaza had become one of the city's sentimental attractions as the picturesque domain of cart vendors selling traditional Mexican goods (fig. 2.4). The proposal to build upon it met with immediate protest. A court injunction halted the project until it was decided whether city officials could legally ignore the Spanish charter and build on the site. Bexar commissioners began to express second thoughts as the controversy brewed for months and legal costs escalated. The Texas Supreme Court ruled in the project's favor in March 1888. Despite the decision, county leaders voted to withdraw from their provisional agreement. Incensed, Mayor Callaghan resolved to continue with his plan to build a city hall on the plaza.[30]

A design competition was held with a May 4, 1888, deadline for entries. Participating architects were invited to explain their designs to the city council on the fifteenth. Six days later the council voted by secret ballot on the plans. This skullduggery caused consternation among the citizenry that intensified when the council chose the plans of Otto Kramer, who had only recently moved to the city from St. Louis, Missouri, and awarded Kramer a $500 prize. Wahrenberger & Beckmann took second place and $250. The $100 third-place prize went to Gordon. The city council's handling of the whole affair drew much criticism, as did the winning design itself. Nevertheless, the project moved forward (fig. 2.5). Braden & Anderson, the firm erecting the Federal Building and personally favored by Callaghan (or at least the *Daily Express* insinuated as much), won the construction contract.[31]

Gordon remained involved with the Federal Building throughout his partnership with Murphy and the city hall competition. Problems accompanying its construction required the architect's continuing intervention. In spring 1888, Gordon condemned the brick used in the basement walls as inferior and compelled the contractors to replace it. Afterward, Julius Holmes revisited the city for the Supervising Architect and

2.4.
Market on Military Plaza, San
Antonio, Texas. *1887 photograph,
courtesy Prints & Photographs
Division, Library of Congress.*

2.5.
San Antonio City Hall, San
Antonio, Texas (1888–91,
altered). Otto Kramer, architect.
*1892 photograph, The Albertype
Company.*

praised the work in the basement as the finest he had seen in his travels from Maine to Texas.

In July, when a considerable portion of the above-grade walls was completed, Gordon deemed the stone improperly cut and laid. The contractor on the site, D. C. Anderson, ignored Gordon's direction to take down the walls and rebuild, citing Holmes's earlier approval as an overall endorsement of the quality of his work. Gordon then ordered all work stopped until the matter was settled. Anderson appealed to the Supervising Architect's office to send another inspector in hopes of having the job accepted, saving the cost of the rework. Instead, Gordon received a telegram from Washington supporting his judgment. The walls were rebuilt.[32]

Such battles of wills were increasingly played out in public view. While Gordon usually prevailed, his conscientious execution of his duty made an enemy of the contractor. As the architect later disclosed,

> Mr. Anderson . . . has frequently become incensed and made threats, all of which I have utterly disregarded, among the last was, that as soon as he could find the right man that I should lose my position.[33]

Anderson's threats eventually found fulfillment, although he may not have been directly involved.

The US presidency returned to Republican Party hands following the election of Benjamin H. Harrison in 1888, and William H. Windrim replaced Freret as Supervising Architect. Fearing Gordon's position may be jeopardized by the political realignment, over 270 leading citizens signed petitions supporting his retention. Letters on Gordon's behalf were also sent to Windrim, some of which were authored by prominent Republicans who noted that Gordon, while a Democrat, was "not in the *least* degree 'offensively partisan'" (emphasis in original) and "more popular with the mass of Republicans than any other architect in the city."[34]

Nevertheless, James P. Newcomb, a fervently Republican newspaperman, wrote to Windrim on May 1, 1889, urging Gordon's dismissal in favor of a Republican like Albert F. Beckmann or W. R. Freeman. In this letter he reasoned simply that the Democrats "have had their day, it is our turn now." By June Newcomb had ratcheted up the rhetoric, writing to a national party official that Gordon's credentials were fraudulent and his negligence resulted in inferior workmanship on the Federal Building. He also charged Gordon with taking credit for the building's design.[35] (While arguably true to the extent he revised the plans, Gordon denied making the claim at the time.)

Gordon wrote Windrim to refute the accusations. Noting that local members of the building trades scrutinized every step of the Federal Building's construction and the work met with overwhelming approval, he continued,

I am a comparatively young man, and determined on this building to make a reputation for ability and integrity.... The building will be completed in a very few months and aside from my financial interest, I have taken great pride in the work, and will show my appreciation of being permitted to finish it by strict attention to duty.[36]

Alas, Gordon was replaced by W. R. Freeman by the end of June. There is little information on Freeman, but there is no reason to doubt he was a competent architect and engineer. Given Gordon's popularity, however, it is unlikely that Freeman's appointment met with wide community approval, and he probably felt a keen need to find nonpolitical justification for his employment. In July Freeman requested the Supervising Architect stop all work on the Federal Building. He then publicly aired a long list of alleged defects in the construction. He sent photographs of the points of concern to Washington and requested an inspector come and inspect the work that Gordon had previously approved.[37]

Gordon took exception to the timing of Freeman's pronouncements—made on the day that it was widely known that he would be in Rockport evaluating construction bids for the Aransas County Courthouse (Chapter 3). He was therefore unable to comment immediately, but on his return a few days later Gordon explained:

I don't want to talk very much until the expert has been here and made his inspection of the building. I sent for one as soon as I saw that the [Balcones] stone in the columns was going to prove defective. The design was made to use granite in the columns and in the base of the turret, and Braden & Anderson, the contractors, had ordered the granite. They afterwards claimed that they didn't have to use it, and the supervising architect sustained them and directed me to allow the use of the limestone. I could do nothing but follow instructions.... There is not a crack or a flaw in the foundation.... There is nothing of the kind in the building which amounts to anything except in the columns. In every building, even the smallest, there are some little things which may be found fault with if a person only wants to find fault.[38]

The Supervising Architect sent an inspector who photographed the building and reported back to Washington. Lethargy ruled the decision-making process yet again, and no direction to the San Antonio group was forthcoming. Eventually growing impatient, the contractors took the initiative to resume work in August with no guarantee of being paid for rework should officials agree with Freeman. September 14 saw a 20-foot US flag, presented by James Newcomb, hoisted atop the turret to announce completion of the Federal Building's exterior. Newcomb then bought a round of drinks for all the workers to commemorate the day.[39]

2.6.
James Riely Gordon.
*Photograph ca. 1890 by Alonzo
Newell Callaway, San Antonio,
Texas. Courtesy Lucy Virginia
Gordon Ralston.*

Finally, on November 20, 1889, a telegram arrived from Washington in response to Freeman's charges of faulty construction under Gordon's superintendence. It abruptly ordered the firing of W. R. Freeman. The government's local superintendent of repairs, George F. Sacrey, was promoted to replace him. Sacrey shepherded the construction through to completion in the following year.[40]

In 1890 a Washington-based correspondent wrote a critique of the Supervising Architect's efforts that was carried in the *Daily Express*. While disparaging federal buildings in many cities, he found praise for others. He wrote,

> Another fine example of the use of local tradition or history in a government
> building is the new post office at San Antonio, Tex. It suggests the Alamo, that
> famous citadel whose heroic defense will live in song and story until the end of
> time. By itself the San Antonio post office is art. Considered in connection with the
> Alamo, near the ruins of which it stands, it is poetry.[41]

Whatever poetic value the Federal Building possessed (it was razed in 1937 following a fire) was due in no small part to its orientation towards the plaza as revised by Gordon.

Although the plodding pace of the federal project frustrated many San Antonians, in retrospect it benefited Gordon immensely. The protracted appropriation process coincided with his fundamental education as an architect. By the time Congress finally approved the project, he was well positioned to take advantage of the opportunity. By that time, too, San Antonio's growth justified a larger federal investment, resulting in a grander structure. With a final cost of $200,000, the Federal Building was among the most expensive buildings in the city.[42] Gordon's appointment as its superintendent of construction marks a major milestone in his career. He was still using its image on his letterhead a decade after being removed from the position. Despite the blow of that removal, his practice and reputation were now established, and he alone could boast such personal involvement with the structure that would be for many years one of the most significant buildings in San Antonio.

Gordon later credited his "thorough knowledge of the government system" to his tenure as superintendent of construction for the United States Court House and Post Office, San Antonio.[43] He probably meant that he learned much about design and construction in accordance with stringent federal standards. Given the history of the project, however, he might just as easily have been referring to the sometimes brutal politics of public building work. Although Gordon desperately tried to hold onto his job as the Federal Building's superintendent, it was ripped from him for purely partisan reasons and Freeman's subsequent attempt to justify the act threatened Gordon's fledgling reputation. But, far from being discouraged, Gordon drew valuable lessons from the experience.

CHAPTER THREE

Aransas

Gordon's travels in search of prospective clients surely would have taken him to the Texas Gulf city of Rockport in 1888. That year saw the completion of the San Antonio and Aransas Pass (S.A.P.) Railway, making travel to Rockport convenient and infusing the community with a booming economy that provided Gordon with his first true courthouse commission. The nature of the community inspired him to create an unusual but appropriate design in what proved to be a waning style. Despite its eccentricity and unique place in Gordon's opus, the Aransas design possessed features that would evolve as his personal artistic vocabulary matured.

Rockport is located on Aransas Bay, which is separated from the Gulf of Mexico by a string of barrier islands. Although naturally situated as a shallow-water port, it could not be fully exploited until an economical means of commerce connected it with points inland. Nevertheless, the town saw some modest development after incorporation as a city in 1871 and designation as the seat of the newly formed Aransas County.

The community experienced marked change seventeen years later with the coming of the S.A.P., which linked Rockport with San Antonio and its growing rail network. To promote tourism, the line was dubbed "The Mission Route" in recognition of Spanish colonial ruins along the road. Rockport quickly became a bustling terminal as intercoastal freighters and passenger ships docked to exchange lading with the train. As the city invested $100,000 in new building in 1889, Rockport's population was in the midst of a tenfold expansion. The city simultaneously developed into a popular year-round resort and commerce flourished. Plans were made to dredge a deep-water port to serve oceangoing trade. One optimistic promotion predicted that the community would soon "be to the mid continent what San Francisco is to the Pacific and New York to the Atlantic."[1] (Later the city was even renamed "Aransas Pass" for a while, thus strengthening its identity with the railroad.)

The city's new prosperity prompted a call to build a permanent home for the county, which had been operating out of rented quarters since its inception. In early April 1889 the Commissioners' Court placed advertisements requesting plans and specifications for a courthouse and a jail in the newspapers of Dallas, Fort Worth,

Rockport, and San Antonio. It was a competition open to anyone interested in preparing designs based on simple criteria: the courthouse was to be built of brick for a cost between $16,000 and $20,000. The jail was to cost between $3,000 and $5,000 and be built of the same material. A May 13 deadline for submissions gave architects about a month to prepare their plans.[2]

Such competitions represented a dilemma for architects. Some clients—public and corporate officers in particular—often sought security in competitions when charged with erecting a substantial building, believing they could obtain the best plans by pitting architects against one another. Decision makers were often ill equipped to select a designer or plans and open contests seemingly shielded them from criticism. (Individual entrepreneurs and home owners could make their selections without such concern.) For architects, participation often required production of a complete set of plans, which could easily involve three months of intensive work, on a speculative basis. (The intervals between calls for entries and deadlines were rarely that long, so it was not unusual for submissions to be incomplete or recycled.) Some argued that compensation for the architect, usually a percentage of the overall cost, was not worth the risk. Architectural groups generally condemned competitions and discouraged members from participating.

One argument, as it relates to government building, was that attorneys, engineers, physicians, and other professionals were selected for public work without being subjected to such demeaning reviews. (Of course, the AIA's own lobbying to have federal work opened up to competition undercut its credibility in condemning the practice.) A committee of the Texas State Association of Architects, which Gordon had joined in January 1889, was studying the problem but had yet to devise an official policy on the subject. It appears that Gordon found competitions to be an unavoidable evil. Later in life he described them as being a terrible waste of time and effort. It would be better, he thought, if clients simply chose architects whose work they admired and in whom they had confidence.[3] Some local officials conducted their contests honestly, but clearly others manipulated the results for personal gain or to reward friends at the expense of taxpayers. Despite intentions, the competition process could not guarantee the best design, the most cost-effective construction, or the elimination of corruption.

In light of these professional condemnations, costly disappointments, and slanderous accusations (potentially leading to criminal prosecution), one may wonder why architects—some of high stature—flocked to courthouse competitions. Desperation for work could be the motive in only some cases. The prestige accompanying this type of public commission is likely a more encompassing answer. In the public realm, county courthouses represented the highest caliber of design work obtainable to most architects. Federal work was closed to them by the Supervising Architect regime. State capitol work was rare. Other state commissions such as hospitals and municipal work like city halls, while potentially lucrative, usually did not garner the broad publicity attending courthouse work. This may explain why numerous architects from as far away as Nebraska responded to the rather small prize offered in the Aransas competition.

Among this group, San Antonio architects Alfred Giles, Gordon, Otto Kramer, and James Wahrenberger traveled to Rockport to present their entries on May 13, 1889. Aransas County officials spent three days examining submissions, which included "quite a number of handsome designs," before finally selecting Gordon's in a competition unmarred by controversy. During his presentation, Gordon undoubtedly listed among his accomplishments his superintendency of San Antonio's Federal Building and his design for Val Verde's jail. He may also have been able to cite some work in Rockport, but this is uncertain.[4] While the young architect had the beginnings of an impressive portfolio, it is doubtful this was enough to elevate him above his competitors. (His fellow San Antonians enjoyed more substantial credentials; the rest of the competitors remain unidentified.)

It appears, therefore, that Gordon won the contest not so much by his reputation, but by a daring plan (fig. 3.1). An article with a May 18, Rockport, dateline describes his entry as "different from anything else in the state, the whole structure forming a most pleasing effect. The conveniences of the building, together with the artistic manner in which the design has been treated, indicate a thorough and careful study of the architect." Gordon's winning submission was identified as being of "Mooresque architecture,"[5] and his use of the style in this particular commission does attest to his knowledge of his art. While it may seem bizarre to modern eyes, the Aransas County Courthouse was a manifestation of its times and an appropriate response for a city that was the terminus of "The Mission Route." To place the Moorish (as it is more commonly called) style in context requires an examination of its appropriation in American architecture and Gordon's exposure to it.

The Moorish style falls under the umbrella of picturesque architecture, which is such a broad classification that it is sometimes of little use in scholarly evaluation. In the study of Gordon's work, however, it is the genus that establishes the relationship of his buildings in many styles designed over many years. Simply put, a building could be considered picturesque if it made a suitable subject for an artist's painting. English critic John Ruskin was the most influential proponent of the picturesque, but he often quibbled with his peers over which buildings qualified. Certain traits were shared by structures passing such a test, however: a heavily textured surface, a sense of movement within the design, irregularity (as in an uneven roofline or asymmetry of plan), variety of masses and parts, and an element of intricacy that invites close examination. The picturesque ideal blossomed in the Victorian era, but it can be detected in buildings in a wide variety of styles.[6] For example, one can find all these traits in San

3.1.
Aransas County
Courthouse, Aransas Pass
(Rockport). James Riely
Gordon, architect. *From
Frank Leslie's Illustrated
Newspaper, October 18,
1890.*

·THE·COURT·HOUSE· ARANSAS·PASS· ·

Antonio's Federal Building, which was indeed picturesque while solidly in the Richardsonian Romanesque style. This picturesque quality is also a unifying thread throughout Gordon's courthouse work, regardless of the style he was working in. As discussed in Chapter 1, he may have inherited this proclivity for the picturesque from his early mentor, W. K. Dobson.

In addition to the picturesque mode, Gordon's appropriation of a historical style, such as the Moorish, was a device used by many architects of the time. As they struggled to reconcile modern building methods and needs, designers often applied historical details to give structures expressive identities.[7] The Moorish was among a group of Islamic- and Asian-inspired styles collectively referred to as "Orientalism." Historically, these cultures had a real effect on the development of Western architecture, but Orientalism was a direct and often superficial application of their architectural vocabulary to capitalize on their exotic appeal.[8]

Because these styles employed rather expensive, nonfunctional ornament, their use was usually restricted to applications where their unique features served as an attraction, such as casinos, resort hotels, theaters, and exhibition halls. One of the most famous early appropriations of Orientalism in America was Iranistan, the residence of the well-known showman P. T. Barnum (built at Bridgeport, Connecticut, 1848). Designed by noted New York City architect Leopold Eidlitz, the impresario's prominently positioned home could be seen from passing trains on the New York to New Haven line (one of the country's busiest at the time). Its unusual style drew attention to Barnum and, by association, his famed circus. Its reported $150,000 cost was therefore balanced by its promotional value. Iranistan was destroyed by fire before Gordon's birth, but he was surely aware of some of the prominent American applications of the style that followed.[9] For instance, it can be assumed that he learned of the exotic Vine Street Temple in Nashville while working for Dobson.

Another fine example, by the son of Iranistan's architect, stood not far from the Gordon family's boardinghouse on Commerce Street. The National Bank Building (fig. 3.2), designed by Cyrus L. W. Eidlitz, was described in the *San Antonio Daily Express* as "a happy blending of the ancient Moorish with modern architecture." This ostentatious display of wealth was intended to impress the bank's customers as well as its president's peers. It worked. Not only did the bank draw local publicity as one of the city's costliest buildings for its size, it also garnered notice in architectural journals.[10] This neighboring design by an architect of national reputation could not have escaped Gordon's notice.

A less successful structure in this mode was the United States Courthouse and Post Office, Houston (1888–89), which was under construction while Gordon was designing the Aransas County Courthouse (fig. 3.3). Although smaller than its predecessor in San Antonio, Houston's Federal Building also enjoyed much publicity. Newly appointed Supervising Architect William Freret therefore gave Moorish styling additional currency by choosing it for this structure.[11] Given the excitement generated by this building and the National Bank, this type of historicism could easily appeal to a young designer.

The state's Spanish heritage provided further argument for Gordon's choice of this historical style. Medieval battles between the Christian Spaniards and the Islamic Moors of North Africa over the Iberian Peninsula led to a cultural blending. As Christian forces gradually reconquered areas of Spain long occupied by the Moors, artisans used to working in the mode imposed by the Islamic regime tailored their craft to the norms of the returning dominant culture. The resulting transitional style is termed *Mudéjar*. Vestiges of *Mudéjar* styling were later carried to the Americas in the customs of early Spanish colonizers, as is evident in the missions and other architecture in and around San Antonio (see fig. 1.1). By adapting these qualities where he felt recognition of Spanish traditions was appropriate, Gordon exhibits early on a regional sensitivity that contributed to his success in Texas. With it, he establishes an intimate bond

3.2.
San Antonio National Bank, San Antonio, Texas (1886). Cyrus L. W. Eidlitz, architect. *Photographed 1892, The Albertype Company.*

3.3.
United States Courthouse and Post Office, Houston, Texas (1888–89, demolished). William A. Freret, supervising architect of the United States Treasury, architect. *From Art Work of Houston, 1894, courtesy Houston Metropolitan Research Center, Houston Public Library.*

between his buildings and their communities. Of course Rockport, having seen its development in the era of Texas statehood, could not claim the long Hispanic heritage enjoyed by some other cities. This is a town that was trying to create its image, and the architect responded with a most exotic courthouse design.

While Gordon's choice of Moorish styling may have been reasoned, the brashness of his design was worthy of Barnum himself. The extraordinary appearance of the Aransas temple of justice was mated with a practical plan, however. A report from Rockport carried in the *Daily Express* provides a description of the design as approved by the commissioners. The line illustration appearing in *Frank Leslie's Illustrated Newspaper*, drawn from on-site sketches or photographs, shows the building shortly after its completion (see fig. 3.1). Both are valuable early references since the building was altered over the years. Later archival photographs and firsthand reminiscences augment the following reconstruction.[12]

According to the *Daily Express*, the building was to be 56 x 74 feet "with four entrances and two large stairways, four verandahs exclusive of the entrance vestibules made of brick and stone with Mooresque arches. In the center of the building is a rotunda [this term was commonly misused at the time; *atrium* is the correct term] with a series of Mooresque arches on each of the four sides." Gordon arranged the first-floor administration offices so that they would all open to one of the verandas "with handsome stone balustrades and Mooresque arches overhead." Judicial offices and a jury room were relegated to the second floor where the district courtroom, planned to measure 34 x 56 feet, occupied the east side. A 13-foot-wide spectator's gallery with wings extending along the north and south walls was accessed from the third floor. This floor also housed a 22 x 34 foot grand jury room, witness room, and storage. The report is silent on plumbing, electrical, and heating considerations, but chimneys built into the dormers suggest that individual stoves heated rooms.

A trio of exaggerated onion-domed roofs (not true onion domes) over the central tower and the entrance pavilions of the north and south façades dominated this three-story structure (fig. 3.4). Horseshoe arches graced every portal, including the tower observatory. Oversized doors marked the entrances. The north and south façades shared identical treatment, each divided into three projecting pavilions separated by the verandas. Main entrances were placed in the central pavilions, which were capped by the previously mentioned onion-dome roofs with flagpoles rising from their peaks. Flanking end pavilions were gabled and their third-story windows revealed an eclectic mixing of styles; Gordon placed classical Palladian windows within their horseshoe openings. A scalloped fan radiated from the window's lunette to fill the horseshoe, creating an effect somewhat like a seashell.

The east and west elevations were simpler. A single, central pavilion projected from the plane of the wall. It mirrored the end pavilions and was mimicked by flanking

wall dormers combined with single, centered chimneys. This three-part arrangement provided balance to the triple pavilions on the adjacent sides. The entrances opened to the east-west axial hall, which converged with the north-south hall at the atrium. The east and west halls also accommodated stairs leading to the upper floors. On the western side a porch (possibly a later addition) shaded that entrance from the afternoon sun.

The architect's first real foray into courthouse design foreshadows work to come. The most significant aspect of the Aransas project, as far as the evolution of what became his Signature Plan, is the way in which the arrangement provides an integrated, passive ventilation system to cool the structure. According to Gordon, this was a major selling point for the Aransas Commissioners' Court in choosing his plans.[13] Central to this, physically as well as functionally, was the masonry tower rising from the concrete and stone foundation to create an interior atrium through the three stories to an observatory above the roofline. As hot air escaped from the interior of the building through the tower observatory, cooler air from the shaded verandas was drawn through the offices to replace it (see Appendix III).

Also important is the near-identical treatment of the opposite façades. This appears to be the architect's response to the relationship between the courthouse and the city. As noted in Chapter 1, Spanish colonial town planning specified that a central

3.4.
Aransas County Courthouse, with jail to the right, Rockport, Texas (1889–90, demolished). James Riely Gordon, architect. *Undated photo by Gildersleve, from the collections of the Texas/Dallas History and Archives Division, Dallas Public Library.*

plaza be kept open for public use, faced by a public building on an adjacent block. This practice was largely continued during the Mexican period of what is now Texas. Towns settled after Texas Independence were plotted on American community precedents, which also feature a public—or town—square, but in county seats the courthouse was usually placed directly on it. In such situations the value of surrounding property could be impacted by the view of the courthouse. A courthouse with a definite front could increase the value of property facing it at the expense of property facing the back.[14] Gordon's design for Aransas attempted to balance the importance of its four sides to minimize its effect on landowners' assets.

Archival photographs reveal that the exterior was enlivened by playful brickwork, which was later obscured by paint. Horizontal bands of rough-faced stone unified the design, and the structure rested upon a battered stone foundation. Details of this stone are unrecorded, but it likely came from one of the many quarries along the S.A.P. line. Pressed brick was employed for the superstructure, and, according to a witness to its demise, no structural iron was employed in the building.

In this early courthouse commission, Gordon establishes his originality in design. While he followed stylistic fashion with his Moorish treatment, his plan reveals a genius for efficiency and provides the strongest expression of his individuality. Here the young architect rejects some of the design elements that were popular to the point of cliché in courthouse architecture at the time. While costlier and in a different style, J. N. Preston & Son's design for the Bell County Courthouse (see fig. 1.4) provides two points for comparative study. The Prestons topped their courthouse with a pressed metal cupola. This feature was quite popular in public buildings as it provided an elaborate crown at a relatively modest cost: its light weight could be supported by wood construction or slight masonry walls. Some contemporary critics considered the use of metal passing as stone to be architecturally deceitful. For them, Gordon's solid masonry tower would be more honest and would result in a more substantial design. Time has established the practicality of Gordon's methods in this area, since the masonry towers for his extant courthouses remain sturdy to this day while metal cupolas for the Bell County Courthouse and many other courthouses of the era were later deemed unsound and were removed. (Happily, Bell County's have recently been restored.) The masonry tower became a prominent part of Gordon's trademark design, and its efficient functionality would contribute to his success. The architect also takes a step away from the Second Empire–style corner pavilions typically employed by his peers. The outside pavilions on the north and south façades of the Aransas courthouse were end pavilions, flush with the extremities of the building rather than extending around to the adjacent sides as seen on the Bell courthouse. Gordon's next courthouse brought the pavilions in further still.

The construction contract for the courthouse went to Emil Niggli and William Witte of San Antonio on July 16, 1889, for $19,595. The contract for the jail appears to

have gone to the Pauly Jail Building and Manufacturing Company for $8,250. The jail was to be stylistically similar to the courthouse and consist "of all conveniences for the jailer and his family, containing all the necessary cells for prisoners, both male and female, and insane." In addition to security, care was given to fireproofing and ventilation. The county took possession of the completed structures eleven months later. Final costs on the courthouse stood at $20,000. The less elaborate jail cost $10,000.[15]

Few buildings in the city approached the height of the courthouse. In addition to its size, the colorful courthouse was conspicuous because of its styling. This bold effect was entirely appropriate for a booming nineteenth-century resort community on the Gulf. The exotic building drew comments from the press and attention to the port city. Like P. T. Barnum's Iranistan, the courthouse had a promotional value that offset its cost: it was a celebrated landmark.

Rockport's prosperity following its connection with the Mission Route was sadly short-lived. Its population boom leveled off, leaving an overbuilt community where investments languished. A particularly destructive hurricane devastated the community a few years later. While the port enjoyed some physical improvements, the deep-water effort was shifted to rival Corpus Christi in the 1920s. Through it all, Gordon's romantic structure served Aransas County for sixty-five years, its sound construction providing haven to the populace during times of storm (fig. 3.5).

Over the years alterations were made that compromised Gordon's design. Photographs show that verandas on both sides of the courthouse were extended and enclosed, and the atrium was filled in with offices. While these changes satisfied a need for space, they surely had a detrimental effect on the passive ventilation system.[16] The

3.5.
Storm tide over Austin Street, Rockport, Texas. The courthouse can be seen near the center of the photograph. *1919 photograph, UTSA's Institute of Texan Cultures at San Antonio, #101-0302, courtesy Helen Shipman Cunningham.*

building fell into serious disrepair by the middle of the twentieth century when voters, taking advantage of windfall oil revenues, chose to replace it in 1955.

Gordon's first courthouse was a success for the architect and the officials who placed their faith in him. Even with this early project, some aspects of his personal style emerged. He established his picturesque approach and commenced the evolution of his trademark floor plan, which is chronicled in the following chapters. He occasionally employed Moorish styling on later commissions, but never again so blatantly on a courthouse. Orientalism soon fell from architectural fashion, partially due to its expense. Indeed, shortly after the completion of the Aransas courthouse the *Daily Express* carried a Washington-based review of recent federal buildings that condemned the use of exotic motifs. In it the author goes as far as suggesting that Supervising Architect Freret be hanged for his use of the Moorish in Houston.[17]

Gordon had reflected the bold optimism of a booming, late nineteenth-century Texas Gulf city with his design. Given the community's aspirations and mainstream architecture's abandonment of Orientalism, the structure takes on an almost quixotic appeal. Still, it must have been quite an experience approaching Rockport from the water, or crossing the flat, coastal plain in those days, to see Gordon's Aransas County Courthouse rising above the tidal marshes like a vision from the tales of the *Arabian Nights*.

CHAPTER FOUR

Fayette

Exotic styling suited the Aransas County Courthouse and the community it served. Rockport's situation was rather unique, however: most county seats in Texas are inland towns oriented toward more traditional economies. As Gordon's courthouse practice expanded, it was appropriate to seek a style more suitable for those economies and local cultures. He settled on the Richardsonian Romanesque style used for the San Antonio Federal Building. In doing so, he entered into the period's mainstream of architectural fashion. This fashion was the result of trends that had been building in the United States for some time.

As discussed earlier, American architects struggled to find a stylistic approach suitable to modern building needs. Much thought and effort were also devoted to the quest for an "American" style that would define the architecture of the nation. Given the breadth of the country and its regional idiosyncrasies, this would prove to be largely unobtainable. A stylistic vogue that came close was the Greek Revival that flowered across the country in the years prior to the Civil War. Its strict classical orders did not allow much latitude for variation in plan or individual expression, but they did provide a common standard to build to. The hegemony of the Greek Revival faded as tastes changed and building needs evolved beyond the style's ability to accommodate. The Gothic, Romanesque, and previously discussed exotic styles then rose in prominence. Accompanying them was a hodgepodge of Victorian creations that were sometimes brash and—more damning in late nineteenth-century America—increasingly identified with the war between the states and Reconstruction era that many wanted left in the past. Spurred on by their growing sense of confidence as professionals, many architects yearned to create something fresh and uniquely American.

There was little agreement on what form a new national style should take, however, and some continued to look toward Europe for inspiration. In this struggle, a new approach to classicism arose that cast off the shackles of ancient orders that had so bound the Greek Revival. Practitioners in this camp included Richard Morris Hunt, who drew from French Renaissance and *Néo-Grec* sources to create excellent designs for prominent clients. Classic design rules were bent and many times broken in this stylistic trend as the nation's architects searched for a focus.[1]

4.1.
Trinity Church, Boston,
Massachusetts (1872–77).
Gambrill & Richardson,
architects. *Photograph ca. 1890,
The Union View Company, Rochester,
New York.*

The path of Romanesque styling turned into an unprecedented architectural movement following the completion of Henry Hobson Richardson's highly regarded design for Boston's Trinity Church (1873–77) (fig. 4.1). With Trinity, the architect tapped a source with a history of variation. The original Romanesque filled the void in European architecture following the collapse of the Roman Empire. Literally "Roman-like," the style is comprised of a multitude of disparate manifestations that sprouted locally from the classical precedents Roman builders left behind. Richardson focused on the styling of the Provençal region of southern France, but fused it with Byzantine and other architectural elements to create his own stylistic vocabulary that transcended historicism. Indeed, he became personally identified with the style. Common Richardsonian elements include massively treated arches; short, polished columns; and polychromatic use of rough-cut, or quarry-faced, stonework. Through this monumental and rugged interpretation Richardson struck a chord with the American self-image.

The term *Richardsonian* had already entered the architectural lexicon before the architect died in 1886 at age forty-eight. His early passing left a void that invited others to pick up his standard and spread the style across the country. Professional journals contributed to the phenomenon by devoting illustrations and lengthy articles to the Romanesque, its revival in the United States, and Richardson's work in particular. Supervising Architect Mifflin Bell furthered the style's dissemination by employing it in government structures throughout the nation. Ultimately, Richardson became one of the most influential figures in the history of American architecture. Many of Richardson's followers embraced the severe styling of his later commissions. Gordon, with others, turned to the picturesque, and therefore still somewhat Victorian, nature of the architect's earlier work for inspiration.

The Richardsonian style proved an ideal vehicle for Gordon's talent because it possessed unexplored potential for individual and regional expression. As described in a treatise from Richardson's library shelf, the Romanesque was solemn yet monumental, lending itself equally well to great richness in execution or extreme simplicity. With no dogmatic rules it could be adopted to a wide range of uses, budgets, and materials.[2] Gordon successfully blended in other styles to complement local cultural tradition as a continuation of the regional sensitivity he demonstrated in the Aransas design. The style also offered many practical advantages for the specific needs of late nineteenth-century Texas courthouses. Its pliancy to local building materials was important given the rudimentary state of transportation in many regions of the state. It was often most advantageous to cut stone from a quarry near enough to the construction site that it could be efficiently carried by a local railroad or team-drawn wagons. Contracting the work and material locally, as much as possible, also wrought political advantage as it kept voter tax money close to home. The rugged nature of Richardsonian stonework allowed local quarries to supply the stone without investing in the expensive equipment needed for finer work.

Gordon gained intimate knowledge of the federal take on Richardson's Romanesque style during his superintendence of the US Courthouse and Post Office in San Antonio. He likely saw more examples, such as Richardson's own John Hay and Henry Adams Houses, during his travels to Washington, DC, in connection with that commission. Other popular professional sources of information on the style were the aforementioned architectural journals and the books and photographic collections advertised therein.

Another opportunity for the architect to study the latest trends in his art was the honeymoon following his October 9, 1889, marriage, in Washington, to Mary Lamar Sprigg (fig. 4.2). The new Mrs. Gordon was the daughter of Colonel James Cresap Sprigg, an engineer in the District at the time of her marriage. She was born in 1871 in Petersburg, Virginia, but spent her youth and received her education at the nation's capital. After their wedding the couple toured the North, including a visit to New York City, before returning to San Antonio. Surely the architect took in a few noteworthy buildings during this trip.[3]

Gordon appears to have been the first San Antonio architect to embrace the Richardsonian Romanesque. A prominent, early application by Gordon was his bank building for W. B. Wright. Gordon completed the plans and specifications for this elaborate, three-story structure by mid-February 1890.[4]

4.2.
Mary Lamar Sprigg,
ca. 1889 (later Mrs.
James Riely Gordon).
Photographer unknown,
courtesy Lucy Virginia
Gordon Ralston.

The Richardsonian Romanesque style, however, did not enjoy immediate or universal acceptance. At the May 1890 meeting of the Texas State Association of Architects, then-president James Wahrenberger used his address to emphatically denounce the style. The German-educated architect, who practiced his own brand of Victorianism, began with an apparent attack on the San Antonio Federal Building:

> It has always appeared to me absurd that public buildings like court houses, post offices, etc., at this age of steam cars and electricity, should be of such antique architectural styles as to remind us of the dark days of the inquisition.

He continued with a diatribe against designs like the Aransas courthouse and their

> peculiar misapplication of the misunderstood Byzantine and Moresque forms, in which some of the younger brethren of the profession seem to take a special delight to show their ignorance in architectural styles and esthetics, and which to a great degree may account for the depraved taste displayed in much of our modern architecture.[5]

One almost suspects that the TSAA president meant to single out Gordon, the protégé of his former partner W. K. Dobson, with these remarks.

At that meeting, Gordon and three other architects were suspended for nonpayment of dues. They appear have to been boycotting the organization to protest actions by some of its founders who were blocking newer members from admission to the American Institute of Architects. The Western Association of Architects consolidated with the AIA under the latter's name in 1889. Since the TSAA enjoyed a preexisting association with the Chicago organization, eight of the TSAA's founding members, including Wahrenberger, automatically became AIA fellows (the highest rank of membership). The old New York gentlemen's club attitude survived in the new organization and some TSAA founders were quick to take advantage of it. They promptly drew up the drawbridge behind them and used their status to veto most subsequent applications for AIA membership by fellow Texans, including Gordon's.[6] It is evident that the spirit of unity that attended the founding of the TSAA four years earlier had faded.

Despite Wahrenberger's reproach, Gordon used Richardsonian Romanesque in his growing practice for commercial buildings, churches, and residences. Like most of his peers, however, he remained eclectic and employed other styles for concurrent commissions. Of course, design decisions in the private sector catered to the tastes of an individual client while public commissions, such as courthouses, tended to be reflective of prevailing stylistic trends due to their representative nature. With the appropriation of Richardsonian Romanesque for his courthouse work, Gordon acknowledged this trend. He first employed it for Fayette County at the town of La Grange.

In late February 1890, the Fayette Commissioners' Court appointed three men to examine the county's existing courthouse and to recommend a suitable course of action regarding its condition. The court's appointees were C. Michaelis of La Grange, Robert Allert of Flatonia, and George F. Sacrey of San Antonio, whom the *La Grange Journal* described as "first class architects," but this seems a bit hyperbolic. After all, a mere three months earlier Sacrey was the US government's superintendent of repairs in San Antonio, before being promoted to replace W. R. Freeman as construction superintendent for the Federal Building. Allert appears to have been a contractor and Michaelis was hired to install shutters and water closets in the new courthouse after it was completed. On March 11 they reported that the old courthouse, a stone structure completed in 1856, was "in anything but safe condition" and not worth repairing. The Commissioners' Court accepted this appraisal and unanimously voted to build a new courthouse to cost between $65,000 and $90,000. Gordon, who attended this session, happily offered to sketch a ground floor plan for such a structure on the spot. This being done, officials approved the sketch and agreed to have the architect present proper plans and a sketch of "one of its fronts" on May 10. Gordon had successfully thwarted the competition system as the Commissioners' Court accepted his design at its May 1890 session.[7]

While it was not unusual for those hoping for county work to attend such sessions, that Gordon traveled to La Grange before the decision to build suggests he had prior knowledge of the examiners' recommendations. He surely knew George Sacrey, who may have informed him.

In June the construction contract went to Martin, Byrnes & Johnston, who also built Gordon's Val Verde County Jail. The old courthouse was razed, and work on the new foundation began late in 1890. The cornerstone was laid in May 1891 amid much Masonic pomp and circumstance. County workers started to occupy some offices in November and the people of Fayette County officially received the building on December 1, 1891. Celebrations surrounding this event drew visitors from considerable distances, swelling the population of La Grange.[8]

Gordon acknowledged Fayette County's cultural background with a German-inspired variation on the Richardsonian Romanesque. His plan drew from Richardson's well-publicized Allegheny County Courthouse (Pittsburgh, Pennsylvania, 1883–88) (fig. 4.3). The three-story Fayette County Courthouse is basically in the shape of a hollow square with an open courtyard in the center. Evolving from the Aransas design, which had a triple-pavilion treatment for its major façades, Gordon eliminated the central pavilion and brought the two on the ends inward. These paired pavilions frame the entrances as they are repeated around the building. A clock tower unmistakably marks the east entrance as the principal façade, however (fig. 4.4; also see Appendix III). Opposite this, on the west side, the pavilions are fused above the rear entrance by the outer wall of the second-story courtroom.[9]

Quarry-faced blue sandstone, supplied by the Fayette Rock Company in nearby Muldoon, comprises most of the exterior. Horizontal bands of red sandstone from Pecos County encircle the building as sill courses. Smooth dressed Belton white limestone adds chromatic and textural contrast to the rough bluish sandstone. The latter two alternate as voussoirs in the arches and create checkerboard patterns in the gable ends of the pavilions. Limestone is used where strength and durability are considerations, such as for the hood moldings and water table that deflect rain runoff away from the windows and foundation. It is also used for the arches of the interior court and the carved details of the exterior. Crenellated parapets top the exposed corners of the main block. Below the crenellations is a dentil frieze, beneath which is a wide terracotta frieze of a rinceau (scrolling floral) pattern.

A fine portico featuring an arch with deeply pronounced intrados provides shelter for the main entrance on the eastern façade. This arch is framed by a semi-octagonal hood molding and supported by polished, clustered columns of the same red Burnet granite that the architect futilely recommended for the San Antonio Federal Building. The portico extends beyond the pavilions, and its top serves as a balcony accessed from a second-floor hall. A smaller balcony bridges the two pavilions on the third-story level and leads higher to three arches accented by two columns similar to those

4.3.
Allegheny County Courthouse,
Pittsburgh, Pennsylvania
(1885–88). Henry Hobson
Richardson, architect. *Pre-1914
view, photographer unknown.*

4.4.
Fayette County Courthouse, La Grange, Texas (1890–91). James Riely Gordon, architect. *Early 1890s photograph (by Louis Melchor?), UTSA's Institute of Texan Cultures, courtesy Verna Reichert.*

clustered on the portico. The triple arcade marks the height at which the splendid masonry clock tower separates from the mass of the building. Above this demarcation Gordon set a 14 x 5 foot limestone slab with an extraordinary carving of an American eagle. Stone dragons project at angles from the tower immediately above this panel. The structure tapers to an observation deck offering views from all four sides. Each of these portals is treated with a diminutive version of the entrance portico with paired columns and a clock face above the arch. Behind the clock faces a steep pyramidal roof takes the tower to its weather-vaned apex, 100 feet above the ground. By reducing the width of the tower and the scale of its features as it rises, Gordon created a false sense of perspective that increases its perceived height.

Gordon employed several techniques to further animate the exterior of the Fayette courthouse. In addition to the dragons on the tower, grotesques carved from the same Belton stone serve as sentinels atop the gabled entrances on the north and south sides. High chimneys and stone finials on the pavilion gables and the clock faces add an upward grace to the bulk of the building. The slate roof is enhanced by Spanish tile along its ridges. His program of various arches—segmental, round, and stilted— inspires further interest. In addition, Gordon threw in two types of pressed metal decoration for the spandrels separating some of the windows. One is a floral medallion design used throughout the building. The other is a garland used below the lunettes in the gable ends. The latter is a classical element somewhat at odds with a ruggedly Romanesque design.

Burnet granite steps lead up to the entrances. At the entrance portico, the steps give way to alternating black and white tiles of Maine marble that continue inside. Passageways from all entrances converge on a hall surrounding the 30-square-foot open courtyard (fig. 4.5). Doorways to the courtyard are in line with the east and west entrances, and numerous windows perforate the courtyard's brick walls. In addition to admitting natural light to the interior of the building these windows could be opened for ventilation previous to air conditioning. As with the Aransas design, warm air rose up through a central shaft (the courtyard), drawing in cooler air through the office windows on the exterior of the building. Air traveling through open doorways and transoms created a gentle breeze. The courtyard was landscaped with shrubbery, a central fountain, and walkways.

The interior of the Fayette County Courthouse is finished with Texas curly pine painted a faux natural wood finish. Stairs in the north and south halls lead to the second and third stories, where the district courtroom occupies the west end of the building (fig. 4.6). Attention is appropriately granted to this two-story courtroom, designed to accommodate 500 people with opera-style seats beneath a coffered plaster ceiling. Neatly molded, 6-foot-high wainscoting of curly pine encompasses the main floor and gallery. Lincrusta (a linoleum-like product finished to appear like tooled leather and

4.5.
Fayette County Courthouse, view
of central courtyard. *Photographed
2004.*

known in Gordon's time as Lincrusta-Walton in recognition of its inventor) provides facing for the gallery's balustrade with a foliated pattern similar to that of the exterior frieze.

All interior walls received "occidental finish, and tinted to suit each story." George D. Barnard and Company of St. Louis supplied the oak furnishings. Fireproof record rooms and racks came from the Fenton Metallic Works in New York, and Cincinnati's Hail Safe and Lock Company made the vault doors. The building was equipped with electricity and plumbing, and lavatories were placed on the first and third floors. Coal and wood were stored in the cellar to fuel the heating stoves during the winter. The

4.6.
Fayette County Courthouse,
view of district courtroom.
Photographed 2004.

third floor included a large room with beds, a closet, and other amenities for jurors sequestered overnight. Above it all, the tower housed a No. 16 Seth Thomas clock with an 800-pound bell.

Detailed plans reveal the architect's thorough knowledge of the construction art at this early point in his career (fig. 4.7). He employed I beams above the windows to allow for larger openings, increasing lighting and ventilation. He incorporated relieving arches that were built into the brick walls to diffuse the downward pressure on entrance openings. Stone veneer on the exterior and plastering inside hid engineering devices such as these arches, which give the building its stability. Gordon also planned for interior walls of solid brick that swell in width to support the tower. Bricks were made on- or near-site, from local clay with a steam press provided by the contractor.[10]

Complaints about the project were raised in the *La Grange Journal*. Its editor generally opposed the Commissioners' Court, and his bone of contention was being denied the county printing contract. Be that as it may, some of the Commissioners' Court's actions were indeed irregular, including a January 1891 decision to hire C. Michaelis, one of the original building examiners, to superintend construction of the courthouse on a full-time basis. Gordon was already contracted to superintend through monthly visits and could be compelled to come more often as required. The editor questioned why Michaelis should be hired at an additional cost to do a job that Gordon was being paid for. Furthermore, the newspaperman criticized the lack of a competition and opined that Gordon was overpaid, suggesting that there was not "an architect in the state who would not have gladly furnished plans and specifications . . . for five hundred dollars." While the editor clearly placed little value on the architectural profession, he had a legitimate point about the Michaelis arrangement. Since records indicate Gordon was still expected to fulfill his duties, it is hard to view Michaelis's hiring as anything besides superfluous patronage.[11]

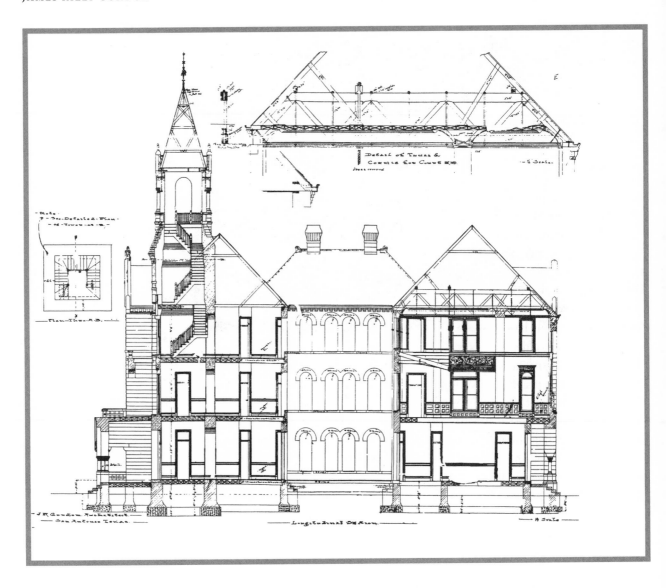

4.7.
Fayette County Courthouse,
section view. *Original plans by
James Riely Gordon, courtesy Fayette
County.*

This is but the first instance of Gordon working with a redundant, county-appointed superintendent. It is doubtful he ever encouraged the practice, which destabilized his authority and double-billed taxpayers, but it was not his position to question a decision by elected officials. Whether Michaelis actually contributed to the work is unknown, but all went smoothly and officials continued to be pleased with Gordon's performance even after the election of a new Commissioners' Court. The court approved paying the balance of Gordon's commission upon the building's acceptance from the contractors. The total cost of Fayette County's new courthouse was about $103,450, including Gordon's commission of about $4,950 for the design and superintendence services.[12]

Although well received, the Fayette courthouse was not completely successful. Complaints of inadequate space for county operations arose immediately, and bats found a favored roost in the courtyard, eventually necessitating installation of netting at the roofline. On the exterior, the east entrance is prominent while the west is treated somewhat as a backdoor, thereby favoring the surrounding property in an uneven manner. Such drawbacks were eclipsed by praise for the Fayette courthouse inside and beyond the county line, however. Perhaps a succinct description supplied at the time of the building's completion serves best, summarizing Fayette as "an imposing structure and a cynosure for all eyes."[13]

On July 9, 1890, right after the letting of the Fayette construction contract, Gordon announced his partnership with Ditlev C. Ernest Laub. Usually identifying himself as D. Ernest Laub, he was for a number of years in the employ of the Office of the Supervising Architect. The two met over the plans for the San Antonio Federal Building during one of Gordon's trips to Washington, DC, probably in 1887. They formed an immediate friendship based upon their mutual interest in their art. A photograph indicates that Laub was older than the San Antonian, and his tenure with the supervising architect indicates that he was a fully capable designer. Mifflin Bell typically charged his draftsmen with responsibility for preparing drawings for entire buildings from foundation to completion, including decoration. Laub reportedly enjoyed a position of authority in the office and many delineations of federal architecture bear his name. For a while, Laub operated his own architectural office in Brooklyn, New York, concurrent with his federal employment. Three years after they met, Gordon invited Laub to assist him with his burgeoning San Antonio practice.[14]

The partnership continued in Gordon's suite of offices in the Smith Block. Major George M. Gordon, the architect's father, moved his real estate business there by the fall of 1890. Family tradition asserts that George also served as the office manager for the architectural practice. Although newspaper accounts of the Fayette courthouse's completion credit the firm of Gordon & Laub, the building had been designed before Laub's arrival and the architectural drawings bear Gordon's name alone. Laub's involvement with Fayette, if any, would have been limited to a superintending role.

CHAPTER FIVE

Bexar

As construction of the Fayette courthouse was under way, the long-running effort to replace the Bexar County Courthouse in San Antonio finally bore fruit. An intense competitive spirit, enmeshed with local politics, surrounded this project that did not subside with the award of the design and construction contracts. Gordon, having won this commission, again found himself fighting to keep it. It was a battle that put his future as an architect at risk.

Bexar County's prosperity has always been linked to San Antonio's. Indeed, as the county lost vast tracts of land through the creation of new counties, its population saw marked growth largely due to the success of San Antonio. During the 1880s the city's population grew more than 83 percent to 37,673. Particularly prosperous years following 1885 coincided with the mayoralty of Bryan Callaghan II. Introduced in Chapter 2, Callaghan headed a political machine that was responsible for many improvements that accompanied—or fueled—the city's growth. Miles of streets were paved and lighted, water improvements reduced the threat of fire, and electric power promised to further industry. Streetcars facilitated cross-town commerce and made new, outlying residential developments possible.[1] The situation was a boon for those involved in building trades. Callaghan's crowning achievement as mayor was the construction of the new San Antonio City Hall, which was as much a monument to him as to the city.

As the new city hall rose on Military Plaza, envious Bexar County officials grew more dissatisfied with their quarters, formerly the Masonic Hall, on Soledad Street. The county acquired this structure in 1872. Eleven years later it spent $40,000 renovating and enlarging the building according to plans by Alfred Giles. Shortly afterward, in 1886, a newly elected county judge recommended building an entirely new courthouse. When critics questioned the necessity of this in light of the recent work, the county judge responded by charging that the existing edifice was structurally unsafe. This local criticism surely stung architect Giles as he continued his struggle to clear his name regarding the El Paso County Courthouse, as mentioned in Chapter 1. In defense of his renovation work, Giles inspected the structure and reported to the press that he found only cracks in the plaster from settling and shrinkage of the timbers. He maintained that such problems were to be expected considering the age of some parts of the structure and poor maintenance. He also noted some cracks had been gouged out to appear worse than they were.[2] Nevertheless, county officials continued to press for a new courthouse. As discussed in Chapter 2, an 1887 plan to build to James Murphy's design was abandoned in favor of the ill-fated city-county project. Afterward, the county acquired additional space in surrounding properties to house growing bureaucratic and judicial obligations. During the 1890 political campaign season, with the $200,000 Second Empire–style San Antonio City Hall nearing completion, Bexar officials renewed their drive for new quarters.

The movement began to take definite shape after the election of County Judge Samuel W. McAllister. On March 11, 1891, the Bexar Commissioners' Court considered buying property facing Main Plaza for a new courthouse. Such a move had the virtue of restoring a permanent government presence to the plaza, as originally decreed by the Spanish Law of the Indies. Most of the property belonged to the influential family of Commissioner Joseph Dwyer, however, and although he recused himself from the vote, purchasing the land was a source of controversy. The plan was approved nevertheless, committing the county to buy lots on the corner of Main Plaza and Dwyer Avenue for a total of $110,000. Two days later the court voted to solicit plans and specifications for a new courthouse, with an estimated cost of nearly $300,000. According to the *San Antonio Daily Express*, "Judge McAllister remarked, with noticeable pride, that architecturally and otherwise the new building will be superior to the new city hall or the new federal court house and the finest county building in the state."[3]

The competition notice imposed no stylistic limitations on the participants but did specify that the building should be fire-resistant, four stories tall, and have a basement and a tower. It needed to be fitted with electrical wiring, steam heat, plumbing, and electric elevators. The notice also stipulated necessary rooms and vaults. A $1,000 prize would go to the entry that the Commissioners' Court deemed to be the best, and $500 would go to the second-place winner. Along with newspaper placement, the notice appeared in the *Journal of Commerce and Building News*.[4]

Architects of unusual geographic breadth and quality responded. Professional rivalry became intense as they checked into local hotels. Some dropped out of the contest before it began, perhaps feeling outclassed or suspecting a foregone conclusion. Excitement grew as the contest spilled into the realm of public opinion. Descriptions of various plans appeared in the press prior to their official consideration, and renderings were displayed in hotel and bank windows. County records document twenty-five architects and firms, from as far north as Chicago and east as Philadelphia, participating. The *San Antonio Daily Express* remarked that the submissions represented "several thousand dollars worth of good professional work."[5]

In addition to Gordon & Laub, James Murphy, Gordon's former partner and author of the unexecuted 1887 design, entered the contest. James Wahrenberger, a severe critic of the competition system, could not resist involvement. Kansas City's esteemed

Henry Van Brunt, formerly of Boston, came from Missouri. Otto Kramer hoped to follow up his San Antonio City Hall design with this prize. Noticeably missing from the field was Alfred Giles. Although by now cleared of the accusations in El Paso, their lingering stigma or perhaps bitterness over earlier claims that his Bexar renovations were substandard may have caused the respected architect to sit out this competition.[6]

Entrants presented and explained their designs to the Commissioners' Court in the week following the May 11 deadline. On May 18, on the first ballot, all votes went to Gordon & Laub. The *Daily Express* reported the estimated cost of building to this design as $300,000. A second unanimous vote designated Wahrenberger the recipient of the second-place award.[7] Such definitive votes in favor of two local architects cast doubt upon the integrity of the contest. If nothing else, the choice shielded county officials from hard feelings like those resulting from the award of the city hall design to newcomer Otto Kramer.

Along with the design award, Gordon & Laub were contracted to "prepare all plans, specifications and detail drawings for the new Bexar County Courthouse, including all furniture and fixtures and superintend and manage the construction, accept same from the contractors and issue vouchers for the payment thereof." The Commissioners' Court chose to keep unusually close control over construction, however. It divided up the project and let the work out piecemeal. Contracts specified that an individual chosen by the Commissioners' Court and another chosen by the contractor would arbitrate any disputes. The arbitrators' decisions would be final. A third arbitrator could be chosen if the two did not come to agreement. (Under this arrangement, a majority of the Commissioners' Court could conceal collusion with a contractor by choosing sympathetic arbitrators.)[8]

Perhaps in response to the plan to divvy up the work, Gordon & Laub designed the courthouse to be built in stages, using a method known as cage construction. Once the foundation was laid, the exterior walls and roof, collectively referred to as the superstructure, would be put up. These were self-supporting and independent of interior walls and flooring. Interior construction, along with the finishing, constituted the last stage of the project.

When bids for the foundation work were received in October, Gordon was concerned that the lowest seemed unrealistic. He asserted that the stability of the whole building depended upon its foundation, and any problems resulting from poor work there would be very costly later. Knowing that rejecting the lowest bids in favor of a higher one would be questioned, the architect recommended that the Commissioners' Court take charge of the work. With the county purchasing material and hiring laborers and a project supervisor, Gordon's role, as he later stated it, was to "look after the accounts, and see that nothing was wasted." While his fees were partially based upon a percentage of the foundation costs, he did not control the prices agreed to by the Commissioners' Court. Work began in November 1891. The ground turned out to be softer than expected and several wells were encountered during excavation that needed filling. Both these factors necessitated the use of more cement than originally anticipated.[9]

Letting of the first construction contract, for the basement and superstructure, was convoluted and portentous of things to come. Initial bids were received from seven contenders on February 15, 1892. After considering the matter for over a month, the Commissioners' Court ordered the contractors to provide bids based on three different combinations of building materials. These bids were due on March 26 and four days later the court chose the one submitted by John Cormack for $193,000. On April 11 the Commissioners' Court then rejected Cormack's bid as not being in accordance with the specifications and instead selected George Dugan's bid for $224,967.[10]

Dugan was president of a Kansas City, Missouri, operation that cut granite and stone for building material. While his business was sizable, he appears to have been fairly new to actual construction and the San Antonio project was probably his most distant job to date. A week after winning the job, Dugan brought Otto P. Kroeger, one of the other competing contractors, "into an interest with him in the erection and completion" of the courthouse. Kroeger was local and had been successful in securing Bexar County's building contracts in the past. He also had a reputation for bringing innovative technology to the local construction industry.[11] Although the exact reasons for Dugan and Kroeger's alliance is unknown, they both brought assets to the partnership. They set to work quickly on the city's most impressive construction project to date.

During the following three months they assembled the equipment and built the facilities necessary to meet the challenge of Gordon & Laub's monumental courthouse design. This included setting up offices at the San Antonio and Aransas Pass Railroad depot and across the street from the construction site. At the depot, stables, workshops, and tool houses were built to facilitate the trimming and transportation of stone as it arrived. The contractors erected two parallel, elevated tracks, 50 feet apart and 150 feet long, over a sidetrack at the depot. A "traveler" consisting of a second pair of tracks transversed the first and was used to lift stones weighing up to 20 tons from incoming flatcars. A specially designed locomotive powered this apparatus to carry the suspended stone in any direction within a 7,500-square-foot area. The stone was then trimmed and loaded onto wagons that hauled it to the site next to Main Plaza.

Upon arrival at the construction area, the stone was lifted off the wagons with steel cable by one of four immense derricks located at the corners of the work site. Cable ran underground from these derricks to a central structure where it was taken up on massive, electric-powered reels. Derrick arms enabled the crew to swing the stone to any part of the yard and set it into position. This machinery operated under power from a huge motor supplied by the electric power company. It was the first time that electricity was used to power construction in San Antonio (fig. 5.1).[12]

With this system in place, construction work began in earnest in July 1892. Sixty carloads of sandstone from the Brackenridge Quarry in Karnes County were added to the concrete slab, completing the foundation. The contract called for five courses of Burnet granite above the sandstone, but Dugan and Kroeger's great derricks were capable of moving much larger blocks of stone than was specified. Believing that fewer courses of larger stones would add to the strength and appearance of the building, the contractors proposed a change to three courses of increased size. An addendum to the contract allowed for such changes to be made if approved by the architect, which Gordon did.[13]

Laub, who had left the partnership and the city in March 1892 (see Chapter 6), was not present to see the superstructure go up. Work continued into the fall, as the county's political scene was changing in ways that would affect the courthouse project and Gordon personally. Local politics—which previously had been largely divided into pro- and anti-Callaghan camps—were realigning as an anti–county administration movement gained popularity. This movement challenged the status quo and became organized as the "Citizen's Party."

Some of this anti-county sentiment can be attributed to investigations instigated by George H. Noonan, judge of the 37th District Court of the state of Texas. Although elected locally, district judges presided over courts of law operated by the state. The state also empowered them to appoint grand juries, which heard evidence in criminal cases to determine if indictments were warranted. In addition to this, grand juries could investigate aspects of local government and report their findings. This watchdog role served as an important check against official malfeasance and could also champion unpopular projects, such as costly jail or courthouse improvements, which might be necessary but politically hazardous for officeholders accountable to taxpayers. Of course, grand jurors could also be manipulated or corrupted for political ends. Typically, Noonan's grand juries embarrassed the Bexar County Commissioners' Court with critical reports on various aspects of county administration, often based on information readily available in the public record. In late summer 1892 one such grand jury reviewed the county's finances and filed a report on September 15. It condemned the bookkeeping practices of county officials as being deficient and questioned transfers of funds between dedicated accounts by the Commissioners' Court. The validity of these charges was debated, but the report made news and its timing further agitated the campaign season.[14]

Per the common practice of the time, voters were restricted to straight tickets listing specific candidates for the offices being decided (as opposed to the present system where the option to pick and choose exists). On the fourth of October, the anti-administration Citizen's Party fielded a slate of candidates to largely replace the current

5.1.
Bexar County Courthouse under
construction. *Photographed 1893,
photographer unknown, courtesy
Alexander Architectural Archive,
University of Texas, Austin.*

county government. Democrats dominated the county government but other politicos
also felt threatened by the Citizen's Party. This was enough to cause the formation
of an unusual coalition that supported candidates likely to preserve the status quo.
Promoting a "County Ticket," the Democratic, Republican, and Workingmen's Parties
united behind the Bexar incumbents, save one. County Judge McAllister sought reelection but was abandoned by the County Ticket in favor of Bryan Callaghan's candidacy.
The political exigency made for strange bedfellows. Callaghan, considered a nominal
Democrat, was sharing the ticket with Commissioner Joseph Dwyer, a prominent
attorney and leading figure in both the Democratic Party and the anti-Callaghan camp.
Likewise, District Judge Noonan, a Republican, was running alongside officials he
continued to embarrass through grand jury investigations.

The Citizen's Party courted Noonan and the few other Republicans in office, particularly Commissioner Peter Jonas. Ultimately, Noonan and Jonas allowed their names
on *both* tickets in defiance of the Republican leadership. They thereby managed, as one
newspaper put it, "to ride both horses and make themselves solid" regardless of which
ticket won the election.[15]

The County Ticket carried the November 8 election, but it would be almost a
month before Mayor Callaghan was sworn in as county judge. With McAllister still
presiding, the Commissioners' Court appointed Henry B. Salliway as the county's

superintendent for the courthouse construction at $100 per month. Of course, Gordon was already contracted for this service. While qualified, Salliway's appointment was likely a political payoff for delivering the votes of a number of workingmen for the County Ticket. His hiring was a redundant expense that undermined Gordon's authority. Directed to inspect the courthouse work to date, Salliway filed a report on November 26 stating that all was in order.[16]

Old political divisions soon reappeared following the election. District Judge Noonan swore in a grand jury to investigate the courthouse project. It presented its report on December 6—McAllister's last day in office. While finding the quality of the work to be satisfactory, jurors concluded that the people of the county had been defrauded: Gordon and the contractors had drawn too much money for the work done to date, the cement foundation was too expensive, and the change of five granite courses to three resulted in a savings of between $5,000 and $7,000, which should have been returned to the county. Although all of the courthouse work had been done in the open, with decisions documented in the public record and the press, the grand jury urged an official investigation into the matter.[17]

According to a pseudonymous contributor to a local newspaper, however, members of this grand jury were far from impartial. Three had been candidates opposing present commissioners in the recent election. Other members were reported to be "not on speaking terms" with some of the accused. The grand jury foreman, a disappointed bidder for the foundation work, had also been its principal witness against the implicated parties.[18]

This appearance of partiality did not discourage Bryan Callaghan from seizing a political opportunity. Indeed, he and some jurors may have been working in concert to take control of the courthouse project. Upon being sworn in as the Bexar county judge on December 7, 1892, his first order of business was to read the grand jury report into the minutes. After considering the matter the Commissioners' Court appointed a committee consisting of Callaghan, Commissioner Peter Jonas, B. F. Jones, and Otto Kramer (who now held the office of San Antonio city architect) to investigate the charges against Gordon and the contractors.[19] Jonas, who had cast a vote for Gordon's winning design and was party to the letting of contracts, was likely the only committeeman not biased against the accused going into the investigation. This committee could not have been authorized without at least two commissioners siding with Callaghan for a majority of the five-member Commissioners' Court. Their motive for approving such an investigation is not known, but being ultimately responsible for the project they may have believed that supporting the inquiry could shield them should controversy arise.

At any rate, the committee worked in secret for more than a week with its members declining all public comment. Rumors and speculation on the investigation were rife in the city. It soon became apparent to Gordon that his career was suddenly in grave danger. With sizable budgets involved in most construction, architects traded on their honesty as much as their talent and knowledge. Now gossip was already gnawing at his nascent reputation. A criminal indictment, whether it had real grounds or not, could be devastating. After all, while Alfred Giles was much better established when similar scurrilous charges were made against him in faraway El Paso, his practice was still impaired, and he incurred considerable legal expense clearing his name. If similar charges against Gordon were allowed to stand in San Antonio, he would likely have to abandon the city, his career, or both.

Gordon began his counter offense on December 15, possibly after some coaching by Alfred Giles, who had a reputation for helping fellow designers.[20] On that morning the young architect went before the full Commissioners' Court and requested to be heard. This being granted, Gordon protested that

> Ever since the Grand Jury report I have been resting under a cloud, which I should have cleared up long since by a statement of facts and figures had not this court appointed a committee to investigate this report. I have waited a week since its appointment and have not offered a word in public in the way of explanation. This committee that you have appointed are conducting their meetings in secret and have refused to hear any explanation from me, or [*sic*] refuse to take the records of my office into consideration, and I now come before you and request that this investigation be conducted openly and before this court. I have nothing to conceal and think the public should know the proceedings of this investigation, and that at once.

The architect's forcefully delivered demand caused a sensation in the courtroom. As reported in the *Daily Express,*

> At the conclusion of Mr. Gordon's remarks, Judge Callaghan arose and objected most strenuously to an open investigation. Mr. Gordon could have his say when the committee had made its report. He concluded his remarks saying: "If this investigation is made in open court, I will not serve on the committee."

Contractor Otto Kroeger was then allowed to address the court on behalf of his partner George Dugan and himself. He stated, "we join Mr. Gordon in requesting an open investigation, conducted by men who are competent to judge. As Mr. Gordon stated, we have nothing to conceal." In response, Callaghan asked Kroeger if he had the opportunity to state his case to the grand jury. Kroeger replied that he had not, and the newspaper continued "that it was on this account that he demanded an open, public investigation. There had been enough star chamber proceedings in the grand jury."

In a pivotal move, Commissioner Dwyer then proposed the investigation be continued in open court, which met strenuous objection by Callaghan. Suddenly, the problems of an architect and two contractors faded, and the courthouse controversy became a game board for a political power struggle. Joining with Dwyer, the other commissioners asserted their combined authority to override Callaghan's opposition to an open investigation. In response, Callaghan moved that his committee be disbanded rather than operate in public view. This caused considerable heated debate but ultimately he prevailed and the committee was discharged. In reporting its dissolution, the *Daily Express* correctly predicted, "What their researches showed will probably never be given to the public."[21]

With Callaghan's secret committee disbanded, the Commissioners' Court resolved to start a new, open investigation—a trial.[22] With their petitions, Gordon and Kroeger triggered a process wherein the Bexar County Commissioners' Court assumed the mantle of a court of law, with county attorneys bringing the case against the defendants: the architect and contractors. Knowing of Alfred Giles's previous experience in El Paso, Gordon surely understood the forces he had set in motion and it was a high-stakes gamble. In effect voluntarily putting himself on trial, Gordon placed his trust in the fairness of the entire Commissioners' Court and laid his actions before public scrutiny, both of which he apparently trusted more than Callaghan. While four members of the Commissioners' Court had approved the contracts with Gordon and the builders, their continued support was not certain, and it appears every effort was made to prosecute the case without bias.

An announcement published in all the city's newspapers requested anyone with information pertaining to the accusations to come forward and address the court. The members of the Commissioners' Court sat in judgment. As county judge, Callaghan would have presided, but he refused to participate and the gavel was passed to Commissioner Dwyer. Defense attorneys for Gordon and the contractors squared off against the county prosecutors. As reported in the press, a sizable crowd gathered in "anticipation of a spicy session" that began the inquiry. It continued for two weeks, with spectators packing the courtroom as the proceedings held the "interest of the greater portion of the businessmen in the community."[23]

The only witness to offer damaging testimony was Frank Teich, a quarry owner who testified that the work on the courthouse was poorly done (even though the original grand jury had reported just the opposite) and that the contractors had profited substantially by changing the number of foundation stone courses. The defense suggested that Teich was motivated by a dispute with contractor Dugan. Other witnesses substantially agreed that Gordon and the contractors had acted professionally and properly. Architects John A. Ettler of San Antonio and S. L. McAdoo of Austin and contractor Emil Niggli were among the notable witnesses supporting the accused. As competitors of Gordon and the contractors, their favorable testimony is particularly significant. The four members of the secret committee were called as witnesses. Callaghan's testimony strained belief, asserting the committee had barely started its work before being disbanded and that he knew nothing about it. Similarly, B. F. Jones said he had not examined anything while a member of the committee. As an architect *and* secret committee member, Otto Kramer was considered to be the most important witness in the investigation. When he claimed to be too ill to travel to the courthouse, the proceedings were moved to his home. Testifying from his bed, the city architect provided nothing of use to either side. Commissioner Jonas was the only member of the secret committee to offer anything besides evasions. He testified that, as far as he knew, he was the only member to examine the construction site and found nothing wrong.[24]

As the hearing drew to a close on December 30, Gordon and the contractors expressed satisfaction that it had been conducted fairly. The Commissioners' Court returned its judgment a few weeks later. It found (1) that the grand jury's initial charges were without grounds, (2) that Gordon acted in accordance with his contract, which was within the AIA guidelines, (3) that deviations from the original specifications for the cement foundation were justified, and (4) that any possible savings gained by quarrying and laying three courses of large stones instead of five courses of smaller stones for the foundation, as originally specified, were negated by the additional cost of handling the large stones. Furthermore, they agreed with many of the witnesses that the use of large stones increased the soundness of the structure and enhanced its appearance.[25]

Perhaps the interest exhibited by the local business community in these proceedings reveals the real motive behind the original grand jury accusations. Callaghan's power base as mayor involved bestowing city contracts upon his friends and supporters,[26] and the courthouse scandal was likely no more than an attempt to oust Gordon, Dugan, and Kroeger in favor of his cronies. Businessmen may have viewed the investigation as a presage of the distribution of future county spoils. Callaghan's aversion to a public inquiry betrays his doubt in the charges. Conversely, Gordon's bold demand for an inquiry testifies to his faith in his own actions.

Of course, Gordon now owed very much to the Bexar County commissioners. Whatever their motivation, their support for the open investigation allowed Gordon to exonerate himself as he openly challenged Callaghan, one of San Antonio's most powerful figures. The ordeal also seems to have forged a bond between the architect and fellow accused Otto P. Kroeger. In the next few years they formed a close working relationship that eventually raised ethical questions.

Work continued on the courthouse throughout the investigation process. The 3-ton, polished granite cornerstone was laid with an impressive Masonic ceremony on Saturday, December 17, 1892. Despite inclement weather, a large crowd filled Main Plaza while others watched from the windows and rooftops of nearby buildings. The cornerstone had been ordered the previous August with the direction that names of the McAllister Commissioners' Court members be inscribed on it. Gordon is listed as the sole architect. (While Gordon had been magnanimous in sharing credit for Fayette with Laub two years earlier, he seems to have had reason—as detailed in Chapter 6—to snub his former partner now.) Dugan and Kroeger share the designation of "Builders," along with David Hughes, who was vice president of the Dugan Cut-Stone Company in Kansas City and a surety for the contractors' bond.[27]

As work proceeded into 1893 Callaghan became an obstructionist to the project, often with the aid of Commissioner William Boemer. While they did not constitute a majority, they could impede the progress of the Commissioners' Court through endless debates and boycotts. Another tactic that Callaghan employed was refusing to sign documents needed for the project to proceed. While Callaghan provided a needed check to the sometimes-questionable ways of the commissioners, it may be wrong to assume he was motivated by fiscal responsibility. As mayor, he had a reputation for being quite liberal with taxpayer monies, with the City Hall serving as a good example.[28]

On February 23 Callaghan refused to sign Henry Salliway's warrant for pay as superintendent. In defending his action, the county judge rightfully argued that Salliway duplicated work Gordon was already contracted to do. Salliway won a subsequent lawsuit to force Callaghan's signature, but the county judge appealed. While the lower court's decision was reversed, it proved a somewhat Pyrrhic victory: while Callaghan could not be compelled to sign, the appellate court also determined that the mayor's signature was not needed to execute the will of the Commissioners' Court—the county clerk's signature would do equally well.[29] Twice beaten by the Bexar County Commissioners' Court majority and his influence significantly diminished, Bryan Callaghan II became more acquiescent.

Architect Gordon saw his influence on the courthouse project diminish as well. For instance, Dugan and Kroeger recommended additional ironwork to strengthen the piers in the district courtroom. After listening to Gordon's report agreeing with the contractors, the Commissioners' Court voted its approval. It then voted to have the additional cost of $785 deducted from the architect's compensation. The contractors also proposed using iron trusses and other modifications to the roof specifications, which Gordon did not consider crucial, but he allowed that it would make the structure more fire-resistant and be money well spent. The Commissioners' Court approved the modifications to the plan for an additional cost, after arbitration, of $15,556.44. Gordon was not penalized for this change, however, presumably because the original plans were acceptable as well.[30]

Up to this point, Dugan and Kroeger had only been contracted for the basement and superstructure. While this construction was under way, Gordon was at work on plans and specifications for the interior. Beginning in February 1893, the architect prepared different proposals and estimates for consideration. The cage method of construction allowed the interior plan to be developed at this late date; the only restriction on the design was that it fit within the space already defined by the superstructure. Unfortunately, this freedom gave officials license to demand numerous, and at times capricious, changes. It was not until April of the following year that the Commissioners' Court was sufficiently satisfied to give its approval and order Gordon to advertise for bids. For unknown reasons, Otto Kroeger did not participate in the May 1894 competition for the finishing contract. Entering on his own, George Dugan's bid for $143,364 was the lowest.[31]

Lack of funds delayed commencement on the interior work for over half a year. In the meantime, another county election was held in November 1894, but the balance of power within the Commissioners' Court remained unchanged. Later in the month they were able to get Dugan to agree to split his earlier bid. The contractor would provide only part of the work at the present time for $35,299 and on December 21, 1894, the Commissioners' Court entered into a contract with him. He was through with this first phase of the interior work by the end of June 1895. There was no further progress on the building until more bonds were issued in November. Gordon was then ordered to submit an addendum to the specifications that cut the cost of the remaining work. A statue and clock for the tower were eliminated, as were window blinds and bathtubs (presumably for sequestered jurors). The amount of jail cells, hardware, gas fixtures, wainscoting, and other items was reduced by half.[32]

Dugan apparently had no interest in negotiating with the county for the reduced remainder of the work. The Commissioners' Court solicited new bids and on January 6, 1896, the contract went to Otto Kroeger for $69,900. Dugan did not participate. Kroeger agreed to complete the work within seven months, but this stretched into twelve.[33]

Gordon was not closely involved with this last phase of the Bexar County Courthouse construction. The Commissioners' Court minutes during this time contain scant mention of the architect while its members became overly involved with minutiae. For instance, along with approval of Callaghan's requisition for curtains for his new office, the minutes note that the janitor was authorized to purchase "24½" nickel plated screws, round heads." The group also deliberated over electrical fixtures, fire hoses, mops, buckets, and cuspidors. While the county's superintendent, Salliway, consulted the architect on occasion, it is obvious that Gordon did not control the project.[34]

County workers began to occupy the building as the job dragged on. The Commissioners' Court held its first session in the new building on September 23, 1896. Five weeks later the court appointed arbitrators to resolve "all questions between the architect and contractor" regarding the courthouse. Gordon found some aspects of the work to be wanting, but the arbitrators sided with Kroeger.[35]

On January 27, 1897, after four and a half years of construction, scandal, delays, and redesigns, Gordon submitted his final report on the Bexar County Courthouse. His brief message to the Commissioners' Court suggests some dissatisfaction with the project as it ended. His anticlimactic postscript is evidence of the architect's wry sense of humor. The report concludes

> As the contract recites that the decision of the arbitrators shall be final and binding upon all parties, I have this day issued vouchers accordingly.
>
> I have the honor to be, with respect,
J. R. Gordon, Arch't.
>
> p.s. I would therefore suggest that this building be accepted, under contract dated Jan. 20th, 1896.[36]

Despite the long and troubled construction history of the Bexar courthouse, the exterior is quite faithful to Gordon & Laub's original design. This is likely because the contract for the basement and superstructure was let before the scandal and subsequent impediments to the project.[37]

The building faces north onto Main Plaza (fig. 5.2). A 134-foot tower, rising near the northwest corner and topped by a beehive dome, must be considered the most distinctive feature of a very distinctive courthouse. With three observation levels, the tower exudes a minaret-like quality that suffers not one bit from the elimination of the originally planned clock and statue of *Justice*. A pyramidal-roofed, belvedere tower to the west continues the program of high architectural quality, rising 104 feet and accented by a carved eagle with a 12-foot wingspan. These towers and two more belvederes on the south façade served as ventilating shafts.

Between the north towers is the main entrance, which is situated beneath a stunningly massive, 30-foot segmental arch exhibiting engineering prowess, with two engaged towers buttressing its outward thrust. These towers rise 45 feet and feature large bronze lamps and beehive domes. Their second stories are incorporated into a loggia that spans the space above the arch. Above the loggia, at the fourth-story level, an arcade of windows fills the space between the larger towers. A foliated frieze of red terra-cotta wraps around the entire building below the line of its hipped roof, and a similar frieze decorates the loggia above the entrance. A tall, second-story sill course of dressed stone mirrors the water table and sets off the ruggedly treated first floor from the more ornate stories above.

To the east, the mass of the building is carved out for a splendid courtyard, leaving the structure U-shaped (fig. 5.3). The courtyard is oriented to harness the cooling breeze from a nearby bend in the San Antonio River, forcing it through the windows (fig. 5.4). (Gordon was familiar with the nuances of the site; his office was a block away

5.2.
Bexar County Courthouse,
San Antonio, Texas (1892–97).
Gordon & Laub, architects.
*Postcard view published by Nic.
Tengg, ca. 1907.*

and his home not much farther.) With obvious pride, the architect described this 50 x 50 foot open court to the press:

> It is entered by ascending very large and spacious granite steps, with immense granite columns and bronze lamps on each side, to a platform floored in marble with a granite balustrade. Over this is a magnificent 26-foot fountain, surrounded by various kinds of tropical plants, the silvery sprays of the fountain as it plays over them producing a beautiful and cooling effect.
>
> From the first platform, which is flanked by stairs of granite, turning to the right and left, one enters into the colonnades which surround the entire court and fountain. They are floored with marble and surmounted with polished granite columns, with magnificently carved capitals and granite balustrades and, from this court, entrance is had to the spacious hall on the right and left.[38]

The colonnade's roof was designed to provide cooling shade to the first-story windows and entrances. The walls above the courtyard colonnades are richly decorated and pierced by window arcades.

The west façade is not as successful as the others, which can be attributed at least in part to funding problems. The architects planned for a western entrance, but its execution was deferred to an undetermined future date that never arrived. This would have included a carriage porch of heavy granite arches, but what was built is a relatively austere wall of windows. As a result, the west side appears somewhat neglected compared to the other façades.

To the south, however, Gordon & Laub placed another entrance behind an impressive arcade supported by polished granite columns. While imposing, the overall composition of this façade suffered somewhat by an unbalanced treatment of the roofs of the flanking towers.

On the whole, the stylistic program is an adept blending of Moorish, Spanish, and Romanesque elements with splendid effect. Detailed newspaper accounts illuminated the architects' objectives. Using information most likely provided by Gordon himself, they established his intended sensitivity to regional culture. As previously discussed, Moorish styling was appropriate for the Aransas courthouse and Richardsonian Romanesque suited Fayette County, albeit with a German twist. An amalgamation of the two, with a strong Spanish influence, befitted Bexar County and San Antonio's historically multiethnic population. It is interesting to note that this design was reported during the competition as being Spanish or Moorish, as opposed to other entries that were described as Romanesque or in the school of Richardson. One account described it as a "very pretty design [that] possesses the merit of having found something worthy in San Antonio's antiquities to weave into its strictly modern fabric."[39]

5.3.
Bexar County Courthouse,
east porch under construction.
*Photographed ca. 1894, photographer
unknown, courtesy Alexander
Architectural Archive, University of
Texas, Austin.*

5.4.
Mill Bridge Ford and Bexar
County Courthouse. *Postcard
view published by Alling Paper Co.,
ca. 1907.*

Besides the features already discussed, a plethora of ornamental elements further enlivens Bexar's exterior. A variety of window treatments are employed, including heavily bracketed balconies that intensify the Spanish flavor. Hip-dormers interrupt the Spanish tiled roof to ventilate the attic. A gently bowed oriel appears on the front of the main tower. The carving of capitals varies from column to column. Polished columns soften window jams while human faces provide the corbel stops to decorative colonettes.

This well-developed program of exterior ornamentation for the Bexar County Courthouse is muted by the monochromatic color scheme. The choice of brownish-red Pecos sandstone for the entire superstructure, instead of just for trim, was made during construction. Gordon & Laub originally specified yellowish-white Muldoon or Brackenridge sandstone, but, in response to concerns about its durability, Gordon supported the substitution of the Pecos stone, and its consistent use yields happy results.[40] Subtle variations in shade and surface treatment exist for those who look for it, but the overall effect is one of a homogeneous mass of stone. Such cohesion, when viewed from a distance, increases the visual presence of large-scale projects. Gordon called it "a mammoth structure, devoid of gaudiness of color or other flashy effect."

While the outside of the building drew much acclaim, the layout of the inside drew much criticism. The arrangement suffered from Gordon's zeal to harness the winds for passive ventilation. Some felt that the large courtyard, while beautiful, virtually divided the building into two parts with only a narrow corridor and a single row of small offices connecting the north and south sections. Other problems were likely due to the late design revisions imposed by county officials and which resulted in some hallways that were narrow, dark, and confusing with tortuous corners and turns. Some offices were criticized as being too small, inconveniently placed, or dependent on artificial light. Since Gordon's other designs are so well considered, these gaffes seem likely to be the aftermath of official meddling.

The two district courtrooms on the second floor, each two stories high with galleries accessed from third-floor halls, were the most meritorious interior features. Expanses of these 50 x 70 foot courtrooms were uninterrupted save the minor columns supporting the galleries. Galleries were faced with Lincrusta, which was also used for decorative wainscoting on the courtroom walls. Ceilings were heavily paneled and acoustics were reported in the press to be perfect. Prisoners accessed the courtrooms via private stairways, as did justices and juries to separate them from "seductive influences."

Brick comprising the interior walls was made with clay from nearby Calaveras. The floors consisted of steel beams separated by fire-resistant terra-cotta and topped with four inches of concrete. The first-floor halls were laid with marble and the second-floor halls with tile. Wood was used for flooring in appropriate offices.

Cost-reducing measures imposed late in the project affected the interior. Shafts were built for four elevators, but only one was installed at the end of construction. The original specifications called for oak finishing, but this was changed to Texas pine. Marble wainscoting, as originally specified, was out of the question. The architect suggested using panels of Acme cement plaster, combed and painted, instead of pine for the wainscoting. This material had been employed in the rotunda of the city's Grand Opera House, and was also used in Gordon's Ellis County Courthouse. The commissioners approved this change, and this material was apparently used throughout the building, excepting the courtrooms.[41]

Bexar represents a meander in the evolutionary track of Gordon's courthouse designs. This could reveal the hand of his partner, Laub, since the asymmetrical façade and U-shaped arrangement owes much to federal buildings designed during his tenure in the Supervising Architect's office. Imagine filling the courtyard with a one-story postal workplace and the similarity to the typical federal template becomes more apparent. Of course, Gordon also became familiar with this template while superintending the construction of the San Antonio Federal Building, and it was Gordon who revised that plan to take advantage of the prevailing winds for natural ventilation, as the Bexar courtyard does. The tall tower that creates the asymmetry may also have been devised to win the support of then–county judge McAllister, quoted above as wanting the courthouse to surpass the Federal Building. The courthouse's tower is 30 feet taller than that of the post office.

There is some evidence to suggest that the beehive dome on the tall tower can be credited to Laub. An alternative design for Bexar that Gordon later used for self-promotion depicts the tower with a pyramidal roof and treated more like his previous tower designs (fig. 5.5). It also shows symmetrical towers at the south entrance. The rest of the rendering is quite close to the structure as built. It was this alternative design that Gordon submitted to *The American Architect and Building News* under his own name and used on his letterhead at least as late as June 1897.[42] There is no evidence that this alternative design was ever presented for consideration, however. Perhaps Gordon used this discarded design in his promotion because it more closely represents his own vision than the domed version that was built. While the architects possibly had differences over some aspects of its design, Bexar's exterior is still the result of collaboration between spirits kindred in their art.

Near its completion, the *Daily Express* made this observation of the Bexar County Courthouse:

It is an interesting structure and attracts a great deal of attention from visitors and strangers, but it possesses a very pathetic interest for the taxpayers of the county who reflect every time they gaze upon its brown walls and the cone-shaped tower

5.5.
Bexar County Courthouse, alternative tower design, Gordon & Laub, architects. Proposed
carriage porch visible on right. *Courtesy Alexander Architectural Archive, University of Texas, Austin.*

that bonds to the amount of $621,000 have been issued to pay for its construction
and to meet such other incidental expenses as have arisen in connection with it.[43]

Far exceeding the original $300,000 estimate, the total cost of the structure was a
source of much local discord. Responsibility for the overruns, with the exception
of unforeseen problems with the site, clearly lies with the elected officials, but some
project costs included in the $621,000 figure had nothing to do with the construction.
Among these are the $110,000 purchase price of the site property, cost of clearing
the property, $2,232.62 for drain and sewer work, legal fees, and Salliway's $100-per-
month salary.[44]

The members of the Commissioners' Court maintained a tight grip on the work
and it is evident that Gordon was not one of their cronies. As superintendent, perhaps
Gordon can be faulted for losing his authority. It must be remembered, however, that
he was compromised by the debt he owed the commissioners who allowed him a
forum to defend himself against the grand jury charges and Callaghan's secret investigation.

Still, competitors used the runaway Bexar project to impugn Gordon's character.
An example appears in Chapter 10, where a figure of $700,000 is tied to the court-
house and used against him in Mississippi. To be fair, it must be acknowledged that
Gordon was not above citing the $700,000 figure himself when trying to impress later
clients with the large sum.

The Bexar County Courthouse served its purpose with little change until 1914,
when a five-story addition was added on the south end. The addition stayed true to the
original building with respect to materials and decorative scheme, as stipulated by the
1914 Commissioners' Court. A major remodeling, initiated in 1926, further increased
floor space with the *Express* reporting that the "Bexar County Commissioners' Court
provided that the same style selected by Gordon be retained. The present building has
been outgrown, but its architectural lines are still considered as beautiful as when it
was first erected." Both the 1914 and 1926 renovations utilized Burnet granite and Pecos
sandstone in sympathy with the original design. Unfortunately, renovations included
destruction of Gordon's prized courtyard to provide space for offices. The center part
of the building gained a fifth story, and the west side saw the addition of two wings.
The interior was gutted: the original steel beams and masonry arches of the cage
construction were replaced with reinforced concrete framing. Artificial heating and
cooling was installed. Further additions in 1963 and 1970 made little or no attempt to
maintain the stylistic integrity of the building's exterior.[45]

Despite changes made to the Bexar County Courthouse through the years, its
largely unaltered main façade still towers proudly over Main Plaza, where it has provided a fitting pendant to the nearby San Fernando Cathedral for over a century (fig. 5.6).

5.6.
Main Plaza, San Antonio, Texas.
Bexar County Courthouse
at center with San Fernando
Cathedral on right. *Photograph ca.
1905, photographer unknown.*

Its massive arch welcomes those having business with the county, and its minaret-like tower is a distinctive feature of San Antonio's skyline. Part of the courtyard's grand arcade can still be seen in the first-floor corridor where a surviving mass of clustered columns, ornately carved capitals, and subtly detailed arches provide a glimpse at past beauty. The same can be said of the courtyard fountain, which, after standing for decades in Waterworks Park, has recently been relocated in front of the courthouse. Although topped with a jarringly new statue of *Justice*, its silvery sprays can still produce a beautiful and cooling effect on a hot Texas afternoon.

The Bexar County Courthouse marks an advance in Gordon's artistic evolution. Here he blends seemingly disparate but locally significant historic architectural references, along with other picturesque ornamental elements, subtly and in harmony. Bexar also represents a step, if a bit out of line, in Gordon's quest for the optimal design for a Texas courthouse. It appears that the passive ventilation of the U-shaped building worked well, but at the expense of convenience and natural lighting. While stunning, it is evident that Gordon had not yet found his ideal courthouse for the Texas climate.

Gordon was already enjoying a thriving San Antonio practice when his firm won the Bexar competition in 1891. The prestige of this commission further established his courthouse credentials. Winning this prize on top of the Federal Building superintendency secured his ranking above James Wahrenberger in the San Antonio architectural hierarchy.[46] By his boycott of the courthouse competition, Alfred Giles, while still held in high regard, allowed himself to be eclipsed by Gordon.

Although Gordon took justified pride in this courthouse and used it in his self-promotion, the scandal and final costs provided fodder for his critics. Despite his exoneration in court and the disingenuous nature of the budget charges, the slander against his character surely cost him some commissions. Through the end of the decade, the Bexar County Courthouse was both a feather in his cap and an albatross tied about his neck.

CHAPTER SIX

Erath and Victoria

Gordon & Laub began two more courthouse projects shortly after winning the Bexar competition. While Laub likely had a role in the designs for Erath and Victoria Counties, Gordon's hand appears dominant. They are derivative of his earlier work for Aransas and Fayette Counties, respectively.

Fire destroyed Erath County's first courthouse in 1866. All of the county records were lost as flames consumed the ten-year-old, wood frame structure on Stephenville's town square. Its replacement was completed in 1867, but the loss of the records had a long-lasting impact on the citizens and continues to vex historians today. Marriage licenses, records of births, deeds, liens and releases, probate and Commissioners' Court proceedings—all were cinders. Reestablishing land titles was an arduous task that lasted years as property lines were defined and recognized through neighbors' affidavits. Although the new courthouse was built of limestone, it was not much of an improvement over its predecessor as far as fire-resistance was concerned.[1] No doubt memories of this ordeal weighed heavily in the minds of citizens as nearby counties built new courthouses employing modern fireproofing technology developed in the wake of the 1871 Great Chicago Fire and other conflagrations.

In 1891 petitions in favor of building a new courthouse circulated among Erath's citizenry. Before these reached the Commissioners' Court, Erath officials placed a notice in the *San Antonio Daily Express* in May. Although unusual for its candor, the callous lack of respect for architects' labors was not unheard of in its time:

> On the 17th day of June, 1891, the Commissioners' Court of Erath County will decide whether they will build a court house or not. Architects who wish to present plans and specifications for the consideration of the court are invited to be present at that time and present them. It is the purpose of the court to build a good court house if they build at all; one that is as near fire proof as possible. For further information, address H. H. Hardin, of Stephenville.[2]

Although it gave no hint of a budget or compensation, nor even a commitment to building at all, this notice drew some ten or fifteen architects from as far away as

St. Louis. They arrived in Stephenville at the appointed date to watch the Erath County Commissioners' Court formally receive the petitions. The court then announced it would begin considering plans and specifications for a new courthouse to cost $75,000. Designers explained their plans before the court during the following week. The *Fort Worth Gazette* reported that the review process was prolonged owing to "the spirited and close competition of the rival architects." Gordon & Laub prevailed in the contest even though the price tag for executing the firm's design was estimated to be as high as $100,000. The court stipulated that the architects make some unrecorded changes to their design and that the cost could not go over the previously stated $75,000. They were given until July 9 to return with the remodeled plans.[3]

The political scene in Erath County heated up immediately after Gordon & Laub secured the commission. Although the petitions for the new courthouse were signed by nearly two-thirds of the county's voters, many now claimed that they did not fully understand the document they were endorsing. Another petition circulated demanding a special election on the matter. This proved to be the opening salvo in a politically acrimonious summer for Erath County. Some saw the construction of a new courthouse as an opportunity to move the county seat. The community of Dublin, near the county's western edge, became a contender, offering to cover the cost of moving the county records. As an indicator of the benefits of a county-seat designation, developers and speculators flocked to Dublin during the summer to profit from increased property values. Conversely, uncertainty caused development in Stephenville to dwindle. There was talk of appeasing both factions by splitting Erath into two counties. A special election held on July 28 settled the matter, coming down in favor of centrally located Stephenville.[4]

Thus decided, county officials could return to the issue of the courthouse, but nearly two months of intra-county bickering had sapped enthusiasm for the project. Gordon & Laub had supplied the county with two versions of the revised plans, which were made available for contractor bids by August 31. The most prominent difference between the two was that the more expensive version featured colonnades that wrapped around the corners of the building. The contract went to S. A. Tomlinson of Fort Worth, whose bid for the less expensive version was $58,823. The Commissioners' Court opted for this design, knowing that additional costs and fees (including the architects') would bring the total near $73,000, close to the original budget cap. Officials feared exceeding that amount could reignite passion smoldering from the summer's political battles. The *Stephenville Empire* reported that the colonnades added "very much to the beauty of the building, but they cost about $5,000, and it was with regret that the court dispensed with them." In the quest for economy, perspective renderings of the final design were considered a nonessential expense, and therefore the architects prepared none.[5]

6.1.
Erath County Courthouse,
Stephenville, Texas (1891–92).
Gordon & Laub, architects.
Photographed 1992.

Work began in mid-September 1891, with Gordon & Laub superintending. The construction methods for the Erath courthouse provide a sharp contrast to the electricity-powered mechanization employed about the same time for Bexar. At Stephenville, teams of oxen pulled plows and moved dirt for the excavation work. Stones, as large as roughly 10 x 18 x 36", were raised and placed with a single, mule-powered derrick.[6]

The final design for Erath blends features from the central tower plan and the hollow square plans previously utilized by Gordon (fig. 6.1).[7] Like Aransas, the tower is located in the center of the building, over a ventilating shaft. Like Fayette, the four façades of the roughly 80-foot-square plan feature paired pavilions and the doorway opposite the courtroom end is treated as the main entrance. This is given slight prominence by a shallow porch featuring an arch supported by clustered columns with Romanesque capitals. The surmounting balustrade protrudes slightly from the flanking pavilions. That said, all façades are similar enough to avoid the pronounced "back door" effect seen with the Fayette courthouse, which is similarly located on a town square. On the opposite side of the building, the southern entrance features a distinctive square headed arch. Above this, a stonework faux balustrade leads to the three large, arched windows that light the second-story courtroom. Identical east and west entrances have simple post and lintel surrounds topped by balustrades that are flush with the pavilions. The windows at the first floor are arched. Second-story windows, excepting those for the south side of the courtroom, have flat arches. Flat and round arches alternate for the third-story windows. Ocular portals in the gables assist in ventilating the attic.

S. Moffat provided the stonework. The preponderant white limestone for the exterior came from area quarries.[8] The familiar red Pecos sandstone provides the accent color as quoining, arches, and window surrounds. This stone is also employed for stringcourses, dentilated eaves, and at the gables, which culminate with blunt tabs at their peak, as opposed to the somewhat delicate finials at Fayette. Above the roofline, Erath's central clock tower rises to a height of 95 feet. The red-and-white stonework is used in a simulated balustrade that provides a transition from the original red slate pyramidal roof to the masonry tower. Above this, on each side of the tower, are observatories divided by two columns surmounted by large, arched ventilation portals. Faces of the clockwork are set in shallow dormers in the steep pyramidal tower roof.

North and south entrances lead to short halls with doorways to offices. These rooms were originally sparingly appointed with fireproofing being a primary concern. Although naturally finished granary pine is used for doorways throughout the building, vaults and other metal features are numerous reminders of the county's wariness of fire. Cast iron stairways in the east and west connect the Gilbert system floors.

At the center of Erath's courthouse an arcade of rough-cut white limestone leads to an interior atrium court. Here the architects used the masonry tower supports to create a quite dramatic centerpiece (fig. 6.2). Three tiered, triple-arch arcades comprise each of the four sides of this court. A wooden platform, accessed from the eastern stair, clings to the bare stone interior of the tower above the third floor. From there, wooden flights of stairs lead up to the observatory. Here hardy visitors took in a panoramic view of the county and gazed down a dizzying 75 feet to the white and gray Georgia marble tiling of the first floor. This tower functioned as the building's ventilator, like Aransas's central shaft and Fayette's open court. Although sheltered from the weather by the tower roof, the openness of the observatory and the ashlar colonnades establish the shaft as part of the building's exterior. Nevertheless, it has an intimate relationship with the surrounding plastered corridors and offices. It is unique among Gordon's extant work. During construction, a visitor reported that "On first entering this corridor one is immediately struck by the number of high arches tying the tower to the many walls of the building, and giving to the vast structure an air of solidity and strength that is indescribable."

The same nineteenth-century narrator reports that "the crowning glory of the whole structure" was to be found on the second floor—the district courtroom (fig 6.3). Occupying the southern portion of the second and third stories, the room measures 38 x 72 feet, accommodating about 400 spectators with theater-style tiered seating.

6.2.
Erath County Courthouse, atrium view looking up toward tower. *Photographed 2006.*

The judge's bench is placed against the south wall, backlit by the three large arched windows mentioned above. A semi-vault springs from the wall above the bench to launch the ceiling and the voices of trial participants toward the spectators. The deeply coffered metal ceiling reaches a height of 24 feet above a third-floor gallery that wraps around the northern side of the room "in the form of a half oval."

6.3.
Erath County Courthouse, district courtroom. *Photographed 2006.*

Erath possesses remarkable interior features and some noteworthy elements on the exterior, but the smaller budget precluded much of the ornamentation seen in Gordon's contemporary courthouses. Perhaps most notably missing is a transition to the roof like Bexar's terra-cotta frieze or Fayette's crenellated parapet. Erath's walls abruptly give way to the roof. Also absent is a reference to an architectural heritage. The county and its seat were founded in 1856 and settled by diverse immigrants from the southern states. With no specific heritage to draw from, it is fitting that Gordon & Laub kept the design culturally neutral.

Concurrent with the design and construction of Erath was Gordon & Laub's courthouse for Victoria County, whose first courthouse had served since 1849 in the city by the same name. Its site is adjacent to the open main plaza, one of the few reminders of the city's 1824 founding by Martín De León. Originally named Guadalupe Victoria, the town was plotted during Mexican rule recalling the dictates of the Law of the Indies. By the end of the nineteenth century the county's German population exerted a strong influence, however.[9]

On May 13, 1891, the Victoria County Commissioners' Court voted to replace the old courthouse, authorizing the clerk to solicit plans and specifications for a structure to cost between $50,000 and $65,000. Submissions would be considered three months later at its August session. This solicitation was made via an advertisement that ran for four days solely in the *Houston Daily Post*. Even this minimal advertising effort drew fifteen architects to the competition by the August 11 deadline. Gordon & Laub's entry was chosen, with Galveston's Alfred Muller running a close second. Participating architects reported the competition to be spirited, but fair. Terms of the architects' contract, which included superintending, totaled 5 percent of the construction cost, with 3.5 percent to be paid upon the letting of the contract and the remainder in regular installments. Plans were placed on display at Victoria's First National Bank the next day. By November, construction was let to Martin, Byrnes & Johnston for $64,487. County officials moved to temporary offices in December and the old courthouse was demolished to make way for its successor after the New Year.[10]

Prospects seemed quite positive for Gordon at this time. In addition to Victoria, he and Laub were working on the Bexar and Erath courthouses (the brouhaha in San Antonio had not yet flared). Things soon began to sour in the architectural office and in Victoria, however.

On March 9, 1892, Laub formally announced his withdrawal from the partnership. Publicly, he only cited "personal reasons" for his departure.[11] While exact causes for the dissolution may never be known, a letter cited below makes it clear that Gordon and Laub had a falling out.

Laub's departure undoubtedly left Gordon shorthanded in dealing with the office workload and reliant on his superintendent in Victoria, where excavation was nearing completion and construction was soon to begin. The Victoria Commissioners' Court found the superintendent's work to be unsatisfactory and without further explanation demanded, on March 14, either Gordon or Laub come to inspect the work personally. It is not clear whether the Victoria officials realized Laub was out of the picture at this time, but surely Gordon would have apprised them at the first opportunity. Nevertheless, the Commissioners' Court minutes continued to reference "Gordon & Laub" in all matters related to the courthouse contract.[12]

Gordon & Laub had sent James T. Hull to oversee the Victoria work, but whether he was the "unsatisfactory" superintendent remains uncertain. Hull was clearly well qualified, having superintended Gordon's out-of-town work for a number of years as well as heading the firm's short-lived Corpus Christi branch office. Once in Victoria though, Hull took the opportunity to establish an independent architectural practice that included a jail project in Beeville. The Commissioners' Court would have reason for dissatisfaction if he neglected the courthouse in favor of his own business. Of course, Hull also may have quit Gordon's employ altogether, leaving the San Antonian pressed to quickly find a replacement who may not have measured up. Another possibility, given the events that followed, is that Victoria officials simply sought an excuse to sever ties with Gordon. [13]

For reasons that are unknown today, the courthouse work continued to slip away from Gordon and toward William L. Martin, senior partner in Martin, Byrnes & Johnston. On May 7 the *Victoria Weekly Advocate* opined, "the architect for the court house seems to have 'gone back on' the county, but fortunately we have a contractor who will do his duty." Martin was personally supervising work in Victoria for the firm that had just built Fayette without incident under Gordon's superintendence. About forty-seven years old at the time of the Victoria construction, Martin claimed many years of experience constructing public buildings in Missouri and Kansas before his firm moved to Texas. [14]

Gordon spent several days in the city trying to salvage his superintendency following the *Advocate*'s published charge of dereliction, with no success. Victoria Commissioners' Court minutes accuse Gordon & Laub of "having failed and refused to superintend the erection and construction . . . having failed and refused to furnish vouchers to the contractors as the work progressed . . . and having totally neglected to comply . . . with other provisions" of the contract. On May 13 the Commissioners' Court then declared the county's contract with Gordon & Laub null and void, declining any further connection with the architects. The decision was final, and compensation was limited to the design work and superintendence to date. Contractor Martin agreed to finish the work under his own supervision at no extra charge. He was quite faithful to Gordon & Laub's plans. [15]

Hearing about the troubles from "a friend," Laub weighed in on the subject from Brooklyn, New York. In a June 7, 1892, letter to the *Advocate*, he wrote,

> Referring to this matter, and in justice to my name, which, during my two years' stay in your great state, I worked hard to and always was anxious to leave behind me fair and pure, I desire to state that on March 9, 1892, for personal reasons, I withdrew from the firm of "Gordon & Laub," signing an agreement that Mr. Gordon would wind up and settle the firm's business. This was duly advertised in the "San Antonio Express" at the time.
>
> How this winding up of said firm's business, as far as your Court House is concerned, is being done you will be better to judge, as you will see from this statement that I am not personally responsible for the state of affairs.
>
> I regret this exceedingly and assure you that up to the day of my withdrawal all business on hand was taken proper care of, and not the least the beautiful building for Victoria County which I *personally designed* and took great pride in. [emphasis in original]
>
> Believe me,
> Sincerely yours,
> D. C. E. Laub [16]

Having thus exonerated himself, Laub fades into obscurity.[17] It should be noted that while he likely contributed to Victoria's courthouse, his claim to have "personally designed" it lacks credibility given its similarities to Fayette, which Gordon designed alone.

This entire episode is curious for it seems out of character for the principals involved. Though perhaps overtaxed after Laub's departure, Gordon seems too industrious and too congenial for the obstinate behavior cited in the minutes. Plus, the *Advocate*—hardly a friend of the architect—documents his effort to rescue the commission contrary to the official charge of total neglect. For its part, Martin, Byrnes & Johnston enjoyed a fine reputation and it is hard to imagine the firm delivering poor work. It is equally hard to imagine Gordon unjustly refusing good work, especially in light of his past relationship with the contractor going at least as far back as the Val Verde jail. With the events in Victoria contradicting our knowledge of the participants, it is reasonable to suspect some sort of collusion was afoot to remove Gordon as superintendent, one comprised of local officials and perhaps the contractor and perhaps James Hull. Supporting such conjecture are later efforts to undermine Gordon by Martin and possibly Hull (discussed in Chapter 10), which may have roots in this period.

In addition to their designer and builder, the Fayette and Victoria courthouses have a number of properties in common. They share the same hollow square design with interior court and paired pavilion façades with central entrances. Both have a tower designating the eastern façade as the primary one. The plan is better suited to the Victoria site, however, because the courthouse faces the open public plaza rather than sitting upon it. With extreme dimensions of 88 x 101 feet, Victoria is slightly smaller than Fayette. The exteriors of both buildings are primarily covered with ashlar blue sandstone from the Muldoon quarry in Fayette County. Interior furnishings were again supplied by George D. Barnard and Company. Their bricks were even made with the same steam press.[18]

These two courthouses also have significant differences. While exuberantly detailed, Victoria's exterior color scheme is more subtle than Fayette's (fig. 6.4). Gone are the animal grotesques and the dark bands of red Pecos sandstone. Arches here are of dressed white limestone with no alternating treatment to the voussoirs. Where Fayette has a terra-cotta frieze below the crenellations of the main block, this courthouse sports a checkered pattern of rough-cut and dressed stone runs with tourelles gracing the corners. Only the tourelles have carved stone finials along the lines of those that grace Fayette's gables. As at Erath, blunt tabs mark Victoria's gable points. As at Fayette, the window bays in the pavilions are recessed, and again the architect employs classical garland decoration on the spandrels, but their scale is much reduced at Victoria.

Most noteworthy are the colonnades that wrap around Victoria's corners. Rejected

6.4.
Victoria County Courthouse,
Victoria, Texas (1892). Gordon
& Laub, architects. *Photographed
1992.*

as too costly for Erath, Gordon saw this innovation as an important step in the evolution of his courthouse design. Like Fayette, the building was ventilated as warm air rose in the open center court and was replaced by relatively cooler air drawn through the office windows on the exterior. Like the horseshoe-arched porches of Aransas, Victoria's colonnades provided shade to further cool the incoming air on the first story, increasing the effectiveness of the airflow. This is the primary function of these colonnades, as evidenced by the absence of doors leading to them: one must climb through a window or over a balustrade to gain access. Aware that the unique features of his plan held value, the architect filed a copyright on his design for the Victoria courthouse.[19]

Massing of the Victoria courthouse is more complex and yet more unified than that of Fayette. Arches over the entrances continue the rhythm of the colonnade arches. Gabled pavilions and the projecting exterior of the courtroom provide agreeable interruptions to the resulting arcade and its second-story balcony. Stonework of the balcony balustrades echoes the checkered frieze at the truncated third-story level, which gives way to a hip roof. This two-and-a-half-story design, in concert with the first-story colonnade, creates a sense of massiveness as the bulk of the building recedes from the street-level observer while it climbs in height. In contrast, the pavilions rise straight to their three-story height and thereby grow in prominence.

Victoria's clock tower also rises straight to its hip roof, topping at 103 feet. Just below the Seth Thomas Number 16 clockworks is an open observation deck, or belvedere, that offers a commanding view of the nearby Guadalupe River as it winds through the city and surrounding farms and prairies. Engaged limestone corner posts run up the tower to support the clockworks and roof. Visually harmonizing the open observatory with the massive masonry clock housing above was likely a challenge for the architects. Modern methods enabled the load to be carried on relatively slight structural ironwork, but Romanesque building traditions establish the expectation of more massive masonry to perform the task. Seemingly in response to this dilemma, Gordon & Laub visually "pierce" the hip roof with the tops of the corner posts. This treatment expresses the physical dynamics of the upward thrust of the posts countering the downward push of the clockwork housing, as if the piercing is a consequence of the conflicting forces. The effect returns a sense of massiveness to the top portion of the tower. Some ninety-eight polished pink granite columns adorn the building. Frank Teich supplied these, presumably from his quarry near Fredericksburg.[20] (This is the same Frank Teich who testified against Gordon, Kroeger, and Dugan in the Bexar investigation.) Heavy brackets under the eaves lend a German flavor to the design in deference to the county's then-dominant population.

As at Fayette, the entrances opened to passageways that converge on the hall surrounding an atrium courtyard. At the time of its completion, a reporter described the flooring as "being of pretty and artistically colored tiling which makes the floor look like the palace of 'ye olden time.'"[21] The plaster covering the brick walls along the halls was incised to simulate stonework, and tinting of the plaster varied from story to story, suggesting different types of stone. These walls were also decorated with Texas curly pine wainscoting and painted stencil work. Gilbert corrugated iron vaulting was left exposed in hallways (fig. 6.5). The King Iron Bridge Company provided the structural ironwork. Diebold Safe and Lock Company supplied the vaults. The rectangular atrium was accessed from doorways in the short ends, along the north-south axis. The third floor held rooms for jurors and witnesses, who used a separate entrance off the north staircase to enter the courtroom on the second floor.

A contemporary account hails the district courtroom as "the finest courtroom south of Dallas . . . furnished with luxury and taste . . . it reminds one of a vast theatre."[22] Measuring 85 x 47 feet, it occupies the west side of the second story with a third-floor gallery. As at Erath, its 24-foot-high ceiling curves into a semi-vault above the judge's and witness stands to allow for the exterior pitch of the roof. Cast iron

6.5.
Victoria County Courthouse, interior corridor. The courtyard can be seen through the arch on the left. Gilbert system fire-resistant vaulting is visible above stairs. *Photographed 2006.*

columns with Romanesque capitals support the gallery and its foliated Lincrusta-faced balustrade. An entrance along the northern side of the room allows for the egress of jurors and witnesses, as well as the accused, coming up from a first-floor holding area. A carved railing separating spectators from the participants leads from the stairway around to the west, past the bailiff, and before the stands. Afternoon light filters in through colored glass panels behind the judge, falling upon the rich carpeting.

For the most part, William Martin dutifully followed Gordon & Laub's plans for the Victoria courthouse, but an exception is the addition of two third-floor restrooms included at the request of the Commissioners' Court. This revision necessitated the addition of two dormers to the southeast and northwest corners of the roof.[23] Obviously an afterthought, they are awkwardly placed but provide only minor distraction to an otherwise excellent composition.

Construction was completed by the end of the year. At Martin's suggestion, the Commissioners' Court called upon Houston architect Eugene T. Heiner, who designed the county's jail ten years earlier, to inspect Martin's work. Heiner declared "that Victoria county has one of the best court houses in Texas and that Martin, Byrnes & Johnson [sic] carried out their contract to the letter—and did even more." The building was accepted on December 17, 1892.[24] William Martin was praised for his service to the county and for a while his firm claimed Victoria as its address.

The total cost of the Victoria County Courthouse, including plumbing, electrical wiring, and furnishings, was reported to be about $85,000. As with the Fayette courthouse, the Victoria temple of justice was highly praised. At the time, Gordon himself considered the design to be one of his master achievements. He submitted an elevation rendering of it to the editors of *The American Architect and Building News* for publication. Although it did not appear in the journal until 1896, it is noteworthy that the editors felt the design to be still relevant and worthy of publication.[25]

With the courthouse earning acclaim, Gordon returned to the city of Victoria in February 1893 to explore business prospects. According to the *Advocate*, "Mr. Gordon's action in the new court house matter did not make many friends here, and he was not enthusiastically received." It went on to state that Victoria already had a resident architect with a claim "to all the work to be done here for years to come." This was James T. Hull, who, in the midst the superintendence controversy, established his own practice and went on to become, in the *Advocate*'s words, "Victoria's popular architect."[26] To recall the 1889 TSAA presidential address of W. C. Dodson, an architect appears to have been elevated upon the ruins of another's reputation.

CHAPTER SEVEN

The Texas State Building

The 1893 World's Columbian Exposition would prove to be a pivotal event in American architectural history. Planned to mark the 400th anniversary of Columbus's 1492 voyage to the Americas, anticipation mounted as promoters from cities across the United States lobbied Congress for the opportunity to host a fair predicted to surpass all previous world's fairs. For James Riely Gordon, who would be the architect of the Texas State Building for the exposition, it was an opportunity few regional architects experienced. Designing the Texas pavilion for the great world's fair would garner national attention for the energetic San Antonian and put him in contact with some of the leading lights of his profession. Publicity accompanying the fair probably did more to raise his countrymen's awareness of architecture than any other single event. In addition, after two redesigns, the Texas State Building as built represents an important step in Gordon's development of his signature courthouse plan.[1]

In an era before broadcasting, the great fairs of the latter half of the nineteenth century were important vehicles for promoting commerce. They afforded an opportunity for leaders of business and industry to present their wares and resources to an international audience. To attract as many as possible, the fairs were planned as grand and spectacular events. The decision was made to hold this fair in Chicago, Illinois, and Jackson Park was developed as its site. American pride demanded that the World's Columbian Exposition be the greatest fair ever, and the celebration had to be delayed until 1893 to allow for adequate preparation.

Initial plans for the layout of the grounds were formulated in the fall of 1890 by a small group of consultants that included Frederick Law Olmsted, the nation's foremost landscape architect, and Daniel H. Burnham, a partner in one of Chicago's most successful and progressive architectural firms, who would later be designated chief of construction for the fair. As the exposition's centerpiece, they conceived a man-made lake surrounded by a grand assembly of huge buildings dubbed the "Court of Honor." As plans progressed, the north end of the fairgrounds was reserved for pavilions representing states and territories of the Union. This gathering was envisioned as a "diminutive United States" where foreign and domestic visitors would have a rare opportunity to view and compare the assets, resources, customs, and residents of the participating states. Therefore, the state building grounds offered more valuable information to individuals and commercial concerns interested in relocation than could the industry-oriented Court of Honor.[2]

Seeing a benefit in having Texas represented at such an event, the Texas World's Fair Exhibit Association was formed by promoters across the state and set to the task of raising funds and organizing exhibits. Fund-raising lagged behind expectations, but it was necessary to proceed with other plans to stay on schedule. Although unable to post the requisite bond to secure a lot, the association nonetheless managed to reserve one of the finest parcels on the fairgrounds in July. This was achieved with the help of John T. Dickinson, a San Antonian known throughout the state as a tireless promoter of Texas. He was then serving as secretary for the National Commission, a group of notables selected to oversee the fair's execution. The site he helped secure was the third-largest parcel on the state building grounds and ideally located next to the fair's primary north entrance. On it the ambitious Texas group planned to erect one of the largest state exhibit structures.[3]

The association contacted seventy-five Texas architects to solicit designs and in early September sent out a circular requesting "preliminary studies (floor plans and elevations only), line drawings without color, . . . for a building for the Texas exhibit at the World's Fair, Chicago." The frame structure was to be two stories in height, constructed as far as possible of Texas materials, and cost was not to exceed $100,000. The association's desire for a design evocative of the state's old Spanish missions was well publicized and likely communicated at some point in the correspondence.[4]

Construction on the Court of Honor had already begun before the Texas association initiated its correspondence with architects. For a number of reasons, including the pressing deadline of opening day, Burnham and the other planners had chosen to employ Renaissance-inspired, neoclassical styling for the fair's magnificent centerpiece. Most of the architects chosen to design the primary buildings were from the eastern United States, where exuberant adaptations of classical forms were replacing Richardsonian Romanesque as the latest stylistic trend. Many of them studied at Paris's Ecole des Beaux-Arts, the famous design academy that promoted "modern" variations on classical ideals. They decided to employ neo-Renaissance styling in order to meet the desired criteria of uniformity of design, monumentality of appearance, and expeditiousness of execution. There was precious little time to coordinate the design process of the Court of Honor buildings, and the architects' common experience with this classical vocabulary ensured their individual compositions would integrate into a unified whole. The planners also developed a uniform set of building standards for the Court of Honor, specifying such aspects as cornice height, bay width, and color—which was white. This gave rise to the fair's nickname, "The White City."[5]

Gordon traveled to Chicago to personally inspect the lot allocated for Texas before preparing his entry. Professional journals and the popular press had carried news of the excitement attending the design and construction of the Court of Honor around the world; now the architect could see for himself the magnificent endeavor rising in a flurry of activity.[6]

Surely just as professionally invigorating was the opportunity to meet some of the leading architects in Chicago. A letter from Gordon documents his stopping at the offices of Adler & Sullivan, where Dankmar Adler, then AIA secretary, extended "many courtesies" to his guest. Presumably these included a tour of the firm's offices in the tower of the famed Auditorium Building, making it likely that Gordon also had an opportunity to meet Adler's partner, Louis Sullivan, and their head draftsman, Frank Lloyd Wright. It seems this was more than purely a social call. Gordon likely thought personal contact with an officer would improve his chances for acceptance into the AIA. Institute fellows from the Texas State Association of Architects continued to block his application, however. Gordon later confided to Adler,

I regret to feel that a few of my brother architects, all of whom treat me with every degree of courtesy to my face, should, prompted by jealousy alone, stoop to league themselves together to stab me in the back, under the cover of secrecy. It is cowardly to say the least.

He took pains to make it clear that he did not blame Adler for this setback.[7]

Gordon may have hoped to meet Daniel Burnham during this trip as well. Although the chief of construction was operating out of a temporary office in Jackson Park when Gordon inspected the Texas exhibit site, it is doubtful that any such meeting took place.[8] Burnham had endorsed the association's desire for a building evocative of the Texas missions, so it seems he would have indicated as much had they discussed the matter. Furthermore, subsequent correspondence from Burnham to the association (cited below) does not indicate any familiarity towards the San Antonian at this time.

At any rate, Gordon & Laub entered a design into the competition that was at odds with the association's published stylistic desires, Burnham's desires, and the physical parameters specified in their circular. (Although Laub's departure has already been discussed, the firm was still intact at the time of this competition. There appears to be no record documenting an active role by Laub on this project, however.) The sketch shows an Italian Renaissance–styled building dominated by a massive dome that was undoubtedly inspired by the buildings of the Court of Honor (fig. 7.1). A three-story administration wing was to project from the west side, housing offices, sleeping quarters for officers, a museum of natural history, a library, a pressroom, and exhibits. The architects felt that this imposing structure could be built for the specified $100,000.[9]

Gordon & Laub's entry was among twenty-two taken to the Texas State Fair in Dallas, where October 30, 1891, was declared "World's Fair Day." Unable to decide on

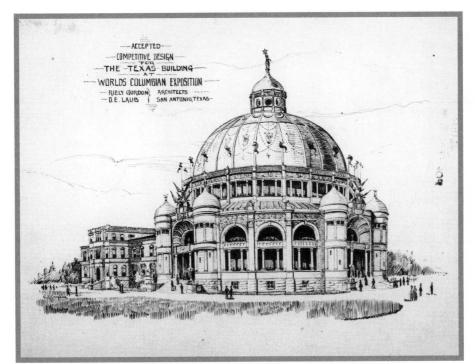

7.1.
Competition design, Texas
State Building. Gordon &
Laub, architects. Not built as
designed. *1891 office delineation by
C. A. Coughlin, courtesy Alexander
Architectural Archive, University of
Texas, Austin.*

one as best, the association selected five to forward to Daniel Burnham for him to choose. The finalists were Gordon & Laub, Alfred Giles, Eugene T. Heiner, Patrick S. Rabitt of Galveston (who may have been representing Nicholas Clayton), and Dallas's George W. Stewart. That Gordon's entry survived this first cut despite its variance with the association's stylistic wishes suggests there may have been a scarcity of compliant entries.[10]

On December 8, Burnham reported to the association that, after carefully examining the plans, he found "none of them are entirely satisfactory, but that, on the whole, the sketches of Messrs. Gordon & Laub, of San Antonio, Texas, can be made to do, and we hereby accept and approve the said sketches, with some changes in plans and modifications of exterior which can be better explained to the said architects personally than by letter."[11]

John Dickinson, the guardian angel of the Texas World's Fair Exhibit Association, may have again interceded. Had Burnham flatly rejected all the submissions the association would have had to return to square one in the design process. Given the caliber of many of the competitors, it seems more likely that Burnham rejected the forwarded plans on stylistic grounds rather than architectural incompetence. Dickinson, the powerful secretary of the fair's National Commission, was likely privy to Burnham's dissatisfaction and may have urged him to consider allowing one of the submitted designs to be revised in order to avert a disaster for the Texas effort.

Whether Dickinson helped Burnham see the merit of Gordon & Laub's submission in particular is impossible to determine. The secretary had a long and close friendship with Gordon, but the chief of construction enjoyed near-autonomous authority

where the fair's architecture was involved. Regardless of whether Burnham arrived at this decision on his own, Gordon proved a good choice and was committed to see the project through. With the decision came a request by Dickinson that a member of the winning firm travel to Chicago immediately, presumably to receive Burnham's instructions.[12] It may be assumed that Gordon made the trip, and he soon set down to the task of revising the plans to the chief of construction's satisfaction.

Gordon rushed to complete the new design, which was published in late February 1892.[13] While he changed the shape of the main hall, the revised design was little more than a repackaging of the Italian-style competition entry with Spanish Renaissance ornamentation (fig. 7.2). This could be the result of the pressure to produce the revised design as soon as possible. It may also represent a compromise between the individual aspirations of the parties involved. The architect was able to design a state building whose classicism reflected that of the already acclaimed Court of Honor. At the same time, the design referenced the state's colonial heritage, as Burnham willed. Contemporary accounts described the revised design as being patterned after the old missions, indicating that the subtle differences between the Moorish-influenced missions and the more Italian-influenced Spanish Renaissance style either eluded or were ignored by the Texas association's publicists. Gordon seems to have shunned the mission association, later describing the design as "a piece of Spanish Renaissance."[14]

This design was never realized, however. Like fair committees for some of the other states, the Texas World's Fair Exhibit Association continued to be perilously

7.2.
Revised design, Texas State Building. Gordon & Laub, architects. Not built as designed. *1892 unsigned office rendering, courtesy Alexander Architectural Archive, University of Texas, Austin.*

behind schedule in its fund-raising. This was largely due to the widening economic collapse that would come to be known as the Panic of 1893, which already had the state suffering the double blow of depressed cotton and beef prices and had a negative impact on people's willingness or ability to donate funds. Gordon and Laub ended their partnership in March and the following months saw Gordon's loss of the superintendence for the Victoria courthouse construction and his entanglement in the Bexar scandal. Despite these professional setbacks, he continued his involvement with the building for the great fair.

By mid-July it became obvious that Gordon's revised design for the Texas State Building could not be built for lack of funds. It was recommended that a structure costing $45,000 to $50,000 be considered, but at the end of the month the Texas World's Fair Association disbanded as the likelihood of raising even this reduced amount seemed nil. Through all of this, the women's department of the association had been raising funds to commission renowned artist Elisabet Ney to create statues of Sam Houston and Stephen F. Austin for the exposition. Unwilling to accept that there would be no building to house these works, the group reorganized itself as the Women's World's Fair Exhibit Association of Texas on July 26 and took on the challenge of fund-raising for the whole endeavor. Under the leadership of president Bene-dette Tobin, the new group appealed directly to the state's wealthy families, as well as to its schoolchildren, for donations to supplement funds already committed.[15]

Clearly, the scale and cost of the exhibit structure would have to be reduced, sending Gordon back to the drawing board once again. It is not likely that the architect was paid for his efforts: his motivation was probably a mix of civic pride, personal commitment, and the promise of widespread publicity. On September 3, the women's association accepted Gordon's plans and specifications for a building to cost $25,000 (fig. 7.3). The plans were forwarded to Burnham in Chicago, who approved the new design.[16]

The lowest bid for construction of the temporary structure was $25,650, $650 over the authorized amount. Gordon and John Dickinson signed a personal note for the balance and work began by October 1892.[17] The Women's World's Fair Exhibit Association of Texas continued its heroic efforts and finally, according to Tobin, "thanks to the generosity and chivalry of gentlemen who control some of the principal railroads and other large interests in the state, work on the Texas Building was commenced and brought to completion." The final cost of the enterprise was reported to be $40,000. Far from being one of the largest state buildings, as originally planned, Texas's entry came in twenty-second out of a field of thirty-six state and territorial pavilions.[18]

The World's Columbian Exposition lived up to the massive, worldwide publicity campaign that preceded it (fig. 7.4). According to noted critic Montgomery Schuyler, "it was a common remark among visitors who saw the Fair for the first time that nothing they had read or seen pictured had given them an idea of it, or prepared them for what

7.3.
Final design, Texas State Building. James Riely Gordon, architect. *1892 unsigned office delineation, courtesy Alexander Architectural Archive, University of Texas, Austin.*

they saw." After visiting the fair for himself, Gordon exclaimed, "the World's Fair is the grandest thing that one's imagination can picture. I do not think any one could possibly come away dissatisfied." The impression of the Court of Honor was overwhelming, but as Schuyler noted, its success was largely based upon illusion. The magnificent buildings were not grand marble edifices as they appeared to be from a distance and in photographs. They were all temporary structures covered with staff—a plaster, concrete, and hemp composition that required constant repairs throughout the summer.[19]

Overall, the architecture of the state building grounds was a mixed bag (fig. 7.5). California was widely recognized as having the most impressive showing with its large, mission-style building. The Illinois pavilion appears to have been exempted from Burnham's stylistic direction, with hapless results. Its neoclassicism invited unfavorable comparison to the superior designs of the Court of Honor. The largest of the state buildings, it was topped by a dome structure clumsily stretched to attain the highest point on the fairgrounds.

The Texas State Building was finally completed on July 8 (fig. 7.6). While much of the Spanish Renaissance styling from the previous design was retained, the floor plan

7.4.
Court of Honor at the World's Columbian Exposition. *From* Shepp's World's Fair Photographed.

7.5.
View of the state building grounds at the World's Columbian Exposition. The Texas State Building is at the left. The Palace of Fine Arts (now the Museum of Science and Industry) is the large structure at the upper right with the *in antis* portico. *From* Portfolio of the World's Fair, Art Series No. 9.

of the final design was radically changed. As built, the Texas State Building was patterned after a modified Greek cross, about 85 x 85 feet. The main entrances remained on the east and south sides of the structure. On the west side was a service entrance; the north side had no doorway since it bordered the fair's elevated electric railway. Only two of the four towers survived to the final design. These were located on either side of the east entrance, facing the visitors as they entered the fairgrounds via the north gate. A stand of trees obscured this view and prevented photographers from documenting the front of the building. Porches filled three of the reentrant angles of the cross, nearly filling the foundation plan out to a square. The exterior was fashioned from staff painted to have the appearance of white marble. The building was roofed with light red Spanish tile. The main doorways were decorated with plateresque surrounds accented by sculpted heads of longhorn steer and the Lone Star motif.[20]

One of Gordon's objectives was to suggest Texas's tropical climate through his design. Since the building was only intended to last the summer, it did not need to be designed to face the harshness of the Chicago winter. Open porches and belvederes created an inviting, airy effect. Inside, spacious 19-foot ceilings on the first floor, rising another 17 feet in the assembly hall, carried this theme through. Furthermore, landscaping with foliage shipped from Texas and planted around the building was an integral element of Gordon's overall scheme.[21] This attention to landscaping was evident throughout the fairgrounds and due in part to the influence and participation of Frederick Law Olmsted.

Montgomery Schuyler praised Gordon's use of historical design, but he also noted the Italian influence in the Texas State Building that seems to have lingered on from the original competition design. As Schuyler wrote in *The Architectural Record*,

> the general composition of the building, with its double low-crowned belvederes, resembles an Italian villa as strongly as it does any Spanish or Spanish-American erection, though much of the profuse detail is distinctly Spanish. It is in all events distinctly festal architecture, and ingenious provision has been made for heightening this effect by ornamental and characteristic planting.

He was less complimentary to other state buildings, especially those that more closely emulated the Court of Honor's styling on a small scale.[22]

Accolades for Gordon's design came from other quarters as well. While it was under construction, the *Fort Worth Gazette* reported that Daniel Burnham publicly pronounced the structure to be one of the best on the grounds. According to Gordon, this appraisal was supported by "a great many letters, highly praising the design, from some of the most prominent architects in the United States," that he received. The architect wrote to Tobin in February that his design had "been published in the *Inland Architect*, *Harper's Weekly*, the *World's Fair Illustrated*, the *Manufacturer's Record*, the *Southern*

Tradesman, many papers in New York, Chicago and San Francisco, besides a number of Texas newspapers." Photos and praise in other publications followed as the fair progressed. The world's fair editor of the *Chicago Record* deemed Gordon's building "one of the most attractive at the Fair." Gordon was also honored by the World's Columbian Commission with a medal and certificate commending the Texas State Building's "picturesque general appearance, with motives derived from Spanish Architecture."[23]

Throughout the summer, receptions and musical recitals were held in the hall of the Texas State Building, which, like Gordon's courtrooms, had fine acoustics. A piano of native Texas woods, specially made for the fair, provided accompaniment. Furnishings and exhibits were somewhat sparse, but work by Texas artists seems to have compensated for any privation. Contemporary accounts report that Elisabet Ney's statues flanked the rostrum, but it seems that *Stephen F. Austin* was not finished in time to be displayed at the fair. Paintings of Sam Houston by S. Seymour Thomas and of David Crockett by William H. Huddle adorned the walls. Visitors from Texas registered their names, which were duly reported in newspapers back home.[24]

Saturday, September 16, was "Texas Day" at the great fair, and the building was lavishly draped in the state's colors for the ceremonies. A capacity crowd listened to speeches by Tobin and former Texas governors John Ireland and Richard B. Hubbard.

7.6.
The Texas State Building at the World's Columbian Exposition, Chicago, Illinois (1892–93, destroyed). James Riely Gordon, architect. *From* The Dream City, World's Fair Art Series, I, No. 14.

Gordon was present and played a role in orchestrating the celebration. The air was filled with the scent of abundant Cape Jasmine from Texas. Professor Katzenberger's Columbian Chorus from San Antonio provided musical entertainment.[25]

Despite its financial setbacks and the disappointment of would-be exhibitors, Texas's participation in the fair was widely regarded as a success and Gordon received credit for his efforts as well. A release from the Texas Press Bureau at the fair glowed:

> The Texas building is an architectural gem in this fairy land of architecture, and may be said to represent the chaste and beautiful public and private architecture of the Lone Star State. It reflects a great credit to the master mind that designed it; the name of J. Reily [sic] Gordon, the Texas architect, is now on the lips of thousands of admirers of the World's Fair.[26]

Such exposure in the state's newspapers was particularly opportune as the continuing economic depression caused the architect to seek work from a wide geographic area. Furthermore, his name and design received notice in many of the national periodicals and books chronicling the World's Columbian Exposition. The Texas State Building was surely the most widely publicized commission of Gordon's career. Forty-four years after its demise, numerous obituary notices cited it among his prominent works (although, as noted in Chapter 21, the fair was often confused with the 1933 Century of Progress Exposition, also in Chicago).

The architectural legacy of the fair has been debated in academic circles, but the lavish praise for its buildings in numerous publications lent legitimacy to the neo-Renaissance styling of the Court of Honor. This later came to be called Beaux-Arts classicism in reference to the French architectural school, although the chaste teachings of the Ecole were not always reflected in the exuberant work of American designers. The Richardsonian Romanesque was already on the wane in some areas, accelerated by a public campaign waged by architects designing in the classical style. These architects were concentrated in the eastern United States, and the movement was strongest there and radiated outward, but it gained an undeniable and formidable boost from the Chicago fair. For the many reasons that made the Richardsonian practical in the first place, however, the style remained popular in the West through the turn of the century. Gordon returned to the Richardsonian Romanesque for his courthouse work through the remainder of the decade.

The evolution of the floor plan of the Texas State Building had a more immediate impact on Gordon's oeuvre than its style. As discussed in previous chapters, the architect explored different plans to allow for passive ventilation—a prime consideration in the Texas climate. In its final, reduced form, the structure built in Jackson Park was in the shape of a Greek cross with colonnaded porches in three reentrant angles.

This design was foreshadowed by the arcaded loggias wrapping around his rectangular courthouse for Victoria County and planned for, but not executed at, Erath. In the Erath design, the cooling porches were dispensed with, but a ventilating tower occupied the center of the courthouse. With the Texas State Building plan, air entered at the porches and exited through the central skylight. This created a natural updraft that cooled the building during the Chicago summer.

The Erath courthouse and the Texas State Building, considered together, take the evolution of Gordon's ideal courthouse plan to the brink of realization. Both designs were the result of constrained budgets that forced deviations from the original designs, but the process yielded efficiencies that brought the architect a clearer vision of his goal, which would be achieved in the next temple of justice he would design.

CHAPTER EIGHT

Gordon's Signature Plan

The Panic of 1893, which lasted about four years, proved to be the worst financial calamity to date in the United States. The West was hit particularly hard as numerous railroads and banks failed. Gordon noted that architects were among the first to suffer as nearly all building stopped.[1] The dwindling size of the Texas State Building is symbolic of the dwindling prospects for Gordon and his peers. All the while competition within the profession grew more intense and courthouse work became even more coveted.

During this period Gordon's family was dependent on the performance of his architectural practice. His father closed the land agency business by fall 1891 and apparently was now primarily, if not solely, engaged in managing his son's office. Likewise, it seems the architect's mother ceased taking boarders around 1888, when the entire family moved to a frame house at 405 San Pedro Avenue (which family tradition holds Gordon designed). Lucy Virginia Gordon, Mary and Riely Gordon's only child, was born on February 6, 1893.[2]

Farmers across the country were battered by the panic, too, and such troubled times gave momentum to an agrarian-based, grassroots populist political movement called the People's Party. On a state level, the People's Party in Texas grew to have a significant political impact in counties with large numbers of poor farmers. For the first time since the end of Reconstruction, the Democratic Party's hegemony in Texas was threatened, disturbing traditional power bases and affecting some courthouse projects. Even in counties Populists did not control, their strident opposition to anything they saw as extravagance sometimes curbed spending. One of the merits of the movement was its raising public awareness of the crooked political practices of the day, even though leaders of the People's Party were not always above corruption themselves.[3]

In this political climate, Gordon's Democratic Party credentials, surely a positive consideration in some earlier public projects, now posed a potential liability. From the populist perspective, in addition to his party affiliation Gordon was further distrusted as a professional man from a large city.[4] As discussed in this chapter, he assumed a less prominent role in courthouse projects for counties where populism held significant sway.

During this time, Gordon expanded his participation in the Texas State Association of Architects and joined the recently formed Southern Chapter of the American Institute of Architects on January 10, 1893. Given the troubled times, he probably saw involvement in the Southern Chapter as a springboard to a wider market. (Many used membership in regional chapters as a stepping-stone to acceptance in the national organization, but the AIA remained closed to Gordon.) The architect's first allegiance remained with the TSAA, however, where he began serving as secretary in 1892. His involvement with the Southern Chapter seems to have been limited to paying dues and occasionally submitting designs to its official organ, the Atlanta-based *Southern Architect*.[5]

Any courthouse work would be particularly appealing in this economic climate, but an exceptional opportunity arose at Fort Worth in January 1893. That month the Tarrant County Commissioners' Court solicited plans and specifications for a new courthouse with a tempting $2,500 award for the winning submission. It drew seventeen architects and firms from across the country. Given two months to prepare entries to unusually exact and thorough requirements, those who entered generally agreed it was "one of the longest and hardest fought contests ever had." Highly motivated by both the prize and the estimated $400,000 project to follow, participants took the contest to the streets of Fort Worth while the Commissioners' Court deliberated. Perspective drawings of their entries were displayed in storefronts and the lobbies of banks and hotels. One contestant sent the county judge a letter essentially offering a bribe. Indignant officials publicly displayed the letter and the author's entry was dropped from further consideration.[6]

Gordon's submission represents an intriguing addition to his Romanesque work (fig. 8.1). As with Bexar, the large budget and multiple courtrooms diverted the architect from his path toward an efficient Texas courthouse plan. Gordon's Tarrant entry called for an H-shaped structure of four stories resting on a high basement. The plans included a huge clock tower with an observatory rising from one side of the crossbar. The tower's battered base added to its massiveness, but a large arch for the main entrance defied the weight above. Its scale and structural demands would have exceeded Bexar's entrance arch. Gordon used decorative cartouches to relieve large expanses of wall. He also borrowed many details from his previous work, including loggia-type porches on the first and fourth floors that hearken to those over Bexar's entrance and around its east-side court. The inclusion of massive arcades to shade entrances on the building's extreme ends recalls the porches of Victoria. Close examination reveals fanciful dragon grotesques that the architect had not used since Fayette.[7]

As at Erath, noticeably missing from this design is any specific cultural recognition. In Gordon's previous courthouses, historic inspiration was most pronounced in the tower. Fort Worth began as a military outpost in 1849; its relatively short history

8.1.
Competition design for Tarrant
County Courthouse. James Riely
Gordon, architect. *1893 unsigned
office rendering, courtesy Alexander
Architectural Archive, University of
Texas, Austin.*

offered little architectural heritage to draw from. Gordon responded to this with a
tower that emphasized geometry over ornament. The result was a rather remarkable
design that may have had its inspiration in the avant-garde architecture of its day.
Housing for the clockwork was carried above the belvedere on machicolated, square
tourelles at the corners of the tower. Between the tourelles a steep slate roof rose to the
clock faces. The tourelles themselves were terminated by individual pyramidal roofs
that progressed into the base corners of a single, tall, pyramidal roof for the tower
proper.

The intriguing geometry of the tower, successfully wedded as it was to a
Romanesque design, was perhaps a result of Gordon's exposure to new architectural
trends he saw in Chicago. He met Adler, surely Burnham at some point, and probably
a host of other leaders in their profession as a new architectural spirit was developing
in the Midwest and West, evolving from the movement Richardson initiated. The latest
Windy City architecture also offered pronounced geometric forms characteristic of
what would later be called the Chicago School and the seeds of its kindred Prairie Style.
Judging from the Tarrant tower, this was the immediate inspiration Gordon brought
back from the great fair.

His entry survived into the second round of consideration in April, but it was ultimately bested by a neo-Renaissance design.[8] While surely a disappointment, Gordon
could take comfort in losing to worthy opponents in a fair contest. The Tarrant County

Courthouse, as designed by the Kansas City firm of Gunn & Curtiss, is a remarkable structure (fig. 8.2).

Another courthouse opportunity began to germinate at the end of 1893 in Brazoria. The town was laid out on the bank of the Brazos River in 1828 as one of Stephen F. Austin's land grants. Despite a troublesome sandbar at its mouth on the Gulf of Mexico, the river offered natural navigation for some 250 miles inland. Brazoria was situated at a comfortable distance from the Gulf, where it could prosper from the traffic. A county of the same name was established after Texas Independence.

The town's position as the county seat was threatened by the 1890s because it lacked a railroad connection. By this time rail commerce superseded what the Brazos River could offer. Nevertheless, the citizens of Brazoria County resisted efforts to move the seat of government: they defeated two proposals for relocation in 1891. Two years later voters approved the building of a new structure to replace the original small, wooden courthouse. This commitment to a new courthouse seemed to guarantee that Brazoria would remain the county seat for years to come. Plans to extend the International-Great Northern rail line and other improvements augured a prosperous future for the town.[9]

In December 1893, the Commissioners' Court appointed a building committee of eight citizens to examine several recently built courthouses around the state. From this investigation they were to determine the best design trends and select an architect who could provide plans accordingly. Numerous, unsolicited plans were submitted to the committee by hopeful architects as news of its work spread. Eventually, four architects were invited to Brazoria on February 13, 1894, to present plans for a courthouse and jail to total $55,000. Although his design required "a little more money than was first accepted," the committee ultimately recommended Gordon as the architect for the new courthouse, which the Commissioners' Court approved. It was the San

Antonian's first new courthouse commission since securing Erath over two and a half years earlier. The jail project was postponed, presumably to allow for a greater courthouse budget.[10]

Among the virtues of Gordon's design, in the mind of the committee, was "the system of ventilation throughout the whole of the building," which Gordon himself saw as an improvement on his earlier courthouses.[11] At little more than a tenth of the Tarrant budget, the needs of Brazoria forced him to consider efficiencies just as he had in the Texas State Building. This drove him back to his earlier courthouse designs for inspiration, but with significant innovations.

Brazoria's design marks the crystallization of Gordon's ideal Texas courthouse, referred to here as his Signature Plan (fig. 8.3).[12] The Texas State Building's modified Greek cross floor plan inspired a cruciform layout for the Brazoria courthouse with porches introduced in all four reentrant angles to cool incoming air, à la Victoria. Gordon placed public entrances at these porches where they would share equal prominence to equally benefit surrounding property values. This also brought the entrances closer to the center of the building, greatly reducing corridor space. Two of these porches, opposite the district courtroom, were two-tiered. As hallways disappeared Gordon had to find a new place for the stairs. He solved this by combining a single stairwell with the central ventilation shaft, which had been an atrium at Aransas and Erath, a courtyard at Fayette and Victoria. At Brazoria, this dual use furthered the efficiency of the design. Massive, arched piers encircled the 13 x 13 foot central stairwell/ventilation shaft and supported the masonry tower above. Corridors surrounded these piers, providing access to the various offices on all three floors. During the long Gulf Coast summers, shaded and hence cooled air was drawn in from the porches, past the arcaded piers, and up through the tower. This updraft, in turn, drew outside air in the windows, creating a breeze as it passed through the offices and up the ventilation stairwell shaft.

Gordon's mastery of engineering and fire-resistance further enhanced the merits of his plan. In their recommendation, the Brazoria building committee noted a further attribute of his proposal: acoustics, which they deemed to be very good.[13] A detailed description of the acoustical considerations in this building does not exist, but the plans show significant modifications of the district courtroom. The sides of the courtroom flanking the judge's stand were rounded following the curves of the porches below, while the ends of the wall opposite the judge's stand were beveled inward. According to accounts of later Gordon courtrooms, these features greatly enhanced the acoustics, typically allowing court proceedings to be clearly heard by jury members and spectators alike.

Another notable aspect of Gordon's design is its pyramidal massing (fig. 8.4), which, while practical, seems directly inspired by Henry Hobson Richardson's Trinity Church in Boston. As Richardson wrote of his own inspiration for Trinity:

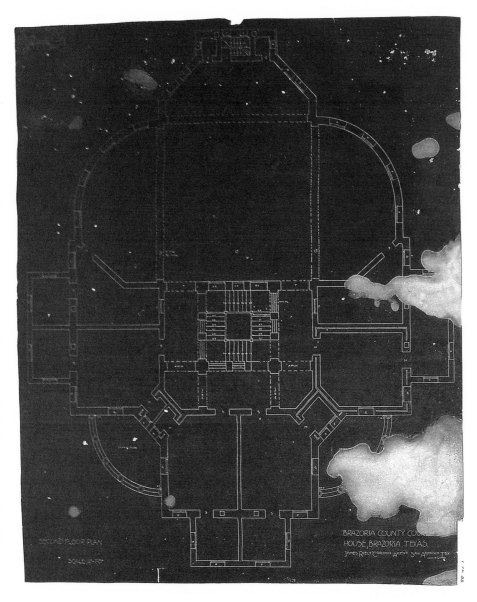

8.3.
Brazoria County Courthouse,
second-floor plan. James Riely
Gordon, architect. *Courtesy
Brazoria County Historical Museum,
photo by Gary Young.*

Among the branches of the Romanesque in Central France, nowhere were the peculiar characteristics of the style so strongly marked as in the peaceful, enlightened and isolated cities of Auvergne. The central tower, a reminiscence, perhaps, of the domes of Venice and Constantinople, was here fully developed, so that in many cases the tower became, as it were, the Church, and the composition took the outline of a pyramid, the apse, transepts, nave and chapels forming only the base to the obelisk of the tower.

In studying the problem presented by [Trinity's site,] fronting on three streets, it appeared desirable that the tower should be central, thus belonging equally to each front. . . . For this dilemma the Auvergnat solution seemed perfectly adapted. Instead of the tower being an inconvenient and unnecessary addition to the Church, it was itself made the main feature.[14]

Richardson had not yet studied churches of the Auvergne Region in person at the time of Trinity's design. Like other architects (including Gordon), he worked from photographs (figs. 8.5, 9.11) and other reference material. While the pyramidal form served Trinity's three-fronted site, it also suited Brazoria's four-sided town square, where—to paraphrase Richardson—the tower becomes the courthouse. In fact, Gordon realized this pyramidal form more fully than Richardson. The western side of Trinity, its primary façade, was initially truncated to create a monumental entrance. Richardson's pyramidal intention is therefore more clearly seen from an eastern viewpoint (fig. 8.6). Apparently not satisfied with the result, the architect proposed a west porch shortly before his death, which his successor firm executed in the mid-1890s. Richardson also considered pyramidal designs for the Connecticut State Capitol and the Brookline, Massachusetts, Town Hall, but these were not built.[15]

Gordon filed a copyright on the Brazoria plan as he had with Victoria's.[16] Along with its virtues, this plan did have what might be considered drawbacks. For instance, it lacked an inspiring hall to greet the visitor upon entering the building. Some may dismiss a grand entry as unnecessary and extravagant space, but visitors to Gordon's signature courthouses are confronted by an impressive but somewhat close collection of thick piers. This plan is also suited for smaller communities needing just one courtroom. Furthermore, while Gordon's design met the needs of the day, it did not lend itself to alteration as needs changed with time. Like Greek temples, Gordon's ideal temple of justice met its initial requirements but was not very flexible. As a result, Signature Plan district courtroom galleries were often converted to additional floor space and the stairwell/ventilation shafts given over to elevators after a few years, robbing these chambers of their drama. Fortunately, a recent series of restorations to the extant courthouses have undone many alterations imposed over the years.

Brazoria's construction was let to Brownwood contractors Tom Lovell and William Hood for $57,000. During construction the Brazoria officials continued to exhibit

8.4.
Brazoria County Courthouse, Brazoria, Texas (1894–95, destroyed). James Riely Gordon,
architect. *Photographer and date unknown, courtesy Brazoria County Historical Museum.*

8.5.
Église de Clermont Ferraud, Auvergne Region, France. *Photograph from H. H. Richardson's collection, courtesy of the Frances Loeb Library, Harvard School of Design.*

Trinity Church.

8.6.
Trinity Church, viewed from southeast. *Line art illustration ca. 1877.*

the studied prudence shown during their selection of an architect. They hired George Meiguard to superintend the daily work of the contractor for $500. Then, Gordon and George Dickey (a Houston architect previously invited to compete) were brought in to double-check Meiguard's work. Such scrutiny assured the people of the county the highest quality of materials and workmanship. Brazoria's courthouse was completed by October 30, 1895.[17]

Gordon utilized the tower he developed for the Tarrant courthouse in this design but carried the geometric scheme further by using devices such as horizontal lintels, as opposed to arches, to top the columns on the first-floor porches. While his use of pressed brick may have been dictated by an economic need to transport materials by water (the brick was from St. Louis), it lent itself to the geometry of the tower. The architect mixed these features with standard Victorian elements that seem a bit fussy in this context, however. Ultimately, it is the plan that gives the Brazoria County Courthouse design its merit. The building's overall massing admirably expressed this plan, but one must see past a confused decorative scheme to appreciate it.

Reports vary, but by the time it was finished and furnished, the citizens had invested between $80,000 and $90,000 in the courthouse. This expenditure was not enough to keep the county government in the city of Brazoria, however. Less than a year after completion, another vote to move the seat led to the most bitterly fought campaign in Brazoria County history. In the end it was decided to move the government to Angleton, which already enjoyed rail service. To limit the costs of relocation, county officials simply purchased Eugene Heiner's plans for the courthouse in adjacent Matagorda County. Abandoned by the county government, Gordon's courthouse became known as "Brazoria County's Folly."[18]

On February 24, 1894, less than two weeks after Gordon secured the Brazoria commission, Karnes County officials reviewed eleven submissions for a courthouse at their new seat in Karnes City. The contest was open to both architects and contractors. Gordon was among the former and Otto Kroeger, one of the builders for Bexar's courthouse, was among the latter. By day's end the Commissioners' Court selected the plans of James Wahrenberger.[19]

Wahrenberger's victory proved to be short-lived, however. After allowing contractors a scant four days to submit construction bids, the populist Karnes County Commissioners' Court rejected them all. Next, on March 15, they annulled their decision to use Wahrenberger's plans. They reversed themselves again in favor of the architect on April 4, but on May 18 they ultimately decided against him and returned his plans. At the same session they considered five plans submitted by contractors. The next day the Commissioners' Court finally decided on plans by contractor John Cormack of San Antonio.[20] This circus in Karnes County may have induced Gordon to occasionally ally himself with contractor Otto Kroeger rather than lose out on future courthouse projects under populist governments.

At the time of Wahrenberger's futile entanglement over Karnes, another opportunity took shape at Sulphur Springs. Fire claimed nearly an entire block there on January 12, 1894. Included in the ruins was Hopkins County's twelve-year-old courthouse; only its vault survived. The Commissioners' Court quickly arranged to build a replacement on the same site. Five architects responded to a competition held in March, with Gordon and Austin's Arthur O. Watson selected as finalists. The Hopkins county judge, three commissioners, and the sheriff then toured Austin, San Antonio, and other points to inspect Gordon's and Watson's recent work. They decided upon Gordon's plan, and the $52,000 construction contract went to the Dallas firm of Sonnefield & Emmins in May.[21]

Gordon retained the best features of his Brazoria plan for the Hopkins County Courthouse, modifying it by filling the reentrant angles on the east side with curved offices on the first floor instead of porches (fig. 8.7). This was entirely appropriate for the site adjacent to the Sulphur Springs town square, where the east façade was unavoidably the backside.[22] Another modification was the inclusion of third-floor, arcaded loggias on the north and south sides of the structure. These are unique in the architect's courthouses of this period and likely added ventilation in compensation for the loss of the east porches. Together, these changes demonstrate that Gordon and his Signature Plan could accommodate change as circumstances warranted.

Some features appear little changed from Gordon's previous courthouse, such as the open staircase rising through the center of the structure until it gives way to a spiral stair servicing the tower (fig 8.8). A dense group of columns surrounds the stair (fig 8.9), as would have been the case in Brazoria. Like the earlier courthouse, Hopkins's district courtroom has rounded sides (fig. 8.10), although other details of their treatments may have varied.

The exterior treatment is more sculpted and elaborate than Brazoria. In Sulphur Springs the architect wielded Burnet granite trimmed with his typical red Pecos sandstone, rearranging many elements of its predecessor into a more coherent composition. Gordon employed arches for the first-floor porches and major windows. Second-story window lintels blend into stone courses initiated by the porch lintels on the same floor. This consistency went far in uniting the design while Gordon's previous Romanesque work lent detailing to Hopkins's exuberant program. Contrasting quoining around the windows recall that of Erath. The gentle swelling at the center of the loggia balustrades hearkens back to the balcony on Bexar's main tower. As at Brazoria, cartouches document the construction date. Its Richardsonian checkerboard frieze was last seen at Victoria. Spirelets in the reentrant angles, which mask the beveling for the doorways under the porches below, evoke Victoria's tourelles. These spirelets provide a segue for the tourelles of the tower, which are capped by conical roofs and in turn give way to a pyramidal roof, recalling Brazoria's tower. Hopkins is more Victo-

8.7.
Hopkins County Courthouse, Sulphur Springs, Texas (1894–95). James Riely Gordon, architect.
1995 photograph.

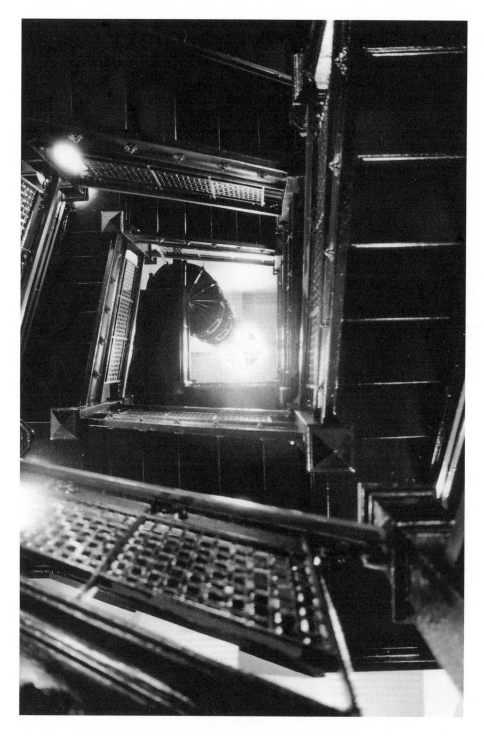

8.8.
Hopkins County Courthouse,
view looking up stairwell from
basement. *2005 photograph.*

8.9.
Hopkins County Courthouse, corridor surrounding stairwell. *2005 photograph.*

8.10.
Hopkins County Courthouse, courtroom. *2005 photograph.*

rian in execution, however, and therefore it represents a retreat from the avant-garde—but with splendid results.

The Commissioners' Court called for several structural changes to the plan during construction. In October and November 1894 the court authorized Sonnefield & Emmins to use more iron, terra-cotta tiling, and metal lathe in the work than originally called for. The contractors employed the Gilbert system with cement instead of wooden floors. It appears that the primary goal was increased fireproofing, although these changes enhanced the building structurally as well. It is entirely possible that Gordon proposed cheaper and more combustible materials to fit the original budget; then later all agreed it was worth spending more for safety. It is also possible that the architect and the Commissioners' Court planned all along to use the more expensive material but thought to present it to the voters in more palatable pieces. Either way, the cost to the taxpayers of Hopkins County for these changes ran an additional, and likely controversial, $5,060.[23]

In the following months the Commissioners' Court hired Watson, their runner-up choice for architect, to assess the work. His subsequent report was entered into the court minutes on March 22, 1895. Watson began his report by regretting that the building's architect was not present for the inspection and urged that Gordon review and comment on the report. As recorded in the minutes, Watson went on to state that "your building is of a very neat clear design conveniently arranged and substantially [sic] in its general construction." He reported that the tower walls were designed adequately, but the brick employed in their construction was not suitable. In his words, "a serious error or mistake has been made while owing doubtless to a desire to use local material . . . only the best brick obtainable should have been used regardless of cost." Watson determined that the inferior brick combined with the effects of some water, which was allowed to stand around the foundation, resulted in adverse settlement. He noted that "this settlement is not of a serious or dangerous character at present and I am hopeful that no further settlement will occur." Watson also found that the "general workmanship of the tower above the balcony floor is poorly executed and not up to the standard of the [rest] of the building." He suggested several remedies that for the most part involved ironwork.[24]

With no available information on the circumstances surrounding Watson's investigation, it is impossible to evaluate his report with certainty. One possible conclusion is that the Hopkins County Commissioners' Court was dissatisfied with Gordon's performance and the report documents his failings.[25] If so, this would be a rare instance of professional negligence on Gordon's part. To give Gordon the benefit of the doubt, however, Watson may have been brought in for an expert second opinion in some sort of dispute. For example, if Gordon had ordered costly rework of a poorly executed tower or changes to compensate for mandated, but inferior, local brick it would not be unreasonable to seek another architect's advice on the matter. If this were the case, then Watson's report likely corroborated Gordon's position. In either scenario, Gordon's absence during Watson's inspection is a reasonable safeguard against the San Antonian influencing the resulting report. Perhaps the fact that the Commissioners' Court paid Gordon the balance of his fee establishes that his performance was indeed satisfactory. The building was received from the contractor on August 22.[26]

Concurrent with the Hopkins courthouse construction was that of another in the town of Gonzales. Founded in 1825, the town played an integral role in the Texas War of Independence as the location of the legendary first shot fired in that conflict. After the Texans' victory Gonzales became the seat of a newly formed county of the same name. Its third courthouse, an 1857 sandstone structure, was destroyed by fire on December 3, 1893. At its February 1894 session, the populist Commissioners' Court ordered advertisements calling architects to submit designs for "a first class, fireproof courthouse . . . not to exceed sixty-five thousand dollars." A special session was called for March 26 to consider submitted plans and specifications.[27]

Eleven architects and firms answered the call, including some of Gordon's strongest competitors. The contest even drew a submission by Elijah E. Myers of Detroit, who authored the Michigan and Texas State Capitols. Conspicuously missing from the list of participants is Gordon himself. It may be tempting to attribute his absence to his involvement in the simultaneous contest in Sulphur Springs, but somehow A. O. Watson found time to compete in both. Perhaps after the Karnes shenanigans Gordon was now wary of populist governments like Gonzales County's. The prize went to T. S. Hodges apparently for political reasons. He did not have long to savor his victory, however: the Commissioners' Court rejected his plans a month after they had approved them.[28]

Hodges surely appealed to populist sensibilities as a local man (raised within the county but later removed to Lockhart). Although the *Gonzales Inquirer* described him only as "a builder and contractor," he is also credited as the author of the Italianate courthouse for Tyler County (1891, Woodville). Hodges's plans for an estimated $59,000 courthouse at Gonzales were not the lowest, nor were they, in the minds of many, the best or even complete. Critics suggested his award was the result of political influence and the *Inquirer* maintained, "the people do not care who the man is or whether he is a republican, democrat or people's party man, but when they pay out sixty to seventy thousand dollars they want . . . a good courthouse and the best one their money will bring." Official records merely state that the plans proved to be unsatisfactory.[29]

A second call for plans and specifications was announced in May, this time directed at contractors and builders. Watson entered again—it seems he presented himself as a contractor on occasions that called for it. The award went to Otto Kroeger, whose $64,450 bid included an unattributed Signature Plan design provided by Gordon.[30]

Kroeger's compensation to Gordon for this design is not known, but the arrangement was akin to that of the Val Verde County Jail nine years earlier. Unlike that jail, Gordon's name does not appear in county records or any known contemporary newspaper accounts of the Gonzales courthouse construction. The architect did include it in a promotional portfolio (discussed in Chapter 10) a few years later, however. While the TSAA had long denounced the practice of architects anonymously supplying plans to contractors, it is difficult to fault Gordon given the depressed economic times and the influence of anti-professional populist politics. There were later accusations that Kroeger colluded with county People's Party leaders and provided a kickback in the form of a $2,500 campaign contribution, but a grand jury investigating the matter did not issue any indictments. Kroeger completed the structure under county-appointed superintendents in early 1896.[31]

Gordon appears to have designed this structure specifically for Gonzales's Mexican heritage and he did so in a way unique in his opus (fig 8.11). At the time of its completion, the *Inquirer* noted that "the design of the building is of the Spanish-Venetian type and thus emphasizes the historical relations of our quaint and heroic town." The architect deftly added Romanesque and Gothic elements to the pressed brick exterior. Typical for Gordon, the tower provides the foremost expression of his architectural inspiration. Here, Moorish domes cluster around the low-pitched, pyramid-roofed clock tower. While eclectic, the program is masterfully executed. It should be noted, however, that the architect returned to the Brazoria plan of having all four reentrant angles occupied by entrance porches. This is curious since the Gonzales courthouse is located adjacent to the traditional, Spanish Main Plaza; it would seem more practical to have followed the Hopkins plan with offices opposite the plaza side.

The *Inquirer* article also provided an account of the interior that lauds Gordon's Signature Plan:

> In arrangement it is novel and cozy. It is different from most public buildings as it is almost devoid of the usual long, misleading and space consuming halls. . . .
>
> The building is 91 x 103 feet, and from the ground to the apex of the tower 100 feet. As one enters the building from the step balconies the [interior] arcade is entered and a forest of arches is presented to view supporting the stairway shaft. A double stairway leads from the first to the third floor, and the base of the tower. The tower is reached by a winding stairway. . . .
>
> Every room in the building is a corner room with plenty of light and ventilation and convenient balconies.
>
> In fact it is admirable [*sic*] arranged in every particular, but some say, with some

reasonableness that some of the rooms are too small, and especially the district court room. However it is an admirable building in most respects, and one that the county can well take pride in.[32]

In the town of San Patricio, about 130 miles south of Gonzales, fire destroyed the San Patricio County Courthouse in 1889. The lack of rail service to the town and its position in the southwest corner of the county contributed to a strong desire within the county to move the government from the town. Yet, four years later, with a shortage of funds and no consensus for a new location, the county had still not taken action. Officials conducted business in rented quarters until finally the citizens of the coastal county settled upon Sinton, a newly chartered, centrally located town with a station on the San Antonio and Aransas Pass Railway.[33]

On July 14, 1894, the San Patricio Commissioners' Court voted to advertise for

8.11.
Gonzales County Courthouse,
Gonzales, Texas (1894–96).
James Riely Gordon, architect.
1990 photograph.

plans for a permanent courthouse not to exceed $25,000 with submissions due a week later. From a field of five entries, Gordon carried the competition and received orders to return the following month with complete plans and specifications as well as estimates. Officials unanimously approved the architect's work and ordered him to advertise for construction bids "and notify the county judge to call a special meeting to let the contract."[34] While it was rather unusual for county officials to invest this sort of authority in an architect, they may have been so impressed by Gordon's credentials that they simply yielded to his judgment. It is just as possible they realized their minuscule budget provided little room for corruption.

In light of their past relationship, it is not surprising that Gordon recommended the construction contract go to Otto Kroeger for $24,987. The contractor likely enjoyed an "inside track" bidding on this modest project as a return for providing Gordon the Gonzales design. Gordon also designed a jail for San Patricio for which the lowest bid, by Kroeger, was $9,983. This was too expensive for the county so the contractor recommended changes to the plan, such as eliminating the cells and window bars on the second floor, to get the price down to $6,609, which the court accepted.[35]

Kroeger's contract stipulated that the courthouse and jail would be completed by August 15, 1895, and a local man was appointed to superintend. Two days before this deadline, Gordon submitted a report to the Commissioners' Court "showing the defects and what was needed to complete the said buildings and advising the court not to accept" them until the work was done. The officials followed his recommendations and Kroeger was assessed late fees while the project stretched into October.[36]

The new courthouse in Sinton had a severe, geometric treatment (fig. 8.12). Financial considerations surely affected this design, but it was also appropriate for the Spartan, agrarian county and its incipient seat. Little information exists on the construction of this courthouse, but archival photographs show it followed his Signature Plan. The geometric potential previously hinted at in Brazoria found fuller expression in San Patricio. The result was a rather frugal composition of stark brick surface planes slightly interrupted by decorative brick moldings. Implied crenellations provided simple accent below the roofline and above the porches. Clusters of Tuscan columns, unique in Gordon's courthouse work, supported the pyramid roof of the airy tower.

Otto Kroeger, his problems at Sinton aside, was undoubtedly a capable builder of courthouses. He brought the latest construction methods and his own innovations to the industry in Texas. By the mid-1890s, he was also establishing a history of making deals with county governments to secure work. His Van Zandt County Courthouse construction dealings furthered this history.

A push to replace Van Zandt's deteriorated 1857 frame courthouse (derisively called the old "Martin Box," presumably in reference to nesting birds) in Canton began in 1890. Parties interested in moving the county seat managed to put off any work for

8.12.
San Patricio County Courthouse, Sinton, Texas (1894–95, destroyed). James Riely Gordon, architect. Gordon's jail is visible on the left. *Undated photograph, courtesy Loretta M. Moody and the Sinton Public Library.*

four years, but eventually the condition of the old courthouse became intolerable. The Van Zandt Commissioners' Court voted to build a replacement in Canton and at that same August 14, 1894, session entered into a contract with W. C. Dodson to design it and superintend construction.[37]

There was no competition, and Dodson likely received the commission by virtue of his work on the county jail, which he secured at the end of the previous year. According to the terms of his contract and assuming that the courthouse construction would total about $50,000 (based on the initial bond issue), Dodson stood to receive around $2,500, from which he would need to pay a local supervisor and other expenses.[38]

This arrangement lasted less than a month. Before Dodson delivered any work, Otto Kroeger presented a set of plans and specifications by Gordon to the Van Zandt Commissioners' Court in a special session on September 4. Officials then entered into a contract with Kroeger to build according to those plans for $49,000. Kroeger also agreed to pay Dodson $1,000 for any work performed to date under the county's previous contract.[39]

The Commissioners' Court's motives for contracting with Kroeger may never be fully understood, but his allowing the county some creativity in payment may have been a factor. Several years earlier, it loaned some of the county's school funds to the government of Archer County. Archer County bonds were provided as security.

Kroeger accepted these bonds toward payment for the courthouse construction. This enabled the Van Zandt officials to replace the collateral Archer bonds with cash generated from the sale of their courthouse bonds. The Democratic county officials may also have been eager to drop a "big city" professional like Dodson in an attempt to slow populist momentum in the county. If so, the effort was unsuccessful as the county still moved to People's Party control in the November election. Architect Gordon appears to have signed no contract with Van Zandt County, but his authorship of the design appears in its records. The Commissioners' Court employed H. A. Evans to superintend the work, so Gordon's involvement with Van Zandt likely ended with approval of his plans and specifications.[40]

While the Gonzales design that Gordon provided to Kroeger was original and unique to that particular county, his Van Zandt design (fig. 8.13) was very similar to the Brazoria courthouse. Kroeger was again working with a relatively low budget, and it is possible that these previously used plans fit the financial resources. Brazoria's decorative scheme was also appropriate for Van Zandt, given that the latter similarly lacked an obvious historical association to draw from. Scrutiny of archival photos reveals some differences in the exteriors, however. For example, the exaggerated stone voussoirs of Brazoria's arches are replaced by brickwork for Van Zandt with pleasing results. For Van Zandt's stonework, stone was shipped by rail to Wills Point, where it was trimmed and made ready for placement before being loaded on wagons bound for Canton.[41]

Gordon's specifications for the Van Zandt County Courthouse are preserved in the Commissioners' Court records. Like the earlier drawings for Fayette, these specifications document Gordon's mastery of his art as well as the thorough detail of his instructions to the builder.

His specifications strictly defined the composition of the cement used for the foundation and floors. Brick was to be hand-fired and laid close. Mortar was to be flush with the brick face. Timber was specified as well-seasoned, long-leaf Calcasieu pine and methods for fire-resistance were detailed. Gordon provided designs for cast iron support columns, but allowed that an acceptable stock pattern could be used. The courtroom balcony was to be faced "with an approved design of ornamental paneled frieze of a good quality Lincrusta Walton."

The architect specified no particular quarry for the stonework, but he called for first-quality, close-grained natural stone and gave detailed trimming instructions. While the drawings provide direction for stone carving, Gordon intended that it be "executed artistically and spirited." This indicates that the architect followed the highly influential English art critic John Ruskin's decree that carvers be left free to express themselves in their work. It was thought that such freedom would serve to enliven the whole structure.[42]

8.13.
Van Zandt County Courthouse, Canton, Texas (1894–96, destroyed). James Riely Gordon, architect. Photographed shortly before its demolition. *1936 photograph from the collections of the Texas/Dallas History and Archives Division, Dallas Public Library.*

Work on the Van Zandt County Courthouse began almost immediately. Gordon's plans called for a structure measuring 89 x 92 feet with its tower reaching a height of 101 feet. The cornerstone was laid on November 16, but county elections that month installed a populist government that had opposed the courthouse construction. An injunction was filed in April 1895 that forbade Kroeger from continuing work on the structure. (Obviously, any pull Kroeger may have had with Gonzales County populists held no sway in Van Zandt County.) The injunction was eventually dissolved, at the plaintiff's cost, in April of the following year, and the courthouse was rushed to completion.[43]

Gordon's Van Zandt County Courthouse served until the late 1930s. It fell to the wrecking ball after county officials, enabled by Public Works Administration funds from the federal government, voted to replace it (fig. 8.14).[44]

Back in Brazoria, town officials had endeavored to find uses for Gordon's courthouse there following the county seat's removal to Angleton. The structure served as a school, office building, and occasionally hosted balls and church services. It even suffered the indignity of use as a roller rink and dance hall. Through these years, the

8.14.
Van Zandt County Courthouse during demolition. *Photograph from the collections of the Texas/ Dallas History and Archives Division, Dallas Public Library.*

sound structure sheltered the citizenry during storms and floods. In the 1930s, after a storm took off its roof, the county unceremoniously dynamited the building, pulverized most of the material, and scattered it throughout the county as road fill. A few fragments survived the blast and were squirreled about the county and state. They are all that remain of Gordon's first Signature Plan courthouse.[45]

The San Patricio courthouse served for over thirty years. A new courthouse, with a third-floor jail, was built a few blocks to the west of Gordon's and completed in 1927. The older structure was razed the following year. The 1894 jail was torn down in the 1950s.[46]

Happily, Gordon's courthouses for Hopkins and Gonzales Counties are extant.

CHAPTER NINE

Ellis and Wise

In early August 1894 Gordon began to advertise that he had "over one million dollars worth of courthouses alone now under construction." A tally of his known work in progress at the time does not support this claim, suggesting perhaps he optimistically included courthouse commissions that seemed promising but ultimately were not built.[1] The veracity of this promotion aside, clearly Gordon by then had decided that public buildings were the specialty of his practice. These commissions likely made up a good portion of his income, but he had other work as well.

In an interview later that month, Gordon reported having twelve persons working in his office in the Smith Block. Furthermore, he boasted having six satellite offices outside San Antonio that employed an additional nine. The entire enterprise had nearly seventy projects at hand in mid-August, with the majority of the drawings being created at the main office. Building activity overall was still down from previous years, but Gordon was carrying on well enough through the Panic of 1893. He was the only architect to advertise regularly in the *Express* and, as the architect described his practice, "we are always building, and finer buildings, better constructed and more artistic designs than ever before. The people of Texas know what art is and are rapidly becoming more progressive."[2] As he spoke, the genesis of one of his greatest artistic achievements was taking shape in Waxahachie.

At its August session, the Ellis County Commissioners' Court considered building a new courthouse at the seat of Waxahachie, but the cost of doing so flamed resistance. Anti-courthouse (or, more precisely, anti–*new* courthouse) sentiment was strong in these still depressed times, and as a result three of the five-member Commissioners' Court voted against it.[3] The pro-courthouse faction, led by Ellis County Judge D. F. Singleton, was not easily deterred, however.

Democrats, who were the dominant party in the county, comprised both factions, but Singleton and his cohorts were lame-duck officials. Having just lost in the party's primary vote, their chances for reelection as independents in November were nil. With nothing to lose, politically speaking, they continued to press for a new courthouse. One consistent dissenting voice on the Ellis County Commissioners' Court belonged to A. O. Finley, who recounted the subsequent finagling in a letter to the *Waxahachie Enterprise*. Finley won in the primary, making him the only commissioner with a stake in the upcoming general election. His narrative is consistent with information from other sources and provides the basis for the account that follows.[4]

A special Commissioners' Court session was called on September 28, 1894, to vote on a matter unrelated to the courthouse. After that decision was made, County Judge Singleton declared the body was to reconsider building a new courthouse—to the surprise of Finley and perhaps others. Considering a matter not publicly announced prior to the session is suspect, and Finley protested, arguing the issue was dead after the August vote. Singleton countered that one of the commissioners who previously voted against the project requested that it be brought up again. They took another vote and this time the project was approved three to two along with an order to advertise for plans and specifications to be considered the following Friday, October 5. A *Dallas Morning News* account has Singleton stating it was "their intention to have the work in progress within thirty or sixty days."[5] By moving quickly, they could have the county irreversibly committed to the project before the anti-courthouse faction followed them into power at the end of November.

After the special session adjourned, the officials met informally to "hear a contractor talk about the proper method of advertising for courthouses."[6] The contractor was William L. Martin of the construction firm Martin, Byrnes & Johnston, and his presence makes it obvious he had foreknowledge that the Commissioners' Court would approve building a new courthouse that morning. Martin recommended that Ellis County solicit contractors for plans, specifications, and bids, effectively eliminating architects from the competition. In addition to offering his advice, Martin urged officials to take a trip with him to visit courthouses he had built, especially the one at Victoria. As the contractor advised, the Commissioners' Court informally voted to redirect advertising toward contractors with submissions due October 30.

Not privy to the competition changes instigated by Martin, the *Enterprise, Morning News*, and possibly other papers carried the news and advertisements that the Ellis County Commissioners' Court would meet with architects as previously planned. Any designers traveling to Waxahachie for the October 5 session wasted their time and expenses: not enough court members attended to constitute a quorum, and the session adjourned without discussing the courthouse. A notice to contractors ran in the *Morning News* two days later calling for submissions for a $150,000 courthouse for Ellis County.[7]

Two commissioners availed themselves of Martin's offer to travel to Victoria, and later in October the entire Ellis County Commissioners' Court traveled to Kaufman, Dallas, and Fort Worth to inspect additional courthouse projects. In Fort Worth Otto Kroeger intercepted the party and persuaded them to travel, at his expense, to San Antonio to see the work he was doing on Gordon's Bexar County Courthouse.

A special session of the Commissioners' Court opened on October 30 to examine thirteen submissions for the new courthouse. Members unanimously selected Kroeger's entry. Kroeger's proposal, featuring a design by Gordon, came with a $150,000 price tag. A letter from Singleton congratulating Gordon indicates that the architect met with members of the Ellis County Commissioners' Court at some point in the process, possibly on their trip to San Antonio or during the presentation of designs in Waxahachie.[8]

This turn of events must have been particularly galling to Martin, who early on persuaded the Ellis County Commissioners' Court to deal only with contractors and probably fancied the job his. Adding to the insult was the fact that Martin's effort to present his own construction work unavoidably showcased Gordon's designs as well. The architect's work was integral to Kroeger's success in Waxahachie. Despite his anti-courthouse stance, even Finley acknowledged that the Kroeger-Gordon submission was the best of the field.

While agreeing that Gordon's design was best, Commissioner Finley felt that other contractors should have an opportunity to bid on its construction. Kroeger indicated that he was agreeable to the idea, but County Judge Singleton was adamant, arguing they did not have time for any further deliberations. Frustrated in his attempt to open up the bidding, Finley boycotted the November regular session, which needed full attendance to authorize Kroeger's contract. The pro-courthouse, lame-duck faction retaliated by finding a district judge to remove Finley from office and appoint a pro-courthouse replacement for the remaining fourteen days of the term. The Commissioners' Court quickly signed the contract and arranged for stopgap funding out of the county's general revenue until bonds could be approved and sold. This chicanery enraged the anti-courthouse citizenry, and the November 19 order of the Commissioners' Court to turn over the old courthouse to Kroeger for quick demolition further fueled emotions. Opponents to the project filed suit to stop the work but it was too late: the old courthouse was, as a Fort Worth newspaper reported, "a huge pile of ruins."[9] Finley's account ends with the pro-courthouse faction enjoying a fait accompli; the newly elected officials had no choice but to build a new courthouse and Kroeger held the contract.

The pro-courthouse faction of the Commissioners' Court may have truly believed a new structure was in the best interest of the county, but given their actions in pushing the project it is reasonable to suspect ulterior motives. While it appears no one ever formally lodged an accusation of any crime, those with an interest in the project lavishly entertained these officials in hard times. Kroeger did not initiate the project (that credit seems to belong to Martin) and he was not alone in providing favors, but clearly the whole process raised the ire of Ellis County citizens.[10]

On November 30 the new Ellis County Commissioners' Court took office as scheduled. Finley, having won reelection, returned to the commissioner seat from which he had been removed. In the following weeks officials of the new Commissioners' Court worked swiftly to gain control over the courthouse project. They accepted the resignation of a superintendent appointed by the previous Commissioners' Court and began searching for a replacement. They also ordered Kroeger to cease work pending the outcome of litigation related to the project.[11]

The suits came before district court on December 15, and the judge handed down a somewhat Solomonic decision. First he ruled that the old Commissioners' Court did not have the power to pay Kroeger out of the general revenues, voiding its supplemental contract to that effect. Then he ruled that the original contract with Kroeger, to build a courthouse to Gordon's design for $150,000, was legally binding for the county. This resulted in a stalemate. Unless the Commissioners' Court took action and sold bonds, there would be no money to pay Kroeger and the project would be brought to a stop. The county still needed a new courthouse, but Kroeger's contract prevented anyone else from doing the work or making changes to the design without his agreement. This ruling left both parties considering appeals, but a quick resolution was clearly in the best interest of all involved.[12]

While the work suspension remained in effect, the new Ellis County Commissioners' Court hired a Fort Worth architectural firm to review Kroeger's bid against Gordon's plans and the specifications. This firm, Messer, Sanguinet & Messer, had also provided a design for one of the unsuccessful contractors competing for Ellis. The firm took the documents back to their Fort Worth office for examination and returned a detailed report two weeks later. It found the specifications vague and pointed out a few incongruities. Gordon's surviving plans and specifications from this period are typically rather explicit, but it seems sure that Kroeger rewrote anything the architect provided to suit his own purposes, which may account for at least some shortcomings. At the very least, Kroeger would need to purge the document of requirements for architect's approval on materials and workmanship. The vagueness observed by Messer, Sanguinet & Messer could have been the result of sloppy editing, but a deliberate attempt to obfuscate cannot be ruled out.[13]

As part of its report, Messer, Sanguinet & Messer provided two estimates for constructing the courthouse according to the plans. These reflected different interpretations of the specifications with regard to workmanship and material. The Fort Worth firm calculated that the highest-quality courthouse could be built for $121,667.10. Cost could be kept to $102,148.40, however, by building "in a moderately cheap manner under the same specifications, without in any way 'slighting' the work, but following out the specifications, in the less expensive manner." Messer, Sanguinet & Messer may not have been totally qualified to assess a contractor's additional costs of doing business (there was no consideration of payment for using Gordon's plans, for instance), but Kroeger's profit margins seemed excessive.[14]

East
entrance
detail

Tower detail

Fayette County Courthouse

LA GRANGE, TEXAS, 1890–91

C-1

Northwest
tower detail

East side
entrance
detail

Bexar County Courthouse

SAN ANTONIO, TEXAS, 1892–97

C-3

Erath County Courthouse

STEPHENVILLE, TEXAS, 1891–92

Roof and
tower
detail

Porch detail

Victoria County Courthouse

VICTORIA, TEXAS, 1891–92

C-5

Courtroom wing detail

Detail of corbelling beneath logia

Hopkins County Courthouse

SULPHUR SPRINGS, TEXAS, 1894–95

C-6

Roof and
tower detail

Gonzales County Courthouse

GONZALES, TEXAS, 1894–95

Porch capital detail

Terra-cotta and stonework detail

Ellis County Courthouse

WAXAHACHIE, TEXAS, 1895–97

Tower
corbelling
detail

Wise County Courthouse

Comal County Courthouse

NEW BRAUNFELS, TEXAS, 1898

Porch detail

Lee County Courthouse

Skylight and roofline detail

Dome detail

Arizona Territorial Capitol

PHOENIX, ARIZONA, 1899–1900

Harrison County Courthouse

MARSHALL, TEXAS, 1899–1901

C-13

Pediment
and
dome
structure
detail

McLennan County Courthouse

WACO, TEXAS, 1900–02

Ornamental
details

Vicksburg City Hall

VICKSBURG, MISSISSIPPI, 1901–03

C-15

Entrance
detail

Copiah County Courthouse

HAZELHURST, MISSISSIPPI, 1902–03

Wilkinson County Courthouse

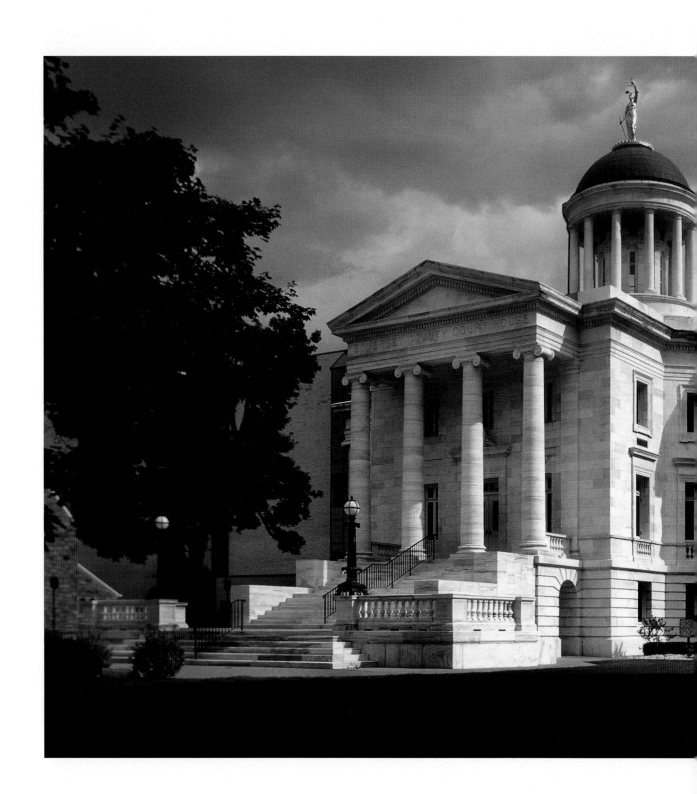

Somerset County Courthouse

Entrance detail

Garrett County Courthouse

OAKLAND, MARYLAND, 1907–08

C-20

Pediment
and dome
detail

Madison County Courthouse

WAMPSVILLE, NEW YORK, 1908–09

C-21

Detail of
drum
beneath
dome

"History" at entrance

Bergen County Courthouse

HACKENSACK, NEW JERSEY, 1909–10

North "Gordon wing" added to M. E. Bebe's original 1880 central section

Cambria County Courthouse

World War I
memorial

Cortland County Courthouse

CORTLAND, NEW YORK, 1922–24

9.1.
Ellis County Courthouse under
construction. *Photograph ca. 1896,
photographer unknown, courtesy
Alexander Architectural Archive,
University of Texas, Austin.*

The Commissioners' Court used the report and its pending legal appeal to leverage concessions from the contractor. Kroeger, with payment for his work to date in
limbo, had interest in negotiating and both parties parleyed for a week in early January
1895. Marshal L. Sanguinet provided his assistance to the effort, but there is no record
of Gordon's involvement. In order "to have a fuller interpretation," Kroeger and the
new Commissioners' Court rewrote "the specifications and made certain alterations
... indicated on the [original] plans." On January 11, all agreed to these revised documents as a supplement to Kroeger's contract, and related litigation was then dropped
so that work could resume. A week later the county engaged Sanguinet, through his
firm, as its superintendent empowered "to order necessary changes and to define the
true meaning of the plans, specifications and details." Records do not indicate any
change to the cost of the contract, so it seems the supplement held Kroeger to the more
expensive manner of building, with Sanguinet enforcing the county's will.[15]

Kroeger had a reputation for bringing innovation to his work, as evidenced by
the apparatus employed for Bexar's construction. He continued in this vein at Ellis
with specialized equipment that he had in operation by July (fig. 9.1). According to
his representative on the site, Kroeger installed two 5,000-pound capacity derricks at
Waxahachie. The representative went on to describe them:

The masts are 65 feet long, booms 50 feet. They will be erected on 15 foot towers,
making the total height 80 feet from the first floor to the top of the masts. From the

9.2.
Ellis County Courthouse,
Waxahachie, Texas (1894–97).
James Riely Gordon, architect.
1901 photograph by Hudson.

first floor the booms will stand at 47 feet. On these booms a track of regular rail-road iron is laid and on the track a carriage runs back and forth. The little railroad will be operated by electricity supplied by a dynamo.[16]

This contrivance was used to help set in place some two million bricks, "160 car loads of Texas granite, 100 car loads of Pecos red sand stone, used in trimming the building, and fourteen cars of iron." The Winkle Terra Cotta Company of St. Louis, Missouri, supplied the architectural terra-cotta. Trimming and carving of the stone is the work of Theodore Beilharz's Dallas firm.[17]

    With these components, Kroeger assembled a courthouse that rivals Bexar in size. Ellis measures 114 x 134 feet and rises 134 feet to the apex of the central tower (fig. 9.2). It is a massive pile of stone that showcases Gordon's originality while giving tribute to the Richardsonian Romanesque style. For the first time in an executed courthouse design, Gordon fully embraced the French Provençal ornamentation that Richardson had employed so ably. Still, it remains a Gordon courthouse: familiar architectural elements from his previous courthouses are present, skillfully synthesized within the Provençal fabric.[18]

A striking difference between Ellis and Gordon's previous courthouses is its loftiness, with 65 percent of its height above the roofline (fig. 9.3). Gordon's earlier Signature Plan courthouses were surely inspired by Trinity Church, but Ellis seems to be drawn from Richardson's (with Charles Gambrill) aborted early designs for Trinity in particular. As noted in Chapter 8, Richardson emulated the churches of Auvergne in his Boston design. Accordingly, he proposed a tall, obelisk-like, octagonal tower rising from the pyramidal mass. Concerns about safety arose after construction began, however, and Richardson was forced by his client to abandon this concept. Trinity's shorter, square tower as built represents a compromise, albeit a masterful one. While the completed church drew wide praise, at least one early biographer appreciated the abandoned design as "strong and individual, and not without beauty." A line cut of this design was published in Marianna Griswold Van Rensselaer's biography of Richardson (fig. 9.4), which Gordon possibly studied.[19] Whether intentional or coincidental, Ellis's tower is a superb manifestation of Richardson's original concept.

The gray granite basement rises to a red, Pecos sandstone water table course. Beyond that, the complexity of the design obscures Gordon's familiar Signature Plan and almost defies narrative. Two apsidal bays project from the northwestern façade and are flanked by two-story, beveled porches. On the southeast side, one-story porches again follow the curve of the district courtroom above. A compound apse off the courtroom wing allows for the judge's chambers, and a spiral stair runs from the basement to the attic. Wall dormers and spirelets, augmented by metal eagles, enliven the rise to a clock tower whose complexity rivals the rest of the structure. The tapering composition furthers the perception of height while relaying a sense of naturally settled mass.

The decorative treatment is equally complex. Horizontal banding offsets vertical elements, such as slender columns and two-story pilasters. Arches as well as rinceau and checkerboard friezes ameliorate the tension between vertical and horizontal thrust. Close inspection of the exterior stonework rewards the observer with what is likely the most elaborate sculptural program of any Texas courthouse. Human and animal faces, ranging from angelic to grotesque and whimsical to demonic, peer from foliated capitals, stringcourses, and elsewhere (figs. 9.5 and 9.6).

Carver and modeler Harry Herley appears to be the artisan behind this splendid work. He claims the courthouse as "Carved by Herley" on the back of a business card from the time. The front lists prominent architects from about the country as his

9.3.
Ellis County Courthouse. *2004 photograph.*

9.4.
Discarded 1873 design for Trinity Church,
detail. Gambrill & Richardson, architects.
From Van Rensselaer, Henry Hobson
Richardson and His Works.

9.5.
Ellis County Courthouse, capital detail. *1989 photograph.*

9.6.
Ellis County Courthouse, tower detail. *1995 photograph.*

references. Sanguinet is among these, making it likely he is responsible for Herley's employment here.[20] Further scholarship is needed before a Gordon or Kroeger connection with the carver can be ruled out, however. Local folklore surrounds the symbolism of this artwork, but regardless it is the product of a talented and imaginative hand given free rein, as Gordon often specified. Over a century after its execution, the carving still serves its purpose by drawing interest to the courthouse.

The familiar Signature Plan layout defines the interior. Corridors and the courtroom feature the combed cement plaster wainscoting that the architect contemporaneously recommended for the Bexar County Courthouse (fig. 9.7). Ellis possesses the only extant example of this unusual treatment as employed by Gordon in a courthouse.

Gordon introduced structural refinements as well. He achieved increased fire-resistance by using iron in place of wood for the wall studs and attic rafters. Another innovation for a Gordon courthouse was the use of the expanded metal arch system of fire-resistant flooring. This replaced the Gilbert corrugated iron arch flooring used previously and likely provided the same level of safety at a reduced cost. These innovations appear to have been part of the original specifications and indicate the architect's interest in structural as well as decorative and plan refinements.[21]

9.7.
Ellis County Courthouse,
corridor with combed cement
plaster wainscoting. *2004
photograph.*

Despite its profuse decoration and polychromatic treatment, the Ellis County Courthouse exudes controlled nobility. A watercolor perspective rendering from the architect's office reveals that, when viewed from a short distance, the exterior of the courthouse as built matches Gordon's vision exactly. The wealth of stone carving raises the possibility that it may to some extent be the result of Marshal Sanguinet's role as superintendent. While the original Ellis plans and specifications with their negotiated annotations appear to be lost, those that survive for other Gordon courthouses demonstrate that he was specific about decorative programs, ordering carving that was "executed artistically and spirited." Sanguinet, tasked with extracting as much value as possible from Kroeger, likely demanded the most elaborate carving that could be deduced from Gordon's orders.

Kroeger may have built such an ornate courthouse if left to his own supervision, but it is reasonable to assume that the execution of Gordon's plans benefited from the adversarial relationship between the contractor and the Commissioners' Court. Sanguinet, in his watchdog role, held Kroeger to the most expensive interpretation of the plans. The courthouse in Ellis County is the superb result of county officials striving to get the most for their constituents' tax dollars.

A permanent reminder of the contentious origins of this project is literally set in stone at the northern porch. In lieu of a typical cornerstone, two polished granite blocks are set into the parapet walls flanking the steps. One lists the officers of the new Commissioners' Court. The other, set on the opposite side of the entrance, notes Gordon as the architect and Kroeger as the builder and lists the county officers at the time the construction contract was signed. The Commissioners' Court ordered the first stone. Kroeger donated the second.[22]

Ellis County began limited use of the building in January 1897. On April 7 Messer, Sanguinet & Messer reported to the court that the Ellis County Courthouse had been "finished according to the plans and specifications," and the building was formally accepted.[23]

Ellis is the fifth and last Gordon-designed public building built by Kroeger. Although no other contractor constructed as many, the number is not too remarkable considering other builders could claim four. The relationship between Gordon and Kroeger deserves some scrutiny, however. There is no evidence of any notable connection between the two prior to the Bexar courthouse project, but they formed a bond standing together in defense of their reputations during the subsequent scandal. In the depressed times following the Panic of 1893, Kroeger, as a builder, provided access to design work that was not open to architects directly. For his part, Gordon armed Kroeger with plans that proved an advantage over other contractors. While mutually beneficial, this arrangement ran contrary to the goals of the AIA and the TSAA, which struggled to establish and protect the legitimacy of architecture as a profession. By allowing a contractor to present his designs as part of a "package deal," Gordon undermined these efforts. Granted, he may have been desperate for work when the Gonzales and Van Zandt Commissioners' Courts considered Kroeger's proposals, but his practice was apparently doing well when the Ellis contract was signed. Gordon likely steered San Patricio's construction toward Kroeger, but it was a unique situation where the small budget required efficiencies already present in their familiar working relationship.

While Gordon's relationship with Kroeger may have compromised his ideals as a professional, he clearly did not let it compromise his responsibility as an architect. It is quite significant that Gordon advised against accepting San Patricio until the work was completed, and a dispute between the architect and builder over Bexar went to arbitration. Of course, the architect had no control over the three projects he did not superintend and where ethical questions surround Kroeger's contracts. Gordon also demonstrated that he was not dependent on Kroeger as he continued to participate in, and win, courthouse design competitions where the contracts went to other builders. Indeed, he competed *against* Kroeger for the Karnes County Courthouse. Furthermore, construction contracts for Gordon's concurrent non-public commissions, where he had more control over the process, often went to other builders as well. Finally, even while members of the new Ellis County Commissioners' Court were trying to straighten out the courthouse project left by their predecessors, they entered into a contract with Gordon to design its furnishings. Although this arrangement did not see fruition, it establishes that they considered the architect free of any taint they may have attached to Kroeger.[24]

Nonetheless, his affiliation with Kroeger developed into an embarrassment for the architect. It opened him to professional criticism at a time when cost overruns on the

Bexar project reflected poorly on all involved. By 1897 the architect and the contractor had distanced themselves from each other. That year, Gordon assured a fellow architect in connection with a Galveston courthouse contest (discussed in Chapter 10) that "Mr. Kroeger is not in any way, shape or form interested in me nor in my plans. I have his written agreement that he will not bid on the Court House if my plans are adopted."[25]

While construction was under way in Waxahachie, Gordon obtained another courthouse commission through the more orthodox competition system. Wise County's third courthouse, a wood frame Second Empire design built in 1881, burned on January 8, 1895. This was the second courthouse that Wise lost to a suspicious fire. It is therefore understandable that fire-resistance was high on the list of concerns as officials contemplated a replacement from their rented space in a commercial building.[26]

In mid-February three Wise commissioners traveled to San Antonio and other points to inspect courthouses. Their purpose appears to have been to become informed on the subject quickly enough to judge the submissions, which were due March 4. Meanwhile, promoters of other communities tried to use the opportunity to get the county seat removed to their towns. As the *Decatur News* put it, "the roof of the courthouse had hardly fallen in before petitions were being circulated and money raised" to move the government. A quickly organized election settled the matter in Decatur's favor on February 26. Debate followed as to where the new structure should be built—adjacent to the town square, where the previous courthouse sat, or directly on it.[27]

The eventual decision to build on the square likely gave Gordon's Signature Plan an edge as he prevailed in a field of ten architects and firms on March 4, 1895. He was also hired to superintend the work. The construction contract went to J. A. White, whose $97,225 bid was the lowest, but officials worked with the architect and builder to make some minor changes to get the price down to $95,000.[28]

The project was the source of controversy of the familiar type. In some circles the cost of the courthouse was questioned, as was the conduct of county officials. Specific charges could not be resurrected at this writing, but an irritation during these still-lean years was a junket taken by the Commissioners' Court, at Gordon's invitation, to inspect building materials in St. Louis. (Ellis County officials who made a similar trip were rather pampered.) Cries of jobbery were also raised. The *Decatur News* dismissed the majority of the complaints as coming from "people that have an axe to grind." Be that as it may, the matter appears to have cost officials reelection.[29]

Construction began on June 1. Work on Wise proceeded without any problems related to the architect or his design. Adverse weather and labor strikes delayed the completion past the May 1, 1896, deadline to the following January, however. The final cost paid to the contractor was $109,500 plus $5,126.37 for "extras" such as sidewalks

and fences to keep horses off the square. Wise County officials received the courthouse on January 5, 1897.[30]

Although smaller, Wise is similar enough to Ellis in plan and composition to be considered a "sister" courthouse. Ornamental differences establish its own, unique merit, however (fig. 9.8).[31] In contrast to the polychromy of its predecessor, Wise is sheathed in Burnet pink granite and homogenous terra-cotta. The result is a more sober composition that still follows in Richardson's Provençal precedent. Its monochromatic, but fictile, exterior program also aptly demonstrates the decorative potential of sunlight and shadow in architecture as surfaces change dramatically during the course of the day.

Corbelling below the roofline gives way to terra-cotta that is employed as a frieze filling the spandrels between the third-story arches and encircling the structure. The use of terra-cotta extends to corbelling on the tower, friezes on the smaller turrets on

9.9.
Wise County Courthouse,
roofline detail. *1998 photograph.*

the apse extending from the courtroom side of the building, and other applications. As
at Ellis, the Winkle Company provided the terra-cotta work, although here the foliation approaches art nouveau expression (fig. 9.9).[32] Lion heads at the tower hearken
back to the Ellis tower and provide the only figurative decoration. The capitals for
the Wise courthouse are carved from granite, a much harder material than that used
at Waxahachie, so the ornament appears less plastic here. Because of this, the Wise
ornament has resisted weathering quite well and appears little changed from when the
scaffolding was taken away well over a century ago.

Gordon also explores the compositional potential of smooth surfaces in the
Wise design. Voussoirs for the third-story arches are dressed smooth in contrast to
the quarry-faced treatment of the porch arcades. Windows with minimal ornament
punctuate flat expanses of the dormers. Likewise, the circle-motif balustrades at the
tower and above the courtroom roofline are also dressed smooth. These balustrades
are unique among the courthouses built to Gordon's Signature Plan. Given the cost
difference, it is unlikely Wise's interior was as ornate as that of Ellis, but Gordon did
specify Vermont marble wainscoting along with mosaic tile.

Together, Ellis and Wise mark the zenith of Gordon's Richardsonian Romanesque
work as applied to his Signature Plan. The relatively generous budgets of these proj-

9.10.
Église de Issoire, Auvergne Region, France. *Photograph from H. H. Richardson's collection. Courtesy of the Frances Loeb Library, Harvard School of Design.*

9.11.
Wise County Courthouse, telephoto view. *1998 photograph.*

ects allowed the architect to elaborate upon this plan with complex augmentation and ornamentation, resulting in highly personalized statements that once again demonstrate the Richardsonian style's capacity for innovation. In their full pyramidal massing and lofty towers, Gordon comes closer to realizing the "Auvergnat solution" than Richardson was ever able to execute (figs. 9.10 and 9.11). While legions of imitators recycled the massing of Trinity Church as built, Gordon, through either scholarly intent or aesthetic intuition, found his way back to its source. Surely the maverick in Richardson would have admired the effort. Considered in this narrow context, it seems Gordon out-Richardsoned Richardson with Ellis and Wise.

CHAPTER TEN

Commissions Lost

The Ellis and Wise temples of justice mark the highest development of J. Riely Gordon's Signature Plan. These masterworks could have served as the beginnings of a series of comparable public edifices, but political and professional maneuvering prevented it. Instead, more than two years lapsed before ground was broken for another Gordon courthouse. During this period, he lost one design contest to a competitor who appropriated his Signature Plan. Another courthouse commission was wrestled from the San Antonian after he had seemingly prevailed. Yet another was similarly wrenched from a distinguished peer whose design had been chosen over Gordon's. A state house contest demonstrates Gordon's own machinations to get his plans adopted and the lengths his enemies would go in order to foil him.

Gordon appears to have been rather philosophical about his travails; rarely did he grouse about commissions lost. There were times, however, when the architect felt he had been unduly wronged. For example, the suspected theft of intellectual property (his plans and designs) or threats to his reputation provoked him to pursue satisfaction. The setbacks chronicled in this chapter shed further light on this architect's career and character.

Lamar County's twenty-five-year-old courthouse at Paris was deemed unsafe in 1895. At its February session, the Commissioners' Court voted to issue $84,000 in bonds to fund its replacement.[1] Details of the events that followed are sketchy and largely reliant upon a sworn affidavit filed by Gordon against one of his competitors: Arthur O. Watson of Austin.

As Gordon relates, he drew up plans and specifications that were similar to Ellis and Wise, but individualized to meet Lamar County's needs (fig. 10.1). Early in the discussions and during the competition he pointed out that his plans were copyrighted. After the Commissioners' Court rejected his entry in favor of Watson's, Gordon examined Watson's drawings and found them, in his words, "to be the same general plan, with slight variations in immaterial points, as my plans." He urged the Austin architect to change the plans to avoid infringing upon his copyright. Watson refused, so Gordon took the matter to the Commissioners' Court, which was equally unsympathetic. In

10.1.
1895 competition design for
Lamar County Courthouse.
James Riely Gordon, architect.
*Unsigned office rendering, courtesy
Alexander Architectural Archive,
University of Texas, Austin.*

early July 1895, he filed suit in the US Circuit Court, Eastern District of Texas, to enjoin
Watson from using the plans.[2]

Two sentences from a Carthage, Missouri, newspaper corroborate Gordon's version of events in Paris. The article, concerning building stone for Lamar's courthouse,
reports, "it was discovered that the plans chosen were not original with the architect
who presented them. A controversy in the courts was gotten up among the architects
which resulted in the plans being rejected, new ones chosen and new bids taken." Enig-
matic entries in the Lamar County Commissioners' Court minutes simply note that it
was engaged in an architect's competition in April 1895 and, after a period of silence on
the subject, again engaged with courthouse matters in June and July—about the time
of Gordon's suit. On August 20, the county awarded a contract to Messer, Sanguinet
& Messer for new courthouse plans. Ten days later the construction contract went to
Martin, Byrnes & Johnston. In September, Watson filed suit against Lamar County for
damages totaling $4,333, possibly related to the rejection of his plans.[3]

It is impossible to know if Lamar County officials actively conspired with Watson
to appropriate Gordon's Signature Plan, but the tight-lipped nature of the minute
entries suggests some conniving was afoot and they did not want details made public.
Cribbing from Gordon's work does seem to have been to the Lamar Commissioners'
Court's liking, however; even the subsequent courthouse designed by Messer, Sanguinet & Messer is suggestive of the Signature Plan (fig. 10.2). (Could it be more than

10.2.
Lamar County Courthouse,
Paris, Texas (1895–97, destroyed).
Messer, Sanguinet & Messer,
architects. *Postcard view published
by Art Manufacturing Co., ca. 1907.*

coincidence that both Watson and Marshal Sanguinet previously had ample time to
study sets of Gordon plans—Hopkins and Ellis, respectively?) In a departure from the
Fort Worth firm's earlier Ellis County proposal, they adopted a somewhat cruciform
floor plan and moved entrances into the reentrant angles for Lamar. They placed these
entrances awkwardly beneath foreboding octagonal turrets rather than behind Gordon's more inviting airy and cooling porches. Perhaps Messer, Sanguinet & Messer
made these and other deviations from the Signature Plan to avoid further litigation
from the San Antonian, but the resulting structure did not function as efficiently as a

Gordon courthouse. Lamar is remembered as "poorly arranged inside, poorly lighted and ventilated. The court rooms were on the north side of the house and were dark and inconvenient to access."[4] There may be no better demonstration of the success of Gordon's tightly integrated plan than the failings exhibited by Lamar's departure from it.

While Gordon endured his share of issues and controversies associated with his courthouse work, problems attending the Lamar construction demonstrate that this was not unique to Gordon. Charges that work on Lamar was not in accordance to the specifications caused the Commissioners' Court to install one of its members as superintendent. Costs rose well beyond Martin, Byrnes & Johnston's bid price of $88,190, which may have been a factor in the ouster of the entire Commissioners' Court in the 1896 primary. The building, upon its completion in October 1897, reportedly cost from $135,000 to $150,000. It was destroyed along with much of Paris in the great fire on March 21, 1916.[5]

Denton County's 1877 courthouse had also fallen into disrepair by 1895 and many felt that a replacement was long overdue when its Commissioners' Court finally concurred in May. After traveling to other counties to examine new trends in courthouse design, officials advertised a competition in the *Dallas News* for the design of a structure not to exceed $100,000. Entries were due June 24 and fifteen architects responded, including Gordon. The court found none of the entries satisfactory, but voted on July 2 to employ Gordon "as architect to make plans and specifications for the courthouse." Commissioners C. W. Bates and J. M. Miller were opposed to hiring Gordon.[6]

The next day the Commissioners' Court thoroughly reviewed Gordon's entry and specified the changes they deemed necessary. Bates urged his colleagues to take stringent, and not totally unreasonable, measures to ensure the architect was held to his estimates for the courthouse as specified with the revisions. This met with approval, and the commissioners required Gordon to post a bond to guarantee his fidelity to the desires of the Commissioners' Court. Destruction of the old courthouse began shortly thereafter, and Gordon went home to San Antonio to make the changes.[7]

He returned to the city of Denton, the Denton County seat, on July 22 and presented revised plans. Bates and Miller found even these deficient, but the other members were quite satisfied, suggesting only minor revisions. On July 25 Commissioner J. C. Brannon proposed the revised plans be accepted. Gordon seemed to have clinched another victory, but, just as they were about to vote on the revisions, Commissioner Bates asked that Commissioner Miller be allowed to make a statement. This being granted, Miller shocked the assembly by declaring that he had been offered money to vote for Gordon's plan. In the commotion that ensued Gordon demanded to know who made this alleged bribe. Miller would only disclose that the offer was not made by Gordon and that the incident occurred in June. The architect demanded an investigation as the Commissioners' Court took a short recess to recompose. Commissioners

Bates, Brannon, and Miller then withdrew to another room for a private conversation. When they returned Brannon moved that the decision to hire Gordon be reconsidered. Upon approval of this Bates quickly followed with a motion that the order employing the architect be rescinded, which was seconded by Miller and approved. Gordon demanded an explanation. Brannon provided the only response, stating flatly, "it is my privilege."[8]

Parallels between this series of events and Alfred Giles's trouble in El Paso are eerily close, and Gordon knew he could not allow this allegation to stand. As with the Bexar scandal, he was confident a fair inquiry would clear his name, but the Denton County Commissioners' Court chose not to investigate Miller's story. Gordon's competitors and enemies would soon use the bribery allegation against him, so his only recourse was litigation.

He returned to Denton on August 6 to file a $3,325 claim against the county for services rendered while employed as the courthouse architect. This was rejected, so Gordon sued in district court arguing county officials made a verbal agreement to employ him to revise his competition plans and specifications. The county's defense argued that his employment was dependent on his revisions being accepted, but the bribery charge preempted that vote. Witness testimony supported both sides but the jury sided with the county. Gordon appealed.[9]

In the meantime, the courthouse project continued without Gordon. On August 9 Commissioner Bates motioned that W. C. Dodson be hired as the architect for the Denton County Courthouse. This carried and Dodson set to work creating the plans and specifications for a building estimated to cost $80,000. Having lost the Van Zandt project to Gordon's design, Dodson may have found satisfaction in this turn of events. He was compensated for his troubles in Canton, however, with no injury to his character. The Denton project was completed a little more than a year and a half later at a final cost of nearly $150,000. It appears that Commissioner Bates's strict standard of fiscal accountability for Gordon was not applied to Dodson.[10]

Gordon eventually lost his appeal, but the decision provided vindication. The appellate court conceded that Bates and Miller opposed hiring Gordon and, after the vote to have him make revisions, continued working to sway some other member of the Commissioners' Court to their side for a majority. They succeeded when Brannon changed his vote following Miller's charge of bribery—a charge that the court noted, "*seems to have been without foundation in fact*" (emphasis added). Regardless, the court ruled that Gordon failed to prove that his work would have been accepted had the vote to approve his revisions not been abandoned. Denton County therefore had no obligation to pay Gordon the money he claimed. Nevertheless, Gordon had cleared his name in the public record by discrediting Miller's bribery allegation. Unfortunately, this decision did not come until 1899—long after Gordon lost the Denton project.[11]

As Gordon sought vindication in Denton a new opportunity arose in the state of Mississippi. In early 1896, William S. Hull and Lundie Monroe Weathers were hired separately as disinterested experts to inspect the 1839 state house in Jackson. Although identified as an architect, Dallas city directories listed Hull and his brother, Francis B. Hull, as jail builders and contractors as well as general agents for the Pauly Jail Building and Manufacturing Company. Weathers had designs for a number of public buildings to his credit, including courthouses for Caddo and Bossier Parishes in Louisiana. Both advocated replacing the building, with Weathers going so far as to report, "the capitol is dangerous and liable to fall at any moment." This was enough to spur the state legislature to action (even though the building stands to this day).[12]

On March 20 the legislature appointed a committee composed of Governor A. J. McLaurin, the state attorney general, and the secretary of state to advertise for plans and specifications for a new capitol. Submissions for a structure to cost between $550,000 and $1,000,000 were due on July 15. Compensation for the adopted plans would be $1,000, unless the same architect was chosen to superintend construction. In that case compensation would be limited to the percentage of the total cost allowed for superintending. In no case would there be any compensation for a design not actually used. While viewing competitions in general as degrading, the editors of the *Inland Architect and News Record* found this one particularly insulting: the prize, if awarded, would amount to a fraction of 1 percent of the projected cost.[13]

Be that as it may, more than fourteen architects and firms, representing at least six states, participated. Gordon was among them (fig. 10.3). The governor's committee was to review the submissions and then pass its recommendations along to the legislature. While the nature and number of the recommendations were not defined, several of the competing architects, including Gordon, signed letters petitioning the committee to forward only one design. The committee settled on one entry, submitted by Lundie Monroe Weathers.[14]

Immediate criticism arose from this selection of the architect who had already been paid for his "disinterested" recommendation to replace the old building. The resolution creating the governor's committee did not actually bind the legislature to follow its recommendations, and Gordon seized upon this as an opportunity to salvage the commission. In the subsequent months, the San Antonian began a remarkable lobbying effort to win lawmakers over to his plan. His engaging personality likely carried him a long way to this end, but he did not hesitate to draw upon other resources at his command. His professional accomplishments and medals for his Texas State Building design impressed some legislators. Others were moved by letters of endorsement from prominent persons and architectural organizations. Some placed importance on his family connections. His father's service to the Confederacy was noted and probably overstated. Georgia Governor General John Brown Gordon, CSA, Gordon's second

10.3.
1896 competition design for
Mississippi State Capitol. James
Riely Gordon, architect. *Unsigned
office rendering, courtesy Alexander
Architectural Archive, University of
Texas, Austin.*

cousin, provided a letter of recommendation that was read before the Senate. It was also recognized that the architect's wife was cousin to the late Mississippian and US Supreme Court justice Lucius Quintus Cincinnatus Lamar.

When it came time to vote on the capitol bill in the House and Senate in May 1897, anti-Gordon forces went into action. One congressman addressed the Senate saying William L. Martin, of the Texas construction firm of Martin, Byrnes & Johnston, informed him that Gordon was unreliable and had taken "a contract at $350,000 and the building cost $700,000." Furthermore, Martin was present on the floor and "ready to back up all he said." The congressman then urged that these charges against Gordon be investigated.

Although sensational, the ploy of bringing Martin in at the eleventh hour backfired. According to newspaper reports, at least two votes went to Gordon because of it. A senator who had previously endorsed Weathers's plan took exception to the last-minute attack on Gordon's reputation. Summoning southern conventions, he changed his support to Gordon, declaring that "character, and a man's honor had been assailed on the floor of the Senate; honor was dearer than life, and was to a man what chastity was to a woman." He dismissed as not credible "the idea that a *disinterested* person [Martin] would come all the way from Texas," supposedly paying his own expenses, to bring this accusation that contained "spite and meanness" (emphasis added). The senator then urged the legislature "to set the seal of disapprobation on Gordon's accuser."

Another congressman who was formally of the Weathers camp "denounced Martin in unmeasured terms."

One of Gordon's backers maintained that it was "too late to spring charges of unreliability on Mr. Gordon. Unaided by a powerful lobby of this state he has single-handed and alone won the over-whelming endorsement of the House and Senate." Besides, he added, such charges mattered more in considering the choice of a superintendent. Lawmakers could simply avoid the issue by choosing Gordon's plan and then selecting someone else to monitor construction. In the end, the Mississippi legislature passed a bill to build a new capitol according to Gordon's plan.[15]

Getting to this point was an impressive feat for Gordon, but the capitol project was stopped dead in its tracks with Governor McLaurin's veto of the bill. Knowing this would cause controversy and widespread disappointment, McLaurin prepared a carefully crafted explanation of his action. He addressed questions surrounding the propriety of the committee's selection of Weathers's plan, arguing that, at the time the architect was hired to inspect the old building, he did qualify as "disinterested" since he did not pay taxes in Mississippi, but that did not bar him from the subsequent competition. McLaurin also suggested Gordon was a hypocrite for petitioning the committee to forward only one entry but not accepting his loss. The governor disputed some constitutional aspects of the new capitol bill, but he clearly understood he had to thoroughly discredit the well-liked Texas architect if his veto was to stand.

Conceding Gordon's popularity, McLaurin cautioned the cost and permanent nature of this project required that officials look beyond the architect and concentrate on the plan. He then accused Gordon of trying to pass off an old courthouse design for the new Mississippi Capitol. He offered as evidence Gordon's specifications, which are fully transcribed in the governor's message with annotations where the original typewritten document had sections erased or struck through and penciled notes added to change the terminology specific to a courthouse to that of a state house. On this basis the governor charged Gordon's plan was insufficient for a state capitol.[16] McLaurin's attack was thorough and successful, if not altogether fair.

Although the architect accepted the defeat and returned to San Antonio, it is clear he had advocates in Jackson who disputed McLaurin's charge. A month later Gordon wrote to a Mississippi legislator thanking him for past kindness. He went on to write, "I have received a great many letters from friends insisting upon my explaining that portion of the Governor's veto message bearing upon my preliminary specification. I have up to the present time, avoided any comment whatsoever."[17]

Gordon seems to have maintained his public silence on the subject for three years, until events in the Mississippi legislature (discussed in Chapter 14) compelled him to return to Jackson and address the matter. He then told his side of the story to a *Jackson Daily News* reporter:

Well, when I submitted my plans . . . my specifications were lost here in Jackson and they were never found. . . . [But, f]or a fine courthouse the [specifications], especially as relates to the ceilings and plastering, are about the same, and when I found that my [specifications] were lost, I did take out some court house specifications and write the words House and Senate over the words district court room, but when I handed them in to the governor I told him that the plans were just preliminary and that the real work of getting up the specifications would come after the bill was signed. I do not feel hard at the governor for vetoing the bill, although I do not think that I was treated exactly right.[18]

Gordon is correct that specifications detailing technical information such as cement mixing instructions and fireproofing methods for a sizable courthouse would be largely applicable to a state house. His story that he was forced to substitute specifications from a courthouse, which he hastily revised by hand, is borne out by the public record and contemporary newspaper illustrations.[19] These illustrations from Gordon's plans make clear that he submitted a unique, Beaux-Arts design for Mississippi, complete with a dome derived from Michelangelo's dome for St. Peter's in the Vatican. However, the transcribed specifications quoted in McLaurin's veto message show that Romanesque features were erased or struck through, verifying Gordon's assertion that the latter originated with a completely different design. (They probably were created for the Lamar competition or the aborted 1895 Galveston competition discussed below.)[20] It is not known how Gordon's capitol specifications came to be "lost," but surely he would have explained the substitution rather than try to fool officials with an erased, struck-through, and otherwise marked-up document as McLaurin alleged.

Be that as it may, the governor's veto stood and Mississippi did not build a new capitol at that time. McLaurin's assertion that Gordon tried to pull a fast one in Mississippi is one of the most persistent myths associated with the architect's career. Unfortunately, it has been taken at face value in many accounts since 1897.[21] Clearly, the governor's primary justification for his veto was untrue.

In 1896 Gordon self-published a promotional booklet titled *Sketches from the Portfolio of James Riely Gordon, Architect, San Antonio, Texas*, which he gave out to potential clients. Such monographs were fairly common marketing tools for enterprising architects at the time. *Sketches* contains reproductions of office drawings and photographs of projects, executed and unexecuted. The endeavor was supported by a few advertisements from interested concerns such as the St. Louis Expanded Metal Fire Proofing Company, the San Antonio Foundry Company (makers of architectural ironwork), the Globe Furniture Company, the Winkle Terra Cotta Company, and the Hydraulic-Press Brick Company (the latter two both of St. Louis). These monographs eventually fell from favor in the profession due to fear that such advertising support could compromise architects.[22]

10.4.
1895 competition design for
Galveston County Courthouse.
James Riely Gordon, architect.
*Unsigned office rendering, courtesy
Alexander Architectural Archive,
University of Texas, Austin.*

Gordon's *Sketches* is a problematic resource for scholarship. Its value is that it identifies which projects up to that date Gordon regarded as most noteworthy and photographs provide helpful documentation. Some of the drawings and titles, however, are at odds with other sources of information. Such contradictions and incongruities cast doubt upon the booklet, suggesting it should be cited with caution.

This being said, an illustration in *Sketches* titled "Preliminary Competition, Court-House, Galveston County, Texas" (fig. 10.4) was likely prepared in response to a competition announced in October 1895. The existing, antebellum courthouse in the island city of Galveston had been much modified over the years yet many felt it was still inadequate for the county's needs. The Commissioners' Court had high aspirations and voted to build a new $375,000 courthouse, but the population did not share their enthusiasm. Opposition was so strong that the commissioners cancelled the competition and the project the following month.[23] Gordon likely had already commenced work on his entry before the project was dropped, which explains the unique title of "Preliminary Competition" in his portfolio booklet.

Although the citizens' reaction cancelled the expensive new edifice, the need for some sort of courthouse work remained and was exacerbated by a December 16, 1896, blaze that left the building seriously damaged. County Judge Morgan M. Mann advocated repairing the structure, while Commissioner Charles Vidor pressed for a new courthouse. Two days after the fire the Commissioners' Court sided with Vidor, voting to solicit plans for a replacement.[24]

Authorities placed advertisements for plans and specifications for a four-story, fireproof courthouse not to exceed $200,000 in the *Galveston Daily News* and the

Dallas News. The contest drew twenty-six entries by the February 23, 1897, deadline, and the court spent nearly two weeks reviewing them. Gordon was among the entrants but, engaged at the time in his lobbying effort in Mississippi, he relied on a representative, architect Charles W. Bulger.[25] His submission is an intriguing reworking of his 1895 design, exhibiting Beaux-Arts tendencies perhaps reawakened in Gordon with the Mississippi Capitol effort (fig 10.5). Of particular note are twin towers imparting a Mediterranean air for the island city, not unlike his Arabian fantasy for Aransas.

Galveston's 1897 architectural contest was markedly different, at least on the surface, from the aggressive contests reported elsewhere in this volume. Perhaps the allure of the island with its long beaches tempered competitive passions among the architects. Another possibility is the participants were resigned to the likelihood of the award going to the city's revered resident designer, Nicholas J. Clayton. Whatever the

10.5.
1897 competition design for Galveston County Courthouse. James Riely Gordon, architect. *Unsigned office rendering, courtesy Alexander Architectural Archive, University of Texas, Austin.*

reasons, the interval devoted to the review of plans became an idyllic respite for the architects. According to the *Galveston Daily News*, Henry W. Wolters, a veteran architect from Louisville, Kentucky, was "unanimously elected chaperone of the visiting delegation . . . as an entertainer he is a brand success, and in consequence all members of the craft are having a delightful time." Another report tells of the architects uniting for a fishing expedition.[26]

Probably few were surprised when the court decided in favor of Clayton for a "modernized French renaissance"–style design. When asked for details, Commissioner Vidor displayed unusual candor.

> The choice of the plans had been reduced to three architects—Mr. Gordon of San Antonio, Sanguinet & Messer of Fort Worth [by this date Arthur Albert Messer had departed] and N. J. Clayton & Co. of Galveston. The plans of these were all equally good, and it was difficult to choose from them. But I am frank enough to say that, other things being equal, I preferred to give it to the home firm, believing that its experience in construction in Galveston, where there are peculiar foundation and climatic conditions, gives it some advantages.[27]

The commissioner's reasoning has merit, given that the city is built on a Gulf Coast barrier island where it is exposed to hurricanes and other ravages of the sea. With the decision made, the out-of-town architects ended their impromptu sojourn.

Forces were at work to undermine Clayton's hold on the Galveston County Courthouse, however. Questions were raised as to whether his design could be built for the $175,000 he had estimated. County Judge Mann made this an issue, claiming Clayton's entry was selected solely because of its price (in contradiction to Vidor's earlier statement). The Commissioners' Court then voted to make the architect post a bond personally guaranteeing the construction cost before any contractor bids were opened. When Clayton protested this after-the-fact requirement the Commissioners' Court nullified its contract with him, setting in motion a second competition.[28]

Gordon wrote two brief letters to Clayton concerning events surrounding the Galveston courthouse. From Jackson, Mississippi, where his capitol plans had just been approved by the legislature, Gordon wrote on May 23, 1897:

> I have been informed by the County Clerk of Galveston County that your plans have been rejected and I have been invited to be present on Monday. . . .
>
> I hope however you will arrange your differences and proceed with the work according to your own plans. I learn there is a combination between Sanguinet, Hull the Jail Man and Martin the contractor. They tried to do some very mean things over here to defeat me for the capitol.
>
> With kind regards
I am Fraternally yours
J. R. Gordon[29]

Entries for the second competition were due May 24, 1897. Clayton entered the second competition as well. Once aware of this, the San Antonian did not participate. A four-man committee that included Commissioners B. F. Barnes and B. F. Johnson was appointed to further review three entries with their authors to verify suitability for bidding. After the committee reviewed and approved of Sanguinet & Messer's entry and reviewed and rejected J. B. Legg's (of St. Louis), Johnson said he did not care about seeing the third entry, Nicholas Clayton's, and left the room believing it would be rejected as well. Barnes then went over those plans and specifications with Patrick Rabitt, a former draftsman in Clayton's office who worked his way up to become a partner. Barnes suggested changes, which Rabitt made in the form of penciled-in notes and went on to write more on separate sheets. Where the specifications originally allowed for a choice of materials for some features, the revisions allowed only the cheapest. In the process, a sidewalk originally specified was excluded. Rabitt signed the separate sheets for N. J. Clayton & Company and dated them May 27. Later that same day the committee returned to the Commissioners' Court and reported the entries of Sanguinet & Messer and N. J. Clayton & Company were satisfactory. The Commissioners' Court formally adopted Clayton's entry (fig. 10.6), requiring that he post a $25,000 bond, as stipulated before the second competition, to guarantee the courthouse could be built for $175,000. Two days later, while Clayton was away in Florida, Rabitt's revisions came to the attention of the Commissioners' Court and a ruckus ensued.[30]

There was plenty of suspicion and blame to go around. Commissioner Johnson's behavior was bizarre: he clearly favored Sanguinet and was negligent in leaving the room as Clayton's entry was examined. It seems the committee's instructions did not categorically exclude working with the architects as they reviewed the entries, but Barnes's unilateral actions are suspect. Although Rabitt acted at the behest of Commissioner Barnes and in the presence of the other committeemen except Johnson, he appears to have been naïve, if not culpable, in doing so. The committee simply approved Clayton's and Sanguinet's plans as suitable for bidding; the Commissioners' Court chose between the two afterward. Had that body revisited the plans before making its final decision, the obvious revisions would surely have been noticed before it selected Clayton's design and accepted his bond. Finally, having been forewarned by Gordon, Clayton should have been more vigilant—not delegating this work to Rabitt and perhaps not leaving town so soon afterward. (As seen in these pages, mischief seems to happen when the architect is out of town.)

Had it been handled differently, perhaps Clayton could have salvaged his contract. After all, Rabitt put the date on his revisions—hardly the act of a person trying to pull a fast one. Unfortunately, Clayton relied on attorneys whose haughty and demanding attitude managed to solidify the entire Commissioners' Court against him, including once staunch allies Barnes and Vidor. Even what was perhaps the best evidence in

SOUTH FRONT ELEVATION

Clayton's favor, a potentially incriminating $5,000 check from Sanguinet & Messer in Johnson's possession, was rather lamely explained away as "earnest money" without further question by the now unified officials. In the end, they rejected the architect's plans a second time and the Commissioners' Court kept his bond. A motion was made by Commissioner Johnson to accept Sanguinet & Messer's plan on the spot, but he was persuaded to withdraw it and allow time for further consideration.[31]

On June 3, Gordon wrote to Clayton from San Antonio:

> I notice by yesterday's *Galveston News* that the Court has rejected your plans. I deplore this fact and extend to you my earnest fraternal feeling. Now if this is final, I would like to re-enter the field, as I know something of the methods employed to bring about the present state of affairs, and I would like very much indeed, to see them rewarded as they deserve, aside from a desire to now have my plans adopted. The same methods were used against me in Mississippi and by the same parties.

10.6.
1897 competition design for Galveston County Courthouse. N. J. Clayton & Company, architects. *Unsigned office rendering, courtesy Alexander Architectural Archive, University of Texas, Austin.*

You have had my kindest feeling all the way through, as I believe you already know. . . .

[I] stand ready, as I said before, to assist you in any way I can consistently.[32]

Gordon's offer of assistance was likely sincere: he may have similarly benefited from Alfred Giles's counsel when defending himself in Bexar. While there appears to be no documentation of Clayton taking advantage of this offer, Gordon was in the island city on June 8 when the Commissioners' Court again took up the matter of the new courthouse. Any attempt to reward the cabal "as they deserve" failed to stop the adoption of Sanguinet's plans (fig. 10.7). In fact, officials did not consider any others. Perhaps Gordon's efforts did discourage William Martin's firm from bidding on the construction contract; the work went to a local concern. Clayton later sued for the return of his bond money but ultimately lost. Refused this prestigious commission in his hometown, lacking a judgment vindicating him, and financially damaged, Clayton saw his commissions begin to decline, and his career never recovered.[33]

Galveston's courthouse saga provides a glimpse into the professional relationships of Texas architects at the time. Clearly, Gordon held respect for Clayton but did not hesitate to compete in an apparently honest contest. Once he felt the Galvestonian had been wronged, Gordon stepped away. Believing Sanguinet had crossed a line, Gordon took Clayton into his confidence and expressed himself more candidly than he would in public, identifying those he thought to be conspiring against them both.

Newspaper accounts provide support to Gordon's conspiracy theory. Contractor William L. Martin was indeed in Jackson and doing some very mean things to prevent Gordon from winning the Mississippi Capitol design. Martin's motivation for pursuing Gordon to the halls of the Mississippi legislature is uncertain. He could have been angry over his loss of the Ellis County Courthouse contract. There may have even been bad blood between the two dating back to Victoria. At any rate, it seems a shame that a member of the firm that gave Gordon his start in public architecture (the Val Verde County Jail) should end such an enemy.

In his denunciation of Gordon in Mississippi, Martin charged that the architect took a contract for $350,000, but the building cost $700,000. Although loose with the figures, this was obviously a reference to the Bexar courthouse and deliberately misleading. It was also hypocritical, since Martin's firm was currently at work on Messer, Sanguinet & Messer's Lamar courthouse, about which similar insinuations regarding cost overruns could be made.

Sanguinet competed for the Mississippi Capitol design, but nothing found in the research for this volume ties him to Martin's efforts there. The events in Galveston, however, bore out Gordon's warnings to Clayton concerning the Fort Worth architect. Clearly Sanguinet had supporters in Galveston who were a determined lot. They succeeded in securing the courthouse project for their man on their third attempt.

Court House, Galveston Texas.

10.7.
Galveston County Courthouse, Galveston, Texas (1897–98, destroyed). Messer, Sanguinet & Messer, architects. *Detail of postcard view, ca. 1905.*

The identity of "Hull the Jail Man"—as named in one of Gordon's letters to Clayton—remains uncertain, but three likely candidates appear in the pages of this volume. Francis B. and William S. Hull both qualify for the designation by their work for the Pauly Jail Building and Manufacturing Company. They also had a connection to the Mississippi capitol due to Francis Hull's inspection of the old state house. Later they moved to Jackson and eventually competed against Gordon as architects.[34] The title "Jail Man" could also apply to Gordon's former superintendent, James T. Hull, who was involved with a Gordon & Laub jail for Nueces County and later designed the jail in Beeville. Of course, Hull would have known William Martin through the Victoria County Courthouse project, where many people's opinion of Gordon became soured. Francis and William Hull possibly had a connection to Martin as well, through a fellow agent for the Pauly Jail Building and Manufacturing Company named S. Pickens. Pickens held the contractor in high regard and provided the cells for Gordon's Val Verde and Nueces jails.[35]

Whoever its third member, Gordon's claim of an alliance against him seems well founded. Irrespective of professional courtesies and personal charm, his uncompromising and competitive approach surely made other enemies. It is therefore impossible to ascertain what share of other attacks on Gordon's professional character may be attributed to this Hull-Martin-Sanguinet cabal. In contrast to their devious methods, it is worth noting that Gordon conducted openly his very determined efforts to persuade the Mississippi legislature to adopt his capitol. Furthermore, research for this volume found no evidence that Gordon ever maligned fellow architect L. M. Weathers's work or character while promoting his own design in the Mississippi contest.

CHAPTER ELEVEN

Comal and Lee

Lean times continued for Texas architects as a group through 1896 and 1897. Repeated, optimistic press reports that the depressed building trades were "turning the corner" indicate the paucity of the times.[1] As architects vied for the available work they surely boasted any credentials they could, and membership in the American Institute of Architects was becoming more esteemed. The issue of the Texas State Association of Architects founders, now AIA fellow members, blackballing other Texans' membership in the national organization became more divisive.

J. Riely Gordon was elected to the position of first vice president of the TSAA for its 1894–95 session. During this period he led a faction of designers intent on circumventing this barrier to their membership in the AIA. In 1895 Gordon appealed directly to the AIA for a state charter designed to admit TSAA members en masse. Opposition from the Texas AIA fellows, led by W. C. Dodson, resulted in denial. (The AIA still had the air of a gentlemen's club and here it appears the fellows united in maintaining their hegemony.) Gordon was elected TSAA president at its September 1896 meeting in Austin, where mediocre attendance foreshadowed the demise of the group. In an attempt to avert a total breakdown of professional organization within Texas, the AIA granted a separate, provisional state charter to Dodson, but the damage was done. As Dodson informed the AIA in 1897, "it was impossible to get men together to organize under it." The TSAA disbanded completely.[2]

On another front, Gordon's career as a courthouse architect brightened a bit in November 1897. Comal County's Commissioners' Court voted to replace the dilapidated courthouse in New Braunfels and authorized County Judge Adolph Giesecke to consult with "reputable architects" on how to proceed. On November 23, the Commissioners' Court met with Gordon and his fellow San Antonio architect Albert F. Beckmann. Meeting minutes reveal that both "advised strongly that the court should not ask for competition plans, but should engage an architect of acknowledged ability, in whom they could place full confidence, and let him prepare plans for the contemplated courthouse." On November 30, A. O. Watson of Austin also appeared, but the details of that meeting went unrecorded.[3]

Comal officials continued their architectural education into December, accepting Gordon's invitation to visit San Antonio and inspect Bexar County's courthouse and the Federal Building. Finally, after consulting several architects, the Commissioners' Court announced that they had concluded that the most proper method for selecting a design was through competition. While disregarding Gordon's initial advice to forgo a contest, the officials resolved "to investigate some specialties copyrighted by Mr. J. R. Gordon and claimed by him to be far superior in the construction of court-houses." They traveled to Gonzales to inspect his Signature Plan design.[4]

Despite its particular interest in Gordon, the Commissioners' Court advertised in the *Galveston Daily News* for plans to be considered at its January 17, 1898, session. Six architects responded to the call for submissions. While each of the entries possessed unique advantages, the field was narrowed to the plans of Alfred Giles and Gordon. Gordon carried the vote of three commissioners to win the contest, but County Judge Giesecke and Commissioner August Schultze, Jr., were quick and vocal in their disapproval. As recorded in the minutes, in session they "protested against the adoption of the plans of Mr. Gordon and against employing him as superintendent," claiming "that there is too much evidence against his integrity and character, and also evidence of some of his buildings being badly built."[5]

Such slander was becoming part of a familiar routine, and its source was surely a competing architect: Schultze admitted he heard it while reviewing the submissions. Fresh charges involved the soundness of Gordon's Alamo Baptist Church and Alamo Fire Insurance Building, both dating to 1890. Schultze apparently did not inspect the church while in San Antonio, and, in light of his other comments, his vague and unsubstantiated claims about its faults can be easily dismissed. He did tour the massive commercial block that Gordon designed for the insurance company, possibly at the architect's request. The commissioner's charge that it had almost fallen in during construction probably stems from foundation difficulties due to its site on an unstable bank of the San Antonio River. Since this property was purchased five months before Gordon was invited to compete for that design, he can hardly be blamed for the decision to build there. To the contrary, he is probably due praise for stabilizing the riverbank through a system of piling that allowed the work to proceed. The issues that Schultze had with Gordon's Signature Plan amply demonstrate that architectural expertise was not a requirement to be a county commissioner. He objected that a great shaft of wasted space ran from the ground floor up through the roof at the center of the courthouse. Furthermore, he complained that the corners of the building were cut away to make room for the doors, which he found senseless and feared weakened the building.[6]

Schultze's three fellow commissioners dismissed his complaints of Gordon's integrity and ability as hearsay and argued that the Signature Plan's perceived faults were actually virtues designed to improve ventilation. They remained resolute in their vote and Gordon entered into a contract to provide plans and specifications for the Comal County Courthouse, as well as superintend its construction, which the entire Commissioners' Court signed.[7]

Before signing, Schultze asked that Gordon be forced to post a bond insuring that no cracks would occur in the building. The majority rightly found this absurd, but compromised by ordering that

> Mr. Gordon shall enter into a bond in the sum of $10,000 . . . that the plans and specifications shall not be taken out of the County Judge's Office by said Architect before the completion and acceptance of the building. That the plans and specifications are perfect in every aspect, that the building is to be a complete Court House and that there will be no other outlays and nothing needed in addition to what is mentioned in the plans. That only first class material and of the best quality will be used in the construction of the building. That the workmanship and construction shall be first class and free from faults and defects.[8]

Although Gordon estimated that the building could be built for $36,200, the construction contract went to the Austin firm of Fischer & Lambie for $36,900. Most of the extra cost can be attributed to the commissioners' desire to use white limestone, quarried within the county, instead of brick. The building was accepted from the contractor on December 6, 1898, and formally dedicated on the following January 22.[9]

Comal again demonstrated versatility within Gordon's Signature Plan (fig. 11.1). After two years pursuing larger courthouse commissions without success, the architect reworked his design, scaling it back to meet a much lower budget. At 78 x 92 feet, this was the architect's smallest courthouse since Aransas. Stripped of the elaboration of Ellis and Wise, this generation of his plan was a succinct and refined statement.[10]

This grace owes much to the choice of local stone, which harmonizes with the bleached outcroppings of the surrounding Hill Country. As with Wise, the color scheme is largely monochromatic, with relatively thin, polished, red granite columns supplying contrast. Smooth and quarry-faced surfaces provide variety and subtle horizontal cohesion that does not interfere with the verticality of Comal's 83-foot tower, which Gordon called the "climax to the picturesquely grouped building it surmounts."[11]

At first glance this square belvedere may appear simple, especially in comparison to his earlier towers, but this is deceptive. Gordon deftly reduced the detail and neatly divided each side with three tall and narrow arches that drive its perceived height. He further enhanced this effect by tapering the tower by two degrees, creating a false sense of perspective. While perhaps a contrivance, it is one that works exceedingly well as narrow windows elsewhere contribute to this perceived loftiness.

COMAL COUNTY COURT HOUSE, NEW BRAUNFELS, TEXAS

11.1.
Comal County Courthouse, New Braunfels, Texas (1898). James Riely Gordon, architect. *Postcard view ca. 1915 by L. A. Hoffmann.*

Gordon's familiar porches fill the reentrants. Proportionally quite-wide Romanesque capitals, unique in his courthouse opus for their flatness, appear distorted by the weight above. Granite steps lead up to the entrances beyond which blue-and-white tiling on interior floors contrasts with terra-cotta paint on the walls. Reduced structural demands afforded by the smaller tower allowed the central shaft to be more open than those of Gordon's previous courthouses. The large and acoustically balanced courtroom is semicircular on the ends with a succession of proscenium-like arches above the bench. A newspaper reported with pride its forty-two electric light fixtures to "dispel the darkness in the event that justice has to be dealt out after daylight."[12]

Comal is curious as an application of Gordon's Signature Plan to a site that was not the town square. German colonists established New Braunfels in 1845 following their own traditions of town planning, which included open central squares or plazas fronted by a town hall or church. In this case, a long, rectangular plaza serves as the central focus of the town plan (fig. 11.2). While Comal County officials initially considered placing their new courthouse directly on the square, it was clear before the competition that the city would not consent to the plan.[13] In light of this, it is surprising that Gordon did not modify his plan along the lines of his similarly situated Hopkins County Courthouse.

A one-story addition on the northeast side was added in later years. While sympathetic in exterior treatment, it disrupted Comal's original massing and closed off two entrance porches. As of this writing, this and other alterations are being removed in an extensive effort to restore the building to Gordon's original vision. The structure has withstood the passing of a century, vindicating the three commissioners who championed Gordon's abilities and design.

While working on Comal, Gordon secured a courthouse project for Lee County, about 100 miles to the northeast. Lee had been carved out of Bastrop, Burleson, Fayette, and Washington Counties in 1874. Four years later the county designated a

square just south of the existing business district in Giddings and built a courthouse. This structure was destroyed by fire in November 1897. On February 18, 1898, the Commissioners' Court voted to advertise for plans and specifications to be received by March 15. The courthouse was to be built of brick and stone at a cost that was not to exceed $35,000. A week later, after some consultation over the matter, the officials decided to visit several counties in the state to determine "the best way of building a courthouse with all modern improvements." It is not known which courthouses they visited, but a stop to inspect the similarly budgeted Comal courthouse seems likely.[14]

The Commissioners' Court met in secret session to examine the submissions. Reasons for this secrecy and the number and identities of the competing architects are not known. On March 17 the court announced that Gordon's plans and specifications had been selected, subject to changes agreed to by the court concerning the size of the building, number of rooms, and so forth. Gordon did not personally superintend the construction, but he was required to post a $5,000 bond and later paid half of the superintending costs with the county picking up the balance. Like so much else about this project, the reason for this unusual superintendence arrangement is uncertain. After initial construction bids were all rejected as being too high, Sonnefield, Emmins & Albright returned with a $32,270 bid that the county accepted on April 22. The Commissioners' Court repeated this tactic for obtaining lower bids on other aspects of the project.[15]

All indications suggest that the design proposed to the Lee County Commissioners' Court was likely the same as the initial brick design for Comal. The exterior pro-

11.3.
Lee County Courthouse,
Giddings, Texas (1898–99).
James Riely Gordon, architect.
Photographer unknown, ca. 1908.

files of the two structures are quite similar, although the footprint of the courthouse in Giddings is about 2 feet shorter in both dimensions. Its tower, however, is about 3 feet taller, allowing room for clockworks. The clock faces, incidentally, were black with gold hands and numerals—a rather unusual color scheme. Like Comal, Lee's tower is tapered for an enhanced sense of height (fig. 11.3).

While the two courthouses are similar, Gordon creates distinctions through the materials used and their application. Lee's exterior presents stark contrasts between red brick with white limestone. This was a popular Victorian motif that drew comparisons to lean bacon. Quarry-faced stone features such as arches, lintels, sill courses, and friezes interrupt smooth expanses of brick. Polished gray granite is employed for the porch columns. It is interesting to note that the capital designs, while all Romanesque, are different on each of the four porches. This treatment appears to be unique for the architect.

Inside, the second-story courtroom has remained largely intact for over a century and echoes what the architect described for Comal. Seating was arranged in a fairly novel manner with jurors placed behind the accused and the counsel, opposite the judge, with their backs to spectators. The philosophy behind this arrangement was to position the judge to observe (and presumably control) the entire courtroom from a single perspective. Furthermore, jurors were less likely to be influenced by spectators if they could not see them. This seating caused debate within the Lee County Commissioners' Court, but Gordon's vision won out.[16] It is uncertain whether it was also employed in Comal, but Gordon returned to it for later courthouses.

H. W. Clusky was installed as superintendent on January 1, 1899. It is unclear who was responsible for hiring Clusky, but Gordon paid half of his $125-per-month salary. In June an inspector representing Gordon reported some defects including a crack in an exterior wall and problems with a gravel roof, but otherwise the structure was in accordance with the plans and specifications. Members of the Commissioners' Court inspected the work for themselves and elected to accept the building with the understanding that the contractor would correct the defects before final payment was made.[17]

Structural problems manifested themselves not long after completion of the building. Wood trusses above the courtroom proved inadequate, and iron columns were installed in the courtroom to brace the ceiling in 1901. In 1905 the slate roof was replaced with galvanized shingles to lighten the load on the structure. Second-story columns on the northwest porch needed repair in 1910. The following year the court authorized the expenditure of $5,808 to replace the foundation and for remodeling work. Steel reinforcements were added to inside walls in the 1930s. A twenty-first-century restoration ran $4.5 million, largely to correct structural shortcomings from this patchwork.[18]

Such flaws are not characteristic of Gordon work. Many of his surviving courthouses have recently gone through extensive restorations, but this is reasonable after a century of uneven maintenance, and much of the work involved removing alterations and returning the structures to their original appearance. Lee's problems manifested themselves within a few years, and Gordon seems possibly more culpable here than at Hopkins, for instance, where existing information is ambiguous regarding any possible fault. While not personally superintending the construction, he is responsible through his representatives who vouched for the work (although Clusky's role remains a bit mysterious). As has been seen, it was not unusual for an architect to specify cheaper materials to fit the competition budget and then persuade officials to "upgrade" to more durable ones. This may have been Gordon's initial intention, but the Lee County Commissioners' Court could have been too thrift-minded to consider it. Still, one would expect even cheaper materials to last a reasonable span for the times, say twenty years. Why Lee is an anomaly is unknown.

Comal and Lee are the last of Gordon's courthouses in the Richardsonian Romanesque style. As discussed previously, it was a style particularly responsive to the needs of late nineteenth-century American architecture. It was also one that Gordon could apply with variety to his Signature Plan and forge into some of his most masterful works. These are among the finest and most original examples of the fashion that aspired to be the "American Style" of architecture.

CHAPTER TWELVE

The Arizona Territorial Capitol

An 1898 act of Congress authorized the Arizona Territory to build a permanent capitol. For Arizona's leading citizens, this was another step on a long but deliberate procession toward statehood. For James Riely Gordon, it developed into another opportunity to author a state house or, more precisely, a building destined to become one. It was also a chance to refute the Mississippi governor's false charge that he tried to pass off a courthouse design for that state's capitol. It seems the rarity of capitol work and a great desire to clear his name enticed the San Antonian to enter a competition far from home and with a relatively meager budget.

After vacillating between the cities of Prescott and Tucson for a number of years, Arizona's territorial government moved into the second floor of the Phoenix City Hall in February 1889. Shortly afterward it appointed a capitol commission to bring a permanent home to fruition. Members of this commission as well as the government changed over the following years, but the methodical quest for statehood remained constant, and it was believed building a permanent territorial capitol that could also accommodate a state government would grease the necessary federal approval process. Lack of authorization limited their actions, but it seems they did as much preliminary work as possible to ensure approval before actually appealing to Washington.

Among the commission's first tasks was soliciting a donation of land for a capitol site. In July 1889, they selected an area west of the town site (as originally plotted in 1870) with a promise by developers to extend Washington Street and a streetcar rail line to the future capitol. Over the next eight years the commission enhanced the site with irrigation, walkways, and an ambitious landscaping program. Ten acres of desert were transformed into a lush oasis. The *Arizona Republican* remarked, "It appears as though every part of the world has been ransacked to furnish the plants and trees that are the main ornament to the grounds."[1]

When the site was ready and the territorial government had sufficient financial and political backing, a bill to build a capitol was taken to the US Congress. On February 8, 1898, a telegram from Washington announced that it had passed, authorizing the issue of $100,000 in bonds for construction. Included in the legislation were strict guidelines for the conduct of the design competition and the letting of contracts. One of the stipulations barred the winning architect from superintending the work.[2]

The capitol commission published its call for plans and specifications, accompanied by cost estimates not to exceed $90,000, on May 20. The award for the winning design was $500. Submissions were due by July 20, 1898, and the entrants' identities were kept secret from the commission and public by pseudonyms. Eleven architects and firms entered, but it appears that the contest was cancelled after allegations of corruption circulated in the press. It is also possible that the measly prize failed to attract suitable entries. Due to the secrecy imposed, it is not known if Gordon entered this initial competition.[3]

Officials announced a second contest on August 20, 1898, with submissions due November 1. Interested parties could request a detailed prospectus from the commission. This included a site plan and the stipulation that the designs allow for possible future additions without detracting from the capitol's immediate completeness or appearance. No particular style was imposed, but the commissioners expressed their desire "that the designs include a suitable dome for the building, the upper part thereof to be erected in the future, and to be excluded from estimates of the present cost." The winning architect was expected to provide sets of drawings and specifications and scale details in return for 2½ percent of the construction cost. The commission reserved the right to also use part or parts of the second-best design as well. This time the names of the sixteen competitors were made public. The participants represented a geographic range from New York to California, and Gordon was among them.[4]

After considering the submissions for over two weeks, the commission settled on Gordon's plans. While some of the final details had yet to be decided, descriptions of the design appeared in numerous periodicals, including the *Arizona Republican*, which reported:

> According to these plans, Arizona's capitol building will be massive and dignified. The design is of the renaissance. Though the building will be symmetrical and complete within itself, the plans look to extensions with increasing needs. The building will be 184 feet long and 84 feet deep. It will be entered from four sides, but the main entrance will be on the eastern or Washington street side, up an ascent of granite steps through a massive colonnade into a large vestibule.

The account continued to describe a central rotunda, open from the second floor to the dome, and assembly and council chambers.[5]

Gordon believed that such a structure would meet Arizona's needs for twenty years. If the design was later expanded according to his plans, he predicted that the capitol "would compare with the best in the United States and the total cost of the first structure and the additions to ultimately be about $750,000."[6]

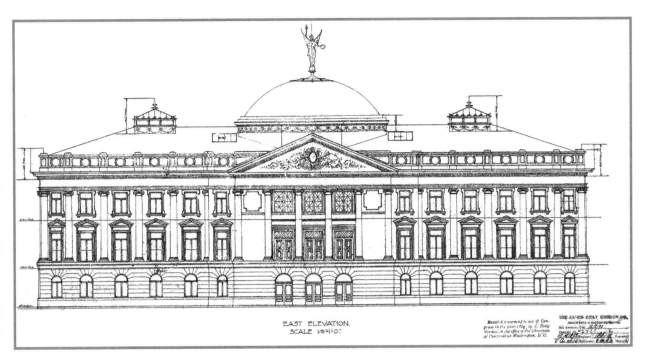

EAST ELEVATION.
SCALE 1/8"=1'0".

12.1.

1898 revised plan for Arizona Territorial Capitol. *East elevation view by the J. Riely Gordon Company, courtesy Lucy Virginia Gordon Ralston.*

With the selection of a design, the nine-year-old capitol project suddenly quickened its pace. Gordon revised his plans in accordance with the commission's wishes, and they were ready to solicit bids in December. Gordon kept a set of these revised drawings, dated December 8, 1898, which vary slightly from descriptions published right after his design was selected (fig. 12.1). For instance, the granite flight to the colonnade was deleted, making the main entrance through the first-story arcade of the central portico. This was surely a cost-reducing measure that Gordon agreed to since the steps could be added later. He did open the rotunda down to the first-floor level to complement this change, however. Additional changes were made, such as substituting the less expensive Ionic order for the Composite Corinthian as originally described.[7]

On January 12, 1899, the commission awarded the construction work to Tom Lovell, the Denton, Texas, contractor who built Gordon's Brazoria County Courthouse. The revised specifications allowed bidders latitude to suggest building materials, but local stone was preferred. Lovell provided estimates on a variety of materials and the commission chose a combination amounting to $88,383. Superintendence went to an unsuccessful bidder on the construction, Phoenix contractor Joseph Fifield.[8]

Gordon was quoted in an article appearing the day after the contract was awarded as saying,

I think that Arizona will have one of the best public buildings that has ever been built for the amount appropriated. The building will be so built that the additions may be built without destroying the first work done. When the territory becomes a state and the wings are added to the building it will be a state house which the people will have reason to be proud of. Mr. Lovell, the successful bidder, will be found at work from morning until night with his coat off and assisting his men. He is a competent man, and I have every reason to believe that his work will be highly satisfactory.[9]

With the project in good hands, Gordon returned to San Antonio shortly after this interview. It was anticipated that the architect would return to Phoenix as his services as a consultant were needed, but there is no indication that any such trips were made.[10]

Groundbreaking took place on February 16, 1899, without fanfare. While capitol backers hoped to use the building as leverage toward statehood, a portion of the citizenry felt it was too extravagant for the territorial government. Others resented having such an investment being made in Phoenix. As a result, commission members found themselves under much scrutiny and wary of the appearance of wastefulness. Therefore, they avoided any unnecessary items or pomp, including a cornerstone, and kept expenditures to a minimum.[11]

Tom Lovell followed Gordon's revised plans quite closely (fig. 12.2).[12] The foundation is built of malapai rock taken from the nearby Camelback Mountains. It extends 4 feet below the first floor, resting on an 8-foot-deep base of cement and broken stone. Gordon designed inverted arches beneath the octagonal rotunda to disperse the concentrated downward thrust of the piers.

Above this is the first floor, which is treated on the exterior like a Renaissance basement with rough-cut granite quarried some ten miles to the southwest along the Salt River. Arches above all doorways and windows on this level (except the west entrance) convey mass and strength. Facing the original town site, the main east entrance is announced by a central pavilion where three heavily treated arches on the first floor lend visual support to six Ionic columns above. The arches correspond with the three bays of an *in antis* portico providing a second-floor balcony. Unornamented panels accent the antae (flanking walls) at the third-floor level; there is no indication that any decorations or inscriptions were planned for these. A pediment decorated with scrolling garlands caps the pavilion. To the north and south are wings divided into six bays by Ionic pilasters. These wings are five bays deep with pediments above the north and south entrances. The west entrance is centered in an unusual concave pavilion originally intended to receive the curved end of the permanent assembly hall when a rear wing was added.[13] The second and third floors are faced with tuff, or tufa, a type of granite quarried near Kirkland about 100 miles north of Phoenix. Lovell received permission from the capitol commission to treat the tuff on the walls as quarry faced, implying that Gordon specified smooth dressing. While the quarry-facing serves the executed building well as it stands, smooth dressing would have lent itself better to the enlarged building Gordon anticipated. The windows on the second floor are

12.2.
Arizona Territorial Capitol,
Phoenix, Arizona (1899–1900).
James Riely Gordon, architect.
Postcard view ca. 1908.

pedimented; lintels top those on the third. A smooth frieze, leading to a cornice and pediments of galvanized steel, marks the diminutive fourth-floor attic.

At the center of the roof is a shallow dome resting on a short drum. It is 44 feet wide and topped by a 16-foot statue of *Winged Liberty* holding a torch and laurel wreath that rotates with the wind. There were hopes during construction to cover the dome with native Arizona copper, but they were not fulfilled at the time and a steel alloy was used. The roof was asbestos-lined tin plating with decorative galvanized roofs sheltering skylights illuminating the legislative chambers and, by a system of shafts, the basement below. The capitol is 76 feet from the ground level to the top of the dome. According to the plans, its base measures 183 x 87 feet (varying slightly from the competition entry).

Upon passing through the arches and doors at the east entrance, visitors encounter a vestibule opening to the rotunda, a 42-foot-wide octagon. Its ceiling is broken by a 20-foot diameter light shaft that affords a view to the inner dome, whose center is some 65 feet above the floor (fig. 12.3). Walls flanking the entrance contain office doorways; the north and south sides of the rotunda are arched and give way to the corridor of offices on the building's main axis. The northwest and southwest sides of the rotunda octagon housed iron stairways designed to accommodate elevators at their centers. Only one elevator had been installed by the time the building was complete, however. The rotunda's west side led to an alcove for another exterior doorway.

The second level was designated as the executive floor as it contained the governor's office. Three sets of double doors lead to the balcony above the entrance. A marble plaque near these doors was likely located with the thought that exterior steps would be added one day to make this the main entrance. It records the information usually found on a cornerstone, with the architect's name misspelled as "J. Reilly Gordon." An 11-foot-wide corridor surrounds the rotunda light shaft, which is encircled by an oak balustrade.

12.3.
Arizona Territorial Capitol,
third floor of rotunda. *2000
photograph.*

The third level, deemed the legislative floor, contained the assembly and council
chambers. These chambers, placed at the ends of the north and south wings (fig. 12.4),
each measure 40 x 42 feet. Three sides of these halls are lined with committee rooms
topped by spectator galleries offering seating for 350. In addition to the skylights, oculi
above the galleries provide natural light. These halls became the Senate and House of
Representatives chambers with statehood. The *in antis* portico of the central pavilion
was enclosed on this level for a supreme courtroom and chambers. Gordon likely envi-

12.4.
Arizona Territorial Capitol,
legislative chamber. *2000
photograph.*

sioned opening up this area when more appropriate judicial accommodations were
built with the capitol expansion. As it stood, however, these rooms proved hopelessly
small and the supreme court operated out of rented facilities elsewhere instead.

Fire-resistance methods that Gordon routinely used in courthouses are present
in the capitol, including the expanded metal flooring system. Lovell replaced the few
wood joists Gordon specified with iron to further increase resistance to fire. Dual gas
and electric light fixtures were used throughout the structure, reflecting the even balance of the utility service at the time of construction. Arizona products predominated;
exceptions included the stairways and steel beams from Los Angeles, California, the
Otis elevator from Chicago, Illinois, and the woodwork, which is white oak from the
vicinity of Waco, Texas.

Officials received the building from the contractor on August 4, 1900, although
some finishing work remained. Lovell was paid $117,290 for his work, which included
commission-approved changes. Gordon received $2,250 for his plans, however, so
his compensation reflects only Lovell's initial bid.[14] This, along with the misspelling of
the architect's name on the aforementioned plaque, is evidence that Gordon probably
never returned to Phoenix after the contract was let.

As noted, the Arizona capitol commission sought a design that could be expanded
upon in the future. This Gordon delivered, but he had very specific notions on how to

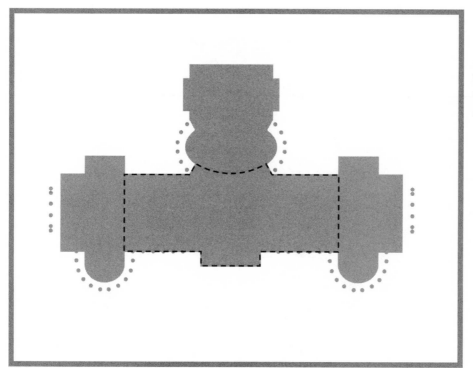

12.5.
Footprint of Arizona Territorial Capitol superimposed on modified (widened by four bays) footprint of Gordon's 1896 Mississippi Capitol entry. *Illustration based on original plans.*

expand, which, if implemented, would have realized his design for the Mississippi State Capitol. Reports of Gordon's initial Arizona design indicate that he also presented his Mississippian expansion plans to the capitol commission during his sales pitch. While the Arizona Territorial Capitol was a complete building, the architect clearly conceived it as the central unit of a structure virtually identical to one he lobbied for in Jackson two and a half years earlier (figs. 10.3 and 12.5). Indeed, Gordon often claimed later that, after the Mississippi governor vetoed his design, he sold it to the Arizona capitol commission. To be precise, the commission only asked for and bought the central portion, but Gordon's proposed expansion surely was also considered during the selection process.[15]

Arizona's territorial capitol was dedicated on February 26, 1901. As reported in the *San Francisco Chronicle*, visitors from all over the Southwest gathered to witness ceremonies that included a large parade and much speech making. The California newspaper noted that the capitol was an imposing structure and the greenness of the surrounding landscape program provided a midwinter delight for northern guests (fig. 12.6).[16]

A visitor from the Magnolia State was also on hand. As he watched the dedication ceremonies he recalled the "acrid discussion and criticisms" of five years before, when Mississippi's governor rejected the same plan as being for a courthouse. Writing for a Jackson newspaper, the reporter relayed his impressions while standing "within the shadows of the stately pile," and concludes with a sarcastic jibe at his former governor:

> I noted its graceful perspective, its height, breadth, width, the magnitude of its general design; I wandered through its marble halls, noted its elegant appointments and wondered, if the plan had been originally drawn for a court house, what

county was so burdened with public officials as to require such numerous and
ample accommodations or so rich as to propose the erection of a building that
covers so much space at the expense of the sweating taxpayers.[17]

Even here, of course, this correspondent was looking at only a fraction of what
Gordon had ultimately envisioned for both Mississippi and Arizona. Changes made in
the late 1898 revision process precluded an *exact* realization of the Mississippi proposal,
however. In addition to some of the changes already discussed, the *in antis* portico
of the central pavilion was pared from four bays to three. Still, the building could be
enlarged in a manner not unlike the growth of the US Capitol over the years, albeit on
a smaller scale, as statehood increased the demands on the Arizona Capitol.

In Washington, on the morning of February 14, 1912, President Taft signed the
proclamation admitting Arizona to the Union as the forty-eighth state. Like the
capitol dedication eleven years earlier, Admission Day was celebrated with a parade
and speech making. At noon George W. P. Hunt entered the capitol to take the oath
of office as the state's first governor. That evening, an inaugural ball was held in the
streets of Phoenix, and all Arizonans were invited to attend. The Admission Day Committee had previously invited "the world to drink a toast on the admission of Arizona,
and the completion of the chain of states from the Atlantic to the Pacific, at 8 o'clock,
Wednesday, February 14th."[18] The Arizona Territorial Capitol that Gordon designed
was now a state house.

The building stood with no substantive changes for six years. It is not known if
state officials remembered Gordon's expansion plans, but the $125,000 appropriation

was too small for serious consideration of it. Instead, plans were made for a sympathetic addition to the west of (behind) the existing building. The design called for a second structure, nearly identical in appearance to Gordon's on the exterior (but without the dome and entrance pavilion), to be built parallel to the original with a 70 x 70 foot connection in between, where Gordon envisioned the permanent assembly hall. The finished building, which would take the shape of an H, was not completed until 1938.[19] Although radically different from Gordon's expanded plan, this solution complements his work and appears almost as natural as if he had designed it himself.

In the late 1950s, plans to replace the structure with a high-rise tower design met opposition, most notably from Frank Lloyd Wright. A seasonal resident of nearby Scottsdale, the architect severely criticized the proposed building and the contract with its designers. Of course, he had a proposal of his own. His plan would move most of the state government to an imaginative, canopied structure off-site and preserve Gordon's capitol for "minor offices."[20] Although never adopted, Wright's proposal engendered enough controversy to forestall legislation to fully fund the high-rise. Only part of the plan was realized; in 1957 two buildings housing new House and Senate facilities were built just to the east of Gordon's capitol. Had the proposed tower been built in between, its rear would be only 16 feet from the entrance to Gordon's capitol.[21] Had the old building been relegated to such an inconsequential and awkward position, its future would have been doubtful.

As executed, the legislative structures produced a plaza in front of the old capitol that opens toward the downtown business district. In 1974, after years of debate, officials built their tower as a new west wing, beyond the 1938 addition. The old capitol is now preserved as a museum and the 1918 and 1938 additions became the home of the state archives and library. Gordon's original plans, provided by his granddaughter, were invaluable in the restoration of the building to its 1912 appearance in recognition of Arizona's first year of statehood. The aspiration of roofing the structure and dome with native copper was finally realized during this work as well.[22]

Gordon's Arizona Territorial Capitol is now the centerpiece of the state's capitol complex. It stands, safely preserved and restored, as a valued architectural survivor of Arizona's territorial period. Small and austere in comparison to state capitols built around the same time, it reflects the circumstances and ingenuity surrounding its design. Built to be complete in its own right, additions over the years have not robbed it of its unique, original character.

The competition for this commission drew designers from across the country. Far from home and apparently unaided by any local associations, Gordon prevailed in this contest. Although the architect's overall plan was never implemented, he was eventually able to claim a state capitol as part of his oeuvre.

CHAPTER THIRTEEN

Harrison, Callahan, and Mississippi Redux

After fire destroyed the ten-year-old Harrison County Courthouse in Marshall on June 7, 1899, county officials rushed to replace it. The stated goal was to have the new structure roofed before winter, but they may have been anxious to commit the county to rebuilding in Marshall before any campaigns to change the county seat were initiated. Within a month of the fire, the Commissioners' Court had contracted with Gordon and Cornelius Grandbery Lancaster to design the new courthouse. Apparently they considered no other architects.

Lancaster was a Marshall native who had studied architecture at the Agricultural and Mechanical College of Texas (now Texas A&M University) and achieved some renown as the designer of a locally prominent hotel. It is likely that county officials approached him and he in turn suggested they call upon Gordon as an expert on the building type. (The relationship between the two architects is discussed further below.) After visiting a number of Gordon's works, the officials were sufficiently impressed to order the preparation of plans and specifications. The courthouse was to have three stories plus a basement and modern fireproofing and cost between $60,000 and $75,000. The Commissioners' Court awarded the construction contract to Sonnefield & Emmins on August 29, 1899.[1]

Construction proceeded at a fast pace even while the court considered and approved changes to the plans and building materials. To avoid interruption of the work, officials deferred arbitration for disputed changes until after the courthouse was completed. Lancaster, who superintended the work, and the contractor settled their disputes swiftly, however. For instance, the superintendent ordered all work stopped when an argument erupted over foundation measurements. While Lancaster considered his own authority final, both parties consulted Gordon in San Antonio by telephone and quickly reached an agreement. The Harrison County Courthouse was accepted on May 13, 1901, although some work remained to be done.[2]

This is the first Gordon courthouse in the Beaux-Arts classical style (fig. 13.1). Beaux-Arts classicism had steadily gained popularity since the World's Columbian Exposition captivated the nation with its fabulous Court of Honor. The style was also

13.1.
Harrison County Courthouse, Marshall, Texas (1899–1901).
James Riely Gordon with Cornelius G. Lancaster, architects.
Postcard view ca. 1906 by the Rotograph Company.

in sympathy with the City Beautiful Movement, another trend popularized by the fair. This movement sought to apply a comprehensive concept, integrating street plan, zoning, architecture, and landscaping, to the urban environment. The Beaux-Arts style became identified with these current notions of comprehensive city planning and so-called progressive government.

Aspects of the Richardsonian Romanesque style that made it well suited for regional building became less advantageous once a maturing rail network could deliver relatively cheap, mass-produced architectural elements. Masterful architects, observing classical rules of order, could combine these elements into exceptional Beaux-Arts compositions. Unversed clients, however, often accepted marginal work by designers of limited ability and training as long as expected features like columns, pediments, and such were somehow present. A résumé that included formal education and AIA membership helped architects distinguish themselves from such competition. The AIA increasingly valued education as a requisite for membership as well. Paris's Ecole des Beaux-Arts was the elite school of choice.

Gordon's motivation for utilizing Beaux-Arts styling at Marshall is uncertain, but he may have been personally ready for a new style or feeling professional pressure to embrace the trend. Harrison's accelerated schedule also may have influenced the choice. Working in a common classical vocabulary surely smoothed communication between Gordon and Lancaster, just as it facilitated work for the White City. While Beaux-Arts styling is often considered antithetical to the Richardsonian movement, Richardson learned his art at the Ecole, where theories on planning strongly influenced his future work. As seen, Gordon also cared much about this aspect of design and in this sense Richardson's spirit continued in the Texan's work in other styles.[3] At any rate, his proposal for a courthouse designed in a modern style associated with progressive government likely appealed to the Harrison County Commissioners' Court.

In this project the architect was quick to exploit the illusory use of materials that was acceptable within the Beaux-Arts style. The Richardsonian Romanesque was founded in the Ruskinian notion of true representation of building materials. Gordon's Romanesque towers, therefore, all but *had* to be masonry. Beaux-Arts offered more latitude and Gordon could cap Harrison with a relatively light metal dome painted to appear as stone. Similarly, he was free to simulate stone as closely as possible with locally made, buff-colored brick. The mortar is flush with the exposed face of the brick to produce relatively smooth surface planes akin to cut stone. This is then embellished by fabrications such as rusticated quoining at the corners, also of brick. Actual stone is used for the foundation, entrance arcades, and accents with polished granite columns.

From the outside, it may appear that Gordon simply draped Beaux-Arts features over his Signature Plan for Harrison. Inside, however, the style allowed Gordon's introduction of a major change to his central core. Relieved from the structural necessity of a forest of piers, Harrison has an open rotunda with a grand flight of steps leading to the second-story district courtroom doors (fig. 13.2). The staircase is made of cast iron with imposing art nouveau newel posts and marble treads. Brackets cantilever from the walls to support the second and third floors of the rotunda, leaving their circular balustrades unobstructed. Acanthus leaves and electric lights decorate these brackets. Ancillary stairways at the corner of the rotunda lead to the third floor and courtroom balcony. Art glass lights pierce the lowest level of the coffers that ring the inner dome. Together, these changes invest fresh drama into Gordon's interior composition. Other interior features, including the acoustically tuned, ovular district courtroom, remain relatively unchanged from his previous work.

Still, Gordon seems to have struggled to reconcile his Signature Plan with classical disciplines. This can be seen in the porticos that extend from three of the wings. Since Attic Greece, porticos comprised of columns supporting pediments have traditionally marked entrances of classic edifices, as seen in Gordon's design for the Arizona Capitol. For Harrison, however, Gordon placed porticos at the ends of the wings while entry remains through his familiar arcaded porches in the reentrant angles. Although the three-bay porticos are nicely set from their five-bay wings and provide fine balconies, this break with tradition is difficult to reconcile given the precepts of classical

13.2.
Harrison County Courthouse, view of rotunda.
2009 photograph.

order. The architect also treated the first-floor brickwork with horizontal banding in simulation of a Renaissance sub-story, but set it atop a pronounced foundation of rusticated granite producing a redundant effect.

Unless Gordon was striving for a Mannerist effect, which seems doubtful, these awkward deviations are at odds with Harrison's more successful classical features. Single-bay balconies accent these porticos at the third-story level. Scrolled pediments top the balcony doors and all second-story windows. Pilasters continue the rhythm of the polished granite portico columns. Paired columns compensate for the reduced scale of the arcade of the balconies above the northeast and northwest entrances. Balustrades encompass the roofline and grace the third-floor balconies above the entrances. Metal eagles provide climax to the gabled ends.

The brickwork continues above the roofline to form the octagonal drum for the dome. Polished granite columns follow the periphery of the octagon to support a metal cornice where more eagles decorate the points of the octagon and clock faces align with the courthouse wings. A statue of *Winged Justice* holding her scale aloft stands above a cupola topping the smooth-surfaced dome.

Following the courthouse's completion, Lancaster became Harrison County's de facto architect for alterations and repairs to the courthouse. His role in its construction certainly qualified him and he performed admirably over the years. In response to the need for more space, Lancaster devised a sympathetic plan for enlarging the structure in 1925, which involved detaching the east portico end and pulling it away from the structure. Gaps created by this were filled with two bays, adding approximately 22 feet to the wing. This process was repeated on the west wing in 1927.[4]

Gordon's association with Lancaster was part of a professional network the San Antonian established under the umbrella of the J. Riely Gordon Company. He initiated the company shortly after his partnership with D. Ernest Laub dissolved in 1892, but he did not typically utilize the business name until the end of the decade.[5] Perhaps disappointed in his past partnerships, this arrangement enabled Gordon to maintain and broaden the geographic range of his practice. By allying himself with competent professionals possessing the benefits of local familiarity, he avoided overextending his resources and imbroglios like the one that led to his dismissal as superintendent at Victoria. As demonstrated by the Gordon-Lancaster collaboration for the Harrison courthouse, Gordon provided the designs and participated in securing the commission while the local associate superintended the work. Gordon remained the architect of record and his authoritative role is evidenced by the dispute between Lancaster and the contractor, where both turned to him to support their positions.

Lancaster proudly advertised his association with Gordon as early as 1896. Other such associations in the late 1890s include Burt McDonald in Austin, Harry A. Overbeck in Dallas, George B. Worcester in Denison, Sam Herbert in Waco, and A. J. Armstrong in Shreveport, Louisiana. Perhaps these were the six satellite offices that Gordon referred to in the 1894 interview quoted in Chapter 9. His association with Overbeck was particularly successful. Born in Cincinnati, Ohio, on July 19, 1861, Overbeck credited his early training to his father, who was a builder and lumberman and for whom he worked for several years. After an education in the public schools he took a college course at Dayton followed by special studies in Cincinnati. He practiced architecture on his own for eight years before moving to Dallas in 1895. Overbeck is listed as the manager for Gordon's Dallas office in the *Dallas City Directory for 1896*. Later the pair advertised themselves with variants of Gordon and Overbeck, Associated Architects when doing business together.[6]

By 1890 Dallas was a formidable commercial center, with a population of 40,720, augmented by a sizable suburban population. The effects of the Panic of 1893 were felt here, but Dallasites recovered in the latter half of the decade.[7] During that time, Gordon and Overbeck managed to secure major projects in the city, including St. Paul's Sanitarium and the Linz Building (1896 and 1898 respectively, both destroyed).

In the fall of 1899 Gordon relocated with his wife and daughter to Dallas. A newspaper account explained the move:

The many friends of Mr. J. Riely Gordon are exceedingly sorry to hear that for business reasons he has moved his headquarters from San Antonio to Dallas. Mr. Gordon has lived in San Antonio for the past 26 years and through energy, industry, perseverance and ability he is now considered the foremost architect in the State. Mr. Gordon has designed more public buildings than any other architect in Texas and is now devoting his talent almost exclusively to the erection of public buildings and Dallas being more centrally located, he was compelled for business reasons to move his headquarters to that place.[8]

The family initially resided in the Oriental Hotel and then moved to a house at 107 Cadiz. Gordon's parents had retired to Washington, DC, at this time. With the move to Dallas Gordon began doing business as "The J. Riely Gordon Company (Incorporated)," officing at 259 Main Street. Although occupying the same office, Overbeck continued to be identified as an associate architect separate from the corporation.[9]

The first courthouse to be built under the appellation of the J. Riely Gordon Company turned out to be a rather humble affair for Callahan County. Callahan had experienced limited growth since its creation in 1858, partially because a Comanche presence discouraged settlement in its early years. County administration was consigned to adjoining counties until 1877. Voters moved the government to rail-served Baird in 1883, where a permanent, stone courthouse was built shortly afterwards. On February 15, 1900, the Callahan County Commissioners' Court voted to solicit plans and specifications for a new courthouse utilizing material from the old and not to exceed $18,500 in cost.[10]

At its March session the Commissioners' Court rejected all the submissions that had been presented. It then ordered that the J. Riely Gordon Company be employed "to prepare suitable drawings and specifications for a new court house . . . approximately 65 x 75 feet, two stories high and to utilize as much of the materials etc. now contained in the old court house as suitable." A month later the court contracted with Sonnefield & Emmins to build the structure for $27,069. Gordon's company was paid 2½ percent for the plans while 2½ percent went to J. E. Flanders for superintendence.[11]

Callahan's courthouse was accepted on December 11, 1900. Information on this courthouse is sparse, but photographs show it to have been the last iteration of Gordon's Signature Plan with entrance porches in the reentrant angles of a modified Greek cross (fig. 13.3). A low dome marking the crossing is reminiscent of the Arizona Capitol and likely capped an open rotunda with a stairway similar to the Harrison courthouse. An ovular courtroom occupied the north side of the second story. This may have featured a low balcony similar to one in Gordon's later courthouse for Madison County, New York (discussed in Chapter 17). The rough-cut stone on the exterior and paired, low-arched windows appear to have been extracted directly from the previ-

13.3.
Callahan County Courthouse,
Baird, Texas (1900, destroyed). J.
Riely Gordon Company, architect.
*Undated postcard view, courtesy Lucy
Virginia Gordon Ralston.*

ous courthouse. Modest and appropriately scaled to the town around it (fig. 13.4), the county judge described the courthouse as being "well and handsomely planned and very conveniently arranged." He went on to say that Gordon, in representing his firm, "won the respect and confidence of the Com[missioners'] Court by his honest, fair and open dealings with the Court." Gordon's courthouse served Callahan County until 1929, when it was razed to make way for a four-story, $150,000 structure.[12]

The Callahan County judge's kind assessment of Gordon's character was in response to events in Mississippi, where a new capitol effort was under way. As chronicled in Chapter 10, the legislature's 1896 bill to build a state house according to Gordon's design was vetoed by then Governor McLaurin, who favored a plan by L. M. Weathers. Legislators revisited the subject in early 1900, and both houses of the state legislature passed "an Act to create a State House Commission, to secure drawings,

13.4.
Baird, Texas, with courthouse
in distance. *Date and photographer
unknown.*

plans and specifications for, and to authorize and provide for the building and erection of a state house," which was signed into law by Governor Andrew Houston Longino on February 21. This act provided for a commission composed of the governor, state attorney general, a member selected by the governor, a member selected by the Senate, and a member selected by the House of Representatives. Commission members, who could not be legislators, were charged under the law to secure a suitable set of plans through open competition or another method they deemed better.[13]

On March 1, before the commission was empanelled, Representative Smith brought the following motion before the House:

> Whereas, The consideration of the Gordon and Weathers plans for the building of the new Capitol has heretofore seriously embarrassed the people of the State in their effort to build same, and has resulted in the loss of a considerable amount of money to the State; therefore be it
>
> *Resolved*, by the House of Representatives, That the person nominated for Capitol Commissioner by this body is hereby instructed to disregard and not to consider either the Weathers or Gordon plan in acting on the Capitol Commission, or any plan with which either of them are connected as architects.

Some House members immediately sought to table the resolution, but Smith prevailed and it was adopted. He may have been trying to clear the field for a favored architect, because he then blocked a motion by dissenters to also disqualify all designers who had recently lobbied the legislature. All other attempts to moderate Smith's resolution similarly failed.[14]

The controversy did not stop there. A writer to the *Jackson Clarion-Ledger* questioned the legality of imposing a restriction not stipulated in the original act and only binding the representatives' commissioner. How could the commission hold an *open* competition if some architects were barred from consideration? If the House could so bind its commissioner, could not the governor and Senate preempt their commissioners' consideration of some other architects? (A Senate resolution barring its commissioner from voting for a Gordon or Weathers submission was in fact proposed, but defeated.)[15]

While debate over the House resolution continued in Mississippi, Gordon's competitors elsewhere were quick to exploit this turn of events. Within days, copies of the resolution were circulating in Texas and finding their way into the hands of potential clients. Gordon first learned of the resolution when confronted with a clipping of it while competing for a courthouse. Fortunately, he had already won the confidence of the officials for that county (most surely Callahan), and this attempt to embarrass him by some fellow architect failed. It was nonetheless clear that Gordon could no longer leave the 1896 competition in the past. The stigma of McLaurin's veto was persistent and far-reaching.

Gordon returned to the Mississippi capital to confront the problem, telling a *Jackson Daily News* reporter, "the resolution the House passed shutting out Mr. Weathers and myself from bidding on the new capitol" was "a great injustice." (To be precise, the two architects were not barred from competing: the commission member appointed by the House was barred from voting for either of their entries.) While he had not decided if he would enter the contest, he suggested that he could "get vindication" by submitting a plan and having it adopted by the rest of the commission. He pointed out that he was not among the bevy of designers that had lately been lobbying for the work. Indeed, this was his first visit in three years.[16]

Taking an opportunity to rebuff his detractors, he crowed to the *Clarion-Ledger,*

I am now building a capitol at Phoenix, Arizona, under the plans submitted in Mississippi in 1897, which was adopted over eighteen [*sic*] competitors from New York, Chicago, San Francisco, and elsewhere, and consequently could not present the same plan in the [current] Mississippi contest.[17]

Gordon used his March 19 rounds of the press to defend his honor in Jackson, but perhaps he was also polling officials for his chances in a new competition. The State House Commission announced it would hold an open competition, suggesting that Gordon and Weathers were welcome—the House resolution notwithstanding. Gordon said he was still unsure whether he would participate when he left Jackson with the morning train on March 22.[18]

Entrants could present and explain their plans to the commission between April 6 and 20, when the selection would be made. Some twenty architects informed the governor of their intention to participate, and they began trickling into Jackson on April 5. Commission members grew frustrated by the slow pace of arrivals and suspected competitors were deliberately delaying their coming in the belief the last presenter might be better remembered and therefore have an advantage. Some of the architects who were in town asked to delay their presentations, claiming heavy rain delayed the trains carrying their plans. While deadly rains had in fact washed out many railroad tracks, the architects may have figured out their absent competitors' strategy and adopted it also.[19]

Weathers arrived on April 17 on the evening train. Incensed over the House resolution, he stated that it was a mistake to suppose that he would not enter or have another architect submit his plans. He vowed to "go before the commission personally and represent his plans in the same manner as the other architects who have appeared heretofore." His plans were reportedly given a careful examination during his presentation the next afternoon.[20]

Gordon arrived on April 20 with a fresh set of plans and specifications for, in the words of one Mississippian, "a magnificent new design." It is tempting to believe he planned this as a dramatic, last-minute entrance worthy of the stage. Any intended theatrics were lessened by the commission's decision to extend the deadline. Gordon likely did not know of this move, made two days earlier because a mere eight architects had entered by that point.[21] (Gordon's 1900 plans appear lost today.)

By April 25 a total of fourteen architects and firms were in contention, and the State House Commission closed the competition. The commissioners then set to reviewing the entries in a process of elimination and nearly all the architects planned to stay in Jackson, anxiously awaiting the outcome. Two days later the commissioners decided to adjourn until May 14, ostensibly to attend to other business while educating themselves on the subject of architecture in order to better evaluate the plans. They also hoped to bring in William Ware, the renowned architect then teaching at Columbia University, as a consultant. Disappointed by the delay, none of the competitors lingered in Jackson to see the commission reconvene.[22]

It appears the commissioners were not entirely candid in their excuses for the delay. During the adjournment they conducted a secret investigation into Gordon's background and presumably those of other entrants. A number of letters were sent to individuals and offices that might have knowledge of Gordon. They were likely identical, and one dated May 5, 1900, reads:

Dear Sir:

I am a member of the Capitol Commission for this State, charged with the duty of having erected a capitol building to cost one million dollars. I write to ask you to inform me by letter to be used confidentially, what you know of the character, ability and general worth of Mr. J. Riely Gordon, architect, late of San Antonio but now of Dallas, Texas. What you may write may be duly appreciated and held to be entirely confidential.

Yours Truly
R. H. Thompson

The promised confidentiality was not fully respected as copies of at least some responses found their way into Gordon's office papers. This letter and the responses to it may be the only surviving evidence of the commission's covert inquiry: it is not recorded in the commission minutes or reported in the press, and the governor made no mention of it in his 1902 official report to the legislature on the State House Commission's work.[23]

While their existence today is the result of a lapse of ethical decorum, these letters assist Gordon scholarship by providing a glimpse into the opinions held by his peers and clients. It is predictable that the sampling of county and state officials generally offered praise while some competitors pointed to the problems with various court-house projects and insinuated culpability on Gordon's part. Officials who had hired Gordon were unlikely to find fault with him lest they cast doubt on their own judgment. Other architects had little incentive to say good things about a competitor unless they knew him personally.[24] Two responses stand out, however, because they offer insight into matters previously discussed, and their authors seem to have no reason for bias.

Recall that Gordon lost the Denton County Courthouse project after accusations of bribery were raised in the Commissioners' Court. While the 1899 appellate court ruling affirmed the falseness of the charge, the judgment nevertheless did not favor Gordon, and some of the architects responding to the Mississippi inquiry cited the Denton scandal as tarnishing his reputation. One of the respondents in Gordon's favor, however, was I. D. Ferguson. Elected Denton County judge after the scandal, Ferguson's assessment can be presumed objective. In his letter, the county judge recounts that the architect "submitted plans for our court-house and they were accepted so I heard and *the county went back on his plans and accepted another plan that suited them better and he lost the contract, but it was not the fault of Mr. Gordon.* I was not a member of the court at that time. Mr. J. Riely Gordon to my judgment is all right" (emphasis added).[25] Unfortunately, the Mississippi State House Commission's promise of confidentiality prevented Gordon from using this endorsement to publicly refute his competitors' slurs at the time.

At least one architect recommended that the State House Commission contact Messer, Sanguinet & Messer for more information, which, combined with the machinations discussed in Chapter 10, suggests that Marshal Sanguinet's efforts against Gordon were well known in the region's architectural community. Commission members followed up, but the Fort Worth firm had by that time dissolved. Their letter found its way to the individual practice of Howard Messer, who seems more kind toward Gordon than his former partner was.[26]

In his response, Messer hints that he is aware of unflattering stories about Gordon being circulated, but declines to comment on them since he had "no direct proof of the charges that have been laid at his door," adding, "I always think that there would be very direct proof to support any accusations brought by one professional man against another." This is perhaps the best substantiation that slanderous allegations regarding Gordon were largely the product of competitive sniping: if Sanguinet really had evidence against Gordon he likely would have shared it with his partner at the time. Again, the promise of confidentiality prevented Gordon from capitalizing on this.

Messer did not confine his response to comments on Gordon's character, however. He took this opportunity to vent his feelings about public projects and the officials who run them, observing, there must be great inducements offered to manipulate public contracts, or there would not be so much of it done.

I was asked to compete for your building, but knowing by experience that it is not so much a question of integrity and ability, as skilful misrepresentation and scheming, I prefer to do less business with more self-respect than vice-versa.

Messer concludes by declaring that most public officials are not competent to judge any architect's work.[27]

The Mississippi State House Commission delayed its return to work until May 16, by which time it likely had received a sufficient response to its covert survey. Professor Ware declined the invitation to consult so members began reviewing the submissions on their own, but their work suffered greatly from a lack of expertise. Perhaps taking Messer's harangue to heart, the commission turned to Bernard R. Green for help. Green was a Washington, DC, civil engineer who superintended construction for the Library of Congress. He arrived in Jackson on June 6 and began scrutiny of the plans, which were numbered to hide the identities of their authors.[28]

It was announced on June 14, 1900, that, on R. H. Thompson's suggestion, the commission unanimously selected the design submitted by Theodore Link of St. Louis, Missouri. Governor Longino's message to the legislature states that, after "a close and thorough study of all the plans and specifications" with the commissioners, Green had "reported in favor" of Link's submission "as being the best."[29]

This was not entirely accurate, however. Part of Green's official report to the State House Commission was made public on June 15. According to the *Clarion-Ledger* and contrary to the governor's message, "it is understood that [, in] the portion of this report not made public," Green actually recommended a total of four submissions as being worthy, including Gordon's.[30]

CHAPTER FOURTEEN

McLennan and the Vicksburg City Hall

Harrison marked James Riely Gordon's courthouse transition to the Beaux-Arts style. Although the budget for the Callahan courthouse was so modest he could barely consider style, in his next two major public commissions he more fully demonstrated a command of the Beaux-Arts, which now had largely eclipsed Richardson's Romanesque in popularity. These projects are the McLennan County Courthouse and the Vicksburg City Hall.

The seat of McLennan County is Waco, a city that in the 1880s considered itself "the Athens of Texas," based upon a number of fine educational institutions in the area. By 1900 the existing, thirteen-year-old McLennan County Courthouse had been outgrown and its Second Empire style considered outmoded. An April special election approved replacing the structure, and officials began seeking a suitable location for the new courthouse. (A dispute over ownership of the original town square caused the county to abandon that site in 1874.) The property selected was a sizable portion of the block along Washington Avenue between Fifth and Sixth Streets.[1]

In June the Commissioners' Court turned to Waco's elder architect, Wesley Clark Dodson, as an expert consultant. As earlier recounted, Dodson served as the first president of the Texas State Association of Architects. He later succeeded Gordon as the architect for the Denton County Courthouse and also thwarted Gordon's attempt to have the TSAA membership accepted en masse as AIA members. Dodson was in his seventies and likely retired from active practice when his services were retained for the 1900 McLennan project.

Under his contract, officials forwarded preliminary submissions from hopeful architects to Dodson for examination and appraisal. Once a design was selected, he was to validate the final plans and superintend construction. Compensation was a $500 payment for reviewing all plans in addition to 1½ percent of the cost of construction for superintendence. The Commissioners' Court considered ten plans. The identities of their authors were kept secret; Dodson referred to them only by number in the official record.[2]

In his report on the preliminary designs, Dodson narrowed the field down to two suitable entries, identified as "8" and "9." He ultimately dismissed 8 as having "many excellent points worth consideration, but others that are undesirable and hard to overcome." Design 9 was Gordon's submission. Dodson noted that it showed "unity of design in every part. The style of architecture is classic Corinthian, and the treatment of all its parts (internally and externally) is delicate and scholarly." Elsewhere he observed rooms that were well grouped and "remarkably well ventilated and lighted." He suggested a few minor changes, however. He found the dome "in keeping with the body of the building, and . . . of fine proportions, except that the plinth and drum are each too low." Be that as it may, he concluded that the "whole makeup of the building is easy and dignified, and if built with changes suggested, will give [the county] a public building with convenience, elegance and repose."[3]

Gordon's submission was substantially different from his previous courthouse work. Wings flanking the entrance are long enough to effectively mask another wing in the rear. Although still cruciform in plan, it appears to be a rectangular block from most front viewing angles (fig. 14.1). As such, it is not far removed from his previous capitol proposals. Indeed, among Gordon's office papers is an alternative design for McLennan that is an elaboration upon the adopted design. It expands the plan with elliptically bayed wings reminiscent of his 1896 Mississippi State House design. The exact role of this alternative plan in the McLennan design process is uncertain. While possibly too extravagant for serious consideration, it presents irony worthy of the architect's sense of humor: instead of trying to pass off a courthouse plan for a state capitol, as he had been accused, Gordon was proposing a capitol plan for a courthouse!

On September 15 the Commissioners' Court minutes recorded that "the plans submitted by the J. Riely Gordon Company of Dallas are recommended as most meritorious by W. C. Dodson." The officials went on to stipulate some changes to be incorporated in the final plans. A fountain proposed for the rotunda was deleted. An underground tunnel connecting with the jail was added. Concerning the use of statuary, they empowered Gordon and Dodson to "carefully study the actual requirements of the building . . . and provide in the most economical manner [only] such statuary . . . as shall be absolutely necessary to a reasonable and proper adornment of the building." Other changes were made to room arrangements and assignments. Officials also left the matter of the height of the dome to be resolved between the two architects. The Commissioners' Court made it clear that Gordon was expected to represent the company in person and be on call to work with Dodson for the duration of the project. Agreeing to this, the J. Riely Gordon Company was to receive 3½ percent of the construction cost for the design.[4]

An unexpected opportunity to purchase additional land west of the new courthouse property arose in November. The county availed itself, extended the site to the

WACO, TEXAS.

COURT HOUSE.

14.1.
McLennan County Courthouse,
Waco, Texas (1900–2). James
Riely Gordon, architect. *Postcard
view ca. 1905.*

entire length of the block, and planned for the courthouse to be centered along Washington. In early December the construction contract went to Tom Lovell for $196,875, making it second to Bexar as the most expensive Gordon courthouse to date.[5] Lovell built Gordon's Brazoria courthouse and Arizona Capitol, as well as Dodson's Denton courthouse.

This entire project, from design review through construction, appears to have been admirably conducted by the McLennan County Commissioners' Court. The officials recognized that the selection of a design and adoption of plans for this undertaking required "technical knowledge possessed only by an experienced architect." By hiring Dodson, they gained his expertise and satisfied the typical pressure to employ local talent but left themselves free in their choice of designing architect. They also had the prudence to leave aesthetic decisions to Gordon and Dodson. There is no evidence of friction between the two architects during this project, so presumably they settled any differences of opinion in a professional manner. The completed courthouse was accepted on October 3, 1902, and the county government moved in shortly thereafter.[6]

With McLennan, Gordon delivered a firm and capable application of Beaux-Arts classicism to the needs of a county courthouse.[7] While he had to abandon his Signature Plan here to accommodate multiple courtrooms, it is significant that he never returned to it for smaller projects. It seems he understood that the plan was ill-suited for the classical styling he now embraced. His "Capitol Plan" remains cruciform, however, leaving him with a minimum of twelve exterior walls allowing windows for light and ventilation. Recessed porches created even more surfaces for windows. The main entrance was placed in the center of the Washington (south) façade with a major second entrance off Fifth Street (fig. 14.2). This configuration reflects the anticipated site during the design stage: the north side of the building faced an alley, across which stood the jail, and the west side faced private property. Although actual construction had yet to begin when the county acquired the adjoining property, it was surely

considered too late to balance the structure with a Sixth Street entrance—a change that would necessitate drastic revisions to the already finalized interior plans.

McLennan's courthouse sits prominently on a hill that gently rises from the Brazos River and lifts the building above street level. Approached from the south, the imposing structure is exuberant yet precise, amiable yet scholarly. Gordon was able to use fluted Composite columns here for the first time on a public building. Rough-cut, Texas granite, laid to produce Renaissance-style banding, defines the first floor and nine flat-arched windows across the front of each wing enumerate the bays. Above this the material changes to light limestone and the windows are pedimented. The third through fifth bays in from each end are recessed, creating porches behind columns that project from the building. These porches are mirrored on the north sides of the wings. The second-floor pattern is repeated on the third, although the windows have no pediments, and the fourth floor is treated as an attic. Consoles above the paired columns marking the extremes of the porches lead to pediments decorated with laurel leaves and oculus lights.

Four tiers of granite steps lead from Washington Street to a second-story, prostyle portico whose treatment expands upon those of the porches to its right and left. Above, two statues expressing *Liberty* and *Justice* flank the pediment, and a splendid dome recalling Gordon's competition design for the Texas State Building (fig. 7.1; see page 92) rises over the crossing behind. It is difficult to assign credit for this dome, given the instructions that Gordon and Dodson work it out between themselves, but Gordon proved himself quite capable of delivering fine domes on his own with his other classic-styled courthouses. The zinc dome sits upon an octagonal drum with paired columns at its points. Between these, tall windows provide light to the inner dome. Eight large-scale eagles proudly ring a dome decorated in relief and surmounted by a cupola. Above it all stands another statue of *Justice*.

Inside, Gordon created formal processional spaces that invoke the majesty of the law. Passing through the main entrance door, beneath a segmental pediment announcing McLennan County, one enters a vestibule, then a wide corridor leading to the impressive rotunda (fig. 14.3). From the white oak balustrade, visitors can look down to the first floor or up, past the third-floor gallery to the inner dome with its exquisite art glass. The building radiates from this point: the largest courtroom to the north, offices and additional courtrooms to the east and west. Extensive wainscoting features light Creole Kennesaw marble.

Although much more elaborate than most of Gordon's previous courthouses, McLennan lacks the efficiency of his Signature Plan. Of course, this commission enjoyed a generous budget and ample site, so the primary restraints that drove earlier designs are absent here. Gordon and his competitors also enjoyed an unusually long design period on this project. This allowed the architect time to adapt features from his

14.2.
(OPPOSITE) McLennan County Courthouse, aerial view with main entrance center and Fifth Street entrance on right. *Photograph ca. 1935, photographer unknown.*

14.3.
McLennan County Courthouse,
rotunda. *2003 photograph.*

previous state capitol proposals to a courthouse design. The result is a superbly detailed composition that is as sure in its embrace of Beaux-Arts classicism as his earlier courthouses are in the Richardsonian Romanesque. This Gordon masterpiece enjoys a prominent position in Waco where its excellent dome is highly visible. It remains a Beaux-Arts jewel worthy of a community aspiring to the title "Athens of Texas."

Late in 1900, a decision to build a new city hall in Vicksburg, Mississippi, provided Gordon with an opportunity to display his command of Beaux-Arts styling on another public building type. It also furthered his reputation beyond the Texas state line.

Vicksburg was the largest city in the state, and on December 17, 1900, its city leaders advertised for plans and specifications for a new city hall due two months later. They called for a three-story building to occupy a narrow lot at the corner of Crawford and Walnut Streets. Total cost, except for furnishings, was not to exceed $37,000.[8]

Ten architects and firms responded, but only eight appeared before the board either in person or by a representative. They agreed amongst themselves to draw lots to determine the order in which they would explain their plans before the mayor and board. Gordon began his presentation at 7:00 p.m. on February 19. According to the *Daily Herald*, the architect

> appeared accompanied by his assistant, Mr. White, and with a mass of matter to be used as reference. Mr. Gordon began by going carefully into questions of technique and detail, explaining terms with the aid of diagrams in perspective, sectional, traverse and longitudinal, his plans for a state house which was entered in competition for the Mississippi State House in 1896. This plan has since been adopted by the state [*sic*] of Arizona, and is a handsome, massive, strong looking building. His design for the City Hall . . . had been made very carefully according to the printed instructions sent him. The exterior presents a massive yet light appearance, and there is no doubt whatever that it would be an ornament to any community or any neighborhood. Mr. Gordon wound up with the remark that he would be pleased to have a representative building placed in Mississippi, and after a pleasant little anecdote [ever the raconteur] closed his argument and left the case with the jury.[9]

Gordon likely suspected some on the board harbored doubts about him, which he addressed head-on. By unrolling the very capitol plans that four years earlier Governor McLaurin claimed to be for a courthouse and using them as an architectural primer, he simultaneously demonstrated his expertise and the falseness of the charge. It was brilliant salesmanship.

After all the presentations had been made, the architects departed Vicksburg, leaving their plans behind for further consideration. Through a series of votes, the officials eliminated plans from consideration until three remained. Perspective views of these three were placed in business houses along Washington Street for the populace to view. Gordon's seemed "to be the most favored by the general public," according to the *Evening Post*.[10]

The finalists were recalled for another presentation on the evening of February 26. As reported, Gordon

appeared with pleasant, smiling countenance, fresh from his victory at Hazelhurst
[see Chapter 15], and at the request of the committee again outlined his design in
all its features. He was closely questioned and cross-questioned, and promptly
answered all queries. He stated this was a matter in which he had taken special
pains and to which he had given close study. He had some good reasons for this,
and cited the competition over the state house plans in 1896 [again], in which it
was sought to besmirch his character. He had hoped, if he could not put up a public building at Jackson he would like to place one as near there as possible, and for
that reason as well as for professional pride he had devoted special care to this city
hall matter. He explained closely every detail of his building, as to construction,
material, heating, ventilation and other features, answering many questions from
different members.

Another vote was taken after all three architects spoke; Gordon won on the first
ballot. Gordon was "a most gratified man" upon being informed of his victory. Afterward, the architect spoke to a gathering of newspapermen at the Carroll Hotel:

Gentlemen. I do not wish to be understood as speaking boastfully or looking too
far ahead, but I assure you the paper work gives only a partial idea of the building
I will give to Vicksburg. I have many reasons for this, one of them is professional
pride and the desire to expand, which is natural. Another reason is that the city
council has shown its confidence in our firm and I am going to show them that it is
not in the least misplaced.

As the press reported, "the action of the committee met with popular approval
from many citizens last night, and it is thought the choice for Mr. Gordon's graceful,
dignified and architecturally fine design has been well made."[11]

Gordon's final plans were adopted on May 27, 1901, subject to a few very minor
changes. On August 6 the construction contract went to the Davis-Larkin Company
of Chicago for $42,140. Arthur Giannini, representing the J. Riely Gordon Company,
superintended the work. The structure was largely completed by February 1903, but
legal squabbling between the city and contractor delayed possession. The city took the
building by force and began occupying it in April, pending resolution of the litigation.[12]

The Vicksburg City Hall is a strikingly original design (fig 14.4).[13] The building has a
quatrefoil footprint with exterior dimensions of 64 x 96 feet. Unusual, curved façades
are visually constrained by four square towers, which are engaged for the three-story
height of the brick building. Gordon capped these towers with small domes serving as
bases for heraldic statues trumpeting the merits of Vicksburg.

The northwest tower houses the main entrance, with a curved flight of granite
steps leading to it from the corner of Crawford and Walnut Streets. Either side offers

entry, and the doors have limestone surrounds above which, on the second-story level, are ocular lights encircled by terra-cotta laurel wreaths. The third floor is separated with a metal cornice and treated like an attic frieze.

To the east of the entrance is a circular lobe of five bays separated by brick pilasters with Composite capitals. To the south, the pilasters give way to limestone columns of an excellent, two-story elliptical veranda. Gordon obviously strove to evoke the romance of antebellum architecture with this wonderful open porch. Another Walnut Street entry centers in this façade. The shape of the north and west façades are reflected on the opposite sides of the building. The southwest tower offers another street entry.

Gordon placed the mayor's court on the first floor of the north lobe and the board of aldermen's chamber directly above it. As the aldermen sat in session, the windows of the semicircular end of the building provided a panoramic view of downtown Vicksburg behind them. Inside the main entrance tower, a cast iron stair negotiates the three floors with irregular trapezoidal flights. Marble is employed for the stair treads and hallway flooring. Oak finishing was used in the major rooms. The third floor was devoted largely to an auditorium and a library. Offices for various city functions, including the police department, filled the rest of the building.

14.4.
Vicksburg City Hall, Vicksburg, Mississippi (1901–3). James Riely Gordon, architect. *Photograph ca. 1905, courtesy Old Court House Museum, Vicksburg, Mississippi.*

193

Gordon designed the Vicksburg City Hall for a community boldly embracing its future. Working with a relatively small budget, he delivered a strong statement to befit its site on the crest of a prominent bluff. While the city hall still stands, man and nature have robbed it of its original splendor. Renovations have obscured Gordon's interior finishing, but most tragic has been the enclosure of the veranda for additional office space. A deadly tornado inflicted further injury in 1953. In addition to its costly toll on the area, the storm carried off the heraldic statues from the city hall rooftop. Although currently deprived of its most inspirational features, this unique structure is both eclectic and elegant, and like Harrison, approaches mannerism in its take on the Beaux-Arts.

While the exuberance of the McLennan County Courthouse and the Vicksburg City Hall betray Gordon's Victorian picturesque background, they also serve as the prologue to his twentieth-century work. McLennan demonstrates that Gordon came to terms with the notion that his Signature Plan, which he so jealously protected, had become obsolete. Circumstances required something new, and his capitol work provided the model. The curved façades of the Vicksburg City Hall are realizations of the elliptical wing design that Gordon proposed for the Mississippi Capitol, the expansion of Arizona's, and the alternate design for the McLennan courthouse. This feature would find its way into the plans of a number of the architect's future courthouses.

CHAPTER FIFTEEN

The J. Riely Gordon Company

In February 1901, as Vicksburg's aldermen were contemplating J. Riely Gordon's plan for their city hall, county officials in another Mississippi town were exploring how best to replace their aged and inadequate courthouse and jail. Gordon's work on this project was a protracted process, but it resulted in a new plan he used as a template for six more courthouses. He designed these buildings and a courthouse addition over a relatively brief period that turned out to be his transition from Texas to New York City.

This series began in Hazelhurst, Mississippi, when the Copiah County Board of Supervisors (analogous to a Texas county's commissioners' court) empanelled a building committee to seek out the best available architect and plans. The committee, in turn, approached fourteen architects and firms through letters of inquiry. Some of the nation's most experienced designers of public buildings were targeted, demonstrating commendable acumen on the part of the committee. In addition to Gordon, the mailing list included names previously mentioned in this volume: Theodore Link, Elijah E. Myers, H. W. Wolters, and L. M. Weathers. Also solicited were John W. Gaddis of Indianapolis, a designer of many midwestern courthouses, and Alfred Zucker of New York City. The letter sought plans for either or both the courthouse and jail with the expectation that they would cost about $40,000 and $10,000, respectively.

Gordon, Link, Myers, Zucker, and five others responded to the letter and appeared before the committee in Hazelhurst. The official report does not differentiate between those tendering plans for the courthouse and those for the jail, however. Not completely satisfied with any single proposal, the committee instead enthusiastically recommended that the Board of Supervisors engage Gordon to develop plans for the buildings. The committee's report provides another account of the architect's renowned salesmanship:

> Without disparagement to his competitors, most of whom are men of eminent
> ability and qualifications, it is but just to Mr. Gordon to say that in the opinion
> of the committee he had more experience in the construction of this class of
> work than any of his competitors, and that his facilities for enabling us to get

competent bidders and competitive prices are superior to his competitors. Mr. Gordon presented to this committee not less than two hundred letters of recommendation coming from Governors, United States Senators, Rail Road officials, Bank officials, Building Committees, Judges of Courts and Commissions for whom he has constructed this class of work. Not only is this true, but it will be remembered that Mr. Gordon's plans for the construction of a capitol for the State of Mississippi were selected over all competitors by the Legislature of Mississippi in 1898 [sic], and if human testimony can be accepted in reference to the character qualifications of any man, his qualifications and integrity are not subject to doubt or cavil.

Conditions of Gordon's engagement with the Copiah project were rather burdensome. He was to work with the committee to develop multiple and varied plans all suited to the particular needs of the county in order that they may have "unlimited choice." In addition to his design work and assistance in attracting contractors, Gordon offered to secure a superintendent for whom the county would bear "but a small portion of his salary."[1]

Developing a plan that met approval and the budget proved challenging. Over the next five months the committee was, in its words, "in constant communication" with the architect. Gordon was required to prepare and submit several plans, to which the committee "suggested many modifications and alterations." Members of the committee found the process to be difficult and time consuming for both the architect and themselves, but on August 10, 1901, they presented a final plan for the courthouse to the Board of Supervisors. The board adopted the plan and let the contract to George T. Hallas and Company, a Jackson firm, on January 7, 1902, for $44,603. (They deferred the jail project until later.) The county accepted Gordon's recommendation for superintendent—probably Arthur Giannini, who also oversaw construction of the Vicksburg City Hall and Wilkinson County Courthouse (discussed later in this chapter).

Questions on the location of the courthouse delayed construction until spring 1902. Although Gordon moved to New York City about this time, county records show that he was still involved with the project, through correspondence, as late as July 1903. Copiah's courthouse was accepted on August 15, 1903.[2]

Just as Gordon's Signature Plan was to an extent the product of the redesigns for the Texas pavilion for the 1893 World's Fair, his Copiah Plan was forged in the protracted process of appeasing the building committee.[3] In a way, Gordon reprioritized his Harrison design; he reduced the height of the three office wings to two stories while enlarging the relative size of the rear courtroom wing. All the wings emanate, again, from a central clock tower with entrances set in the reentrant angles (fig. 15.1). The pedimented east façade features detached stone columns, reminiscent of Harrison's entrance-less porticos. Two primary entrances, set in the northeast and south-

east reentrants, have circular porches supported by a pair of two-story stone columns. All of the columns have Composite Corinthian capitals, as do brick pilasters separating the bays on the north and south wings. Simple piers divide bays further back. Above the frieze, the tower drum adds a third story leading to the dome.

Gordon introduces some economical, yet interesting, innovations to the courtroom wing. Its north and south sides are bowed in an elliptical curve echoing the Vicksburg City Hall design. First-floor porches are recessed behind the plane of the curved walls on both sides, with central openings providing access from which one can proceed west to enter offices in the rear of the building or east to secondary reentrant entrances to the main foyer.

This 20-foot-wide octagonal foyer can also be accessed from the primary entrances. In later iterations of this plan this foyer is the first floor of a rotunda open to the inner dome above, but here at Copiah it may have been floored off (as it is at present), leaving somewhat claustrophobic spaces. Existing plan drawings suggest it was closed, but a side elevation view shows a fine, if modest, rotunda (fig. 15.2). The third floor provides access to the courtroom gallery and minor offices and is illuminated by the eight lights of the drum, which vary in height according to the roofline outside.

Marble flooring and wainscoting meet visitors at the entrances. Doors of the first-floor foyer open to administrative offices. Most of the offices on the second floor were judicial, with double doors leading to the courtroom. On the reduced-height third floor, two separate doors lead to the north and south courtroom galleries.

Elliptical in shape, the Copiah courtroom was a new entry in Gordon's oeuvre. From the doors on the second floor of the rotunda, the walls curve out and then back in as they approach the judge's bench at the west end. Hugging these walls are

15.1.
Copiah County Courthouse, Hazelhurst, Mississippi (1902–3). J. Riely Gordon Company, architect. Jail by Hull & Hull visible at rear. *Courtesy George W. Covington Memorial Library.*

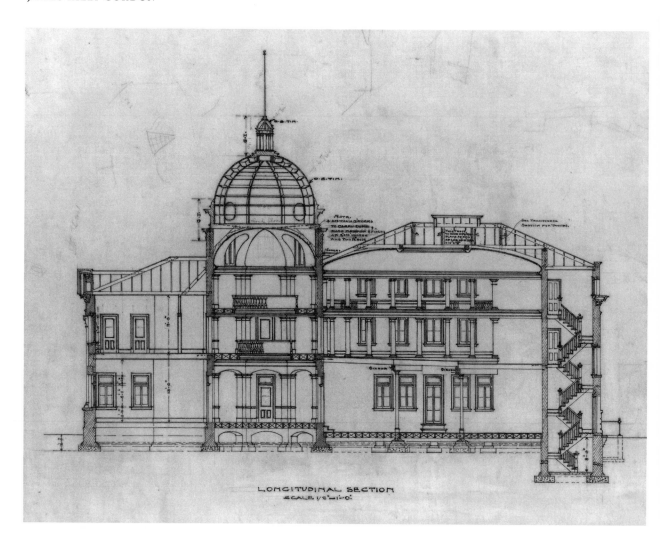

LONGITUDINAL SECTION
SCALE 1/8" = 1'-0"

two rows of gallery seating on risers that are separated from the main floor by Doric columns aligned with the inside wall of the recessed porches below. The main floor slopes toward the slightly raised bench for improved sight lines. Curving back into the main room, a balustrade separates participants from spectators and sets an arc for the seating to follow. Third-floor balconies repeat the seating of the side galleries. Here, Composite columns support a frieze that encircles the room and gives way to the coved ceiling that arcs to a central art glass skylight.

Overall, the Copiah County Courthouse is a clever, economical, and modestly elegant design, but Gordon had trouble reconciling some features. Particularly awkward are the main entrance porches. Their circular form seems detached from the surrounding structure, and their columns appear too spindly for their task. Regardless of such shortcomings, Gordon was sufficiently satisfied with the overall plan to propose it, with some variation and refinements, for his next six courthouse commissions. While engaged with the Hazelhurst project, however, he also designed an addition to an existing courthouse in Lake Charles, Louisiana. For this the architect devised a significantly

15.2.
Copiah County Courthouse, section drawing by the J. Riely Gordon Company. *Courtesy Alexander Architectural Archive, University of Texas, Austin.*

different design. In doing so, Gordon demonstrates his versatility and adaptability to challenging design criteria.

Before delving into Gordon's work in Louisiana, an introduction into some of the state's unique government terminology may be beneficial. Following its 1803 purchase of the territory, the United States government tried to impose a county structure on a resistive, mostly Roman Catholic, population. As a compromise to ease acceptance, Church parish divisions were adopted as the pattern for county-level civic jurisdiction. The elected head of each parish was the parish judge, who assembled a jury of residents to make decisions on taxation, infrastructure, and police matters. The popular term for this body, *Police Jury*, was eventually codified and members assumed the duties of parish administration. Organization could vary from parish to parish, but in Gordon's time individual members were typically elected from ward divisions of the parish. These members chose one from their ranks to act as president.[4]

In May 1901 the Calcasieu Parish Police Jury met to discuss plans for an addition to the existing courthouse in Lake Charles: a two-story brick structure in the Second Empire style, built ten years earlier for $20,000.[5]

Details of what followed are sketchy, but by September 1901 the Police Jury had adopted Gordon's plans for an addition and extensive renovation and selected a contractor, R. W. Abright, a Shreveport builder who bid $50,165. The original completion date was set for March 4, 1902, but funding problems delayed the contract signing until February 1902. While he was clearly personally involved in designing the addition, this delay ran up against Gordon's move to New York, preventing his participation in the actual construction just as it had for the Copiah courthouse. An attorney represented him at the contract signing.[6]

As it stood, the existing courthouse was on a narrow lot that restricted the architect to working along the axis of structure. Gordon wrought considerable change nonetheless, nearly doubling the building's size and leaving little of the original exterior exposed. The majority of the new construction extended 30 feet off the east façade of the old structure (fig. 15.3). A local newspaper described the result as "a splendid specimen of the renaissance style of architecture," but it also owed much to the Federal style. Brick walls resting on a stone foundation were stuccoed with cement and trimmed with limestone. The new east entrance was set behind a two-story, Ionic portico. Similar porticos graced the north and south sides of this addition. Behind rose the tower, originally mansard-roofed, that Gordon squared off and elevated to 90 feet, adding clockworks and a blue-domed observatory surmounted by a 10-foot bronze statue of *Justice*. Photographs show the exterior as a successful and harmonious composition.[7]

On the interior, changes were made to the old structure to integrate it with the modern conveniences of the new. Electric wires were installed via conduit set into

15.3.
Calcasieu Parish Courthouse, Lake Charles, Louisiana. View showing east side addition (1902–3, destroyed). J. Riely Gordon Company, architect. *Postcard view by the Rotograph Company, ca. 1905.*

the walls. Basement excavation made way for the new steam heating furnace, and the building was fitted for sanitary plumbing throughout. Gordon replaced the original roof with one of a higher pitch to accommodate vaulting added to the district courtroom for improved acoustics. Halls were floored with encaustic tile and wainscoted with marble. Walls were tinted hard plaster.

Controversy and hard feelings marred completion of the work. At the end of the year, the Police Jury took issue with some aspects of Abright's work. Reports vary on the details of the dispute, but there was uncertainty as to whether the contractor complied with the plans and specifications and some felt the workmanship to be inferior. The *Lake Charles Weekly American* also found fault with the architect:

> Police jurors recall with bitterness their architect, J. Riely Gordon, who made them glowing promises, waved all suggestions aside with, "That's all right, we'll attend

to everything," talked loudly about his reputation, drew them a set of defective plans which cost them hundreds of dollars extra, got his money and then deserted them.[8]

While the situation may have been frustrating, these complaints about Gordon are surely unjust. When the original projected completion date was March 1902 it is quite possible that everyone, including Gordon, anticipated his company would be superintending the work. It was the Police Jury's funding problem that delayed the start of construction, and newspaper reports of the final contract contain no mention of any continuing responsibility on his part. Whatever his original intentions and promises, available information indicates he abided by the contract as signed. The *Weekly American*'s additional charge that the architect provided defective plans carries little credibility given his other work. True, there were additional charges for work on Calcasieu that ran into thousands of dollars. These were called for by the jurors themselves, however, and include questionable expenditures like $220 to have the contractor install electric lights on the crown of the statue and red and green signal lights on the clock faces. After some negotiation, the Police Jury settled its dispute with Abright, and the additions to the Calcasieu Parish Courthouse were accepted on January 17, 1903.[9]

Gordon's next courthouse was for the Texas county of Angelina. Officials began work toward a new courthouse in the seat of Lufkin in fall 1901, calling for competitive entries due December 2. The Commissioners' Court accepted the J. Riely Gordon Company's submission and also engaged it to superintend construction.[10] Of the courthouse contracts that Gordon entered into during this period, Angelina's appears to be the only one signed before his move to New York was finalized. This probably explains why it is the only one in which he committed his company to superintendence. By all accounts the work went well.

When construction bids were solicited in January 1902, copies of the plans and specifications could be inspected at the company's offices in New York, Dallas, Houston, and Shreveport. While it is clear that Gordon was making the transition to New York at this time, an article from a Lufkin newspaper establishes that he was in the city and personally involved in designing the courthouse.[11]

Gordon used his Copiah Plan with some alteration for Angelina (fig. 15.4). A few reasons may explain this: (1) the site, climatic considerations, and budgets for both were similar, (2) Beaux-Arts styling does not typically lend itself to the expression of existing local culture, so the design was equally appropriate for both communities, and (3) Gordon had much time and effort invested in the Copiah design, possibly motivating him to reuse it to recoup costs.

A review of archival photographs reveals exterior differences between the Copiah and Angelina courthouses. Copiah's decorative portico of detached columns on the primary façade was eliminated at Lufkin; a pilastered treatment identical to the side

15.4.
Angelina County Courthouse,
Lufkin, Texas (1902–3,
demolished). J. Riely Gordon
Company, architect. *Construction
view ca. 1902, photographer
unknown.*

wings was used instead. The circular porches with their freestanding columns were
also dropped. In their place, Gordon simply carried the cornice line and balustrade
across the midway point of the reentrants at a 45-degree angle. Brick pilasters set at the
same angle provided visual support as the roof springs from the wall. These changes
surely helped to get the cost down, yielding a strong, unfussy design even though
Angelina's dome was a bit more decorative with anthemion molding.

The construction contract went to B. B. Shearer, S. W. Henderson, and Theo Miller
for $36,324.30. Alexander Bellis, representing the "southern department" of the J. Riely
Gordon Company, superintended the work. In addition, Bellis superintended a Lufkin
school building, which Gordon's company also designed.[12]

Another version of the Copiah Plan was intended for the Oklahoma Territory.
On January 28, 1902, the Kiowa County Board of Commissioners voted to adopt a
courthouse design submitted by Gordon. The territorial governor's approval was also
needed, however, which may account for the delay until July for the solicitation of
construction bids. In August the contract was awarded to J. W. Stokes, for the allot-
ted amount of $30,000. Gordon was paid $1,050 for his plans in October 1902. By this
time he was in New York, and the county procured its own superintendent.[13]

In February 1903 a newspaper in Hobart, Kiowa's county seat, carried an illustration of the design and noted it was under construction (fig. 15.5). As depicted in the
Hobart Republican, the courthouse was similar to Angelina; the most discernable difference being the introduction of hipped roofs to the side wings. This eliminated pediments and, presumably, pilasters on those wings. Such a deletion would help bridge
the $6,324 difference between Angelina's price tag and what the Oklahoma territorial
government was willing to pay.[14]

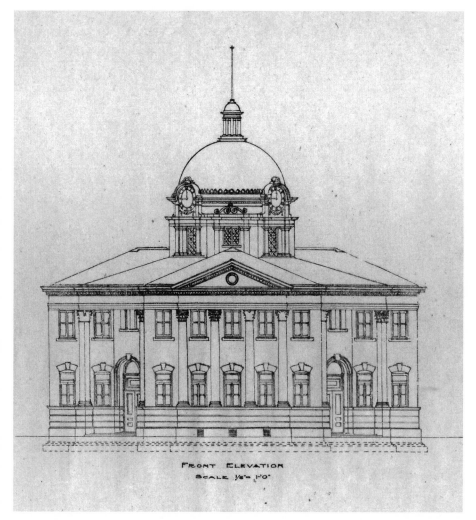

15.5.
Kiowa County Courthouse,
Hobart, Oklahoma Territory
(construction abandoned). *1902
elevation drawing by the J. Riely
Gordon Company, courtesy Alexander
Architectural Archive, University of
Texas, Austin.*

Contractor Stokes had laid the foundation and basement and was commencing work on the walls when members of a newly installed Board of Commissioners ordered construction halted. For reasons that remain unclear, they deemed the work to be substandard and tore it up. Later the county abandoned Gordon's design in favor of one supplied by the U.S. Department of the Interior. Stokes was released from his contract, and Kiowa County built its courthouse to a different set of plans in 1906.[15]

Gordon's next courthouse project took him back to Louisiana, where on February 20, 1902, the Rapides Parish Police Jury met in a contentious debate over replacing its courthouse in Alexandria. Gordon was present, but there seems to be no record of any competition previous to this session. The Police Jury finally agreed to proceed with the project and to solicit bids according to Gordon's design due in April.[16]

An illustration published in March 1902 shows a design based on the Copiah Plan but much more elaborate: a full three stories high with decorative porticos extending beyond the three office wings (fig. 15.6). Eagles are depicted adorning the pediments and dome, the latter being topped with a cupola and statue. Its main entrance treatment

15.6.
Rapides Parish Courthouse, 1902
office drawing by the J. Riely
Gordon Company (not built).
*Courtesy Alexander Architectural
Archive, University of Texas, Austin.*

shows a unique deviation with the reentrants enclosed by first-floor porches continuing the rustication surrounding the building's first floor. The J. Riely Gordon Company's estimate for the cost of the Rapides Parish Courthouse was $100,000.[17]

Familiar contractors competed for the job: R. W. Abright, Davis-Larkin Company,
and Tom Lovell, but the jury rejected all bids. Afterward, with Gordon removed to
New York, the Police Jury appointed a committee to select a superintendent as well as
a builder. It chose the New Orleans architectural firm of Favrot & Livaudais to superintend the project. Although the Police Jury's main complaint in rejecting the bids was
that they did not include removal of the old courthouse, it appears they wanted to get
out of using Gordon's design completely.[18]

After examining the plans, Favrot & Livaudais submitted a report to the Police Jury
on July 17, 1902. It was the firm's opinion that the structure, as designed by the J. Riely
Gordon Company, would not be sound. It also found the specifications to be so vague
as to be almost worthless for quoting purposes. The New Orleans architects "made the

necessary corrections" to the plans and wrote new specifications. They estimated the cost of the structure as amended would be about $112,000.[19] Of course, the assertions in the Favrot & Livaudais report are dubious. First, the judgment that the design was so poor as to be hazardous is contradicted by the sturdiness of Gordon's other Copiah Plan courthouses—two of which still stand. Second, bids by three competent contractors belie the claim that Gordon's specifications were useless.

The committee was under the impression that the J. Riely Gordon Company was somehow obligated to furnish additional copies of the plans so they could also be "corrected" for estimating purposes. Members wrote the architect, requesting that he provide ten or twelve sets without delay. Gordon's response was emphatic. According to a newspaper account, the committee "received a reply sharply refusing to supply any more sets of plans and specifications and in addition added that they were copy righted, and any infringement would be prosecuted." With that, the committee returned the matter to the Rapides Parish Police Jury, which resolved to reject Gordon's plans once and for all. It opted to consider, in concert with Favrot & Livaudais, plans that had been previously submitted by Hull & Hull, architects of Jackson, Mississippi. This design was ultimately adopted and built by the F. B. Hull Construction Company of Jackson.[20]

Almost straight north of Alexandria lies the city of Ruston, seat of Lincoln Parish. On February 27, 1902, the Lincoln Parish Police Jury met to consider a new courthouse. Memphis architect A. J. Bryan appeared before the afternoon session and presented some drawings and photos of courthouses, presumably designed by him, built in other parts of the country. Surely Bryan hoped to seal the deal then, but the Police Jury chose to advertise for plans and specifications for a new courthouse to cost between $25,000 and $30,000, due April 7. After reviewing submissions for two days, it chose the entry of the "J. Riley Gordon Co., architect Dallas, Texas."[21]

Although they misspell his name, Police Jury records fix the architect as still in Dallas at this time. In March 1902 he signed a contract with Alfred Zucker committing himself to moving to New York, but there was nothing to prevent him from continuing sales of plans in the South although personal superintendence would be doubtful. Gordon likely presented his plans to the Lincoln Parish Police Jury himself, as he did the other courthouses discussed in this chapter, but H. M. White (presumably the same Mr. White who assisted Gordon in his Vicksburg City Hall presentation) provided the working plans, specifications, and a contract in June. White is recorded as representing Alfred Zucker in connection with the J. Riely Gordon Company, Architects of New York. The Police Jury sought the advice of an architect named J. W. Smith in reviewing the plans and on July 8 agreed to sign the contract with a few changes in the design still pending.[22]

The pitfalls of working commissions far from his new home soon became evident for Gordon. On September 12, 1902, White, as his representative of the company, agreed to a 3½ percent fee for the design of a courthouse expected to cost $30,000, with construction going to M. T. Lewman and Company of Louisville, Kentucky. On September 15 the Lincoln Parish Police Jury signed a contract with Lewman to build the courthouse for $44,500. Gordon later took legal action against the parish, apparently claiming a 3½ percent fee on the difference between the estimate and the contract cost of the building.[23] Normally an architect's fee is based on the total cost, and it is likely that Gordon's contract clearly stated this, but without an extant copy it is impossible to be certain. The Police Jury's signing—just three days after agreeing to the estimate—of a construction contract for $14,500 more is suspicious, however. By design or by circumstance, the leaders of this northern Louisiana parish were shorting the architect on his fee as normally calculated. The outcome of Gordon's suit is unknown.

The Lincoln Parish Courthouse was accepted as complete on June 24, 1903. The total cost of the project is placed at $54,000.[24] Archival photographs of the exterior indicate that its design was again similar to the Angelina variation of Gordon's Copiah Plan (fig. 15.7).

The next iteration of this plan was for Wilkinson County in southwest Mississippi, where some citizens lamented the demise of the county's antebellum courthouse. The *Woodville Republican* acknowledged that "with this demolition there passes another land mark of the vanished South, so soon to survive alone only 'in song and story.'" Nevertheless, the paper countered, the county had suffered much through the Civil War and its aftermath, but there was finally a feeling of confidence and renewed pride among the citizenry. The paper predicted future growth, "and the new Court House is the first step."[25]

The chancery clerk was authorized to invite architects to submit sketches of their proposals due the first Monday in April 1902. After reviewing a number of preliminary drawings, the board selected the submission of the J. Riely Gordon Company. On July 7 the construction contract went to the Davis-Larkin Company for $41,085. Arthur Giannini superintended the work for Gordon's company.[26]

Again Gordon drew from his work for Angelina, this time facing the foundation with limestone below the water table (fig. 15.8).[27] Wilkinson's rotunda provides another demonstration of the architect's ability to affect drama on a budget (fig. 15.9). Stairs are tucked off to the side, so standing on the first floor one sees a simple, circular opening to the floor above, ringed by a balustrade. Similarly, the second-floor ceiling opens to the inside of the dome encompassed by eight lights from the exterior. Treatment is austere, but superfluous decoration would quickly clutter this relatively small space.

Louisiana's Acadia Parish was Gordon's next courthouse client. Its seat is Crowley, which is divided into quarters by Hutchinson Street and Parkerson Avenue—two long, perpendicular boulevards. The courthouse square straddles their intersection, which made the courthouse visible for a considerable distance in four directions. By creating

15.7.
Lincoln Parish Courthouse, Ruston, Louisiana (1902–3, demolished). J. Riely Gordon Company, architect. *Date and photographer unknown.*

these vistas, the Crowley plan embraced a conceptual ideal of the City Beautiful Movement: traffic and attention were drawn to the symbolic center of parish government. This was a setting made to order for a Beaux-Arts courthouse.

On May 20, 1902, police jurors accepted plans by the J. Riely Gordon Company and W. L. Stevens, associated architects. The $68,418 contract went to Tom Lovell. Stevens was a young Crowley architect who had also designed the city's high school building and the Lake Charles City Hall and Jail, which were constructed about the same time as the Acadia courthouse.[28] Stevens may have been responsible for Gordon receiving this commission, similar to C. G. Lancaster's role in the Harrison County Courthouse.

Photographs of Acadia suggest it was quite similar to Gordon's Rapides design with its semicircular porticos and rusticated stone first floor extending across the primary entrances (fig. 15.10). At a full three stories tall, it was the largest iteration of the Copiah Plan to be built. Lack of information prevents complete assessment of this

15.8.
Wilkinson County Courthouse,
Woodville, Mississippi (1902–3).
J. Riely Gordon Company,
architect. *Undated postcard view
by the Louisiana-Mississippi News
Company.*

15.9.
Wilkinson County Courthouse, rotunda. *1996 photograph.*

15.10.
Acadia Parish Courthouse,
Crowley, Louisiana (1902–3,
demolished). J. Riely Gordon
Company, architect. *Undated
postcard view by the Illustrated Post
Card Company.*

design, but extant images show the courthouse in harmony with its setting. From the four compass points it terminated long, level vistas as the ever-present focus of the community (fig. 15.11). Lighting and landscaping of the boulevards indicate citizens valued the city plan and their courthouse. It was a modest but successful synthesis of architecture and urban planning.

Of the six completed Gordon courthouse projects discussed in this chapter, only the Mississippi courthouses, Copiah and Wilkinson, survive. The years have brought much change to the Copiah County Courthouse. In 1933 the WPA funded the removal of the dome and clock, leaving a short, ungraceful, octagonal hip-roofed structure in its place. Additions that further disrupt the original design were built onto the north and south wings in 1953.[29] Its innovative courtroom remains largely as Gordon designed it, however. Copiah therefore has the significance of housing the only extant Gordon courtroom of this series. In some ways Copiah's sister courthouse in Woodville has fared better. The Wilkinson County Courthouse rotunda is intact and its exterior is virtually unchanged, save an addition off the back. Redesigns of other parts of the interior, including an ill-conceived "new" courtroom, obscure Gordon's genius,

15.11.
Acadia Parish Courthouse, west façade view. *Date and photographer unknown.*

however.

While the Calcasieu Parish Courthouse was only partially Gordon's work, it holds the unfortunate distinction of being his only courthouse to be destroyed by fire. Seven years after the completion of Gordon's addition, a fire ravaged downtown Lake Charles, Louisiana. It was first detected around 3:40 p.m. on April 23, 1910. As it burned wildly through the commercial district, townspeople rushed to remove whatever valuables they could from its path.

Realizing their courthouse was in danger, scores of men bravely joined in an effort to save the parish records. As noted above, the building was on a small, narrow lot and its walls stood close to narrow streets that proved an inadequate barrier from the inferno. Volunteers had just begun their work as courthouse window frames burst into flames and the building had to be immediately abandoned. A witness recalled the flames over the courthouse reaching 100 feet in height and legend holds that the clock had just begun to toll 4:00 o'clock when it fell down into the building as the tower collapsed. By 6:00 p.m., when the winds abated and the flames were finally extinguished, the courthouse stood in ruins, along with a two-block by one-half-mile section of Lake Charles. In all, 109 buildings were destroyed at a loss of up to $750,000. Gordon's columns and the remaining walls of the courthouse were pulled down the following day.[30]

Since Gordon prided himself on his fire-resistant designs, it needs to be asked if any failing on his part contributed to the parish's loss. There are too many extenuating circumstances here, however, to unequivocally place blame on Gordon. It is unknown whether the 1891 courthouse was itself fire-resistant, and it is questionable whether any structure of the time could have better withstood the blaze, given its intensity, once it leapt across the narrow streets. (W. L. Stevens's 1903 City Hall was also lost.) Further- more, Gordon was not contracted to superintend the addition work, so he cannot be held for any unwise deviations from his plans and specifications.[31] Protecting records is one of a courthouse's primary functions, however, and Gordon should have specified the building be equipped with an adequate vault. Perhaps he did and his directions were followed, even though most of the parish documents were lost. Townsmen attempted to retrieve the documents during the fire and—in their sudden flight to save their lives—it is likely they left remaining papers exposed to the flames. The records may have survived had they been properly locked in the vault instead.

A new Calcasieu Parish Courthouse was completed in 1912. This time the Police Jury had the prescience to enlarge the square by acquiring and incorporating adjacent property. The building was set in its center so "should another terrible conflagration come, the flames will not be able to leap across the streets and lick its roof and sides as they did those of the old courthouse in 1910." Favrot & Livaudais designed the new building.[32] Cornerstones of the 1891 structure and Gordon's 1902 addition can still be seen on the square.

The Acadia and Lincoln Parish Courthouses were both destroyed in 1950 to make room for newer structures. Acadia's cornerstone remains on the grounds. That it stood as long as it did further challenges the veracity of the criticism of Gordon's similar Rapides design. Angelina, the last of his county courthouses to be built in Texas, was demolished in 1953. Its cornerstone has been set in an interior wall of its replacement. This block is orientated to display the side listing county officials at the time, so the side remembering Gordon's authorship is sealed within the wall.

Gordon's Copiah Plan was finalized in August 1901, and his plan for the Calcasieu addition was agreed to by September. He sold the other five iterations of the Copiah Plan in the six months beginning December 1901 and ending May 1902. This is a furi- ous pace even for Gordon and he was likely rushing to secure as many commissions as possible before moving to New York, which inevitably would lead to a slow period while he established himself there. Appropriate, in an admittedly generic sort of way, for many communities, the Copiah Plan was well suited for this period—especially once it became evident that Gordon would have to leave superintendence to others. In instances where these courthouses were actually built and the architect arranged for superintendence, things worked out relatively well.

Of course, Gordon's removal from the region surely made it easier for others to undermine his courthouse projects for Kiowa and Rapides. It also seems to have emboldened others to appropriate his designs. For instance, in October 1902 supervisors for the Mississippi County of Harrison approved A. J. Bryan's design

15.12.
Harrison County Courthouse, Gulfport, Mississippi (1902–3, destroyed). A. J. Bryant, architect. *1906 postcard view by the Detroit Publishing Co.*

15.13.
Midland County Courthouse, Midland, Texas (1905, demolished). William Martin, architect. *Undated postcard view by the Haskell Post Card Company.*

for a new courthouse unquestionably derived from Gordon's Copiah Plan, although Gordon does not receive any credit in newspaper accounts or official records. Granted, Bryan added domes reminiscent of a Victorian seaside resort—appropriate for its Gulfport location—and a few curious appendages, but the similarity to the work of the Texas architect who had bested him in recent competitions is undeniable (fig. 15.12). A more bizarre appropriation was perpetrated by none other than William Martin— the contractor who pursued Gordon to Mississippi in 1896 to denounce his character. In 1905 Martin supplied a design for the Midland County Courthouse in Midland,

Texas, which was an extremely pale imitation of Gordon's Signature Plan (fig. 15.13). Like the Gulfport courthouse it is no longer extant, but photographs indicate that it was in the form of a modified Greek cross with a central tower and entrances in its reentrant angles. It possessed little of the genius that Gordon infused in his designs, however. Placed above this forbidding, somewhat Romanesque structure of quarry-faced Pecos sandstone was an incongruent and inadequate little frame tower of vaguely Elizabethan design.[33]

Gordon had a history of copyrighting and defending his plans. Since he appears to have made no effort to fight this looting of his legacy, it may be assumed he was not aware of it. Even if he was, the architect had his hands full in New York by this time.

CHAPTER SIXTEEN

Somerset and Garrett

Despite the family move to Dallas, James Riely Gordon's work remained scattered over a wide geographic area. He was approaching forty years of age and weary of the travel required for his practice when Alfred Zucker, an established New York architect, offered him a copartnership.[1] While the competition would be formidable, the building activity in that city held the promise of abundant work concentrated in a relatively small area.

By 1902 New York City was in the throes of unparalleled renewal to accommodate a surge of activity, population, and capital. Bridges and tunnels were planned or under construction; the subway system was nearing completion; piers and streets were being improved; construction of new buildings, some of them skyscrapers, was on the rise (fig. 16.1). In the process, much of the nineteenth-century cityscape was being obliterated. *Century Magazine* reported:

> One might almost fancy that the town had been bombarded by a hostile fleet, such rents and gashes appear everywhere in solid masonry, ranging from the width of a single building to that of a whole block front, nay, even to a succession of blocks, as where the new East River bridge has made foot-room for itself on the Manhattan shore. The very spine of the island has been split by dynamite in preparing the way for rapid transit; and where excavations are being made in preparations for certain new buildings, it looks as if lyddite [artillery] shells have been exploded, ripping up tons of bed-rock and gravel.[2]

While Dallas was experiencing marked growth at the time, the building industry there could not compare with the remarkable transformation taking place in New York City. No other city could rival the pace.[3] Surely a chance to be part of such phenomenal redevelopment was enticing to an architect of Gordon's talents, and he availed himself of an opportunity when it came to him.

Exactly when Gordon and Alfred Zucker first came into contact with each other is unknown. Zucker was born in 1852 in Prussian Silesia and educated in Germany. He

immigrated to New York in 1873 and then joined the Office of the Supervising Architect of the United States Treasury. It is not inconceivable that he would have known Gordon's father if both worked in Washington, DC, at the same time. He practiced in the South between 1876 and 1882, and then returned to New York City. Zucker built what appeared to be a successful architectural practice in the years that followed.[4] Another possibility for contact with Gordon occurred in 1887, when Zucker provided plans for Joske's department store in San Antonio. The Joske brothers made routine buying trips to New York, where they likely retained the architect's services. Zucker may have visited San Antonio, but there is no record of such a trip and plans could have been drawn up without his visiting the site. Construction on the Joske emporium began early the next year under Wahrenberger & Beckmann's superintendence, but the project was suddenly and inexplicably abandoned. Immediately thereafter, Alfred Giles created new plans for the store, which were eventually realized. Zucker's notable commissions on Manhattan include the Hotel Majestic (1894), the Bolkenhayn Apartments (1895), and the New York University Building (1895).[5]

Regardless of whether he had met Gordon earlier, Zucker had been aware of the younger architect's published designs. He kept a clipping book, presumably for inspiration, of illustrations from architectural journals, and it contained some of Gordon's designs from the 1890s. Of course, the two also competed against each other for the Mississippi Capitol in 1900 and again in early 1902 for the Copiah County Courthouse. They likely discussed partnership while in Hazelhurst; and in March 1902 they signed a partnership agreement. By June Gordon moved his office to New York City, where the two billed themselves as associated architects. They occupied a suite of offices in the commercial section of the New York University Building.[6] What follows is Gordon's account of the partnership. While admittedly one-sided, it appears to be the only explanation available for Zucker's ultimate disappearance.

According to Gordon, he was induced to leave his successful practice in the South by Zucker, who misrepresented the current volume and importance of his business during the partnership negotiations. A rift soon developed between the two architects, likely a result of Gordon discovering the deceit. Rancor reached a point where Zucker initiated action to dissolve the partnership. Gordon retaliated with a $100,000 suit for damages due to fraud and misrepresentation. In the summer of 1903, one year after moving to New York, Gordon began an independent business and removed to an office at 949 Broadway. By March 30, 1904, Zucker fled to Montevideo, Uruguay, with his wife and family. As Gordon told it, in addition to evading his suit, Zucker also fled creditors and an arrest warrant. Zucker "removed all the partnership property he could take away of any value and . . . all of his household furniture and conveyed away his property." The firm's financial books were lost or destroyed as well. Gordon was appointed receiver of the firm's affairs by court order.[7]

Gordon's first years in New York proved tumultuous, but he had little time to doubt his decision to move north. Zucker left with work in progress that Gordon was then obligated to complete. This required capital to keep the office open, so he made the rounds of Manhattan banks, eventually finding one willing to extend him a line of credit. Zucker's unfinished work was a mixed blessing; Gordon had to shoulder its financial burden alone, but it enabled him to maintain the office and establish his own name in the highly competitive market.[8]

Meanwhile, the Gordon family entered New York society with flair probably aided by ancestral ties. Over time, Gordon joined several professional and social organizations where his jovial personality flourished. He belonged to the Elks for some time previous to the move, but the association led to significant fraternal commissions in the East. Daughter Lucy was enrolled in Mademoiselle Veltin's French School in New York and Mrs. Dow's School in Briarcliff.[9]

On January 1, 1905, Gordon entered into a partnership with Evarts Tracy and Egerton Swartwout. Of all his partnerships, Gordon must have found this one particularly rewarding. His new associates' formal education in architecture complemented his self-training and hard-won business acumen. Like Gordon, Tracy was an amiable and engaging fellow. Born in 1869 in Plainfield, New Jersey, he followed his 1890 graduation from Yale with three years' study at the Ecole des Beaux-Arts. He worked for a few years in the office of McKim, Mead & White before opening his own practice in 1896. Swartwout was born in Fort Wayne, Indiana, in 1870 and graduated from Yale with a bachelor of arts degree in 1891. Apparently his love of architecture first manifested itself in 1892 when he, too, began working for McKim, Mead & White. Swartwout remained there until 1900, when he entered into a partnership with Tracy. His later career and writings amply demonstrate his enthusiasm for his art and profession. The young architects were quite talented, but their most notable work was still ahead of them when they joined with Gordon. He later recalled the association: "I headed the firm of Gordon, Tracy and Swartwout, we occupied a whole floor in one of the large Fifth Avenue buildings, maintained a large and competent organization and were eminently successful."[10]

A superb example of their success is the Somerset County Courthouse in Somerville, New Jersey. After the Revolutionary War, the county seat moved to Raritan, where a courthouse was built. This courthouse, in turn, was replaced in 1798 by a combination courthouse and jail. The county used this new courthouse for more than a century, during which time it was radically modified and ancillary buildings were built around it. By 1905 these structures had fallen into disrepair and a grand jury recommended their replacement. (The site, known as the courthouse green, would become part of Somerville when the borough was chartered in 1909.)[11]

On February 14, 1905, the Somerset County Board of Chosen Freeholders unanimously voted to build a new courthouse and jail. The term *freeholder*, or landowner, is a remnant from the colonial era unique to New Jersey government. The board was originally comprised of representatives from each municipality within the county to collectively administer its business. Their numbers (reduced in recent years) proved unwieldy for projects such as courthouse construction. This led to a 1901 New Jersey State law that decreed Boards of Chosen Freeholders appoint a three-man commission from their ranks "to facilitate the acquirement of lands [not necessary in this case], and the erection of buildings for county purposes." Members' tenure was to last the duration of the project.[12]

Somerset's commission chose the firm of Gordon, Tracy and Swartwout as architect. While details of the selection process are not known, surely Gordon's past work and salesmanship were factors. A comprehensive scheme was developed for the courthouse green that included replacing the various county buildings and adding a public fountain. On July 20 Gordon and the commission presented his plans for the new jail to the board, which it approved. Positioning of the two-story jail anticipated the future courthouse to be built on axis to the south of it.[13]

Somerset's Board of Chosen Freeholders approved Gordon's plans for the courthouse on November 28, 1905. The process appears to have gone quite smoothly up to this point, with all board decisions being unanimous. Letting of the building contract did not come until the following May, however, suggesting that finalizing the details dragged on a bit. Construction went to Fissell & Wagner of New York City for $227,589.[14]

16.2.
Somerset County Courthouse,
Somerville, New Jersey (1906–9).
Gordon, Tracy and Swartwout,
architects. Gordon's 1905–6 jail
is visible on the right. *Photograph
ca. 1910, photographer unknown.*

Gordon's design for Somerset is a splendid example of Beaux-Arts elegance (fig. 16.2).[15] The cruciform plan is definitely Gordon's, with subtle details adding to the joy of the design, such as a running course that frames and sets off the three bays of the entrance. Main-floor windows are balustraded in High-Renaissance style to match other parts of the building. A relatively small and simple copper dome sits atop a high peristyle drum, and a gilded statue of *Justice* stands above it all. Its exterior material, entirely Alabama white marble, is one of the finest ever used for a Gordon courthouse.

Somerset's central portico provides a grand entry like that of McLennan County. Gordon outdid his earlier work, however, with a complex flight of stairs that breaks to offer front and side access. This too was executed in marble and augmented by balustrades and cast iron lamps. The ascent leads to a main entrance sheltered beneath an austere pediment supported by four Ionic columns. Similar porticos form balconies on the perpendicular east and west wings.

Passage through the vestibule leads to an octagonal rotunda whose elaboration marks a major step in Gordon's design evolution (fig. 16.3). Eight Corinthian columns run the three-story height to a coffered interior dome. These columns are scagliola (plaster treated to appear as marble), but much real marble appears in the interior as well. All of the public halls feature marble floors and wainscot, the stairs marble treads. It is a magnificent space leading to a stained glass oculus at the center of the inner dome that opened to allow heat to escape. As in his earlier work, Gordon's plan facilitated passive ventilation. Two walls set at 45-degree angles opposite the main entrance

16.3.
Somerset County Courthouse,
rotunda. *2001 photograph.*

each open to stairways and secondary entrances. On the main (second) floor, these
stairs flank the doors to the courtroom, which is accessed through another vestibule,
isolating it from any distracting noise in the rotunda. The two-story courtroom is
also octangular, with vaults springing from the chamfers to lend a curve to the ceiling
as it leads to a magnificent stained glass skylight (fig. 16.4). Detailing throughout the
interior maintains the high standards initiated outside.

16.4.
Somerset County Courthouse,
district courtroom. *2001*
photograph.

All records indicate Gordon led the project, and a cornerstone that credits "James Riely Gordon, Tracy and Swartwout, Architects" attests to this. He worked with the commission and presented the designs to the board. His plan approaches near perfection here in the Beaux-Arts idiom. Contributions by his talented partners may be present in the details, however. For example, the exterior arcade of courtroom windows recalls the façade of McKim, Mead & White's Boston Public Library, which was under construction during both Tracy's and Swartwout's employ with that firm. If ever a county courthouse deserved the appellation "temple of justice" for its architecture alone, this one does.

Somerset County's courthouse was dedicated in March 1909 with a ceremony that drew thousands to the green. Those involved with the project, including the architect, noted with pride that every dollar expended had gone into this splendid structure; it was considered remarkable that none had been diverted by graft.[16] In 1910 the architectural composition of the green came to completion with the installation of the Lord Memorial Fountain, designed by John Russell Pope, on the corner.

Although the jail is now gone, the Somerset County Courthouse remains a precious and stunning example of exquisitely rendered Beaux-Arts architecture. While his partners surely contributed, this triumph belongs to Gordon. With it, he introduced the East to his expertise in courthouses. At the same time he demonstrated that troubles associated with his move to New York were behind him.

In February 1907, early in the construction of the Somerset courthouse, Gordon secured two more significant public projects for the firm. The first was for Maryland's Garrett County, a resort destination nestled in a region of the Alleghenies known as the "glade country." The previous April, the state legislature had passed a bill enabling Garrett County to sell bonds to replace its long-inadequate courthouse in the county seat of Oakland. To shepherd the project, the act stipulated the appointment of a courthouse commission consisting of the three state judges of the fourth judicial circuit, three members of the Garrett County Board of Commissioners, and five citizen taxpayers from the county.[17]

County voters approved the bond sale in November 1906, and the courthouse commission met on December 17. Among the administrative and procedural details discussed, the members agreed to solicit preliminary courthouse plans from five architects and firms. Exactly how these were chosen is unclear, but the commission appears to have been well informed; in addition to Gordon, Tracy and Swartwout, the list included the Baltimore firms of Baldwin & Pennington and Wyatt & Nolting—both having notable public building experience. When commissioners reviewed submissions the following February 1, they also considered entries by two architects that had not been on the invitation list.[18]

The commission reviewed the plans—all entered under a nom de plume—in private for a day and a half and then took a straw vote. They identified three favorite designs and revealed these finalists by opening envelopes containing the submitting architects' names. They were Baldwin & Pennington, J. Charles Fulton, and Gordon, Tracy and Swartwout. The commission offered any finalists still in Oakland that day the opportunity to come and explain his entry. Gordon and Fulton were both present and each allowed an hour before the commission. During his say, Gordon assured the commission that his design could be built for $70,000 or less, excluding furnishings. To guarantee this, he vowed not to hold the commission in any way indebted to him should they choose his design but then fail to receive satisfactory bids within that amount. Afterward the members took another vote, and Gordon's plan was the unanimous choice. The other invited architects received $125 each for their troubles.[19]

Gordon returned to Oakland on March 20 when his plans were formally adopted, pending further modifications ordered that day by the courthouse commission. On May 13 the construction contract went to William A. Liller of Keyser, West Virginia, for $59,962. A separate contract for heating and plumbing went to A. D. Naylor of Oakland for $5,822.[20]

The site for Garrett County's courthouse rises on a slope from Third Street at a fairly steep angle. Gordon set the building back, up on the hill, and designed terraced landscaping with a flight of steps leading from the street to the first floor of the entrance pavilion (fig. 16.5).[21] Garrett's main entry, therefore, is through a ground-floor arcade beneath a columned portico, somewhat akin to the Arizona Capitol. The low

16.5.
Garrett County Courthouse,
Oakland, Maryland (1907–8).
Gordon, Tracy and Swartwout,
architects. *Photograph ca. 1948,
photographer unknown.*

dome also recalls the design as executed in Phoenix. Like the Somerset courthouse, Garrett is cruciform with a main entrance flanked by perpendicular side porticos and the main courtroom opposite, across an octagonal rotunda.

With its smaller budget, the Garrett design differed significantly from Somerset. Its exterior is Indiana limestone for the first floor, columns, and trim. The second and third floors are buff-colored pressed brick. Interior trim is wood and no columns are used in the rotunda. The interior dome is lit by oval windows that are unique in Gordon's opus. Seating less than three hundred, the district courtroom is relatively small. This was a deliberate but controversial decision. Speaking of the courtroom at Garrett's dedication on December 7, 1908, Chief Judge A. Hunter Boyd noted that too much access to the judicial process could have a deleterious effect. Sensational crimes drew large numbers of spectators, including the young, to trials where lurid details were necessarily aired. A school of thought argued for smaller courtrooms, where access to such trials and their damage to public morals could be limited.[22]

The final cost of the building was $79, 949.31. Increases over the original contracts arose from modifications to the plans and specifications that the commission approved. These included changing the exterior columns from wood to stone and flooring the rotunda with marble. To reduce the overall cost, the commission abandoned the original plan to use custom furnishings designed by the architect and employed stock furnishings instead.[23]

Gordon's courthouse for Garrett County served relatively unchanged for over sixty years (fig. 16.6). A continually increasing bureaucracy demanded more space, however. Rather than destroy the structure for a larger replacement or remove the county administration to available space outside town, the county executed a creative but problematic alternative. Beginning in 1977, building began for an addition that houses some county offices and the jail. Built below and in front of the old courthouse, the

addition replaced Gordon's landscaped terraces. The roof of this addition now serves as a courtyard on level with the courthouse entrance. Other offices are located in a further addition behind the courthouse, where a jail previously stood.[24] This solution deprived downtown Oakland of an open, park-like courthouse setting, but it preserved Gordon's fine building for future generations.

16.6.
Garrett County Courthouse, telephoto view. *2001 photograph.*

CHAPTER SEVENTEEN

Bergen and Madison

The Board of Chosen Freeholders for New Jersey's Bergen County voted to build a new courthouse and jail at Hackensack in December 1905. In accordance with the same 1901 state legislative act that governed the Somerset project, the board appointed a three-man committee from its members to facilitate the process. Authorized by the board, this triumvirate, known as the Bergen County Public Building Commission, was to issue bonds to pay for the endeavor. Unlike their counterparts in Somerset, the Bergen commissioners interpreted the act as giving them broad powers, which they soon asserted through unilateral site, building, and financing decisions. Apprehensive of this assumption of power, the remainder of the board sought to regain control through litigation that reached the New Jersey Supreme Court. A July 1906 decision favored the commission and seemingly established its carte blanche.[1] Appraisals of the commission's work are mixed.

The commission determined nothing of the old structure could be utilized and chose a location for the new buildings at the corner of Main and Camden Streets, known as the "Oritani site" after the social and athletic club that stood there. Although somewhat removed from the current government center, arguments in favor of this site included a relatively low water table, proximity to rail service, and a lot size that allowed the jail to be discreetly located behind the courthouse and well off Main Street. Still, the choice was controversial as the board and at least one local newspaper favored using the site of old county buildings.[2]

Commission members inspected several courthouses and jails and, in December, invited four architects to compete for Bergen's buildings. The four were to offer designs for a courthouse and jail that would cost no more than $600,000 to build. With authors identified only by numbers to ensure secrecy, the commission opened submissions on February 26, 1907. They put the plans on display for public review two days later. Early consensus deemed plan number three as the superior entry.[3]

This design was Gordon's (fig. 17.1). Although it was entered under the name of Gordon, Tracy and Swartwout, the firm had officially dissolved by that time.[4] According to Gordon, he and his partners had agreed to disband "probably several months

17.1.
Bergen County Courthouse, 1907
competition drawing by Gordon,
Tracy and Swartwout. *Courtesy
Lucy Virginia Gordon Ralston.*

before" the Bergen competition "but we had a great deal of work at hand [so] we dissolved the partnership and then stayed together and had our offices together for nearly
a year after."[5] Although somewhat unorthodox, this explains why Gordon's submission was initially credited to the firm.

Gordon, Tracy and Swartwout produced some excellent designs during its short
duration. The Home Club in New York and the Connecticut Savings Bank in New
Haven (both 1906) are but two of the firm's notable structures that merit more attention than can be given here. The parting was amicable; Gordon later said he withdrew
so that he could maintain more direct control over his public building projects. Afterward, he relied on specialists whom he retained as needed for assistance. This was not
an unusual arrangement for individual architects of the day. Operating without the
mutual support of partners, they maintained relatively small offices that were enlarged
or reduced as the work at hand warranted. Another notable example of such a practice
was Cass Gilbert's.[6]

Despite the widespread praise for Gordon's design, the commission sent all four
entries to New Jersey's state architect for his appraisal. While he preferred another
plan, the state architect found Gordon's to be suitable also. In mid-May 1907 the commission formally announced the selection of Gordon's entry. By this time, however,
the Board of Chosen Freeholders had launched another effort to regain control of the
project. It withheld funds while lobbying state legislators to amend the 1901 law. For
its part, the commission sued the board, and the project was halted until some sort

of resolution could be achieved. Gordon was paid $600, as were the other competing firms, with the county being under no further obligation to the architect.[7]

While officials in Bergen County worked out their differences, Gordon found another courthouse opportunity in central New York State. This arose from a struggle for the seat of Madison County. The town of Morrisville, in the southern portion of the county, had hosted the government since 1816. By the end of the century, growth of northern districts argued for a change and communities there maneuvered for the designation. By 1907, when the political will to relocate was ripe, the two main contenders were Canastota and Oneida. Separately, however, neither town could muster enough votes to wrench the government from Morrisville. Promoters of the two communities instead compromised and pooled their support in favor of the village of Wampsville.

Besides its location on the rail line between Canastota and Oneida, and an offer of free land, there was little about tiny Wampsville to recommend it as a county seat. Trains did not even stop there. Nevertheless, the village won a county vote on November 6, 1907. The Madison County Board of Supervisors (New York State's term for the elected body overseeing county business) appointed a five-member building committee to bring a new courthouse and jail to fruition on the chosen site, a scrub apple orchard.[8]

Members of the committee visited recently constructed buildings in other counties, including Somerset, and consulted numerous architects on the style and arrangements for the buildings contemplated. The committee then invited a number of reputable architects to submit designs and specifications. While seemingly diligent in their duty for their county, committeemen displayed little regard for the architects. The committee required competitors to prepare entries at their own expense (estimated at $400) and to put up $1,000 to guarantee their design could be built for the specified amount (placed at $150,000 for both buildings). It offered no compensation for the solicited designs that were not selected.[9]

Nine architects and firms responded with designs in late March 1908, but the committee advised the Board of Supervisors that none of the submissions were entirely satisfactory. It recommended, however, that two of the competitors develop further designs: Gordon, for the courthouse, and Poughkeepsie architect William J. Beardsley, for the jail. The committee considered their submissions to be the best, but also in need of some modification to meet the county's needs.[10]

Modifications to Gordon's design were likely minor since he returned to Madison County with completed plans and 459 pages of specifications by the end of May. W. H. Fissell and Company received the $107,584 building contract. A separate contract for the jail construction went to Marcellus, Ballard & Johnson of Oneida for $31,279.[11] Work began shortly after the contracts were signed, and 5 percent commissions for Gordon and Beardsley suggest each superintended the construction of their own designs.

The orientation of the buildings was an early source of controversy. The property sits east of the former Lenox Basin and Cowaselon Valley Road (since renamed Court Street). Tracks for the Oneida Railway ran beyond the fields to the north. The building committee determined that the courthouse's main entrance should face north toward the somewhat distant tracks, with its side to the street, on the premise that the majority of people would see the building from train windows, not the curb. In addition, many believed a boulevard running between the tracks and the courthouse would eventually be built from Oneida to Canastota, validating the northern orientation. A number of other justifications were also offered including noise abatement and sun exposure (north light being deemed more agreeable for the clerical work done in offices). Another benefit of the courthouse's northern orientation was that it allowed the residential portion of the jail structure behind it to face the street. This left the detention area on the other end, where, in the words of the building committee chairman, "its necessarily grim details will be least obtrusive." Beardsley designed his combined jail and sheriff's residence to be in harmony with Gordon's courthouse and of the same materials. The architects also coordinated their efforts so the buildings could be connected by tunnel.[12]

Madison's north entrance is a novel entry in Gordon's repertoire (fig. 17.2).[13] A cluster of three columns at both corners of the portico lends a sort of *in antis* effect to the pair in the middle. These stone columns, topped by Composite capitals, support a stone pediment with a cornucopia relief symbolizing the agricultural wealth of the county. The portico is on a short wing of a cruciform building with relatively long

17.2.
Madison County Courthouse, Wampsville, New York (1908–9). James Riely Gordon, architect. The jail by William J. Beasley is visible on the right. *Photograph ca. 1911, photographer unknown.*

227

wings flanking to the east and west for a total frontage of 148 feet. It reflects Gordon's Capitol Plan from McLennan, but Madison presents a more horizontal sweep: most of the structure is two stories above a low basement. A gallery floor further elevates the courtroom wing behind, recalling the Copiah Plan. From grade level the building rises 38 feet to the parapet top. A dome at the crossing rises another 24 feet, and a statue of *Justice* caps the structure at 72 feet. Ironwork and brick provides the structure and pressed brick with limestone and terra-cotta trim sheath the exterior.

Upon entering Madison's courthouse one passes through a glass-enclosed vestibule to a two-story, octagonal rotunda that is surprisingly intimate for a formal public space (fig. 17.3). This effect is due to its width—25 feet with a wide second-story balcony cantilevering from the walls. The low internal dome seems just above the circular opening to the next floor. Its art glass central oculus and surrounding oval lights bathe the area in soft, natural light.

Opposite the entrance is the supervisors' chamber, arranged as an auditorium providing a forum for county business with seating for 128 spectators, including a small balcony. On the floor above this is the district courtroom, where the elevated judge's stand occupies the southern end. Following Gordon's design, jurors sat directly in front of the judge with their backs to the spectators, who were beyond a semicircular table for lawyers (fig. 17.4). Thus, the judge had an unobstructed view of the witness, jury, attorneys, and spectators. Furthermore, from this vantage point the judge had no clear view out the east and west wall windows to distract him from the proceedings. Likewise, jurors were not distracted by spectators. Although previously employed by Gordon, this arrangement was unprecedented in the state of New York. The main floor originally had 133 oak folding seats for spectators, with 72 more in the Tuscan column–supported balcony.

Gordon placed the grand jury room in the north wing above the vestibule. County and court offices, witness rooms, a law library, a supreme courtroom, and lavatories occupied the east and west wings. Fifty-four rooms in the courthouse were designated for office or court use. All had at least one window to the outside. The building committee chairman claimed, "No other building in central New York approaches it for brilliancy of natural light and easy ventilation."[14] The floor and wainscoting of the rotunda is comprised of Tennessee and clouded blue marble. Dressed oak provides the trim throughout the building. Soft colors were specified for interior walls to reduce glare and enhance the sense of intimacy.

Although there was some grumbling about the project, most thought the taxpayer's money was spent wisely to the credit of all involved. Madison County took possession of the completed courthouse on January 1, 1910. As summed up by the building committee chairman, "in two years there has been erected a Court House and Jail second to none in any rural county, absolutely fireproof, of strikingly handsome

17.3.
Madison County Courthouse, rotunda with the original statue. *Justice* restored and relocated from dome. *2001 photograph.*

17.4.
Madison County Courthouse, courtroom. *2001 photograph.*

appearance and as substantial as the pyramids. There isn't an ounce of shoddy in the whole enterprise; there has been no hint of 'graft.' No litigation has occurred to cause expense or delay." Two and a half years later, Madison County citizens saw Gordon's invitation to compete for the prestigious New York County Courthouse as further proof of their wise choice in architects.[15]

While the years since have brought some change, the spirit of Gordon's court-house remains largely intact. A complex of county buildings has grown up around it, including a new courthouse. These have no architectural affinity with Gordon's work, although one, unfortunately, connects to its east wing. Beardsley's jail was razed and a war memorial built in its place. The hoped-for Oneida-to-Canastota Boulevard was never built, and the old Madison County Courthouse now faces a New York State thru-way. It is currently owned by the state.

As the Madison project sailed smoothly toward completion, the struggle for con-trol of the Bergen County Courthouse and Jail continued to play out in the New Jersey courts and legislature. Both institutions ultimately declined to tinker with the 1901 Act, however, and the power of the Bergen County Public Building Commission was again affirmed. Nonetheless, a slight reconciliation followed in Hackensack. As it turned out, the sale price for the proposed Oritani site was too high even for the spendthrift com-missioners. On December 2, 1908, they yielded to community pressure to utilize the county property on the green and acquire adjacent lots through condemnation.

With the decision made, the commission returned to Gordon, who agreed to revise his plans to fit the new, narrower site. Changes included orienting the jail alongside the courthouse, reducing the depth of the wings flanking the entrance, and increasing the length of the rear wing. As Gordon revised the plans, county engineer Ralph D. Earle oversaw work on the village green property such as surveying, land-scaping, rerouting a stream, and sewer improvements. The commission paid Earle for his courthouse work on top of his county salary.[16]

Despite its authority and the years invested in the project, the commission would not agree to a definite set of specifications. This did not stop it from voting to solicit courthouse construction bids, however. Contractors were instructed to prepare a "base bid" on one set of plans and specifications for a sandstone building. This was to be supplemented by fifty-one "alternate" propositions encompassing variations of building methods and materials. Four firms submitted proposals and security deposits on October 7, 1909. The commissioners charged Gordon and county engineer Earle with the formidable task of determining the lowest bid from the multitude of variable figures. Suspiciously, the commission returned the deposits of two of the bidders just four days later, before the official tabulations were in. On November 1 the commission announced that "W. H. Fissell & Co. were not the lowest bidders," and eliminated them in favor of the John T. Brady Company of New York.[17]

17.5.
Bergen County Courthouse
and jail (left), Hackensack,
New Jersey (1909–12). James
Riely Gordon, architect. *Detail
of ca. 1913 photograph by Haines
Photo Company, courtesy Prints &
Photographs Division, Library of
Congress.*

Shortly thereafter, the commission conferred with the local bar association and others concerning the choice of building materials. They decided upon a marble super-structure above a granite foundation. Extrapolations were made from the morass of figures in Brady's bid, arriving at an estimated cost of $827,672.25, and the construction contract was signed on November 15. Gordon was to receive 6 percent on construction costs for his plans and superintendence, which was the current rate recommended by the AIA. In a questionable yet familiar move, the commission also paid Earle an additional 1 percent for engineering inspection and for services as clerk of the works, both customarily the job of a superintendent.[18]

As the project moved forward, Gordon recommended that concrete pedestal piles be used in the foundation system rather than the type specified in the base bid. Other changes, such as using marble sculpture instead of zinc, were made as the work progressed. On January 6, 1910, the architect submitted plans for the Bergen County Jail, which the committee approved. Contractors again had to deal with a bid package that involved "alternates." In June the jail work was also awarded to Brady.[19]

Gordon's Bergen County Courthouse constitutes another superb entry in his opus and is in the best Beaux-Arts style. He aptly described it as "a massive, yet graceful, classic design of the Italian School."[20] Again Gordon serves up his Capitol Plan with a northern entrance pavilion (fig. 17.5). Wings to the east, west, and south are all seven bays in length. The structure sits on a high basement required by a high water table. Both the basement and first floor are treated with stonework rusticated in horizontal bands. The second and third floors are marked with windowed bays framed by engaged Ionic columns. An entablature topped by a balustrade encircles the building. In a departure for the architect, no pediments interrupt its run. A copper dome sits atop a peristyle drum at the crossing. Gordon returned to an *in antis* central pavilion for a monumental main entrance that boldly relies on stark planes. The porch is recessed behind paired Ionic columns and above a trio of arched entrance portals. An expansive series of steps and landings leads from the street level, up the terraced lot, to the main entrance.

17.6.
Bergen County Courthouse, statuary by Johannes Sophus Gelert. *2001 photograph.*

An exemplary sculpture program enhances this outstanding design. Most of this work is by Johannes Sophus Gelert (1852–1923), an eminent, German-born, Danish-educated sculptor whose work also graces Cass Gilbert's 1907 United States Custom House, New York. Gelert's contribution in Hackensack includes *History* and *Law* flanking the main entrance. Directly above, his allegorical groupings of *Truth, Attended by Justice and Integrity* and *Honor, with Law and Order*, bracket the top corners of the pavilion (fig. 17.6). These are all freestanding compositions carved from Italian Carrara marble. He also designed the figure *Enlightenment Giving Power* that tops the dome. Metallic eagles mark the other corners of the structure. Beneath the dome, a bas-relief frieze encircles the drum with forty panels evoking, in Gordon's words, "the march of progress that has been so wonderful in Bergen County."[21] There are other details, including lion head keystones for the main entrance arcade. Collectively, this is as fine a sculptural overture in the Beaux-Arts idiom as Ellis's carvings are in the Richardsonian Romanesque.

Gordon delivered on the interior as well. The rotunda, a 45-foot octagon running up from the basement level, carries the elegance of his Somerset design to a grander

scale with a more varied programme (fig. 17.7). A relatively small opening between the
basement and first floor is circular and ringed by an iron balustrade. At the second
floor, the opening widens to an octagon lined with a green marble band footing a
white marble balustrade. The opening becomes circular again at the third floor with
an iron railing. Walls with arched portals provide a visual foundation to the rotunda
scheme on the executive-oriented first floor. These give way to paired Corinthian
columns that rise the two stories of the judicial floors. Green marble plinths base the
scagliola columns. Coffers line the interior dome, leading to an art glass oculus.

Two-story courtrooms occupy three wings of the judicial floor (figs. 17.8 and 17.9).
As Gordon put it, these are suited with their own soundproof vestibules so "deep or
shrill voiced Attorneys arguing a case to a jury in one court chamber" cannot disturb
proceedings in the other two. As at Madison, all of the court seating is oriented to

17.8.
Bergen County Courthouse, state supreme courtroom. *Photograph ca. 1912, courtesy Alexander Architectural Archive, University of Texas, Austin.*

avoid potentially distracting views from the windows. Here the architect explained that "where judges, the jury or the audience face the windows, they cannot see distinctly and the glare is frequently blinding and injurious to a terrible degree." This apparently concerned Gordon in the more northern latitudes, where the sun tracks lower in the sky, than it did when he was designing southern courthouses. Acoustics continued to be a virtue in his courtrooms. He eliminated "any square corners in the main outline and provide[d] a coved dome ceiling to give impetus to the voice, that it may travel throughout the chamber without resonance or confusion of echoes."[22]

A tempest that engulfed Gordon blew up around the Bergen County Courthouse and Jail project before it was finished. With costs now exceeding $1,500,000, controversy over the conduct of the Bergen County Public Building Commission, the three-man panel appointed with sweeping authority to shepherd the project, had never abated. Allegations of unlawful expenditures and gross extravagance culminated in action by the New Jersey General Assembly on April 5, 1911. It appointed a five-man committee, chaired by former Bergen assemblyman William H. Hinners, to investigate the work of the building commission. Popularly known as the Hinners Committee, it

was empowered to subpoena and examine testimony and documents associated with
the project and then report back to the General Assembly.[23]

Gordon testified before the committee in October. From his remarks he appears
to have taken the matter seriously and cooperated fully, producing and explaining
requested documents. While straightforward in defending his own actions and fees,
his explanation of the complex computations of the bids as required by the building
commission became quite convoluted. Tedious in sections, Gordon's testimony documents some of the minutiae involved in public building design and superintendence.
At times he appears guarded, as if to avoid sounding critical of some of the questionable decisions of his client, the building commission. This being said, not all parties

were as cooperative as he. Representatives of the contractor, the John T. Brady Company, ignored subpoenas for testimony and documents.[24]

Among the irregularities documented in the Hinners Committee report was the building commission's augmentation of Ralph Earle's $5,000 county engineer's salary with $12,959 for his courthouse work over the years. In a seeming conflict of interest, the commission also paid the county attorney $12,315 in fees on top of his annual salary of $5,500. After an examination of labyrinthine construction bids with their "alternative" prices, the committee determined that the lowest construction bid was that of W. H. Fissell and Company. This cast a shadow on Gordon, since the calculations he made with Earle were used in awarding the contract to the John T. Brady Company. Hinners's committee did not recommend that any action be taken against any of the parties involved but advised the 1901 Act empowering the Bergen County Public Building Commission be amended to prevent future abuses.[25]

Reform had by now become a key issue in Bergen County politics, and some saw the failure of Democrat Hinners to prosecute Democratic officials as a whitewash. Particularly controversial was the pass given to double-dipping in the county coffers. The many court challenges to the courthouse committee's hegemony had left it virtually bulletproof, but it seems other culpable officials also escaped accountability. With the agitation for reform, Republicans were elected to political power and pressed for further action. The county began occupying the courthouse in February 1912, and that April a grand jury began another investigation into allegations already addressed (to some degree) by Hinners. In September, after another set of experts reexamined the bid process, the jurors concluded that Fissell's bid could be calculated as being some $70,000 lower than Brady's and, as a result, accused Gordon and Earle of criminal activity. That said, the grand jury report also spoke glowingly of Gordon's services, adding that his fee was reasonable. Furthermore, it found Brady's work often exceeded specifications and was likely a bargain. Still, the jurors deduced that a crime had been committed, but by this point the statute of limitations had expired on any offenses dating to the bid selection. The grand jury concluded its five-month, often self-contradictory, probe with a recommendation for *further* investigation into the matter.[26]

Despite the grand jury's praise for Gordon's professional services, its allegation of criminal activity cast another cloud over the architect's reputation. He was traveling in Europe and therefore unable to provide an immediate response when the report became public. During his absence, his general manager refuted the charges in a letter to the editor of the *Hackensack Republican*. Edward A. Ward put forth the reasoned argument that Gordon, having had no previous dealings with Brady's company, had no apparent cause to favor that builder in the contract award. If anything, it seems he would more naturally favor Fissell's company, which at the time had completed Somerset and was just finishing Madison. In addition, knowing of the grand jury's actions,

Gordon hired a firm of certified public accountants to independently review the Bergen bids. The accountants reaffirmed that the Brady bid was lowest, establishing that, at the very least, the point was arguable. Regardless, Ward continued, the award of the contract was ultimately the responsibility of the building commission.[27]

When Gordon returned in October, he denounced the grand jury report as unjust and cruel, vowing to take steps to rectify the matter. Confident in his own conduct, he requested the New York Society of Architects, to which he belonged, investigate from a professional standpoint. He boldly declared that "if his charge is true, I am unworthy of your membership."[28]

In contrast, Ralph Earle appears to have limited his defense to condemning his accusers. It is likely that the double-dipping county engineer was the real target of what can be fairly called a smear campaign. While Bergen Republicans clearly sought political gain by fanning the flames of the scandalous courthouse project, they seem to have been reluctant to declare war on all the Democrats involved or to forever stigmatize the county's fine edifice. Hence, they offered the somewhat contradictory praise to the work of Gordon and Brady. Earle appears to have been another matter, however. He was a zealously partisan Democrat who had been particularly bellicose in his denigration of Republican reform efforts. If nothing else, the grand jury report served to undermine his credibility.[29] In support of this hypothesis, the controversy seems to have completely dissipated after the November 1912 elections, and no further action was taken.

Bergen County's majestic courthouse still stands, as does Gordon's brick, five-story, medieval-flavored jail. The composition has been altered since the 1930s by a four-story administration building that connects to both the jail and the courthouse. The newer structure continues the courthouse's style. Aside from the addition, the exteriors of the jail and courthouse are intact. The jail has since been taken over for offices, but the splendid interior of the courthouse is largely preserved. WPA-sponsored murals depicting the history of law were added in the state supreme courtroom in 1933. While competently executed, they run contrary to the architect's goal of limiting courtroom distractions.

CHAPTER EIGHTEEN

The New York Competition

A. D. F. Hamlin succeeded William Ware as the head of Columbia University's School of Architecture and also was appointed consulting architect to the New York County Court House Board. In 1910 the board envisioned building a new structure with up to fifty-five courtrooms. "If the projected plans for the new Court House in this city are carried out," Hamlin predicted, "New York will in the near future have the greatest Court House in the world."[1] Of course, the idea of designing it would tantalize any architect who made such buildings his specialty. Gordon took the concept even further: he envisioned it also being the tallest building on the planet.

New York County's new courthouse was intended to replace the old court building at 52 Chambers Street, which dates to 1862. The old courthouse was a project of city supervisor William Marcy ("Boss") Tweed, whose name became synonymous with corrupt civic government. Fraudulent costs for its construction and furnishings reached such astounding levels that critic Montgomery Schuyler condemned it as "the pretext for the most audacious of the robberies of the Tweed Ring."[2] It became scornfully known as the "Tweed Courthouse," and few New Yorkers lamented the notion of replacing it when the judicial class began agitating for new quarters around 1900. A formidable civic group fiercely opposed any further building on the surrounding City Hall Park, however (fig. 18.1).

In 1903 the state legislature passed an act creating the Court House Board to select the site and build the structure. This board was barred from proposing any plan that took up any more space in City Hall Park than was currently occupied by the Tweed Courthouse. Finding this too restrictive, the board proposed five other sites over the following years, only to have them all rejected. Finally, on February 17, 1910, the law was amended to permit further development of the park. The board officially chose the site eleven days later, a decision which met with immediate opposition for encroaching on the park. In response, consultant Hamlin offered his opinion that a new building, with a foundation of not more than 93,750 square feet and a height of not more than six stories (about 138 feet), would suit the county and the site. At more than double the footprint of the Tweed Courthouse, he believed this would minimize

encroachment and not visually overpower the nearby City Hall. The protests continued unabated, however.[3]

Seeing this controversy as an opportunity, Gordon stepped into the fray with his own solution. With a footprint *half* the size of the Tweed Courthouse, his proposal actually *increased* park space while his building would soar into the sky (fig. 18.2). It was so radical it received widespread newspaper and journal notice.

He unveiled the design on April 30, 1910, accompanied by a lengthy explanation printed in the *New York American* the next day. Gordon envisioned four great clustered

18.1.
City Hall Park, New York, New York. (A) New York County Courthouse ("Tweed Courthouse"), (B) New York City Hall. *Unidentified postcard view, ca. 1915.*

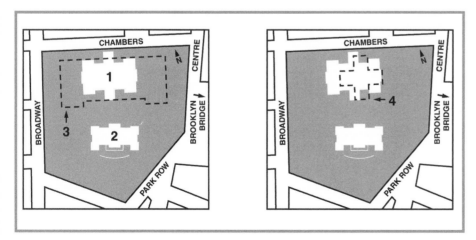

18.2.
Two plans of City Hall Park showing (1) New York County Courthouse ("Tweed Courthouse"), (2) New York City Hall, (3) outline of new courthouse as suggested by A. D. F. Hamlin, and (4) outline of approximate size and location of new courthouse as proposed by Gordon in 1910. *Illustrations based upon drawing published in the* New York Times, *March 13, 1910.*

"Pillars of Justice" standing on a 24-foot-tall plinth in the shape of a Greek cross (fig. 18.3). This base would house the county administration. Above, Doric columns, each 520 feet high and 65 feet in diameter, would emanate from the corners of a square central shaft. Gordon planned for these to contain "sixty circular chambers, jury and accessories, with windows in the flutes." He saw these two-story courtrooms as being acoustically correct (fig. 18.4). A law library would be housed above their capitals, in the 130-foot frieze and cornice sections. This would give way to a 144-foot pedestal section with judges' chambers topped by a huge, 192-foot statue of *Justice* holding aloft a combination of the traditional scales of justice and a Roman torch.

The rise from the ground level of City Hall Park to the top of the torch would be an astounding 1,064 feet. This would surpass the world's then-tallest building, the Metropolitan Life Tower, by some 400 feet. It would even best the Woolworth Building, then still on the drawing board, by over 270 feet. The statue alone would be 40 feet taller than the *Statue of Liberty* in the harbor. Functional as well as symbolic, the statue was to conceal a smokestack running up through its upraised arm to the torch. The torch would feature a 10-foot sculpted flame "formed by numerous electric lights arranged on automatic switches . . . to produce the flame effect." By night this would be visible "throughout Manhattan, for a long distance in New York State, Long Island, New Jersey, and Connecticut, at the same time [be] the beacon light for vessels" at sea.

Such an ambitious structure raised safety and practical concerns, which its architect answered preemptively. Gordon acknowledged that wind resistance was as important as load bearing factors in a building of these dimensions. He explained that the contour of the four round columns would provide bracing and counter-bracing on all sides of his courthouse. With confidence he invited the city's engineers to examine his plans. Accommodating people in such a mammoth structure would be a challenge in itself. Twenty-six elevators would provide vertical transportation. Subways could be built to connect the basement with the Brooklyn Bridge terminal on the east, and all parts of Manhattan, the Bronx, and New Jersey on the west.[4]

Aware that the novelty of this proposal alone would be cause for objection, Gordon included an appeal to professional, civic, and national pride, as well as some flattery for politicians, with his description:

> This would be a monument not only to justice, but to American progressiveness: to the present administration, the Courthouse Board and to the skill of the American engineer, architect and builder. It would be recognized the world over as the tallest, most unique and stupendous structure of even this most progressive age; typical of America in general and New York in particular; possible in no other city in the world and as truly American as it is radical and as logical as it is either.[5]

18.3.
Gordon's "Pillars of Justice"
proposal for the New York
County Courthouse. *1910
promotional composite photograph,
courtesy Alexander Architectural
Archive, University of Texas, Austin.*

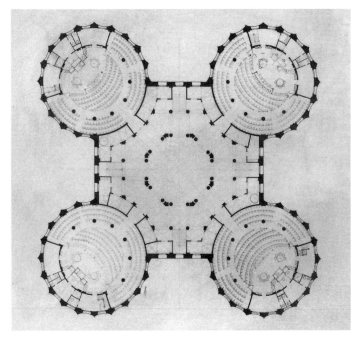

18.4.
"Pillars of Justice" proposal, typical courtroom floor plan. 1910 office drawing by James Riely Gordon. *Courtesy Alexander Architectural Archive, University of Texas, Austin.*

As audacious as it may seem, Gordon's New York County Courthouse proposal is every bit a considered, practical answer to its specialized conditions as his Signature Plan was to the Texas county seat in the nineteenth century. Foremost among these conditions were real estate restraints: property values on Manhattan Island were already at a premium and the "Pillars of Justice" design saved millions of dollars with its relatively small footprint. Its exceptional height accessed natural lighting and purer air, which were also becoming precious commodities, while at the same time raising the courts above the noise and dust of the streets.

Bold, personal, and picturesque interpretations of prevailing styles had also been a hallmark of Gordon's best work throughout his career. For this new proposal, he seems to be taking nineteenth-century skyscraper aesthetics and Beaux-Arts styling to their logical conclusions. Many critics held that a properly composed skyscraper should follow the lead of a classic column by having a visual base (defined by street-level functions), a shaft (of a number of essentially identical floors), and a capital (a cornice marking the vertical termination). Likewise, freestanding columns as monuments were an ancient idea seeing a revival with Beaux-Arts classicism. As a recent scholar noted, Gordon "usurped the commercial skyscraper form, literally translating the column metaphor . . . to give his work predominance in the area and to distinguish his 'Tower of Justice' from the commercial skyscrapers."[6] While perhaps too literal for some, it remains an intriguing concept.

Gordon had pondered such a skyscraper for some eleven years. Among the drawings from his office is a set he called his "Monument Plan," a sixty-story building featuring four gigantic, somewhat overwrought, Corinthian columns rising from a square base (fig. 18.5). Atop this Gordon placed a statue of a US soldier in a Spanish-American War–era uniform, with saber held high and a pistol at his side. From its base to the top of the soldier's hat, the statue would stand 96 feet. Gordon also envisioned heroic statuary on the thirteenth- and fifty-fifth-floor levels. Floors within the columns were divided into wedge-shaped compartments, indicating the building would serve a function other than a courthouse. While these drawings are undated, their captions match word-for-word those on a copyright application Gordon filed in December 1898.[7] This demonstrates the architect's remarkable vision. In 1898 the world's tallest building was twenty stories, which Gordon's Monument Plan would have exceeded threefold. Obviously ahead of its time, the idea sat among his papers until the New York County Courthouse project, with its severely restricted site, presented an appropriate application.

Another drawing, catalogued as "Absurd Interpretation of New York Courthouse," is also among Gordon's papers (fig. 18.6). Again, it shows a tall structure comprised of four columns, this time topped by a statue of a dapper man in modern attire. According to his granddaughter, this is a depiction of a corrupt politician flush with ill-gotten money.[8] This particular drawing seems like much effort in a frivolous pursuit, but perhaps it was the result of some idle hours in the office. Many could appreciate the humor: architects like Gordon with stories of graft-driven officials, beleaguered taxpayers familiar with projects like the Tweed Courthouse, and politicians and bar members inclined to enjoy an inside joke.

Gordon was not the only architect offering solutions for the New York County Courthouse. Although various design proposals received press coverage, continuing protests against using the City Hall Park site overshadowed architectural debate. On October 12, 1911, the law authorizing the project was amended once again, this time *forbidding* building the courthouse in *any* park. In addition, the task of site selection was transferred to the Board of Estimate and Apportionment, which under much pressure decided on a location by the end of January. The cost to acquire the property, just a short distance northeast of City Hall Park, was $6.24 million. Other expenses, like improvements and street diversions, added to the bill—all of which could have been avoided by adopting Gordon's visionary proposal.[9]

Much discussion was given to the method for choosing a design, and the courthouse board hired AIA president Walter Cook as a consultant on the matter. Cook was in a somewhat thorny position. While the AIA had opposed open competitions since its inception, no satisfactory alternative had been developed for commissioning a public building design. Cook and the board arrived at sort of a hybrid solution: ten

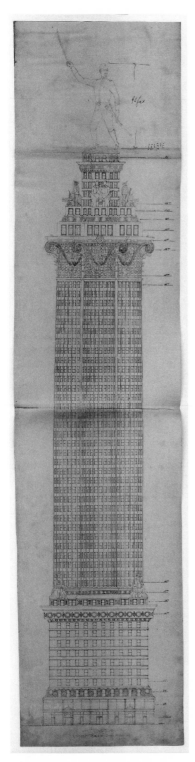

18.5.
"Monumental Plan" project. James Riely Gordon office drawing ca. 1898. *Courtesy Alexander Architectural Archive, University of Texas, Austin.*

18.6.
"Absurd Interpretation of New York Courthouse." James Riely Gordon office drawing ca. 1910 by R. Sunderland. *Courtesy Alexander Architectural Archive, University of Texas, Austin.*

architects, selected by their reputations, would be invited to compete with guaranteed compensation for participating. This met an immediate howl of protest so the board adopted a compromise plan. The competition was opened to a total of twenty architects and firms. In addition to the ten invited, another ten would be selected through a preliminary competition.

As announced on May 28, 1912, the ten invited architects and firms included Carrère and Hastings; McKim, Mead & White; Tracy, Swartwout & Litchfield; York and Sawyer; and Gordon. While controversy about the selection ensued, it is obvious that Gordon had climbed to the upper echelon of his field in the ten years since his move to New York. As could be expected, some took umbrage at being snubbed through omission. A month later the board also invited Cass Gilbert and George B. Post and Sons. While these architects likely lobbied hard for their late inclusion, few would argue their qualifications.

Any architect with a New York address could enter the preliminary contest. First they submitted their names, office addresses, and a record of buildings to their credit. Of the seventy-one so applying, forty-seven were deemed qualified to submit plans, without compensation, according to a tentative program of requirements. These were judged by a panel consisting of architects Robert S. Peabody of Boston, Frank Miles Day of Philadelphia, and John L. Mauran of St. Louis. On October 28, the courthouse board announced that the judges had chosen the ten best from the preliminary competition. Contest rules barred any of the preliminary designs from public display, denying other architects an opportunity to sense the judges' preferences.

The combined, twenty-two final competitors were given until April 1, 1913, to submit plans that met the requirements of a detailed program newly provided by the board. Competitors would receive $1,000 each, and the winning architect would be awarded $10,000 plus compensation for any architectural services subsequently rendered. This new courthouse would accommodate county offices, the courts presently held in the old Tweed Courthouse, the city court, and a number of judicial facilities currently scattered in rented locations. Since the new site allowed for a larger foundation, it was believed that a structure of eight to ten stories would suffice. The projected cost for the building was $10 million.[10]

No stylistic guidelines or restrictions were issued, however, and the subsequent submissions exhibit much variety, offering differing solutions to the shape of the site: an irregular pentagon. Some entries, like those of Carrère and Hastings, George B. Post and Sons, and Tracy, Swartwout & Litchfield, featured central pavilions extending from large, main blocks. York and Sawyer nearly filled the irregular pentagon with an irregular hexagon whose stepped massing rose toward the center where it was capped by a dome. Six others also attempted to fill the lot, including McKim, Mead & White, whose blocky submission was surprisingly lackluster. Foreshadowing his U.S. Supreme Court

Building, Cass Gilbert proposed a rectangular structure recalling an ancient temple. A few entries were variations on tall buildings, including a couple of low-base-with-tower designs. Most submissions were notable designs in a Beaux-Arts or neoclassical mode.[11] Two stand out as particularly individual statements, however.

Guy Lowell, a Bostonian who also maintained a New York office, offered a 200-foot-high circular structure with a diameter of 500 feet (fig. 18.7). Four Corinthian porticos would mark the compass points and serve as primary entrances. A 32-foot-wide annular court would encircle the center of the building, providing light and ventilation. At the center Lowell envisioned a great central hall resembling the interior of the Pantheon, only larger. Exterior statuary would be profuse and include groupings of "the great law-givers of the world, from Moses and Solon to Marshall and Kent." Lowell's entry inspired comparisons to the Roman Coliseum, although some critics thought the Hippodrome to be more apt.[12]

Working with more space than was available at the City Hall Park site, Gordon departed from the soaring design he initially proposed. Nevertheless, his New York County Courthouse competition entry was clearly descended from his Pillars of Justice design. Instead of four tall pillars engaged to a central square, however, the competi-

18.7.
New York County Courthouse, 1913 competition design by Guy Lowell, architect. *Undated postcard rendering, Moses King.*

246

tion design had four massive, squared pavilions extending from an octagonal core (figs. 18.8 and 18.9). Sitting on high basements and capped with tall attics leading to pyramidal roofs, their outward sides would have *in antis* treatments with Corinthian columns separating three multistoried window panels. Gordon planned for a liberal application of sculpture with caryatides, groupings over the entrances, and an ambitious sculptural frieze tracing the evolution of law wrapping the entire building.

In many ways, Gordon's New York competition entry can also be seen as the last, grandest incarnation of his Signature Plan. The footprint was a cross set on a 45-degree angle with entrances set between the pavilions on three sides (an auditorium was planned for the fourth). Somewhat akin to his Texas porches in reentrant angles, these would open to short passages to the center (fig. 18.10). There, banks of elevators, substituting for his Texas central stairwells, surrounded a spectacular rotunda rising seventeen stories from the basement through the lantern of the dome. Even though an office tower surmounted the dome, this rotunda offered Gordon's trademark ventilation and lighting from exterior windows of the octagonal core. On the judicial floors, people exiting the elevators would find it just a short walk to their destination: within each of the pavilions, Gordon layered three two-story, octagonal courtrooms in a cloverleaf pattern. Above, the tower would contain several office floors capped by a majestic law library. A number of studies in Gordon's office papers show he labored over how to top this magnificent composition (fig. 18.11). He finally settled on a stepped dome structure derived from the circular Temple of Vesta.[13]

Each of the twenty-two submissions consisted of twenty-two drawings, making a total of 484 drawings prepared for the final competition at an estimated cost to the contestants of $150,000. When combined with the additional work that went into the preliminary contest, the cost of professional effort ventured for the New York County Courthouse design becomes even more staggering.[14]

The New York County Courthouse design was awarded to Guy Lowell, one of the dark horses battling through the preliminary contest for permission to enter. As the *Times* noted, "Although the choice of Mr. Guy Lowell naturally causes some surprise, as so many other architects of national repute had entered the competition, it cannot be said that he is unknown." Some found the design, more than its author, the cause for surprise. His peers viewed it as too "intensely original" and "an extraordinarily brilliant 'stunt.'" (One wonders what they said about Gordon's Pillars of Justice.) A primary merit in the minds of the judges was its efficient traffic flow.[15] This was similar to the flow of Gordon's entry, suggesting his may have been near the top of the judges' list as well, but such information was not published.

This was just the beginning of criticism Lowell was to face over his design. Naysayers predicted that curved walls would be too costly, but the architect countered there was savings to be had from the repetitious production of segmental sections. Some

18.8.
New York County Courthouse, elevation office drawing, 1913 competition submission by James Riely Gordon. *Courtesy Alexander Architectural Archive, University of Texas, Austin.*

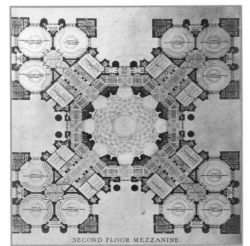

18.9.
New York County Courthouse, second-floor mezzanine plan, 1913 competition submission by James Riely Gordon. *Courtesy Alexander Architectural Archive, University of Texas, Austin.*

18.10.
New York County Courthouse, section view, 1913 competition submission by James Riely Gordon, architect. *Courtesy Alexander Architectural Archive, University of Texas, Austin.*

18.11.
Preliminary drawings for New York County Courthouse, 1913 competition submission by James Riely Gordon. *Sketches of tower proposals, courtesy Alexander Architectural Archive, University of Texas, Austin.*

The New Court House,
New York City.

18.12.
New York County Courthouse,
New York, New York (1910–27).
Guy Lowell, architect. *Undated postcard view.*

argued the design held a host of shortcomings including insufficient lighting and ventilation.[16] Beyond this, selection by the Court House Board turned out to be only the
first step in the approval process; it had to pass a gauntlet of bureaucratic groups and
commissions that demanded changes. Construction finally began in 1919. According
to a fellow architect, "throughout all the necessary compromises, the trying delays and
interference, [Lowell] never lost sight of the essential qualities of the design nor ceased
to labor to preserve its integrity." Be that as it may, he saw his circular courthouse
clipped to a hexagon and much of its elegance diminished (fig. 18.12). The years-long
struggle took a toll. Guy Lowell died at age fifty-six a week before the building's dedication in 1927.[17]

Gordon put considerable thought and effort toward transforming his Monument
Plan into his Pillars of Justice proposal. In addition to the drawings, he made a plaster
model of it that was photographed, sometimes superimposed over a city view, and
distributed to the press. He anticipated objections to the design and answered them
before they were raised. All this suggests that, for all its novelty, it was a serious offering that responded to the client's needs and the site designated at the time. Admittedly
singular in its appearance, had it been adopted as proposed its visibility would have
demanded recognition, similar to the eventual, qualified acceptance granted Minoru
Yamasaki's World Trade Center. Regarding the Pillars of Justice, the *Boston Post* noted,
"Should New York erect such a building it is more than likely that its beauty and
attractiveness will sooner or later find other replicas in all parts of the country."[18] After

all, Bertram Goodhue's tower design for the Nebraska State Capitol was a jarring break with tradition, but it was followed with the Louisiana Capitol and other similarly composed public buildings.

Of course, such speculation only serves to place the design in the context of its creation. Considering the construction history of Lowell's courthouse, it is doubtful that the Pillars of Justice proposal could have been built without many compromises had it been adopted instead. Now the proposal simply seems a curious diversion among Gordon's office papers. While less radical, Gordon's official submission was also well considered, ambitious, and original.

As for the old Tweed Courthouse, it still stands. Remarkably, it escaped destruction for enough years to become sufficiently disassociated from its ignominious past. Now restored, the building currently serves as the New York City Department of Education headquarters.

CHAPTER NINETEEN

Cambria

In spring 1914, as the New York courthouse competition entries were being considered, officials in a western Pennsylvania county contemplated enlarging their courthouse. Several grand juries had concluded that Cambria County had outgrown its twenty-four-year-old structure in Ebensburg, and, in April, the Cambria County Board of Commissioners appointed a five-person advisory committee to select an architect and develop suitable expansion plans. The cost of the addition was not to exceed $300,000.[1]

Historically, Cambria had enjoyed a level of prosperity reflected in this building budget. It was ideally situated as steel manufacturing, coal mining, and agriculture contributed much to the local coffers. Ebensburg was an industrial force in its own right and, like Oakland, Maryland, a popular Allegheny Mountain resort destination. Nevertheless, 1914 was a lean year for many citizens who were skeptical of the courthouse project.

M. E. Beebe of Buffalo, New York, designed the 1880 courthouse, a fine Second Empire composition with central and corner pavilions (fig. 19.1). Philadelphia pressed brick, heavily trimmed with Sandusky limestone from Ohio, sheaths the exterior up to the metal cornice. From there, mansard roofs led to a magnificent clock tower that provided half the building's height. The foundation measured 170 x 80 feet, and the distance from the ground to the top of the tower's statue of *Justice* was 165 feet. Located on a prominent hilltop, the Cambria County Courthouse was a distinctive landmark visible for miles. Its cost, including furnishings, was $109,962.44.[2]

At the time of the addition project, Pennsylvania counties were governed by a three-member Board of Commissioners, all elected at large. To ensure a bipartisan membership, a maximum of two could be from the same political party. The intention of this requirement, born of nineteenth-century reforms, was to limit the influence of partisan politics. The commissioners initially overseeing the courthouse addition were Democrat Thomas A. Osborn, Republican T. Stanton Davis, and A. G. Anderson of the Prohibition Party.[3] Davis opposed the project, as well as other expensive work undertaken by the county during the current lean times, but was repeatedly outvoted.

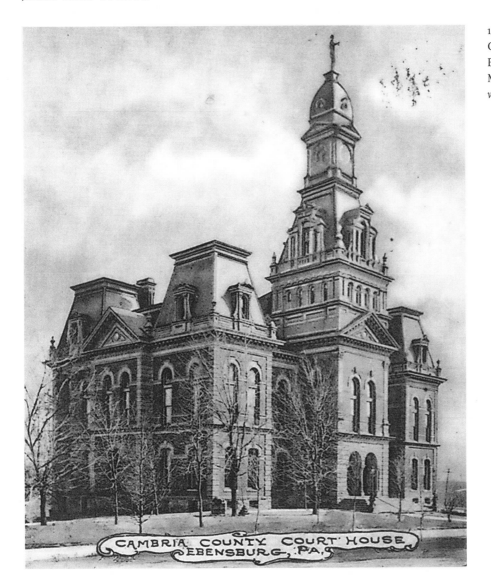

19.1.
Cambria County Courthouse,
Ebensburg, Pennsylvania (1880).
M. E. Beebe, architect. *Postcard view ca. 1905.*

Gordon learned of the project and visited Ebensburg to explore its potential. Afterward, Commissioner Osborn and a member of the advisory committee traveled to the architect's New York office to discuss his ideas further. Gordon later recalled that he was in competition with other architects for the job, but their identities appear lost. On May 12, 1914, following the committee's formal recommendation, Thomas Osborn motioned that "the Commissioners employ James R. Gordon architect for the proposed alterations and additions to the court-house for preliminary conferences and sketches at a cost not to exceed $500." Commissioner Anderson voted with Osborn and the motion carried over Davis's "no." As reported the next day, should Gordon's "drawings be accepted, he will be retained as architect to supervise the improvements."[4]

As agreed, Gordon returned to Ebensburg and conducted a more detailed inspection of the courthouse and the surrounding property. With measurements taken and ideas further discussed, he returned to New York to work up his proposal. Between

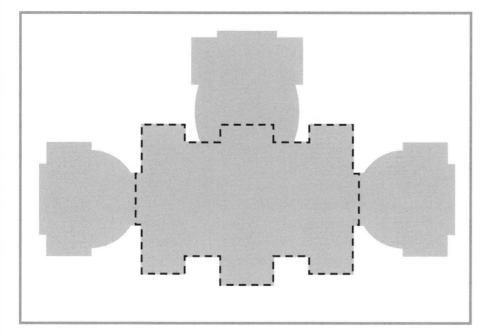

19.2.
1914 plan for renovations and
additions to Cambria County
Courthouse by James Riely
Gordon, architect. Dashed
line represents approximate
footprint of original structure.
*Illustration based upon Cambria
County Historic Site Survey drawing.*

the architect and the advisory committee, weeks were invested creating, scrutinizing, and modifying drawings. Finally, with the committee's concerns satisfied, on July 8 Commissioners Osborn and Anderson approved the plan—estimated to cost around $270,000—for construction, plus Gordon's 6 percent commission and a salary for a "superintendent-of-works" at $100 per month. Gordon was again present and vowed to rework the plans into proper shape to be put out to bid within three weeks. He then returned to his office and had the preliminary drawings redrawn on a larger scale with details while incorporating still more modifications. He also provided specifications for construction and furnishings. In August, after approval by judges of the affected courts, Osborn and Anderson officially approved and adopted the final plans.[5]

Gordon's labors had resulted in a plan not unlike his envisioned enlargement for his Arizona Capitol. In his vision, two wings would flank the existing courthouse to the north and south. A third would project to the east off the rear. As seen from above, these would be semicircular with their flat sides away from the original building (fig. 19.2). The side wings were to hold much-needed offices and courtrooms accommodating about three hundred people; the rear wing's courtroom was planned for about seven hundred. The shape of the additions, which came to be known as the "Gordon Wings" (not always with affection), reflected the layout of the courtrooms within. The existing, two-story courtroom would be divided between floors and remodeled for more offices and a law library. Gordon also included a new roof and interior renovations to the 1880 structure that were to raise its fire-resistance nearer to current standards.

Reports indicated enthusiasm for the plan, but it also had its critics. While some feared the shape of the wings might be too weird, the main objection was their cost. To counter worries over the cost in general and overbuilding in particular, Commissioners Osborn and Anderson decided to structure the bidding process to consider different types of building materials and alternate construction options including building one, two, or all three wings.[6] It was a scenario disturbingly close to the equally controversial, multifaceted Bergen County Courthouse bidding process.

Although Osborn and Anderson were empowered to make this decision, an 1895 state act required that the county controller actually place the advertisements soliciting bids. The commissioners requested the advertising in August, but Controller C. G. Campbell sat on the matter for over two months. Arguing that the structure of the bid, with its base proposal and numerous alternate options, was too vague, Campbell believed that releasing this solicitation would sanction limitless spending for which he could be held responsible. Osborn and Anderson obtained a court order compelling the controller to place the ads or show cause for refusing. Before Campbell could respond, he was stricken with appendicitis and died from complications following surgery.[7]

His successor, George M. Wertz, met with all three commissioners, the advisory committee, and Gordon in January 1915 to resolve the situation. Gordon fully explained his plans to Wertz. A committeeman explained their justification for the improvements and the rationale for the bid structure. This indulgence of the new controller proved all for naught: on February 8 Wertz informed the commissioners that he had decided not to advertise the bids.[8]

Months later, Controller Wertz expanded upon his misgivings saying he had found that the plans and specifications were faulty and gave every opportunity for graft on a level that could proportionally exceed that of the recent Pennsylvania Capitol construction. Raising the specter of the capitol was a calculated move by Wertz intended to cause taxpaying Pennsylvanians to shudder. Perhaps the most notorious example of corruption on a state level and dubbed the "Palace of Graft," the capitol in Harrisburg carried several million dollars in hidden costs, which led to an official investigation and imprisonment of its architect. The controller implied that Gordon was guilty of collusion while narrowly avoiding an outright accusation of criminal intent on the part of the two commissioners.[9]

Commissioners Osborn and Anderson, through the Cambria County attorney, obtained a writ of mandamus ordering Wertz to advertise for bids. When he still refused, the matter went to the courts, where it simmered through 1915. (Many local histories suppose that the project was delayed by the First World War. While anxiety over events in Europe further slowed the economy, the real cause was the protracted battle of wills between officials.) By November's county elections, challengers cited the Gordon Wings among the alleged abuses of the public trust by incumbents. Republicans swept control of Cambria County on a reform platform, including Controller-elect Herman T. Jones, who opposed the courthouse project as excessive and the proposed contract as too loose. Commissioner Davis was reelected and would be joined by fellow Republican Emanuel W. Baumgardner and Democrat Harry B. Heffley in January.[10]

On December 10, Pennsylvania's Supreme Court handed down its decision regarding Wertz's refusal to advertise for bids. It concluded that Wertz held a wildly inflated view of his responsibilities as controller. His role was that of a bookkeeper, the court determined, with no authority to second-guess the commissioners in the absence of any hard evidence of misconduct. The Supreme Court ordered Wertz, now a lame duck, to advertise for the bids. Interested contractors were to submit them by February 25, 1916.[11]

This would follow the installation of the new Board of Commissioners, all apparently hostile to the courthouse addition project. As December 1915 and their terms in office came to a close, Commissioners Osborn and Anderson met at Osborn's residence to wrap up some county business. Both had been quite ill—Anderson was recovering but Osborn surely realized he was terminal (he died the following April at age forty-three). One of their last official actions was to grant an order to pay Gordon over $14,000 for his courthouse addition plans, but actual payment was not made at the time.[12] Whatever their motivations in the courthouse project, they knew its future was now very much in doubt. It appears they at least wanted to get on record that the county owed Gordon for his plans, which he had dutifully prepared to the demands of the committee and the commissioners.

Predictably, the architect's bill was another source of controversy as the new Cambria County Board of Commissioners took office on January 3. The public's appetite for these controversies seems to have waned by this time and perhaps opinions of the former board softened as news of Thomas Osborn's declining health spread. The *Johnstown Tribune*, previously quite critical of the project (new County Controller Jones was formerly its editor), now opined that Cambria deserved the services of a qualified architect and if his bill was just it should be paid. Stopping short of naming Wertz outright, the paper suggested that the time for sanctimonious demagoguery was past.[13]

It seemed the political climate in Cambria County had further improved by February 25. Hopeful contractors had spent a month calculating their complex bids and each posted a $10,000 bond to compete. Gordon was on hand, chatting with a commissioner in the morning where he noted he was "still in the service of the county and would draw up a new set of plans if the present ones were unsatisfactory."

Shortly after 1:00 o'clock Jones brought the bids before the Board of Commissioners. To the surprise of many, the chief clerk of the board curtly announced that all of the bids were rejected, without being opened and without explanation. Gordon was then called before the board to tender his bill for $14,000. The commissioners flatly rejected it and offered instead the $500 authorized for the preliminary work back in May 1914. (It was previously understood the $500 would be rolled into the larger fee.) Outraged, Gordon refused to accept it and later vowed to seek legal redress. The contractors, with their bonds still in the county's possession, considered similar options. Meanwhile, local backers of the project regrouped. There was talk of an effort to oust the three commissioners, who seemed to be acting in unison. Many conceded Gordon would probably prevail in court. It was believed the commissioners were scheming to spring their own improvement plans shortly. The *Tribune* wondered if the taxpayers would ever be delivered from such costly posturing that brings "nothing in the way of results except political gratification to a small few."[14]

In March the commissioners received their own writ of mandamus, issued by a visiting judge from McKean County, ordering them to act on the bids. The following day the board went through the charade of opening the bids and then again rejected them all. When ordered to show cause for their action, the commissioners argued *they* had never approved the plans and specifications. Not accepting this, the judge ordered the contract be awarded by August 1, 1916. While the order seems questionable on a legal basis, the project clearly had powerful backers, and any political capital the reformers had left would disappear if they forced more court costs. The commissioners gave up the fight and invited Gordon to return to Ebensburg and help them tabulate the bids.[15]

On June 22, the contract went to W. H. Fissell and Company. Fissell was the only Cambria entrant to submit a complete bid including all the alternate constructions. The base bid was $253,284. The costliest combination of alternates raised the figure to a possible $394,882. There were other variables, too. Items like excavation were not included and it was still unclear if the old clock tower would need to be removed.[16] Despite the uncertainty, work began shortly thereafter and dragged on for years through several Boards of Commissioners.

Forced into the project, successive boards maintained a hostile relationship with Gordon and, through meddling, obstruction, and inaction, prolonged the work and drove up costs. A typescript of a letter from Gordon to the Cambria County Board of Commissioners is among the architect's papers. In it he states his understanding of his role in the project and recounts his frustration with a Mr. Brown, whose appointment by the board undermined his authority. The letter is so uncharacteristically combative it is possible it was never sent. Nevertheless, it reveals Gordon's state of mind.

Gentlemen:

I regret to feel constrained to write to you that I am the Architect for the Cambria County Courthouse, and irrespective of the lack of support accorded me, and the discourtesy shown me, I have smothered my pride and endeavored to the utmost to do my duty to Cambria County and to you, and shall continue to perform the duties covered by my employment so long as I am the Architect.

I desire to ask if the following interpretation of the status is correct:

The owner is Cambria County, acting through its County Commissioners. The Architect is the Agent for the Owner, and the owner is responsible for the acts of its agent.

The Owner, instead of showing its appreciation of the loyal efforts of its agent, from the inception has, through the instrumentality of Mr. Brown, endeavored to throw every obstacle in the way of the agent and the progress of the work.

I informed Mr. Brown at the inception that I welcomed any conscientious assistance and co-operation, but never once has he been straight forward with me or met me in the same spirit, nor offered a single logical suggestion. I have not dignified by notice the questionable things which he has done behind my back....

Referring to your request ... that I send the hardware specification and schedules to you for Mr. Brown's approval, permit me to say that in no manner do I recognize Mr. Brown. I have reached the limit of my endurance of the humiliation heaped upon me, and my lack of respect for Mr. Brown precludes my compliance with such requests. [If], like the Kaiser, [you have] prepared for [a fight] from the inception, ... then gentlemen, I await your onslaught, and you may consider my hat in the ring, with the consciousness that I have done everything in the power of human endurance to save you and all concerned from such a calamity.[17]

Going as far as to compare the board's actions to those of the belligerent German emperor's, Gordon's words suggest this was the most acrimonious architect-client relationship of his career. Things did not improve as work progressed.

The additions were built first, county workers moved into them, and renovations of the original structure began. Gordon's role was minimized as the commissioners began working directly with the contractor. The board's minutes are rife with examples of changes made outside the original plans and specifications; sometimes Gordon acquiesced, sometimes he was successful in persuading the commissioners to return to the original plans, sometimes the changes were made without his approval. There were instances where the architect protested the contractor's charges for these "extras." At one point Fissell was even taking direction from the county janitor—which the commissioners approved![18]

Among the mutually agreed-upon changes was the 1920 decision to remove the old clock tower; its timber construction posed too great a fire risk. Other changes were required due to the long duration of the work. Gordon kept abreast of changes in Pennsylvania building codes and advised that the courthouse plans be changed accordingly. For example, Gordon recommended the adoption of newly required elevator safety features, which were approved. Also, electrical changes were needed when the Ebensburg power company discontinued direct current in favor of alternating current. Familiar with this scenario of rising costs, Gordon was clearly aware that eventually there would be repercussions. To avoid being scapegoated once again, he made sure the commissioners knew he was keeping copies of all his correspondence with them.[19]

The work dragged with occasional stoppages from 1916 through 1924. All the while county workers and the public had to endure the inconveniences of construction. Grand juries begged for swift completion. Originally contracted to be done by December 1, 1917, Fissell's construction work was completed March 9, 1923. The board, led by T. Stanton Davis (the commissioner who was hostile to the project from its beginning and the only one to hold office through this whole process), stalled on advertising the fixture and furniture contracts until the fall, when it was compelled to do so by yet another court order. In October Gordon inspected the main courtroom, which was getting the last of its furnishings. Demonstrating that at least he had not lost his sense of humor, he declared it to be the "Bee's Knees."[20]

For all the grief involved, the Cambria County Courthouse displays some of Gordon's best work. From the exterior, the three wings are strikingly novel in design while in harmony with the original structure—no small accomplishment (fig. 19.3). The interior balances practical planning with truly dramatic effects. As with the Calcasieu Parish Courthouse in Lake Charles, Louisiana, Gordon did not merely design an addition, he transformed the structure.[21]

M. E. Beebe's mansard-roofed pavilions define the perimeter of his original courthouse. Gordon left the ornate work above the eaves essentially intact, save the tower, which he proposed replacing with a dome after the decision to remove it. Perhaps understandable given the overruns, officials rejected the proposal. As is, the top of the parapet is slightly lower than the flanking pavilion roofs and the result is a bit awkward and perhaps the only flaw in the final composition. While the first-floor façade is largely as Beebe designed it, Gordon refaced the second and third floors, dividing their original two-story window treatments into two distinct levels. Where Beebe's composition had a vertical thrust enhanced by his tower, Gordon's rework is horizontal: the structure stretches about 235 feet between the ends of the north and south wings and 175 feet front to back.

By deftly incorporating Beebe's ornamental program, the Gordon Wings seem a natural extension of the original structure despite their curved surfaces. They connect at recessed points where Beebe placed his secondary entrances and curve out just

short of the plane of the original pavilions. As a result, the wings serve to frame and accentuate the original west façade. Their semicircular shape marks another instance of Gordon using curved lines to tune courtroom acoustics. By showing these on the exterior he followed the fashion of expressing internal function. Also, by resisting the urge to "square off" the exterior, he again optimizes natural lighting and ventilation.

While expertly crafted, little about the exterior prepares visitors for what they will encounter within. A stunning rotunda, ringed by eight scagliola columns, soars through three stories to a coffered dome featuring an art glass representation of the county seal (fig 19.4). Marble abounds as office-lined halls extend in three directions to the Gordon Wings with their amply lit courtrooms. Most impressive is Courtroom One (fig. 19.5). Although the seating was reduced in its final version to 550, it is still the largest of Gordon's courtrooms and among the largest in the United States. From the Gordon-designed furnishings to the trio of apses behind the judge's stand, to the curved gallery, to the dome with its art glass skylight, everything about it is first-rate. As a whole, it competes with some of the finer opera theaters of its day. Inspecting the work at long last must have been very satisfying for its sixty-one-year-old author.

Cambria County citizens had little time to enjoy their completed courthouse before legal wrangling began anew. In April 1925 contractor William Fissell sued the county for $400,000, claiming damages suffered through the protracted construction period. In the end Fissell won a judgment in federal court, which the county settled with payment of $10,052.25.[22]

Gordon's turn to sue came in late 1926, after the Board of Commissioners rejected his final bill. Gordon sought $170,049.30 (surely a high figure but he just as surely knew

19.3.
Cambria County Courthouse, as renovated and enlarged (1916–23) by James Riely Gordon, architect. *2001 photograph.*

261

19.4.
Cambria County Courthouse,
rotunda. *2001 photograph.*

19.5.
Cambria County Courthouse,
courtroom. *2001 photograph.*

he would be settling for less) in the District Court of the United States, Western District Court of Pennsylvania. On May 19, 1930, Cambria County issued payment of $46,611.11 on the verdict in Gordon's favor.[23]

The architect's sixteen-year involvement with Cambria County was finally over. Despite his troubles, he was well compensated and could take much pride in the end product. Most reckonings of the cost for the Gordon Wings settle on $394,882 (based on Fissell's 1916 bid) plus a 6 percent architect's fee ($23,692.92). This does not include a subsequent contract in 1920 for the removal of the tower or the separate fixture and furnishings contract, however. Nor does it take into account legal costs for the internal county wrangling, lawsuits, and settlements. At this point it is probably impossible to come to a full accounting of the cost of the project, but the bill could have been much lower had it not been for political posturing.

Cambria's runaway courthouse project is reminiscent of two others discussed in this volume, Bexar and Bergen. It may be tempting to identify their shared architect, Gordon, as the source of their problems, but this would ignore a more glaring commonality. As their courthouses were being built, all three of these counties became political battlefields as factions (not necessarily partisan) fought for control. Gordon found himself relegated to the sidelines as local figures became more involved in the work. While changes were made to some of Gordon's other courthouses during construction, none were so costly or delaying as the changes to these three after his authority waned. Since ultimate control over these projects rested with the county administrators, Gordon could do little beyond holding them to his contract.

It is true that Gordon's contracts, which were typical for architects, caused him to profit from cost overruns, but there is no evidence he ever advocated waste or fraud. To the contrary, when given the opportunity to counsel officials he sought to steer them away from such pitfalls. A report of one such meeting, regarding Delaware's New Castle County Courthouse, dates to early 1914 when the debacle in Ebensburg was just beginning. In it Gordon advised officials, "you have got to look ahead for 100 years and you should build the very best structure that you can and see that every cent spent goes into the building. It should all be let out in one big contract, so that there will not be an extra for this thing, and an extra charge for that, until the cost runs away beyond all expectations."[24]

CHAPTER TWENTY

Professional Organizations, Cortland, and The World of Tomorrow

The Cambria County Courthouse improvement work was a problematic and demanding project that stretched on for years, but it did not monopolize Gordon's time. He had a number of significant private-sector jobs under his belt by this point, including the Borgfeldt Building, the Bronx and Manhattan Elks Clubs, and the posh, Gothic Revival apartments at 36 Gramercy Park East. Although he did not land another courthouse commission until 1922, he pursued the New Castle project and perhaps others in the meantime. The architect also continued his association in an expanding bevy of professional organizations. On the personal level, Gordon's daughter Lucy married Lieutenant Byron Brown Ralston on June 4, 1919, at St. Bartholomew's Church. Byron's career in the Navy kept him away for long periods, but the couple resided in the Gordons' apartment at 214 Riverside Drive. The apartment was quite spacious, so there was no problem also accommodating their daughter, Lucy Virginia Gordon Ralston, after her birth.[1]

Among his professional organizations, Gordon devoted most of his attention to the New York Society of Architects. This group organized in 1906 to affect reform in the bureaucracy governing construction in the city. At the time, many city offices were sluggish fiefdoms demanding to be appeased before building permits, for example, were processed. Millions of dollars were being siphoned from the building industry to contend with the uncontrolled bureaucracy, with some of it going to payoffs to "facilitate" the process. Therefore, the society worked "with a view to devoting its energies to matters affecting the business and legal interests of the architectural profession in the City and the State."[2]

By 1913 Gordon was chairman of the society's committee on the still-problematic issue of competitions, a member of its board of directors, and elected its vice president. In 1916 he became president of the society, a position he held for many years as it struggled for recognition from city officials, builders, and other architects. During this time its coffers often ran so low that individual members financed efforts like printing its highly regarded yearbook. (The *American Architect* called it encyclopedic and "one of the most complete publications issued by an architectural society.") It is clear that Gordon was usually well liked by those who knew him, and this was an essential asset for the society during stressful times when conflicts between members grew heated. As he once put it, he was "prone to inject a spirit of levity especially at times when I seemed to scent a dangerous proximity of a breach." While others may have been as tireless as he in their devotion to the society, no doubt Gordon's affable yet determined personality was recognized as essential, leading to his repeated reelection as its president.[3]

This is not to say it was all work for the New York Society of Architects. Their regular dinner meetings were preferred affairs held at the Hotel Astor. An account of one annual outing tells of members leaving their headquarters at 29 West 39th Street in a procession of ten autos bound for Long Island's Bayville Casino. Activities included a swimming race, which Gordon won (he was at least fifty-three at the time), dinner, and a baseball game between the members.[4] Professionally and socially, Gordon flourished in this and other organizations. In addition to his aquatic prowess, his humor, engaging personality, and reputation as a raconteur kept him a welcome guest at many events and he was a member, or honorary member, of many regional architectural organizations (fig. 20.1). AIA membership still eluded him, however.

Around 1922 the society created a permanent Advisory Board on Public Buildings, Monuments and Memorials, with Gordon as its chairman. This produced a set of guidelines that, while the work of a committee, clearly embodies Gordon's professional philosophy as he had practiced it over the years. By considering these guidelines with his earlier comments to the New Castle County officials, we can draw a clear picture on the architect's own ethical orthodoxy for public work.

Perhaps first and foremost is his recognition that his client for a public commission was an individual or group representing a community—a county, in the case of a courthouse job. This client was either elected by the citizenry or appointed by its representatives. Either way, the architect—in Gordon's view—was not to question the selection. The client conducted the building project as empowered by the people and was ultimately responsible for his actions and those of anyone hired. While the architect could offer advice, he was not to question the client's wisdom or authority. The architect was to do his own work, including superintendence if so employed, to the highest of professional standards, but his responsibility ended there.[5]

Clearly, Gordon did not consider it his job to make officials behave or to report those who did not. As seen in his Bergen testimony, there were times when this professional ethos placed him in awkward positions. Occasionally, as with Cambria, it became downright humiliating. And when scandal touched a project, as an outsider he could find himself a convenient scapegoat. Such was the arena in which he worked. While perilous at times, the work was satisfying and lucrative.

20.1.
Boat trip, Brooklyn Chapter AIA outing, September 1923. L to R: T. E. Snook, Andrew J. Thomas, Gordon, Henry Bacon, William H. Gompert, Frank H. Quinby. *Photographer unknown, courtesy Lucy Virginia Gordon Ralston.*

Gordon's last temple of justice was for New York's Cortland County, in the seat by the same name. By 1920, the county Board of Supervisors resolved to replace its ninety-year-old structure. The board appointed a building committee, and in June 1921 the committee secured property for the new courthouse and a new jail building. In October the committee was empowered to procure the services of an architect. Details of their search were not preserved, but only one design was considered—Gordon's. He presented his plans and specifications to the board on March 15, 1922. They were approved in the same session.[6]

Described as presenting a "plain, simple, yet dignified and imposing structure," Gordon's plans were well received. While the board again chose to consider construction bids on base and alternative proposals, the choice of building materials was the only variable so the contracting process was less convoluted and controversial than Bergen's or Cambria's. In June the courthouse contract went to the A. E. Stephens Company of Springfield, Massachusetts (competing against The John T. Brady Company and W. H. Fissell and Company) for $532,416. The reorganized Pauly Jail Building Company, Incorporated, won the jail contract for $45,696. The architect complimented board members in their letting of the contracts and their choice of long-lasting Indiana limestone for the exterior. Contracts were let on June 7, 1922, and the Stephens Company began work on the twenty-ninth of the month. On October 5 the cornerstone was laid.[7]

Cortland County Courthouse, Cortland, New York (1922–24). James Riely Gordon, architect. Gordon also designed the World War I memorial in the foreground. *2001 photograph.*

Cortland follows Gordon's Capitol Plan with a short entrance wing on the north side where a flight of granite steps rises to an *in antis* portico with paired and engaged Doric columns (fig. 20.2).[8] Wings extend east and west with engaged columns between the second- and third-story window bays, above a rusticated first floor and basement. This treatment is continued around to the rear wing. As at Bergen, there are no pediments; an austere parapet encircles the top of the exterior walls.

From front to back the building measures 151 feet. Its east-west width is 160 feet. Unlike Bergen, Cortland's rear wing, housing the large courtroom, is longer than the others. Above it all, at the crossing, an octagonal base and balustrade yield to a drum surrounded by twenty-four Corinthian columns supporting a well-executed dome. A 10-foot statue of *Justice* made of copper surmounts it all, rising 132 feet above street level. The structure is three stories, plus basement.

Inside, Gordon once again delivers a stunning rotunda rising 52 feet to a coffered interior dome with an oculus light. A marble arcade lines the octagonal chamber at the ground floor. Above this, paired scagliola columns rise two stories, past marble and iron balustrades. Marble wainscoting is employed throughout the halls. The vaulted supreme courtroom is elaborated with marble pilasters whose flattened, gilded Composite capitals visually support a dentilated frieze encircling the rectangular space

20.3.
Cortland County Courthouse,
courtroom. *2001 photograph.*

(fig. 20.3). Other rooms, such as the law library and surrogate courtrooms, exhibit similar mastery. While not excessive compared to other courthouses of its time, this elegant treatment provides a pleasant surprise given the relative austerity of the exterior. Regarded as a whole, however, the Cortland County Courthouse is an expertly executed composition built with first-rate materials and workmanship.

Gordon also designed the monument standing in front of the courthouse. A ring of Doric columns, it remembers "Cortland County's sons and daughters who served in the World War."

Gordon traveled to Cortland to make his final inspection on May 22, 1924. He approved the work and the courthouse keys were handed over to the county. Cortland makes it clear that a large-scale Gordon courthouse could be built near budget and within two years, in the absence of controversy and political wrangling.[9] The smooth execution of this project must have been refreshing for the architect, considering his recent experiences (his final payment from Cambria was still in litigation at the time).

All in all, Cortland is a fine finale for Gordon's courthouse opus. He may have thought so too. In 1925, at sixty-one, he wrote a nephew that "I am trying my best to get out of active practice but it seems that alluring opportunities are being presented to me that I have never had before and I do not know what the result will be." These opportunities were likely in the private sector: he seems to have secured no more public buildings after Cortland. A few letters among his office papers suggest he had an interest in pursuing some public projects, but the absence of further documentation, such as drawings, indicates his involvement did not go far beyond that.[10] Of course, the days of preparing full-blown drawings and plans just to enter open competitions had largely passed. Now a visit or two could determine whether chasing a job was worth the effort at this stage of his life.

In lightening his workload, the architect found himself able to do something he had wanted for a long time: return to San Antonio for a visit. He had kept in contact with family and social and professional acquaintances in Texas over the years, but work always prevented his making the trip. In February 1927 he finally "just dropped business" and went. There is no record that Mrs. Gordon accompanied him, but he stayed at the home of her sister and brother-in-law. As a reporter for the *San Antonio Express* noted,

> Although he has been away from San Antonio 25 years, many of the works of Gordon are still pointed out here with pride. The most notable example is Bexar County courthouse, which he planned and is now being doubled in size. . . .
> Another example is the Federal Building, also outgrown but still admired.[11]

At the time, the reporter could have cited many more examples by including residential and commercial structures. Some, like the Federal Building, are gone now. Others survive and are still admired and pointed out with pride, including the Staacke Brothers, Stevens, and Clifford Buildings along East Commerce Street and the Kalteyer residence on King William (formerly Kaiser Wilhelm) Street.

Soon after his Texas sojourn, Gordon was invited to join the advisory committee reviewing Mayor James ("Jimmy") Walker's proposed changes to the New York City Building Code. He was among a number of building professionals asked to make sure the changes reflected advances in technology and protected the public from substandard work without unduly constraining progress or development. His experience and work for the New York Society of Architects certainly qualified him for the task. It seems he took the charge with judicious resolve and, overall, the complex review process appears to have been completed in a timely manner. The committee made its recommendations to the city, where they languished in the bureaucracy for years. Most of Gordon's suggestions made it into the final draft, released in May 1936, but other aspects of the code drew heavy criticism from professional groups, including the society. Just before his death, Gordon persuaded the manager of the building code committee to meet with a joint committee representing various architectural organizations to discuss their differences.[12] Once again he proved himself able to bring together disparate parties.

At the December 1929 annual meeting of the New York Society of Architects he announced his retirement as president of the organization. Three years earlier he tried to decline consideration for reelection, citing his age and the need to share the honor with others. Members unanimously prevailed upon him to accept the office again, however. Now, with the society on sound footing, he had to insist. On January 21, 1930, the society held a testimonial dinner in Gordon's honor at the Astor Hotel to an overflow crowd. The society's bulletin observed:

> Men prominent in their respective professions came to voice their tribute to the man . . . who has been our president for thirteen consecutive years, who served with the energy of youth, with a conscientiousness that compelled admiration and whose services have been an inspiration to all who have come in contact with him.

The bulletin also noted that "his genial smile will be missed from the chair." The society amended its constitution to create the office of "Honorary President" for Gordon, which he held for the rest of his life. No other president has served the society more than a two-year term, before or since.[13]

Gordon continued his involvement with the society and other professional organizations after stepping down from the presidency. In fact, the AIA finally admitted him in 1930. He submitted his application form on February 27, which was followed by a letter of endorsement by his former partner and an AIA member, Egerton Swartwout. In it Swartwout expressed "the highest opinion of him in every way." The institute received Gordon's initiation and membership fees on March 26, and the process was complete.[14]

It was, of course, far too late for the distinction of AIA membership to be of much benefit to his career. Gordon had managed to achieve all that he had without it, but still he surely drew satisfaction from the recognition he had sought since the 1890s. The timing and ease of this acceptance suggests that maybe he had simply outlived those

20.4.
Gordon at time of retirement as president of the New York Society of Architects, 1929.
Photographer unknown, courtesy Lucy Virginia Gordon Ralston.

founders of the Texas State Association of Architects who blocked his membership from the beginning. Such an explanation is certainly feasible: while Gordon's enemies in the TSAA remain nameless, founder and AIA fellow James Wahrenberger, for instance, had passed away just four months earlier on October 22, 1929.

Gordon's AIA membership proved to have little tangible value in the years following the stock market crash of 1929. Like the Panic of 1893, the Great Depression took its toll on the building profession as a whole. This reduced the architect's workload quicker than anticipated, but the Gordons managed to get by on rental income. Financial considerations were probably the cause for their move, around 1934, from their sizable Riverside Drive apartment to a house at 159 Corlies Avenue in Pelham. Gordon repeatedly referred to the house, which he did not design, in humor as "a comfortable old barn." Probably for the same financial considerations, he moved his office from Fifth Avenue to 5 East 44th Street two years later.[15]

Through these troubled times Gordon kept his humor and remained as popular as ever in social and professional circles. For example, the president of the Brooklyn

20.5.
Gordon family Christmas, ca. 1935. L to R: daughter Lucy Virginia (Gordon) Ralston, son-in-law Byron B. Ralston, granddaughter Lucy Virginia Gordon Ralston, wife Mary Lamar (Sprigg) Gordon, James Riely Gordon. *Photographer unknown, courtesy Lucy Virginia Gordon Ralston.*

Society of Architects invited Gordon to entertain its annual dinner, putting him on notice that "you will be expected to perform your usual stunt of installing the officers, and telling not more than 30 stories, colored as only you can."[16]

Colorful stories notwithstanding, the Depression continued to burden the economy and psyche despite New Deal promises and inspiring projects like Rockefeller Center. In the mid-1930s a group of New York civic leaders envisioned a great world's fair to rouse the citizenry's optimism for the future. The date set for the fair was 1939, with the excuse of celebrating the 150th anniversary of the first session of the US Congress in New York. Realizing an observance of the first session of Congress might not sufficiently fire the populace, the Theme and Plan Committee later changed the fair's official theme to "The World of Tomorrow." Stephen F. Voorhees headed that committee and the Board of Design as well, making his role somewhat analogous to Daniel Burnham's for the Columbian Exposition.[17]

Gordon was a consultant during the fair's initial organization in the early months of 1936. Later, he was made chairman of the Architects' Division, New York World's Fair Bond Sales Committee. In this role he led the solicitation of his fellow architects to raise funds for the cause. Soliciting donations from this beleaguered profession in such times was a tall order to begin with; making matters worse were the "modernist" and "traditionalist" factions within the professional community. Although adversaries, both factions were suspicious of the stylistic direction of the fair as well as the method for choosing architects. Given the divisive situation, the selection of Gordon as chairman is further recognition of his talent for unifying his colleagues.[18]

Perhaps as a reward for his services, Gordon also received a commission to design a building for the fair. This was quite an honor, but he informed Voorhees that he would only do so in association with Matthew W. Del Gaudio, then president of the New York Society of Architects, and an unnamed architect whom Gordon was sure the Board of Design would find agreeable.[19] Clearly Gordon had concerns about taking on the commission by himself, and by involving Del Gaudio, he was also sharing the honor with a younger architect (then about forty-eight years old) who could benefit more from the distinction.

It is interesting to speculate what sort of building Gordon would have designed. In his competition entry for the Texas State Building he eagerly embraced Beaux-Arts classicism, which was considered by many as the modern fashion then. The 1939 fair planners also envisioned "modern architecture" for The World of Tomorrow, even if they had not quite decided what that should look like. How Gordon would have come to grips with the challenge is debatable. His granddaughter remembers him having little use for the avant-garde designs of the time. (She recalls him particularly admiring the work of Gothic Revivalist Ralph Adams Cram, which is probably an indicator of his stylistic preferences.)[20] As evidenced in this volume, however, Gordon had a history of rising to challenges.

At any rate, a James Riely Gordon building for The World of Tomorrow was not to be. The architect died at his home on March 16, 1937, following a stroke. Although he was seventy-three, his passing was still sudden and unexpected.

Gordon's death was noted in the *New York Times*, the *Washington Post*, and many other newspapers in New York, Texas, and other states. Architectural journals remembered him as well. Obituaries recalled some of his designs and his work for professional and civic organizations. Del Gaudio provided a tribute that concludes, "The architectural profession extends to the family of Mr. Gordon its extreme sympathy at the passing of such a fine character, a man who was loved and respected by everybody who knew him and a man who would do anything possible to assist one of his fellows." Numerous architectural organizations also paid tribute. Fellow architects serving as honorary pallbearers included Del Gaudio and Egerton Swartwout. Some fifty other architects attended the funeral service held in his home.[21] The office of J. Riely Gordon, Architect, closed following his death and most of its contents were moved to the "comfortable old barn."

CHAPTER TWENTY-ONE

Summation

The preceding pages should lay to rest some oft repeated misconceptions about Gordon: that he was to blame for the Bexar cost overruns (the total of which is often misstated), that Denton County officials were bribed on his behalf, that he attempted to pass off an old courthouse design for the Mississippi Capitol, and so on. As previously noted, these accusations can largely be dismissed as political machinations and professional sniping. Other errors that have been recorded through the years seem to be simply mistakes or the result of ambiguous language, sometimes deliberate, on the part of the architect. This folklore should be discussed before considering Gordon's legacy in public architecture.

In the absence of a comprehensive study of Gordon previous to this book, his obituary in the *New York Times* and an entry in Withey and Withey's *Biographical Dictionary of American Architects* seem to be the basis for most subsequent information on the architect.[1] Since Gordon's family surely provided the obituary information, they seem the source of its flaws. The *Biographical Dictionary* is such an ambitious survey of so many (often obscure) architects that its editors may be forgiven for not being able to thoroughly scrutinize its sources. While useful, it should be used with caution.

Among the errors found in the *Times* obituary and the *Biographical Dictionary* is that Gordon designed a building for Chicago's Century of Progress Exposition. Obviously, this has been confused with the Texas State Building at the 1893 World's Columbian Exposition; no trace of a Gordon building for the 1933 fair was found in the research for this book. Another error, that Gordon apprenticed with W. C. Dodson, is perhaps understandable since the Waco architect is more widely known than his actual employer, W. K. Dobson. The *Biographical Dictionary* follows this with numerous inaccuracies that are corrected in the preceding pages.

The *Times* obituary lists the Montana State Capitol among Gordon's work. Inquiries to Helena, Montana, yielded no basis for this assertion, although an explanation for the error is found in a 1922 *Cortland Standard* article listing "Helena" among the locations for which Gordon designed courthouses.[2] This is surely Helena, Texas—seat of Karnes County until 1894. As discussed in Chapter 8, Gordon competed for the new courthouse to be built in Karnes City, and it is understandable that twenty-eight years later he misidentified the old seat as the site for the new building. In another "capitol" error, the *Biographical Dictionary* credits the Mississippi Statehouse to Gordon, working with John G. Link and Charles S. Haire. Of course, Gordon competed twice for the Mississippi Capitol, ultimately losing to Theodore C. Link.

The *Biographical Dictionary* reports that sixty-nine courthouses were built to Gordon's designs while the *Times* places the number at seventy-two. Blame for this misinformation rests on the architect himself, for he told the story differently over the years. In 1911, when asked about his experience in constructing courthouses, he replied under oath, "I have *constructed* over seventy" (emphasis added).[3] Eleven years later, while working on Cortland, the architect referred "with pride to no less than forty-eight court houses for which he has prepared the plans and specifications during many years of active service."[4] One might infer from this Gordon drew a distinction between courthouses he created plans for, whether they were actually built or not, and those whose construction he had somehow participated in,[5] but the architect was not always so precise. Gordon's 1932 vita credits him with sixty-nine courthouses—no distinctions drawn.[6] Other examples could be cited.

I have been able to find documentation of fifty courthouses (including addition work and the Val Verde Jail) for which Gordon provided designs, and correspondence suggesting the possibility of three more.[7] Based on this, it seems the 1922 tally of forty-eight courthouses for which Gordon prepared plans and specifications (not all of which were built) was probably close to accurate. It may not be possible, in the absence of a detailed office log, to assign a definite number to his construction-only projects.

A last, remarkable aspect of the *New York Times* obituary is that it never uses the word *Texas*. The family, in providing the information, may have failed to mention the state where the architect spent almost half of his life and the seminal years of his career, or it may have been edited out. Correspondence and his trip back demonstrate the Lone Star State was never far from Gordon's mind, however, and he never lost his Texas accent.[8]

In addition to flawed sources such as these, local myths associated with some Gordon courthouses contribute to the misinformation (often negative) surrounding the architect. In my travels, I have had many conversations with local history enthusiasts eager to share stories of slick architects selling naïve local officials on building lavish courthouses or otherwise swindling the county. While in some instances this may have been the case, it seems tales of a "big city architect" somehow hoodwinking the unsophisticated are popular and entertaining to retell. Not only do such accounts malign architects in general while perhaps improperly excusing officials, but they fail to recognize that the value of substantial, landmark courthouses could justify their expense.

Of course, a number of historians have managed to circumnavigate the misinformation and publish accurate studies on Gordon, but none have been comprehensive enough to challenge the preexisting errata.[9] Gordon scholars received a permanent windfall in 1979 when The General Libraries of the University of Texas at Austin purchased most of the papers, models, and other memorabilia from his architectural office. Professor Blake Alexander worked with Gordon's daughter and granddaughter to obtain the material, which had been stored in the attic, basement, and garage at the home on Corlies Avenue since his death. A book like this would not be possible without access to the material in the James Riely Gordon Collection in what is now the Alexander Architectural Archive.

Gordon's long career was a success by any measure. While not a stylistic trendsetter, much of his work transcends regional interest to merit consideration within the nation's architectural fabric. Several of his courthouses stand among the finest in their genre while his output in this specialized building type challenges comparison in both quality and quantity.

When architecture was in its fledgling stage in Texas, Gordon fought for prestigious commissions and delivered exemplary designs that raised standards for building within the state. His cutting-edge approach to both aesthetics and engineering challenged his peers, no doubt contributing to the environment that produced a bounty of praiseworthy designs in the region. His courthouses elsewhere in the South shared a common design, but this produced economies that put his work within reach of communities that might not have been able to afford it otherwise—not unlike Frank Lloyd Wright's Usonian aspirations. In the East, Gordon's courthouse work achieved a high level of recognition rarely obtained by outsiders. These achievements are all the more remarkable knowing he was essentially self-educated.

As rewarding as Gordon's work was, he often had to defend his name against public attack. This was part and parcel for his area of specialization, and backing down from a challenge could spell the end of a career. While this was surely wearying, Gordon never seems to have lost his spirit or his sense of humor.

During my research for this book I have been able to document twenty-eight Gordon-designed courthouses that were actually built. Three more can be added if the Val Verde Jail, which served as a temporary courthouse, and the additions to the Calcasieu and Cambria courthouses are counted. The total can be brought to thirty-two by including the foundation work begun for Kiowa. Of this total, twenty-one are extant, as are his Arizona Capitol and Vicksburg City Hall.

That some have been lost is regrettable, and in my travels I have gotten the sense that their loss is most keenly felt in the counties where they stood. While tearing down fine but antiquated and neglected courthouses may seem fiscally responsible in the short run, their replacements rarely embody as much optimism and civic spirit. Because of this, a bit of a county's identity dies with the demise of one of these buildings.

On the brighter side, a high percentage still stand as a testament to Gordon's artistry. During the course of writing this book, many of these courthouses have received praiseworthy restorations incorporating significant advances in that area of the building arts. The broadly supported Texas Historic Courthouse Preservation Program, a legacy of George W. Bush's governorship, recognized the state's surviving nineteenth- and early-twentieth-century courthouses, including Gordon's, as assets and contributed in returning them to their original glory. I have had the honor of contributing the fruits of my research to some of these projects. The value of Gordon's work has been recognized in other states as well, with millions of dollars being spent to remove misguided alterations that have accumulated over the years.

Gordon told prospective clients that a courthouse should be built to last a hundred years. As this book goes to press, nearly all of his extant temples of justice have passed that benchmark. With the current appreciation of his achievement, their continued survival seems more assured than it was just a few years ago. May they stand another hundred.

Acknowledgments

I am indebted to many wonderful individuals and the staffs of many institutions who have lent assistance to my research. Some helped without providing a name; others are mentioned below. I apologize for any misspellings or omissions. This work has stretched over many years, so I have omitted titles because surely the status of many has changed.

A generous grant from The Summerlee Foundation was essential in bringing this project to fruition. Credit for publication goes to the confidence and effort of Texas Tech University Press, especially Judith Keeling, and its editorial, production, and marketing staffs as well as the anonymous readers. A Texas State Historical Association Cecilia Steinfeldt Fellowship for Research in the Arts and Material Culture award greatly helped underwrite the illustrations contained herein. Chapter 7 represents an abridgement, with new information, of an article that first appeared in *Southwestern Historical Quarterly*, and it is printed here with permission.

The Alexander Architectural Archive, The General Libraries, at the University of Texas at Austin is the primary trove of information on James Riely Gordon. I would like to thank Beth Dodd, Lila Knight, and Nancy Sparrow in particular. Sources of relatively broad information utilized in this volume include the American Institute of Architects Library and Archives, particularly Sarah Turner; the Austin Public Library; the Library of Congress; the Dallas Public Library; Daughters of the Republic of Texas Library; the Detroit Public Library; the Frances Loeb Library, Harvard University, particularly Mary Daniels; the Houston Public Library; Institute of Texan Cultures, Patrick Lemelle in particular; Mississippi Department of Archives and History; the National Archives and Record Retention; the New York State Archives; Brown Fine Arts Library, Rice University; the Rosenberg Library, Galveston; the Royal Oak Public Library; San Antonio Conservation Society; the San Antonio Public Library; the Texas Historical Commission, particularly Mark Cowan; the Texas State Law Library, particularly Catherine Harris; the Texas State Library and Archives, John Anderson in particular; Fisher Fine Arts Library, University of Pennsylvania.

Sources of more specific or local information are, for Gordon's heritage and early life: the Bell County (Texas) Clerk's Office, Vada Sutton in particular; the Davidson County (Tennessee) Historical Commission, particularly Terry Johnson; the District of Columbia Public Library; Handley Regional Library Archives, Winchester, Virginia, particularly Rebecca Ebert; Hawai'i State Archives; Hawaiian Historical Society; Iolani Palace; Alan Lessoff; the Tennessee State Museum, James Hubler in particular; the Library of Virginia; and the Winchester-Frederick County Historical Society, Kathy Budrie in particular. For the Acadia Parish, Louisiana, Courthouse: the Acadia Parish Library. For the Angelina County, Texas, Courthouse: the Angelina County Clerk's Office; and the Lufkin Public Library. For the Aransas County, Texas, Courthouse: the Aransas County Historical Society, particularly Raulie Irwin, Jr.; Virginia Shivers and John D. Wendell. For the Arizona Capitol: the Arizona State Library & Archives, Nancy Sawyer in particular. For the Bergen County, New Jersey, Courthouse: the Bergen County Department of Parks, Division of Cultural & Historic Affairs, particularly Ann Romano, Janet Strom, and Schuyler Warmflash; the Johnson Free Public Library, Hackensack; and the New Jersey State Library, Trenton. For the Bexar County, Texas, Courthouse: the Bexar County Clerk's Office and the Special Collections Department of the Kansas City Public Library, John A. Horner in particular. For the Brazoria County, Texas, Courthouse: Brazoria County Clerk's Office; and the Brazoria County Historical Museum, particularly Karen Arvizu-Williams, Michael Bailey, Jamie Murray, and Leslie M. Rankin-Conger. For the Calcasieu Parish, Louisiana, Courthouse: Leslie J. Hartwell, Office of the Calcasieu Parish Secretary; and the Southwest Louisiana Genealogical and Historical Library, Lake Charles. For the Callahan County, Texas, Courthouse: Callahan County Clerk's Office; and the Callahan County Library and Historical Society, Sonya Walker in particular. For the Cambia County, Pennsylvania, Courthouse: The Cambria County Board of Commissioners; and the Cambria County Historical Society. For the Comal County, Texas, Courthouse: the Comal County Clerk's Office;

and the Sophienburg Archives. For the Copiah County, Mississippi, Courthouse: the Copiah County Chancery Clerk Steve Amos; and the George Covington Memorial Library, Paul Cartwright in particular. For the Cortland County, New York, County Courthouse: the Cortland County Historical Society; the Cortland Public Library; and Cathy Barber, Cortland County Historian. For the Denton County, Texas, Courthouse: the Denton County Clerk's Office; the Denton Historical Museum, the Historical Society of Denton County; Mike Cochran and Bullit Lowry. For the Ellis County, Texas, Courthouse: the Ellis County Clerk's Office; the Ellis County Historical Commission, particularly Sylvia Smith; the Ellis County Museum, particularly Shannon Smith; and the Nicholas P. Sims Library. For the Erath County, Texas, Courthouse: the Dick Smith Library, Tarleton State University; the Erath County Clerk's Office; the Stephenville Historical Museum; the Stephenville Public Library; and John A. Wooley. For the Fayette County, Texas, Courthouse: the Fayette County Clerk's Office; the Fayette County Commissioners' Court Office, particularly Ed Janecka; the Fayette Public Library, particularly Kathy Carter. For the Franklin County, New York, Courthouse: the Franklin County Historical and Museum Society, Jean Goddard in particular; and Peggy Case. For the Galveston County, Texas, Courthouse: the Galveston County Clerk's Office, Brandy Chapman in particular; Sarah Lieber; and the Rosenberg Library, Shelly Henley-Kelly in particular. For the Garrett County, Maryland, Courthouse: the Garrett County General Services Department, F. Gary Mulich and Debbie Owston in particular; the Garrett County Historical Museum; the Maryland State Archives; and the Ruth Enlow Library, Oakland. For the Gonzales County, Texas, Courthouse: the Gonzales County Clerk's office; the Gonzales County Historical Commission; the Gonzales Public Library; and the Gonzales Inquirer, Murray Montgomery in particular. For the Harrison County, Mississippi, Courthouse: the Biloxi Public Library, particularly Murella Powell; the Gulfport Public Library; and the Harrison County Chancery Clerk's Office. For the Harrison County, Texas, Courthouse: the Harrison County Clerk's office; the Harrison County Historical Museum; the Marshall News-Messenger; the Marshall Public Library; Preservation Harrison County, Conover Hunt in particular; Gail K. Beil and Michael Smith. For the Hopkins County, Texas, Courthouse: the Hopkins County Clerk's Office; The Hopkins County Commissioners' Court Office, Cletis Milsap in particular; and the Hopkins County Genealogical Society, John Sellers in particular. For the Huntington County, Indiana, Courthouse: the Indiana Room of the Huntington City-Township Public Library; and the Huntington County Clerk's Office. For the Karnes County, Texas, Courthouse: the Karnes County Clerk's Office. For the Kiowa County, Oklahoma, Courthouse:

the Kiowa County Clerk's office, Patty Johnson in particular; the Bizzell Memorial Library, University of Oklahoma; Sandy Miller; and the Southwestern Oklahoma Historical Society, Lawton, Alicia Abbot in particular. For the Lamar County, Texas, Courthouse: the Lamar County Clerk's Office; Paris Junior College Library, Daisy Harville and Larry D. Hunt in particular; and the Paris Public Library. For the Lee County, Texas, Courthouse: the Lee County Clerk's Office; and the Rufus Young King Library. For the Lincoln Parish, Louisiana, Courthouse: the Lincoln Parish Police Jury Office; the Prescott Memorial Library, Louisiana Tech University, particularly Peggy Carter; and Kelly Priestly. For the Madison County, New York, Courthouse: the Office of the Madison County Board of Supervisors; Madison County Historian Deborah Harmon; the Madison County Historical Society, Oneida; and the Oneida Public Library. For the Midland County, Texas, Courthouse: the Midland County Historical Museum, Nancy McKinley in particular. For the Mississippi State Capitol: the Memphis and Shelby County (Tennessee) Public Library and Information Center, particularly Patricia M. Lapointe; and the Mississippi Department of Archives and History, Archives and History Division. For the New York County, New York, Courthouse: the New York Public Library, NYPL Express Research Service. For the Pawnee County, Oklahoma, Courthouse: Pawnee County Clerk Marcelee Welch; and the Pawnee Public Library, Kathy Barnes in particular. For the Rapides Parish, Louisiana, Courthouse: the Alexandria Public Library. For the Somerset County, New Jersey, Courthouse: the Somerset County Board of Freeholders; the Somerset County Engineering Department, Arthur Gerlich in particular; the Somerset County Planning Department, Pat McGarry in particular; and the Somerville Public Library. For the Somerville County, Texas, Courthouse: the Somerville County Clerk's Office. For the Texas State Building at the World's Columbian Exposition: the Chicago Historical Society, particularly Wim de Wit; and The Reyerson and Burnham Libraries, The Art Institute of Chicago, particularly Luigi Mumford and Mary K. Woolever. For the Val Verde County, Texas, Jail: the Val Verde County Clerk's Office and the Val Verde Public Library. For the Van Zandt County, Texas, Courthouse: Elvis Allen; the Van Zandt County Clerk's Office; and the Van Zandt County Genealogical Society, particularly Sibyl Creasey. For the Vicksburg, Mississippi, City Hall: Office of the Mayor, Denise C. Garner in particular; Vicksburg City Council Office; and the Vicksburg Historical Museum. For the Victoria County, Texas, Courthouse: the Victoria County Clerk's Office, the Victoria County Commissioners' Court Office, Helen R. Walker in particular; the Victoria Public Library; and Charles Spurlin. For the Wilkinson County, Mississippi, Courthouse: Wilkinson County Chancery Clerk Thomas T. Tolliver, Jr.; the Wilkinson County Historical

Museum; the Woodville Historical Commission, David Abner Smith in particular. For the Wise County, Texas, Courthouse: the Wise County Clerk's Office and the Wise County Historical Museum.

Individuals whose assistance and encouragement are deeply appreciated include the architect's granddaughter, Lucy Virginia Gordon Ralston, who generously shared family mementos and memories. Ken Hafertepe's enthusiasm and support validated the scope of this work, and Fred Weldon provided guidance in addressing Gordon's litigation record. Warren Lieber, Sherman Lieber, and Gary Young shared photographic expertise.

And of course, most appreciated are my wife, Katie, and our sons Justin and Philip, who grew up with this project and made the journey more enjoyable.

APPENDIX I

Competition Participants

Below is a record of participants in the various architectural competitions discussed in this book. As much as possible, preference was given to relying upon official records in assembling this information. Unless otherwise noted, the dates in parentheses note the day entries were due.

Sometimes the spellings of architects' names are suspect. My research included a cross-check of spellings with other sources, and I selected those that seem most authoritative. The use of initials, abbreviations, and firm names are true to the sources, and participants' hometowns are noted when sources list them. While some architects may be more familiarly associated with different locales or firms, no attempt was made to correct or fill in this information in the belief that this record may aid the study of architects' movement. Those who prevailed in the competition, at least initially, are listed in boldface.

San Antonio City Hall, Texas (May 4, 1888)

J. A. Barton	San Antonio, Texas
Bristol & Clark	Dallas, Texas
Paul Brosing	San Antonio, Texas
Chas. Buckel	San Antonio, Texas
A. F. Giles	San Antonio, Texas
J. R. Gordon	San Antonio, Texas
Kneezell & Vermehren	El Paso, Texas
Otto Kramer	San Antonio, Texas
Jas. Murphy	San Antonio, Texas
Wahrenberger & Beckmann	San Antonio, Texas

SOURCE: *San Antonio Daily Express,* May 16, 1888

Aransas County Courthouse, Rockport, Texas
(May 13, 1889)

Giles and Guindon	San Antonio, Texas
Riely Gordon	San Antonio, Texas
O. Kramer	San Antonio, Texas
James Wahrenberger	San Antonio, Texas

Plus an unspecified number of Texas architects from outside San Antonio and one unidentified architect from Nebraska

SOURCE: *San Antonio Daily Express,* May 19, 1889

Fayette County Courthouse, La Grange, Texas
(Gordon presented a sketch to officials on May 10, 1890)

Gordon tentatively secured this commission without competition on the strength of a sketch he produced after the Commissioners' Court voted to build a new courthouse. Gordon later recalled that his design "was accepted by Fayette county over the plans of numerous architects," but this is not supported anywhere else (see Appendix II).

SOURCE: Fayette County Commissioners' Court *Minutes,* vol. 3, pp. 417–19 (Mar. 12, 1890)

Bexar County Courthouse, San Antonio, Texas
(May 11, 1891)

John Andrewartha	Louisville, Kentucky
Chas. Buckel	San Antonio, Texas
Converse and Reynolds	San Antonio, Texas
A. B. Cross	Kansas City, Missouri
John A. Ettler	San Antonio, Texas
Frankel and Hayden	San Antonio, Texas
Gaensler and McLaren	Philadelphia, Pennsylvania
Gill, Moad and Gill	Dallas, Texas
Gordon and Laub	San Antonio, Texas
Jules de Horvath	Chicago, Illinois

Torgerson, Guissart and Ginder	St. Louis, Missouri
Otto Kramer	San Antonio, Texas
W. W. Larmour	Waco, Texas
Larmour and Watson	Austin, Texas
Jas. Murphy	San Antonio, Texas
Le Sueur and Runge	Atlanta, Georgia
John Meyers	San Antonio, Texas
Orlopp and Kusener	Dallas, Texas
McQuirk and Lewis	Dallas, Texas
Sidney Smith	Omaha, Nebraska
A. Morris Stuckert	Denver, Colorado
John Sutcliffe	Birmingham, Alabama
Van Brunt & Howe	Kansas City, Missouri
Jas. Wahrenberger	San Antonio, Texas
J. W. Yost	Columbus, Ohio [Joseph Warren Yost?]
J. W. Yost	San Antonio, Texas

SOURCE: Bexar County Commissioners' Court *Minutes*, vol. G, pp. 37–38 (May 11, 1891)

Erath County Courthouse, Stephenville, Texas
(June 17, 1891)

Fifteen to twenty architects, including:

A. N. Dawson	Fort Worth, Texas
Gordon & Laub	San Antonio, Texas
(?) Lake	Dallas, Texas
Messer, Sanguinet & Messer	Fort Worth, Texas

SOURCES: *Fort Worth Gazette*, June 23, 1891, and *San Antonio Daily Express*, June 28, 1891

Victoria County Courthouse, Victoria, Texas
(Aug. 11, 1891)

Official records report only that numerous architects submitted plans and specifications. Gordon places their number at fifteen; he and newspaper clippings identify:

Gordon & Laub	San Antonio, Texas
Alfred Muller	Galveston, Texas
Arthur O. Watson	

SOURCES: Unidentified newspaper clippings, JRG Collection, box 29, including Gordon's Affidavit (see Appendix II)

Texas State Building, World's Columbian Exposition
(Oct. 20, 1891)

R. K. Allen	Cleburne, Texas
Buchannan & Hanna	El Paso, Texas
A. N. Dawson	Dallas, Texas

E. T. Heiner	Houston, Texas (submitting three designs)
J. E. Flanders	Dallas, Texas
A. Giles	San Antonio, Texas
Gordon & Laub	San Antonio, Texas
E. Kneezell	El Paso, Texas
Larmour & Watson	Austin, Texas
McAdoo, Wooley & Knight	San Antonio, Texas
M. H. McLaurin	Fort Worth, Texas (submitting two designs)
Messer, Sanguinet & Messer	Fort Worth, Texas
J. S. Moad	Dallas, Texas
P. S. Rabitt	Galveston, Texas
George W. Stewart	Dallas, Texas

SOURCES: *Galveston Daily News*, Nov. 1, 1891, and *Houston Daily Post*, Nov. 24, 1891

NOTE: an unidentified newspaper clipping in the JRG Collection, box 29, includes H. B. Briston (Denison) and substitutes the name of R. H. Adair as the participant from Cleburne.

Tarrant County Courthouse, Fort Worth, Texas
(Mar. 13, 1893)

Anderson Bros.	St. Louis, Missouri
Gerhard Becker	St. Louis, Missouri
Blitz & Allen	Cincinnati, Ohio
A. N. Dawson	Fort Worth, Texas
J. E. Flanders	Dallas, Texas
J. R. Gordon	San Antonio, Texas
Gunn & Curtiss	Kansas City, Missouri
S. B. Haggart	Fort Worth, Texas
Walter T. Littlefield	Boston, Massachusetts
McCurdy & Pulis	Denver, Colorado
Messer, Sanguinet & Messer	Fort Worth, Texas
E. E. Myers	Detroit, Michigan
W. H. Martin	Louisville, Kentucky
M. A. Orlopp	New Orleans, Louisiana
Henry E. Roach & Son	St. Louis, Missouri
A. O. Watson	Austin, Texas
Edwin Williams	Chicago, Illinois

SOURCE: *Fort Worth Gazette*, Apr. 11, 1893

Brazoria County Courthouse, Brazoria, Texas
(Feb. 13, 1894)

This was not an open competition: four architects were invited to present plans to a committee appointed by the Commissioners' Court.

George E. Dickey	Houston, Texas

J. Riely Gordon	San Antonio, Texas
E. T. Heiner	Houston, Texas
A. O. Watson	Austin, Texas

SOURCE: Brazoria County Commissioners' Court *Minutes*, vol. F, p. 366 (Feb. 15, 1894), and unidentified newspaper clipping, JRG Collection, box 29

NOTE: the committee report identifies architects by last name only; the additional information is supplied by the newspaper clipping, which adds F. S. Glover of Houston, apparently an unsolicited entrant, to this group.

Karnes County Courthouse, Karnes City, Texas
(Feb. 26, 1894)

J. S. Calhoun
John Cormack
Dovey & Schott
Alfred Giles
J. Riely Gordon
Hodges
K [? indiscernible, perhaps Niggli & Moody]
Otto P. Kroeger
J. Wahrenberger

Wahrenberger's submission was later rejected, leading to a second contest (May 18, 1894) directed only at contractors in which the following participated:

John Cormack
M. Clark
Dovey & Schott
O. P. Kroeger
S. White

SOURCE: Karnes County Commissioners' Court *Minutes*, vol. 2, p. 243 (Feb. 26, 1894), p. 262 (May 18, 1894), and p. 263 (May 19, 1894)

Hopkins County Courthouse, Sulphur Springs, Texas
(early March 1894)

W. C. Dodson	Waco, Texas
J. E. Flanders	Dallas, Texas
J. R. Gordon	San Antonio, Texas
Lynch & Cann	Wichita Falls, Texas
A. O. Watson	Austin, Texas

SOURCE: Unidentified newspaper clipping, dateline Mar. 17, 1894, JRG Collection, box 29

Gonzales County Courthouse, Gonzales, Texas
(Mar. 26, 1894)

W. C. Dodson	Waco, Texas
F. S. Glover	Houston, Texas

E. T. Heiner	Houston, Texas
T. S. Hodges	Lockhart, Texas
Jules Leffland	Goliad, Texas
McAdoo & Wooley	San Antonio, Texas
Mauer & Wesling	La Grange, Texas
E. E. Myers	Detroit, Michigan
Richter & Lieber	San Antonio, Texas
James Wahrenberger	San Antonio, Texas
A. O. Watson	Austin, Texas

Hodges's submission was later rejected, leading to a second contest (June 18, 1894) directed at contractors in which the following participated:

James Belger	Austin, Texas
Dovey & Schott	Kerrville, Texas
Henry Kane	Houston, Texas
Otto P. Kroeger	San Antonio, Texas
Martin, Byrnes and Johnston	Victoria, Texas
L. S. Pierson	Indianapolis, Indiana
A. O. Watson	Austin, Texas
J. A. White	Vernon, Texas

SOURCE: Gonzales County Commissioners' Court *Records*, vol. 4, p. 361 (Mar. 26, 1894) and p. 391 (June 18, 1894)

San Patricio County Courthouse, Sinton, Texas
(July 21, 1894)

Riely Gordon
Geo. Lewis
Martin, Byrnes & Johnston
A. O. Watson
[?] Williams

SOURCE: San Patricio County Commissioners' Court *Minutes*, vol. 2, p. 78 (July 21, 1894)

Ellis County Courthouse, Waxahachie, Texas
(Oct. 30, 1894)

This competition was directed to contractors. A submission by **Otto P. Kroeger** featuring plans and specifications by J. Riely Gordon prevailed in a field of thirteen. The only mention of other participants found in the research for this volume was a brief *Fort Worth Gazette* report on Messer, Sanguinet & Messer of Fort Worth. It notes that the architects "have just finished and forwarded to Waxahachie the plans for the new court house of Ellis County, upon which they have been engaged for some time past. It will be a three-story stone building and will cost $150,000." There is no mention of which contractors submitted their plans.

SOURCES: *Fort Worth Gazette*, Oct. 31, 1894, and *Waxahachie Enterprise*, Dec. 7, 1894

Wise County Courthouse, Decatur, Texas (Mar. 4, 1895)

A. J. Armstrong	Dallas, Texas
Baker Bros.	Dallas, Texas
Cann & Lynch	St. Louis, Missouri
A. N. Dawson	Fort Worth, Texas
F. S. Glover	Houston, Texas
J. Riely Gordon	San Antonio, Texas
W. W. Larmour	Waco, Texas
I. W. Marlow	Bowie, Texas
Messer, Sanguinet & Messer	Fort Worth, Texas
A. O. Watson	Austin, Texas

SOURCE: Wise County Commissioners' Court *Minutes*, bk. 3, p. 49 (Mar. 4. 1895)

Lamar County Courthouse, Paris, Texas (Apr. 8, 1895)

Commissioners' Court records provide no details on its selection process that ran from April through August 1895. According to Gordon, he and Arthur O. Watson participated and Watson prevailed with a design close enough to Gordon's to inspire litigation. The Commissioners' Court eventually proceeded with a design by **Messer, Sanguinet & Messer**.

SOURCE: Lamar County Commissioners' Court *Minutes*, vol. 6, p. 69 (Aug. 20, 1895), and unidentified newspaper clipping ("Gordon's Affidavit"), JRG Collection, box 29 (see Appendix II)

Denton County Courthouse, Denton, Texas (June 24, 1895)

The Commissioners' Court rejected all submissions and voted to employ Gordon to revise his entry. According to Gordon, he, Arthur O. Watson, and thirteen other architects competed. The commissioners' court later rescinded its arrangement with Gordon and employed **W. C. Dodson**.

SOURCE: Denton County Commissioners' Court *Minutes*, vol. C, p. 502 (July 3, 1895), and unidentified newspaper clipping ("Gordon's Affidavit"), JRG Collection, box 29 (see Appendix II)

Mississippi State Capitol, Jackson, Mississippi (submissions were reviewed in early July 1896)

This list records only those personally attending the competition review; others sent submissions but were not present.

Alsop & Johnson	Memphis, Tennessee
Barnes & Wilcox	New Orleans, Louisiana
Andrew J. Bryan	Atlanta, Georgia
Davis & Postlewaite	Louisville, Kentucky
Favrot & Livaudais	New Orleans, Louisiana
James Freret	New Orleans, Louisiana
J. R. Gordon	San Antonio, Texas
Messer, Sanguinet & Messer	Fort Worth, Texas
A. H. Noorman	Atlanta, Georgia
S. M. Patton	Chattanooga, Tennessee
J. Ryan & Son, Aldenburg & Scott, Associated Architects	Lexington, Kentucky
A. W. Rush & Son	Grand Rapids, Michigan
H. M. Wolters	Louisville, Kentucky
Weathers & Weathers	Memphis, Tennessee

SOURCES: Unidentified newspaper clipping, JRG Collection, box 29, and *Mississippi House Journal*, extr. sess., Apr. 27, 1897, 197

NOTE: Weathers's plan selected by capitol committee; Gordon's plan selected by legislature; neither executed.

Galveston County Courthouse, Galveston, Texas (Feb. 23, 1897)

A total of twenty-six plans were submitted for the Galveston County Courthouse competition. Architects from various parts of the country were reported to have participated, but not all were present to explain their submissions to the court. Those who did were

Armstrong & Fritz	Galveston, Texas
Bird & Siebold	New Orleans, Louisiana
Robert F. Brookes	Paris, Texas
H. C. Chivers	
N. J. Clayton & Co.	Galveston, Texas
H. C. Cooke & Co.	Galveston, Texas
Gunn & Curtiss	
Hawthorn & Kennedy	
E. T. Heiner	Houston, Texas
C. D. Kellogg	
Kilpatrick & Goddard	
H. L. Glover & Company	
J. Riely Gordon	San Antonio, Texas
J. B. Legg	St. Louis, Missouri
Sanguinet & Messer	Fort Worth, Texas
E. J. Schutte	
George B. Stowe	
Hugh Todd	
H. Wolters	Louisville, Kentucky
A. O. Watson	
Wheeler & Wheeler	

SOURCES: Galveston *Daily News*, Feb. 25, 26, and 27, 1897, and unidentified newspaper clipping, JRG Collection, box 29

NOTE: Clayton's plans were later abandoned and those of **Sanguinet & Messer** were adopted.

Comal County Courthouse, New Braunfels, Texas
(Jan. 17, 1898)

Beckmann	San Antonio, Texas
Giles	San Antonio, Texas
Glover	Houston, Texas
Gordon	San Antonio, Texas
Wahrenberger	San Antonio, Texas
Watson	Austin, Texas

SOURCE: Unidentified German-language newspaper clipping, JRG Collection, box 29

Lee County Courthouse, Giddings, Texas (Mar. 15, 1898)

The Commissioners' Court met in secret session leaving no record of number or identities of architects participating. The submission by **Gordon** was accepted.

SOURCE: Lee County Commissioners' Court *Minutes*, vol. D, p. 99 (Mar. 15 and 17, 1898)

Arizona Territorial Capitol, Phoenix, Arizona
(Nov. 1, 1898)

Glen Allen	Houston, Texas
C. H. Brown	Los Angeles, California
J. M. Creighton	Phoenix, Arizona
W. Jones Cuthbertson	San Francisco, California
J. Riely Gordon	San Antonio, Texas
Kilpatrick & Goddard	Los Angeles, California
T. H. Maddox & Son	Phoenix, Arizona
Kenneth McDonald	Louisville, Kentucky
D. W. Millard	Phoenix, Arizona
W. R. Norton	Phoenix, Arizona
D. H. Perkins	Chicago, Illinois
J. N. Preston	Phoenix, Arizona
George Provot	New York, New York
G. B. Stowe	Galveston, Texas
L. B. Valk	Los Angeles, California
R. B. Young	Los Angeles, California

SOURCE: *Arizona Republican*, Nov. 2, 1898 (clipping in Arizona Capitol Restoration Collection, Arizona State Archives, Department of Library, Archives and Public Records)

Harrison County Courthouse, Marshall, Texas (decision to employ architects made around first week of July 1899)

No competition was held. The Commissioners' Court toured several of Gordon's courthouses with **Gordon** and **C. G.**

Lancaster, and afterward they were retained to create plans and specifications.

SOURCE: *Marshall Messenger*, July 7, 1899

Callahan County Courthouse, Baird, Texas (Mar. 12, 1900)

The competitors are unknown, but all entries were rejected and the **J. Riely Gordon Company** was retained to prepare an acceptable design.

SOURCE: Callahan County Commissioners' Court *Minutes*, vol. C, p. 425 (Feb. 15 1900)

Mississippi State Capitol, Jackson, Mississippi (plans considered between Apr. 6 and 20, 1900, extended to Apr. 25)

Moad & Bramlett	Dallas, Texas
Bruce & Morgan	Atlanta, Georgia
Gilbert & Bryan	Atlanta, Georgia, and New York, New York
G. W. Bunting	Indianapolis, Indiana
James B. Cook	Memphis, Tennessee
J. W. Gaddis	Vincennes, Indiana
J. Riely Gordon	Dallas, Texas
T. C. Link	St. Louis, Missouri
George R. Mann	St. Joseph, Missouri
Murdoch Company	Omaha, Nebraska
E. E. Myers	Detroit, Michigan
Henry Wolters	Louisville, Kentucky
Weathers & Weathers	Memphis, Tennessee
Alfred Zucker	New York, New York

SOURCE: *Daily Clarion-Ledger* (Jackson), Apr. 25, 1900

McLennan County Courthouse, Waco, Texas (details are sparse, but proposals were being reviewed in August 1900)

With the architects' identities held secret, the submission by the **J. Riely Gordon Company** was selected from a field of ten.

SOURCE: McLennan County Commissioners' Court *Minutes*, vol. F, p. 266 (Sept. 15, 1900)

Vicksburg City Hall, Vicksburg, Mississippi (Feb. 18, 1901)

A. J. Bryan	Memphis, Tennessee
W. Chamberlain & Co.	Birmingham, Alabama
George and Hunt	Jackson, Mississippi
J. Riely Gordon	Dallas, Texas
Theodore Link	Saint Louis, Missouri

Francis J. McDonnell — New Orleans, Louisiana
Charles Pearson — Raleigh, North Carolina
Snider and Churchill — Shreveport, Louisiana
William Stanton and Son — Vicksburg, Mississippi
Stone Brothers Co. — New Orleans, Louisiana

SOURCE: City of Vicksburg *Minute Book*, vol. H, p. 595 (Feb. 18, 1901)

Copiah County Courthouse, Hazelhurst, Mississippi
(Feb. 1, 1901)

The Courthouse Building Committee sent a letter soliciting plans for a courthouse and/or jail to the following:

Bruce & Morgan — Atlanta, Georgia
Bryan & Gilbert — Atlanta, Georgia
G. W. Bunting & Son — Indianapolis, Indiana
James B. Cook — Memphis, Tennessee
J. W. Gaddis — Vincennes, Indiana
J. Riely Gordon — Dallas, Texas
Theo. C. Link — St. Louis, Missouri
Geo. R. Mann — Little Rock, Arkansas
Moad & Bramlett — Dallas, Texas
E. O. Murdock & Co. — Omaha, Nebraska
E. E. Myers — Detroit, Michigan
H. W. Wolters — Louisville, Kentucky
Weathers & Weathers — Memphis, Tennessee
Alfred Zucker — New York, New York

Responding to the committee were the following:
Bryan & Gilbert
J. Riely Gordon (courthouse)
Hull & Hull (jail)
Hunt & L[? indiscernible]
Theo. C. Link
Frank Milburn
Moad & Bramlett
Alfred Zucker

SOURCE: Copiah County *Minutes of the Board of Supervisors*, bk. H, pp. 436–37 (Mar. 8, 1901)

Calcasieu Parish Courthouse Addition, Lake Charles, Louisiana (construction contract let Sept. 7, 1901)

No information is available on whether a competition was held (the parish records were lost in the 1910 fire). The work went to **J. Riely Gordon**.

Angelina County Courthouse, Lufkin, Texas (Dec. 2, 1901)

The competitors besides the successful **J. Riely Gordon Company** are unknown.

SOURCE: Angelina County Commissioners' Court *Minutes*, vol. G, p. 617 (Dec. 12, 1901)

Kiowa County Courthouse, Hobart, Oklahoma
(plans selected Jan. 28, 1902)

There is no record of a competition, but the plans of **J. R. Gordon** were adopted. Project was cancelled shortly after foundation work was begun.

SOURCE: Kiowa County Board of Commissioners *Record*, vol. 1, p. 35 (Jan. 28, 1902)

Rapides Parish Courthouse, Alexandria, Louisiana
(plans selected Feb. 20, 1902)

There is no information available on whether a competition was held. The work went to **J. Riely Gordon**, but his design was later rejected and the work went to Hull & Hull.

SOURCE: Alexandria *Daily Town Talk*, Feb. 27, 1902

Lincoln Parish Courthouse, Rushton, Louisiana
(Apr. 7, 1902)

After reviewing submissions by an unknown number of architects, the Police Jury selected that of the **J. Riely Gordon Company**.

SOURCE: *Transcriptions of the Parish Records of Louisiana, No. 31 Lincoln Parish (Ruston), Series I. Police Jury Minutes*, vol. II, 1891–1908, p. 181 (Apr. 11, 1902)

Wilkinson County Courthouse, Woodville, Mississippi
(Apr. 7, 1902)

Plans of the **J. Riely Gordon Company** were selected from an unknown number of competitors.

SOURCE: Wilkinson County *Minutes of the Board of Supervisors*, bk. D, p. 313 (Apr. 17, 1902)

Acadia Parish Courthouse, Crowley, Louisiana
(architect selected May 20, 1902)

No information was found to establish if there was a competition before the Police Jury's selection of **J. Riely Gordon Company** and **W. L. Stephens**.

SOURCE: *Crowley Daily Signal*, Oct. 15, 1946

Somerset County Courthouse, Somerville, New Jersey
(architect selected July 20, 1905)

There is no information available on the building committee's selection process. The work went to J. Riely Gordon of **Gordon, Tracy & Swartwout**.

SOURCE: Somerset County Board of Chosen Freeholders *Minutes*, vol. 8, p. 75 (July 20, 1905)

Garrett County Courthouse, Oakland, Maryland
(Feb. 1, 1907)

Invited architects:

Baldwin & Pennington	Baltimore, Maryland
J. Charles Fulton	Uniontown, Pennsylvania
Gordon, Tracy & Swartwout	New York, New York
Holmboe & Lafferty	Clarksburg, West Virginia
Wyatt & Nolting	Baltimore, Maryland

Architects not invited but permitted to compete:

R. G. Kirsh	St. Louis, Missouri
Frank P. Milburn & Company	Washington, DC

SOURCE: Garrett County Courthouse Commission *Minutes*, Maryland State Archives, MSA no. CM537-1, p. 9 (Dec. 17, 1906) and p. 11 (Feb. 1, 1907)

Bergen County Courthouse, Hackensack, New Jersey
(submissions tendered in late Feb. 1907)

Four architects and firms were invited to submit designs for the courthouse and jail, all accepted:

D'Oench & Yost	New York, New York
Gordon, Tracy & Swartwout	New York, New York
Hurd & Sutton	Newark, New Jersey
H. C. Pitman	New York, New York

SOURCE: Newspaper clipping hand identified as the *Evening Record*, May 16, 1907, JRG Collection, box 29

Madison County Courthouse, Wampsville, New York
(Mar. 31, 1908)

Ten architects and firms were invited to compete for the courthouse and/or jail, nine accepted. **James Riely Gordon** was selected for the courthouse, **William J. Beardsley** (Poughkeepsie) for the jail.

SOURCE: *Oneida Dispatch*, Apr. 3, 1908

New York County Courthouse, New York, New York
(final competition Apr. 1, 1913)

Invited architects:
A. W. Brunner
Charles Butler & Charles Morris, Associated
Carrère & Hastings
James Riely Gordon
La Farge & Morris
H. V. Magonigle
McKim, Mead & White
Tracy, Swartwout & Litchfield
Trowbridge & Livingston
York & Sawyer
Added later:
Cass Gilbert
George B. Post & Sons
Architects selected through preliminary competition:
George & Edward Blum
Griffin & Wynkoop
Charles C. Haight, A. M. Githens, and Aymar Embury II
Howells & Stokes
Guy Lowell
Maynicke & Franke
Kenneth M. Murchison and Howard Greenly
Shire & Kaufmann
Walker & Gillette
Wilder & White
All competitors were required to have a New York office.

SOURCE: *Programme of the Final Competition for the Selection of an Architect for the Court House in the City of New York*, The Court House Board, New York County, December 18, 1912, JRG Collection, box 17, folder 3

Cambria County Courthouse, Ebensburg, Pennsylvania
(Gordon employed May 12, 1914)

James Riely Gordon was engaged for the work. He later recalled that the committee investigated other architects, but neither he nor the commissioners' minutes supply their identities or number.

SOURCE: Gordon v. County of Cambria, transcript, 18–24 and 48, JRG Collection, box 11, folder 9

Cortland County Courthouse, Cortland, New York
(Gordon employed Mar. 15, 1922)

A building committee selected **James Riely Gordon** as the sole architect to present plans to the Board of Supervisors.

SOURCE: Cortland County Supervisors' *Journal*, 1921, p. 15 (Mar. 15, 1922)

APPENDIX II

Gordon's Affidavit

J. Riely Gordon filed suit against Arthur O. Watson in connection to the latter's design for the Lamar County Courthouse. The following affidavit, which was part of his case, was reproduced in an unidentified newspaper and appears here courtesy of The Alexander Architectural Archive, The General Libraries, University of Texas at Austin. Unfortunately, some fragments of the newspaper clipping have been lost. The original case files were likely destroyed in the 1916 Paris, Texas, fire and no other copies of this affidavit have been found.

Despite a few missing words, this deposition provides valuable insight into Gordon's aspirations early in his career as a courthouse architect. Missing text is indicated with ellipses. Dashes and misspellings (including that of the architect's name) appear in the original; words in brackets are suppositions from fragmentary text.

Readers will note that some aspects of Gordon's account are at odds with sources cited in the preceding pages. In addition, Library of Congress records show only one unidentified courthouse design entered for copyright at the time of this deposition, although the architect claims two were so protected. While Gordon was surely licensed to use the Ransome twisted iron method for reinforcing concrete, his claim to "own and control" the process seems overstated.

GORDON'S AFFIDAVIT

His Allegations in the Injunction Proceedings.

The following is the affidavit of J. Reiley Gordon in the injunction before Judge Bryant:

> J. Reiley Gordon vs. A. O. Watson, et. al., in circuit court, eastern district of Texas.
> Before the undersigned clerk of the United States circuit court for the eastern district of Texas, at Paris, on this personally appeared J. Reiley Gordon, complainant in the above entitled cause, who being by me duly sworn, states on oath, that he is, and has been for the last fifteen years an architect, engaged in furnishing to builders plans and specifications for buildings, and especially court houses in the state of Texas.
> After nearly ten years of practice in architecture I decided, if possible, to originate a plan and design that would be an innovation to court house architecture, and particularly adapted to this climate. I designed a court house with a ventilating shaft and tower combined built in the center of the building of solid masonry running from the foundation to the top, introducing colonades on the outside instead of the old fashioned porticos so as to give the comfort of galleries, which was adopted by Aransas county over a number of competitors. I then conceived the idea of an open court in the center with fountain, . . . as a ventilating . . . [colonn]ades all around the inside, discarding the flat deck roof,

which was accepted by Fayette county over the plans of numerous architects, including Mr. Watson. Then I added outside colonades and changed the exterior of a plan which was adopted by Victoria county over fifteen competing Architects including Mr. Watson. These plans I had copyrighted on the — day of —, 18—, numbered —. I then modified my plan by uniting the open court, tower and ventilating shaft and changed the exterior design, which was adopted by Bexar county over thirty-two competitors, including Mr. Watson. I then improved upon all these these [sic] plans by arranging the stairway with two platforms between each story, in the combined tower, ventilating shaft and court, and arranged the entrances from the corners, through colonades then into vestibules and a rotunda or colonade around the tower with a series of arches, added consultation room, toilet room and jury and prisoners' stairway to both courts, transformed the district court room upon the theatre principle, with gallery, etc., the stage supplanted by large coves for the benefit of acoustic qualities, added private officers [sic] for each officer, changed the rooms so every one was a corner room and outside room and every office opened upon one of the colonades[.] The jury rooms on the sides of the third story, the grand jury in front with toilet rooms for each and balconies in front of each formed by roofing the private offices with flat roof, placed small towers in the recessed angles, hipped all the roofs except over the court rooms, ornamenting each with a dormer of masonry. This plan was adopted at Brazoria over some dozen competing architects, including Mr. Watson, I had these plans copyrighted on the — day of —. I then omitted the private offices on the sides, used the rear colonades as offices, changed the exterior design and had it adopted by Hopkins county over a dozen competing architects, including Mr. [Watson] . . . Watson. I presented a similar plan at Paris, arranged so as to incorporate the existing vaults as one wing veneered with granite and adding one story for a grand jury room, so as to save some ten or twelve thousand dollars, making the building entirely of granite for seventy-eight thousand dollars, which was rejected, and the present plans of Mr. Watson were adopted by said Lamar county. I presented the same plans at Denton, which were adopted over fourteen competing architects, including Mr. Watson. I exhibited all of the above plans and certificates of copyright to the county judge and commissioners of Lamar county, Texas, several weeks before the competition and again during the competition, and after the plans presented by Mr. Watson were accepted, I examined them and told him privately of the similarity and requested him to change them so as not infringe on my copyright of same, which he refused to do. I told him I would have to explain the matter to the court, which I did in executive session and requested them to have the plans changed so as not to infringe upon my copyright, also stating that I wished them to consider that I had used the proper method for notifying them first. This was before any contract was made with Mr. Watson. I notified the county through its honorable county . . . in writing and wrote him sev[eral] letters in relation thereto. I h[ave] examined the plans submitted [by] Mr. Watson for the Lamar county court house and find them to be of the same general plan, with slight variations in immaterial points, as my plans above mentioned. I have been unable to see a copy of the files and specifications of Mr. Watson. I own and control the patent twisted iron construction of the Ransome & Smith Co., patent No. 305,226.

J. R. Gordon

Subscribed and sworn to before me, this 6th day of July, 1895.

H. H. Kirkpatrick
U.S. Commissioner

Beneath this article Gordon penned, "My injunction sustained."

APPENDIX III

Representative Plans of Gordon Courthouses

With the exception of Bexar and his addition work, Gordon's built courthouses can be grouped under five design types. The representative plans shown here, with titles created for this book, are generalizations culled from actual judicial floor plans.

Hollow Square

Gordon varied this common public building plan with open center courtyards or atriums beneath a central tower.

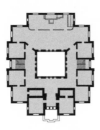

County	Seat	Design Date
Aransas	Rockport, Texas	1889
Fayette	La Grange, Texas	1890
Erath	Stephenville, Texas	1891
Victoria	Victoria, Texas	1891

Signature Plan

Gordon's innovative courthouse plan responding to Texas climate demands.

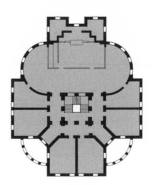

County	Seat	Design Date
Brazoria	Brazoria, Texas	1894
Hopkins	Sulphur Springs, Texas	1894
Gonzales	Gonzales, Texas	1894
San Patricio	Sinton, Texas	1894
Van Zandt	Canton, Texas	1894
Ellis	Waxahachie, Texas	1894
Wise	Decatur, Texas	1895
Comal	New Braunfels, Texas	1898
Lee	Giddings, Texas	1898
Harrison	Marshall, Texas	1899
Callahan	Baird, Texas	1900

Capitol Plan

Gordon expands his cruciform Signature Plan to accommodate multiple courtrooms. By enlarging the wings that flank a central rotunda he evokes the appearance of a state capitol.

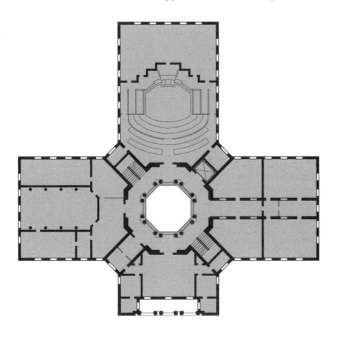

County	Seat	Design Date
McLennan	Waco, Texas	1900
Bergen	Hackensack, New Jersey	1907
Madison	Wampsville, New York	1908
Cortland	Cortland, New York	1922

Copiah Plan

An innovative plan developed to meet the criteria of the Copiah County Courthouse building committee; Gordon designed these variations under the auspices of the J. Riely Gordon Company.

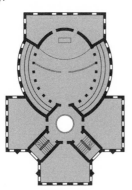

County	Seat	Design Date
Copiah	Hazelhurst, Mississippi	1901
Angelina	Lufkin, Texas	1901
Lincoln	Ruston, Louisiana	1902
Wilkinson	Woodville, Mississippi	1902
Acadia	Crowley, Louisiana	1902

Somerset Plan

An elaboration of the Copiah Plan for larger budgets and northern climates.

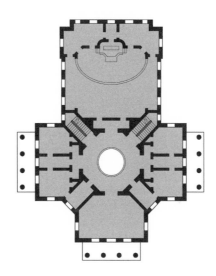

County	Seat	Design Date
Somerset	Somerville, New Jersey	1905
Garrett	Oakland, Maryland	1907

APPENDIX IV

Documented Courthouse Designs
by James Riely Gordon

County or Parish	Seat	Approximate Date of Design	Status	Documentation
Val Verde	Del Rio, Texas	1885	extant	discussed herein, actually a jail initially serving as a temporary courthouse
Aransas	Rockport, Texas	1889	destroyed	discussed herein
Fayette	La Grange, Texas	1890	extant	discussed herein
Bexar	San Antonio, Texas	1891	extant	discussed herein
Erath	Stephenville, Texas	1891	extant	discussed herein
Victoria	Victoria, Texas	1891	extant	discussed herein
Tarrant	Fort Worth, Texas	1893	not built	discussed herein
Brazoria	Brazoria, Texas	1894	destroyed	discussed herein
Karnes	Karnes City, Texas	1894	not built	discussed herein
Hopkins	Sulphur Springs, Texas	1894	extant	discussed herein
Gonzales	Gonzales, Texas	1894	extant	discussed herein
San Patricio	Sinton, Texas	1894	destroyed	discussed herein
Van Zandt	Canton, Texas	1894	destroyed	discussed herein
K	Newkirk, OT (Oklahoma)	1894	not built	*San Antonio Daily Express* Aug. 19, 1894
Pawnee	Pawnee, OT (Oklahoma)	1894	not built	*San Antonio Daily Express* Aug. 19, 1894
Ellis	Waxahachie, Texas	1894	extant	discussed herein
Wise	Decatur, Texas	1895	extant	discussed herein
Lamar	Paris, Texas	1895	not built	discussed herein
Denton	Denton, Texas	1895	not built	discussed herein
Burleson (?)	Somerville, Texas	1895*	not built	drawing in JRG Collection**
Galveston	Galveston, Texas	1895	not built	discussed herein
Galveston	Galveston, Texas	1897	not built	discussed herein
Eastland	Eastland, Texas	1897*	not built	correspondence in JRG Collection
Comal	New Braunfels, Texas	1898	extant	discussed herein
Lee	Giddings, Texas	1898	extant	discussed herein
Harrison	Marshall, Texas	1899	extant	discussed herein

County or Parish	Seat	Approximate Date of Design	Status	Documentation
Callahan	Baird, Texas	1900	destroyed	discussed herein
McLennan	Waco, Texas	1900	extant	discussed herein
Copiah	Hazelhurst, Mississippi	1901	extant	discussed herein
Calcasieu	Lake Charles, Louisiana	1901	destroyed	discussed herein
Angelina	Lufkin, Texas	1901	destroyed	discussed herein
Rapides	Alexandria, Louisiana	1902	not built	discussed herein
Kiowa	Hobart, Oklahoma	1902	abandoned	discussed herein
Lincoln	Ruston, Louisiana	1902	destroyed	discussed herein
Wilkinson	Woodville, Mississippi	1902	extant	discussed herein
Acadia	Crowley, Louisiana	1902	destroyed	discussed herein
Sioux	Orange City, Iowa	1902*	not built	correspondence in JRG Collection***
Huntington	Huntington, Indiana	1903*	not built	drawing in JRG Collection
Somerset	Somerville, New Jersey	1905	extant	discussed herein
Hudson	Jersey City, New Jersey	1906*	not built	drawing in JRG Collection
Blair	Hollidaysburg, Pennsylvania	1906*	not built	drawing in JRG Collection
Garrett	Oakland, Maryland	1907	extant	discussed herein
Bergen	Hackensack, New Jersey	1907	extant	discussed herein
Madison	Wampsville, New York	1908	extant	discussed herein
Lebanon	Lebanon, Pennsylvania	1908*	not built	drawing in JRG Collection
New Haven	New Haven, Connecticut	1909*	not built	drawing in JRG Collection
New York	New York, New York	1910	not built	discussed herein
New York	New York, New York	1912	not built	discussed herein
Cambria	Ebensburg, Pennsylvania	1914	extant	discussed herein
New Castle	Wilmington, Delaware	1914*	not built	drawing in JRG Collection
Erie	Erie, Pennsylvania	1919*	not built	correspondence in JRG Collection***
Cortland	Cortland, New York	1922	extant	discussed herein
Franklin	Malone, New York	1928*	not built	correspondence in JRG Collection***

*Many drawings in the JRG Collection are undated. Approximate dates provided for courthouse designs not discussed herein are drawn from cursory study of the structures that were actually built.

**This drawing is identified in *Sketches from the Portfolio of James Riely Gordon* as "Accepted Design. Court-House. Somerville, Texas." The identification is problematic, however. Somerville is in Burleson County, whose seat is Caldwell. This design and its appearance in *Sketches* suggest it dates around 1895, but no courthouse was built in Burleson County near that time. While the name of another Texas county, Somervell, raises the possibility of confusion, its courthouse was built in 1893—too early for the style depicted in this drawing.

***Correspondence demonstrates Gordon's interest in this project but does not establish if he actually produced a design.

Notes

Many of the newspaper entries cited below are brief passages from local news columns, notices, and advertisements. Newspaper article titles are provided within these notes only when an author is identified.

CHAPTER ONE: CATCHING ON NICELY

1. *Houston Daily Post*, Dec. 2, 1891; and *Handbook of the World's Columbian Exposition* (Chicago: Rand, McNally, 1893), 193. The *Handbook* puts the date of the move as 1873. The *Houston Daily Post* article gives the date of the family's arrival in Texas as 1872, but this is suspect since it also has that year for the family's move *to* Washington. George M. Gordon is listed in the Washington city directory for 1874, but no other year. *Washington, D.C., City Directory for 1874*, 212. For more on territorial Washington, DC, see Alan Lessoff, *The Nation and Its City: Politics, "Corruption," and Progress in Washington, D.C., 1861–1902* (Baltimore, MD: Johns Hopkins University Press, 1994).

2. Dora P. Crouch, Daniel J. Garr, and Axel I. Mundingo, *Spanish City Planning in North America* (Cambridge, MA: MIT Press, 1982), 2, 14, 15.

3. Charles Ramsdell, *San Antonio: A Historical and Pictorial Guide*, rev. ed. (Austin: University of Texas Press, 1979), 12, 19; and Gilbert R. Cruz, *Let There Be Towns: Spanish Municipal Origins in the American Southwest, 1610–1810* (College Station: Texas A&M University Press, 1988), 68.

4. Edward King, "Glimpses of Texas I: A Visit to San Antonio," *Scribner's Monthly* 7 (Jan. 1874): 305, 310, 315, 320, 321.

5. *San Antonio Daily Express*, Sept. 14, 1881, and Nov. 14, 1885.

6. Correspondence, James Riely Gordon (JRG) to the Board of Capitol Commissioners, State of North Dakota, June 21, 1931, typescript in the James Riely Gordon Collection, The Alexander Architectural Archive, The University of Texas Libraries, University of Texas at Austin (hereafter cited as the JRG Collection), box 17, folder 20; and Mary N. Woods, *From Craft to Profession: The Practice of Architecture in Nineteenth-Century America* (Berkeley: University of California Press, 1999), 158–59.

7. *San Antonio Daily Express*, Feb. 21, 1886 (quotation); and Mary Carolyn Hollers Jutson, *Alfred Giles: An English Architect in Texas and Mexico* (San Antonio, TX: Trinity University Press, 1972), 1–2.

8. Willard B. Robinson, *The People's Architecture: Texas Courthouses, Jails, and Municipal Buildings* (Austin: Texas State Historical Association, 1983), 86, 87.

9. Unidentified newspaper clipping (ca. 1902), JRG Collection, box 29.

10. Seymour V. Connor, "Evolution of County Government in the Republic of Texas," *Southwestern Historical Quarterly* 55 (Oct. 1951): 165, 175–76.

11. *San Antonio Daily Express*, Dec. 13, 1886, and Dec. 12, 1887.

12. James Patrick, *Architecture in Tennessee, 1768–1897* (Knoxville: University of Tennessee Press, 1981), 145, 157–58, 183, 200; and *Jewish Messenger* 38 (Oct. 1875), transcription by F. Frank, MS 20:4, 56–58 (quotation), Archives of the Jewish Federation of Nashville and Middle Tennessee.

13. *San Antonio Daily Express*, Nov. 7, 1879; and William Elton Green, "'A Question of Great Delicacy': The Texas State Capitol Competition, 1881," *Southwestern Historical Quarterly* 92 (Oct. 1988): 262–63. This assessment of Dobson's success is based upon a review of San Antonio newspaper reports and advertising during the period.

14. *San Antonio Daily Express*, June 21, 1882; *Houston Daily Post*, Dec. 2, 1891; *Handbook of the World's Columbian Exposition*, 193.

15. *San Antonio Evening Light*, Sept. 28, 1882; and *San Antonio Daily Express*, Dec. 13, 1886.

16. *San Antonio Evening Light*, Nov. 15, 1882. Another report adds that Dobson's daughter accompanied him on the trip. *San Antonio Evening Light*, Dec. 1, 1882.

17. *San Antonio Daily Express*, Jan. 10, 1883; Hank Todd Smith, ed., *Austin: Its Architects and Architecture (1836–1986)* (Austin, TX: American Institute of Architects, Austin Chapter, 1986), 59; Green, "'A Question of Great Delicacy,'" 260, 266–67; and Bob Brinkman and Dan K. Utley, "A Name on the Cornerstone: The Landmark Texas Architecture of

Jasper Newton Preston," *Southwestern Historical Quarterly* 110 (July 2006): 11, 14.

18. *San Antonio Daily Express*, Jan. 10, 1883. The Bell County jail was built in 1883, and the Commissioners' Court solicited plans and specifications for the courthouse competition between Nov. 24, 1883, and Jan. 1, 1884. Vedda Sutton, comp., Bell County Commissioners' Court *Minutes*, vol. F, p. 219 (Nov. 14, 1883) and p. 223 (Jan. 11, 1884).

19. Smith, *Austin: Its Architects and Architecture*, 59. There is no listing for the Prestons in the *San Antonio City Directory for 1885–86*, indicating that the firm had withdrawn to Austin by Sept. 1884.

20. See, for example, *Houston Daily Post*, Dec. 2, 1891.

21. *Texas State Gazetteer and Business Directory, 1884*, 1045; *San Antonio City Directory for 1885–86*, 154; and correspondence, William H. Young to S. B. Maxey, Apr. 28, 1886, Record Group 56, General Records of the Department of the Treasury, Records of the Division of Appointments, Applications and Recommendations for Appointments as Superintendents of Construction, 1852–1904, box 13, National Archives, College Park, MD (hereafter cited as RG 56, box 13, National Archives).

22. *San Antonio Daily Express*, Aug. 12, 1885.

23. Val Verde Commissioners' Court *Minutes*, vol. 1, p. 44 (Dec. 14, 1885), p. 48 (Dec. 19, 1885), and p. 112 (Oct. 12, 1887); and Whitehead Memorial Museum, *La Hacienda* (Norman: University of Oklahoma Press, 1976), 11.

24. Val Verde Commissioners' Court *Minutes*, vol. 1, p. 52 (Jan. 18, 1886); *San Antonio Daily Express*, Jan. 22 and Feb. 24 (quotation), 1886. Apparently well accepted in the male-dominated newspaper profession, Lyons was, along with Judge Roy Bean, among Val Verde County's most colorful citizens at the time.

25. *San Antonio Daily Express*, June 4, 1886, and Aug. 31, 1886.

26. For example, see Andrew Morrison, *Historic San Antonio*, n.d. (1887), 146, photocopy in the James Riely Gordon file, Daughters of the Republic of Texas Library at the Alamo, San Antonio.

27. The six entries are J. C. Breeding & Son, Charles Buckel, Alfred Giles, Gordon & Shelton, Murphy and Company, and Wahrenberger & Beckmann. *San Antonio City Directory for 1885–86*, 340. Shelton and J. C. Breeding & Son disappear from the directory rolls in 1887. Buckel is gone by 1889.

28. *Inland Architect and News Record* 13 (Mar. 1889): 45 (second quotation); and Hank Todd Smith, *Since 1886: A History of the Texas Society of Architects* (Austin: Texas Society of Architects, 1983), 2 (first quotation).

29. Woods, *From Craft to Profession*, 34–39.

30. *San Antonio Daily Express*, Feb. 21, 1886; *San Antonio Daily Express*, Mar. 11 and Sept. 23, 1887, and Jan. 26, 1888 (quota-

tion); Jutson, *Alfred Giles*, 2; and Chris Meister, "Alfred Giles vs. El Paso County: An Architect Defends His Reputation on the Texas Frontier," *Southwestern Historical Quarterly* 108 (Oct. 2004): 181–205. Giles did not completely abandon his architectural practice during this period, as evidenced by his successful bid to design the Mexican government's customhouse at Nueva Laredo. *San Antonio Daily Express*, Sept. 23, 1887.

CHAPTER 2: THE FEDERAL BUILDING

1. For more on the Office of the Supervising Architect, see Antoinette Lee, *Architects to the Nation: The Rise and Decline of the Supervising Architect's Office* (New York: Oxford University Press, 2000).

2. US Congress, House, *Public Building at San Antonio, Tex.*, Rep. No. 459 to accompany H. 4465, 47th Cong., 1st sess. (1882), 1; US Congress, House, *Public Building, San Antonio, Tex.*, Rep. No. 1280 to accompany H. 3441, 48th Cong., 1st sess. (1884), 1; and US Congress, House, *Public Building at San Antonio, Tex.*, Rep. No. 614 to accompany S. 44, 49th Cong., 1st sess. (1886), 1–2; and *San Antonio Daily Express*, Dec. 5, 1885, Feb. 2, Feb. 3, and Feb. 19, 1886.

3. *San Antonio Daily Express*, May 8, 1886.

4. Multiple correspondence, RG 56, box 13, National Archives; *The National Cyclopedia of American Biography*, vol. 28 (New York: James T. White & Company, 1940), 312, s.v. "Gordon, J. Riely"; and interview with Virginia Gordon Ralston, Oct. 29, 2003.

5. James E. Blackwell, "United States Government Building Practice," *The American Architect and Building News* 21 (Feb. 5, 1887): 65; and Lee, *Architects to the Nation*, 135–42.

6. *San Antonio Daily Express*, June 4, 1886; correspondence, Julius C. Holmes to Mifflin E. Bell, Washington, DC, June 9, 1886, RG 56, box 13, National Archives (second quotation); and Donald J. Lehman, *Lucky Landmark: A Study of a Design and Its Survival, The Galveston Custom House, Post Office and Courthouse of 1861* (Washington, DC: General Services Administration Public Building Service, 1973), 78 (first quotation).

7. *San Antonio Daily Express*, Oct. 7, 1889 (quotation); and Alan Lessoff, *The Nation and Its City: Politics, "Corruption," and Progress in Washington, D.C., 1861–1902* (Baltimore, MD: Johns Hopkins University Press, 1994), 61–62, 98–99.

8. Correspondence, Mifflin E. Bell to James Wahrenberger, July 5, 1887, Record Group 121, Public Buildings Service, General Correspondence, Letters Received 1843–1910, San Antonio, TX, P.O., 1888–1889, box 186, National Archives, College Park, MD.

9. *San Antonio Daily Express*, Nov. 11, 1886, and Jan. 27, 1887.

10. *San Antonio Daily Express*, Feb. 19, Mar. 13, May 24, May 31, and June 5, 1887.

11. Correspondence, M. E. Bell to JRG, June 2, 1887, JRG Collection, box 18, folder 4; and *San Antonio Daily Express*, June 12, 1887 (quotation).

12. Correspondence, M. E. Bell to JRG, May 31, 1887, and M. E. Bell to JRG, June 2, 1887, JRG Collection, box 18, folder 4; *San Antonio Daily Express*, June 12, 1887; Percy Clark, "New Federal Buildings," *Harper's Weekly* (May 19, 1888): 368; and Darrell Hevenor Smith, *The Office of the Supervising Architect of the United States Treasury: Its History, Activities and Organization* (Baltimore, MD: Johns Hopkins University Press, 1923; repr., New York: AMS Press, 1974), 13–14.

13. *San Antonio Daily Express*, July 23, 1887 (quotation). In addition to its poor ventilation, the Austin Federal Building was criticized for its slow-paced construction and high cost. Kenneth Hafertepe, *Abner Cook: Master Builder on the Texas Frontier* (Austin: Texas State Historical Association, 1992), 198–99.

14. *San Antonio Daily Express*, July 23 and Oct. 27, 1887.

15. Smith, *The Office of the Supervising Architect of the United States Treasury*, 13, 15.

16. *San Antonio Daily Express*, July 23, 1887.

17. *Inland Architect and News Record* 11 (July 1887): 101; *San Antonio Daily Express*, Feb. 8, 1888; and William Corner, ed., *San Antonio de Bexar* (San Antonio, TX: Bainbridge and Corner, 1890; repr., San Antonio, TX: Graphic Arts, 1977), 39.

18. *San Antonio Daily Express*, Aug. 20 (quotation) and Oct. 27, 1887.

19. *San Antonio Daily Express*, Dec. 9 and Dec. 11, 1887, and Mar. 9, 1888.

20. The description that follows was derived from information gleaned from *San Antonio Daily Express*, July 23, 1887, and July 22, 1890 (quotation); and by examining photographic records and the original drawings as published here and in *American Architect and Building News* 22 (Apr. 7, 1888): 65–67; and unidentified newspaper clipping (ca. 1891), JRG Collection, box 29.

21. Not part of the builder's contract, the intention was to award carving of the frieze to stonecutters separately. *San Antonio Daily Express*, June 26, 1889; and Andrew Morrison, *The City of San Antonio* (St. Louis, MO: George W. Engelhardt [ca. 1891]; repr., San Antonio, TX: Norman Brock, 1977), 10.

22. Lee, *Architects to the Nation*, 163.

23. Sara E. Wermiel, *The Fireproof Building* (Baltimore, MD: Johns Hopkins University Press, 2000), 77–78.

24. *San Antonio Daily Express*, Sept. 14, 1890.

25. *San Antonio Daily Express*, July 10 and July 13, 1889; and Morrison, *The City of San Antonio*, 60.

26. *San Antonio Daily Express*, July 8, 1887.

27. *San Antonio Daily Express*, Apr. 25 and Dec. 1, 1886, and July 10, 1887.

28. It appears that the only other architect invited to participate was Charles Buckel, who received $50 for his efforts. Bexar County Commissioners' Court *Records*, vol. E, p. 137 (Apr. 13, 1887), p. 215 (July 12, 1887); and *San Antonio Daily Express*, July 13 and Sept. 22, 1887, and Sept. 16, 1894.

29. *San Antonio Daily Express*, Jan. 5, 1888. In 1889 Murphy moved to Laredo, where he established an office in anticipation of greater opportunities. Family and business connections caused his occasional return to San Antonio, however. In late 1890 he began a San Antonio association with J. A. Ettler as James Murphy and Company, Architects. *San Antonio Daily Express*, June 3, June 12, and Aug. 12, 1889, and Sept. 1 and Nov. 2, 1890.

30. *San Antonio Daily Express*, Mar. 24 and Mar. 27, 1888.

31. *San Antonio Daily Express*, May 16, May 22, May 23, May 24, July 29, and Aug. 2, 1888.

32. *San Antonio Daily Express*, July 24 and July 27, 1888.

33. Correspondence, JRG to James H. Windrim, June 25, 1889, RG 56, box 13, National Archives.

34. Correspondence, W. H. Huston to James H. Windrim, Apr. 8, 1889 (first quotation); and J. J. Stevens to James H. Windrim, Apr. 8, 1889 (second quotation), RG 56, box 13, National Archives.

35. Correspondence, James P. Newcomb to James H. Windrim, May 1, 1889; and James P. Newcomb to J. C. DeGress, June 18, 1889, RG 56, box 13, National Archives.

36. Correspondence, JRG to James H. Windrim, June 25, 1889, RG 56, box 13, National Archives.

37. *San Antonio Daily Express*, June 28 and July 10, 1889.

38. *San Antonio Daily Express*, July 13, 1889.

39. *San Antonio Daily Express*, Aug. 8 and Sept. 15, 1889.

40. *San Antonio Daily Express*, Dec. 10, 1889, and July 20 and Sept. 14, 1890.

41. Robert Graves, "Uncle Sam's Buildings," *San Antonio Daily Express*, Aug. 31, 1890.

42. This is the generally accepted figure. The *Inland Architect* later placed the construction cost of the United States Courthouse and Post Office, San Antonio, at $185,219. "Cubical Contents and Percentage of Cost of United States Government Buildings Built Since 1818," *Inland Architect and News Record* 39 (Apr. 1902): 23. It is possible that the furnishings accounted for the differences in the figures. Another source identifies five buildings in the city as having equal or higher cost: the Menger Hotel ($225,000), the San Antonio City Hall ($200,000), the Kampmann Office Building ($200,000), the Lone Star Brewery ($200,000), and the Alamo Brewery ($200,000). Morrison, *The City of San Antonio*, 57, 58, 60.

43. Correspondence, JRG to the Board of Capitol Commissioners, State of North Dakota, June 21, 1931, typescript in the JRG Collection, box 17, folder 20.

CHAPTER 3: ARANSAS

1. *Frank Leslie's Illustrated Newspaper*, Oct. 18, 1890; and *San Antonio Daily Express*, Mar. 13, 1891 (quotation).
2. Aransas County Commissioners' Court *Records*, book 1, p. 374 (Apr. 8, 1889).
3. *American Architect and Building News* 11 (Feb. 4, 1882): 49; *San Antonio Daily Express*, Feb. 27, 1886, 5; *Inland Architect and News Record* 10 (Jan. 1888): 94; *Inland Architect and News Record* 13 (Mar. 1889): 45–46; *Inland Architect and News Record* 51 (Feb. 1908): 2; and correspondence, Lucy Virginia Gordon Ralston to the author, June 8, 2000.
4. *San Antonio Daily Express*, May 19, 1889.
5. *San Antonio Daily Express*, May 20, 1889.
6. C. L. V. Meeks, "Picturesque Eclecticism," *Art Bulletin* 32 (Sept. 1950): 226, 227; and Michael W. Brooks, *John Ruskin and Victorian Architecture* (New Brunswick, NJ: Rutgers University Press, 1987), 9.
7. Richard W. Longstreth, "Academic Eclecticism in American Architecture," *Winterthur Portfolio* 17 (Spring 1982): 71–78.
8. The breadth of the style in the United States is treated in Holly Edwards, ed., *Nobel Dreams, Wicked Pleasures: Orientalism in America, 1870–1930* (Princeton, NJ: Princeton University Press, 2000). Some have viewed Orientalism as an expression of Western dominance over subjugated cultures. This notion has many challengers and Gordon's use of it, as evidenced herein, represents a recognition of an indigenous heritage.
9. Clay Lancaster, "Oriental Forms in American Architecture," *Art Bulletin* 24 (Sept. 1947): 183, 185, 186. Also see Kathryn E. Holliday, *Leopold Eidlitz: Architecture and Idealism in the Gilded Age* (New York: W. W. Norton, 2008), 90–92.
10. *San Antonio Daily Express*, Feb. 7, 1887 (quotation).
11. *El Paso Daily Times*, Dec. 16, 1887.
12. *San Antonio Daily Express*, May 20, 1889; and *Frank Leslie's Illustrated Newspaper*, Oct. 18, 1890, 4.
13. See Appendix II.
14. Edward T. Price, "The Central Courthouse Square in the American County Seat," *Geographical Review* 58 (Jan. 1968): 31, 44–45; and Willard B. Robinson, "The Public Square as a Determinant of Courthouse Form in Texas," *Southwestern Historical Quarterly* 75 (Jan. 1973): 344. As will be seen in Comal County, there are also non-Spanish examples of open central squares in Texas county seats.
15. Aransas County Commissioners' Court *Records*, book 1, p. 379 (May 13, 1889), pp. 384–85 (June 19, 1889), p. 390 (July 16, 1889), p. 441 (June 11, 1890); *San Antonio Daily Express*, May 20, 1889 (quotation); *Houston Daily Post*, Mar. 6, 1892; and *Aransas County, a Glimpse at Our Past* (Rockport, TX: Aransas County-Rockport Centennial, 1970), n.p. The *Daily Post* account puts the cost of the courthouse at $25,000, but many other contemporary sources use the $20,000 figure.
16. Former Aransas County Sheriff Virginia Shivers and former Aransas County Judge John D. Wendell both worked in the 1890 courthouse and provided personal reminiscences for this book. Mrs. Shivers's experience in the courthouse dates back to the 1920s, but she does not recall a central atrium. Since Gordon's 1895 affidavit (see Appendix II) cites such a feature, it may be assumed it was executed and later enclosed.
17. Robert Graves, "Uncle Sam's Buildings," *San Antonio Daily Express*, Aug. 31, 1890.

CHAPTER 4: FAYETTE

1. For a discussion of the stylistic struggles during this period, see Longstreth, "Academic Eclecticism in American Architecture," 55–82.
2. The book was the first volume of Léonce Reynaud's *Traité d'Architecture* (1850–58). Elizabeth Greenwell Grossman, "H. H. Richardson: Lessons from Paris," *Journal of the Society of Architectural Historians* 67 (Sept. 2008): 394.
3. *San Antonio Daily Express*, Oct. 12 and Oct. 20, 1889; and Carol Lyn Davis, "The Life and Career of James Riely Gordon, Architect, with an Analysis of Three Specific Texas County Courthouses" (master's thesis, Texas Christian University, 1975), 9.
4. *San Antonio Daily Express*, Feb. 16, 1890, and Jan. 25, 1891 (quotation).
5. *Inland Architect and News Record* 15 (June 1890): 75.
6. *San Antonio Daily Express*, Oct. 2, 1892; Smith, *Since 1886*, 5; and Woods, *From Craft to Profession*, 41–42.
7. *La Grange Journal*, Feb. 27 (quotation), Mar. 20 and June 5, 1890; Fayette County Commissioners' Court *Minutes*, vol. 3, pp. 417–19 (Mar. 12, 1890), p. 433 (May 17, 1890), p. 450 (June 24, 1890), and vol. 4, p. 4 (Jan. 4, 1892); and F. Lotto, *Fayette County, Her History and Her People* (Schulenburg, TX: Sticker Steam Press, 1902), 159. At variance with these sources is Gordon's sworn affidavit against Watson (see Appendix II). Robert Allert's role as a contractor is inferred from an unsuccessful bid for Fayette's construction by Allert and Redmond of Flatonia.
8. *La Grange Journal*, May 16, 1891; and *Houston Daily Post*, Nov. 26 and Dec. 2, 1891.
9. This description of the Fayette County Courthouse is

drawn from the architect's drawings, a detailed article published in the *Houston Daily Post*, Nov. 21, 1891, archival photographs, and personal observation.

10. *Houston Daily Post*, Nov. 21, 1891.

11. *La Grange Journal*, Mar. 6, Mar. 27, and June 12, 1890, and Jan. 15, 1891 (quotation); and Fayette County Commissioners' Court *Minutes*, vol. 3, p. 557 (Feb. 12, 1891).

12. *Houston Daily Post*, Dec. 1, 1891.

13. *Houston Daily Post*, Nov. 28, 1891.

14. *San Antonio Daily Express*, July 6 and July 9, 1890; undated newspaper clippings (ca. late 1890), JRG Collection, box 29; Dennis Steadman Francis, *Architects in Practice, New York City, 1840–1900* (New York: Committee for the Preservation of Architectural Records, 1979), 92; Kenneth L. Breisch, "The Richardsonian Interlude in Texas: A Quest for Meaning and Order at the End of the Nineteenth Century," in *The Spirit of H. H. Richardson on the Midland Prairies*, ed. Paul Clifford Larson and Susan M. Brown (Ames: Iowa State University Press, 1988), n. 151; and Lee, *Architects to the Nation*, 136–37.

CHAPTER 5: BEXAR

1. *San Antonio Daily Express*, Sept. 16, 1894; Department of the Interior, Census Division, *Abstract of the Eleventh Census: 1890*, 2nd ed. (Washington, DC: Government Printing Office, 1896), 30, 36; Edward W. Heusinger, *A Chronology of Events in San Antonio* (San Antonio, TX: Standard Printing Company, 1951), 44–49, 80; and John A. Booth and David R. Johnson, "Power and Progress in San Antonio Politics, 1836–1970," in *The Politics of San Antonio: Community, Progress and Power*, ed. David R. Johnson, John A. Booth, and Richard J. Harris (Lincoln: University of Nebraska Press, 1983), 8–10.

2. *San Antonio Daily Express*, Jan. 21, 1886.

3. The county paid $85,000 for the Dwyer property and $25,000 for property belonging to Caroline Kampmann. *San Antonio Daily Express*, Mar. 9 and Mar. 15 (quotation), 1891, Sept. 16, 1894, and Oct. 4, 1896. The presence of a government building on Main Plaza goes back to 1742, when the *Casa Reales* stood on its east side and housed San Antonio's local governing body. After Texas Independence it housed city and county functions until 1850 when both governments were removed to Military Plaza. The city and county occasionally occupied office space on Main Plaza until the 1891 decision to build the new Bexar County Courthouse. Sylvia Ann Santos, *Courthouses of Bexar County, 1731–1978* (San Antonio, TX: Bexar County Historical Commission, 1979), 2, 3.

4. Bexar County Commissioners' Court *Minutes*, vol. G, p. 15 (Mar. 30, 1891); and *San Antonio Daily Express*, Apr. 16 and Apr. 20, 1891, and May 12, 1891.

5. Bexar County Commissioners' Court *Minutes*, vol. G, pp. 37–38 (May 11, 1891); and *San Antonio Daily Express*, Apr. 16 and May 17, 1891 (quotation).

6. See Appendix I for a list of participants. Wahrenberger's opinion of competitions can be found in *Inland Architect and News Record* 15 (June 1890): 75.

7. Bexar County Commissioners' Court *Minutes*, vol. G, pp. 44–45 (May 18, 1891); and *San Antonio Daily Express*, May 19, 1891.

8. Bexar County Commissioners' Court *Minutes*, vol. G, pp. 168–69 (Aug. 4, 1891); unidentified newspaper clipping (ca. Sept. 1891), JRG Collection, box 29; Bexar County Commissioners' Court *Minutes*, vol. G, pp. 500, 506 (May 20, 1892); *San Antonio Daily Light*, Dec. 16, 1892, JRG Collection, box 29; and *San Antonio Daily Express*, Jan. 1, 1893.

9. *San Antonio Daily Light*, Dec. 16, 1892, JRG Collection, box 29 (quotation); and *San Antonio Daily Express*, Jan. 21, 1893, and Sept. 16, 1894.

10. Bexar County Commissioners' Court *Minutes*, vol. G, p. 406 (Feb. 15, 1892), pp. 475–76 (Mar. 22, 1892), p. 480 (Mar. 30, 1892), and pp. 485–86 (Apr. 11, 1892).

11. *Kansas City: Its Resources and Their Development* (Kansas City: Kansas City Times, 1890), 34; *San Antonio Daily Express*, Apr. 12, 1891; and Bexar County Commissioners' Court *Minutes*, vol. G, p. 495 (Apr. 18, 1892) (quotation), and vol. H, p. 427 (May 10, 1893). Kroeger had previously been contracted by the county to remodel the jail to James Murphy's design and to remove the existing buildings from the new courthouse property. He competed for the courthouse foundation work but was not the lowest bidder. Bexar County Commissioners' Court *Minutes*, vol. G, p. 119 (June 17, 1891), p. 159 (July 25, 1891), and p. 243 (Oct. 12, 1891).

12. *San Antonio Daily Express*, July 14, 1892.

13. *San Antonio Daily Express*, July 14, 1892, and Jan. 16, 1993; and *San Antonio Daily Express*, Dec. 22, 1892.

14. Bexar County Commissioners' Court *Minutes*, vol. H, pp. 152–55 (Oct. 18, 1892).

15. *San Antonio Daily Express*, Oct. 1 (quotation), Oct. 5, Oct. 7, Oct. 9, Oct. 18, and Oct. 27, 1892; and Booth and Johnson, "Power and Progress in San Antonio Politics," 9.

16. *San Antonio Daily Express*, Oct. 5, 1892; and Bexar County Commissioners' Court *Minutes*, vol. H, pp. 179–82 (Nov. 17, 1892) and pp. 215–17 (Nov. 26, 1892).

17. Bexar County Commissioners' Court *Minutes*, vol. H, pp. 227–31 (Dec. 7, 1892).

18. Unidentified newspaper clipping, JRG Collection, box 29.

19. Bexar County Commissioners' Court *Minutes*, vol. H, p. 227 (Dec. 7, 1892).

20. Giles had a reputation as a mentor for other architects. *San Antonio Daily Express*, Feb. 21, 1886.

21. *San Antonio Daily Express*, Dec. 16, 1892.

22. The 1876 Texas Constitution lists county commissioners' courts among the state's courts of law, and county commissioners were recognized as magistrates in the Texas Code of Criminal Procedure into the 1920s. Since commissioners' courts are considered first and foremost administrative in function, their onetime role as courts of law has been largely forgotten. Examples of this power being invoked are the investigations of Alfred Giles by El Paso County in 1885 and James Riely Gordon by Bexar County in 1892. An *El Paso Daily Times* article delineated the process in Giles's case, which seems to have been followed in Gordon's. As this source explains, a commissioners' court, if petitioned, could agree to serve as a court of law with the county becoming the complainant. The county judge would preside, and all members would have an equal voice in the judgment. Commissioners' courts could decline, as Denton's declined a request by Gordon in 1895 (see Chapter 10). Defendants had the right to appeal to higher courts. *El Paso Daily Times*, May 27, 1885; David B. Brooks, *Texas Practice Series*, 2nd ed. (St. Paul, MN: West-Thompson Publishing Company, 2002), 3, 276–88; and Meister, "Alfred Giles vs. El Paso County," 184–85.

23. *San Antonio Daily Express*, Dec. 13, Dec. 16 (first quotation), Dec. 17 (second quotation); and *San Antonio Daily Light*, Dec. 16, 1892.

24. *San Antonio Daily Express*, Dec. 18, Dec. 21, Dec. 22, Dec. 23, Dec. 24, and Dec. 31, 1892.

25. *San Antonio Daily Express*, Jan. 21, 1893; and the Bexar County Commissioners' Court *Minutes*, vol. G, pp. 281–94 (Jan. 21, 1893).

26. Booth and Johnson, "Power and Progress in San Antonio Politics," 11.

27. *Kansas City: Its Resources and Their Development*, 34; Bexar County Commissioners' Court *Minutes*, vol. H, p. 112 (Aug. 29, 1892), pp. 475–76 (Mar. 22, 1892), and p. 427 (May 10, 1893); and *San Antonio Daily Express*, Dec. 18, 1892.

28. Booth and Johnson, "Power and Progress in San Antonio Politics," 9–10. Examples of Callaghan's efforts at obstruction can be found in the Bexar County Commissioners' Court *Minutes*, including vol. H, pp. 309–11 (Feb. 17, 1893), p. 379 (Mar. 4, 1893), and p. 554 (Aug. 10, 1893).

29. Callaghan, County Judge, v. Salliway, 23 S.W. 839 (Tex. Ct. App. 1893).

30. Bexar County Commissioners' Court *Minutes*, vol. I, pp. 5–6 (Oct. 16, 1893) and pp. 168–69 (Mar. 1, 1894).

31. Bexar County Commissioners' Court *Minutes*, vol. H, p. 305 (Feb. 16, 1893), and vol. I, pp. 13–14 (Oct. 21, 1893), p. 62 (Nov. 28, 1893), p. 73 (Dec. 13, 1893), p. 167 (Feb. 27, 1894), p. 213 (Apr. 20, 1894), and pp. 215–16 (Apr. 24, 1894).

32. Bexar County Commissioners' Court *Minutes*, vol. I, p. 244 (May 21, 1894), pp. 472–75 (Dec. 6, 1894), and pp. 502–15 (Dec. 21, 1894), and vol. J, p. 69 (May 20, 1895), p. 287 (Nov. 14 1895), and p. 337 (Nov. 30, 1895); and *San Antonio Daily Express*, Sept. 16, 1894.

33. Bexar County Commissioners' Court *Minutes*, vol. J, pp. 343–44 (Dec. 7, 1895), p. 346 (Dec. 9, 1895), p. 361 (Jan. 6, 1896).

34. Bexar County Commissioners' Court *Minutes*, vol. J, p. 501 (Mar. 14, 1896), p. 535 (Apr. 30, 1896), and pp. 567–68 (May 27, 1896); and vol. K, p. 185 (Sept. 11, 1896) and p. 193 (Sept. 22, 1896) (quotation).

35. Bexar County Commissioners' Court *Minutes*, vol. K, pp. 193–94 (Sept. 23, 1896), p. 224 (Oct. 31, 1896) (quotation), and p. 236 (Nov. 16 1896).

36. Bexar County Commissioners' Court *Minutes*, vol. K, p. 311 (Jan. 27, 1897).

37. The following description of the Bexar County Courthouse was derived from information gleaned from the *San Antonio Daily Express*, May 19, 1891, Sept. 16, 1894, Oct. 4, 1896 (quotations); an illustration of the courtyard published in the *American Architect and Building News* 61 (Sept. 10, 1898), plate; Bexar County Courthouse, Historic American Building Survey, survey no. TEX 3174, 1968, measured drawings; and personal observation by the author.

38. *San Antonio Daily Express*, Oct. 4, 1896.

39. *San Antonio Daily Express*, Apr. 16 and May 17 (quotation), 1891.

40. *San Antonio Daily Express*, Jan. 16, 1893; and Bexar County Commissioners' Court *Minutes*, vol. H, p. 311 (Feb. 25, 1893).

41. *San Antonio Daily Express*, May 21, 1896.

42. "Accepted Competitive Design—Bexar County Courthouse, James Riely Gordon, Architect, San Antonio, Texas," *American Architect and Building News* 46 (Oct. 20, 1894), plate; and correspondence, JRG to Ramsey Wharton, June 30, 1897, Mississippi Department of Archives and History, Archives and History Division. Also see Breisch, "The Richardsonian Interlude in Texas," 96.

43. *San Antonio Daily Express*, Oct. 4, 1894.

44. Bexar County Commissioners' Court *Minutes*, vol. G, p. 119 (June 17, 1891), and vol. H, p. 181 (Nov. 17, 1892).

45. *San Antonio Express*, Feb. 10, 1927 (quotation), and Mar. 17, 1937; and National Registration of Historic Places Inventory—Nomination Form: Bexar County Courthouse, Description Sheets 1, 2. Photostat copy in the collection of the Daughters of the Republic of Texas Library at the Alamo, San Antonio, TX.

46. Chris Carson and William McDonald, eds., *A Guide to San Antonio Architecture* (San Antonio, TX: San Antonio Chapter of the American Institute of Architects, 1986), 131.

CHAPTER 6: ERATH AND VICTORIA

1. Claude W. Bryant, "Historic Erath County Courthouse Stands Test," *Stephenville Empire-Tribune*, Dec. 15, 1961.

2. *San Antonio Daily Express*, May 24, 1891.

3. Erath County Commissioners' Court *Minutes*, vol. 5, p. 172 (June 17, 1891) and p. 175 (June 24, 1891); *Fort Worth Gazette*, June 23, 1891; and *San Antonio Daily Express*, June 28, 1891.

4. *Fort Worth Gazette*, June 27 and July 30, 1891; and *Stephenville Empire*, July 18, 1891.

5. *Stephenville Empire*, Sept. 5, 1891 (quotation); and undated newspaper clipping (ca. 1892), JRG Collection, box 29.

6. Undated newspaper clipping (ca. 1892), JRG Collection, box 29; and Bryant, "Historic Erath County Courthouse Stands Test."

7. The following description of the Erath County Courthouse is drawn from personal observation and an undated newspaper clipping (ca. 1892) in the JRG Collection, box 29 (quotations).

8. The white limestone came from quarries in Erath County, between Stephenville and Alexander, with larger stone being brought from the area around Marble Falls. Bryant, "Historic Erath County Courthouse Stands Test."

9. Staff of the Handbook of Texas, *Handbook of Victoria County* (Austin: Texas State Historical Association, 1990), 129.

10. Victoria County Commissioners' Court *Minutes*, vol. 3, p. 525 (May 13, 1891), pp. 539–40 (Aug. 11, 1891), p. 550 (Sept. 23, 1891), and p. 602 (May 13, 1892); undated newspaper clippings, JRG Collection, box 29; *LaGrange Journal*, Nov. 26, 1891; and *Houston Daily Post*, Dec. 15, 1891.

11. *Victoria Weekly Advocate*, June 18, 1892.

12. Victoria County Commissioners' Court *Minutes*, vol. 3, p. 578 (Mar. 14, 1892).

13. *San Antonio Daily Express*, Nov. 17, 1889, and Apr. 6, 1890; *Corpus Christi Caller*, Nov. 13, 1891; and *Victoria Weekly Advocate*, Apr. 9, 1892, and Jan. 14, 1893.

14. *Victoria Weekly Advocate*, May 7, 1892 (quotation); and *Houston Daily Post*, Feb. 23, 1893.

15. *Victoria Weekly Advocate*, May 14, 1892; and Victoria County Commissioners' Court *Minutes*, vol. 3, p. 603 (May 13, 1892) (quotation).

16. *Victoria Weekly Advocate*, June 18, 1892.

17. *San Antonio City Directory for 1891*; and Francis, *Architects in Practice*, 48, 92. Laub's only known residential address in San Antonio is Saint Paul's Rectory on Government Hill, suggesting he never put down roots during his two years in the community. His letter in the *Advocate* article shows him officing in Brooklyn's Eagle Building immediately after leaving Texas. Francis places him in Brooklyn from 1893 through 1895, and practicing with Anthime W. La Rose at 1 Madison Avenue in New York City in 1894 and 1895. He

was a fellow of the American Institute of Architects from 1894 through 1899, and a member of the Brooklyn Institute of Arts and Sciences in 1895. After 1895 it appears he did not practice under his own name in the area.

18. *Houston Daily Post*, Feb. 23, 1893.

19. See Appendix II.

20. Frank Teich was known about the state as a supplier of architectural and monumental stone. In 1890 he operated quarries at Cherry Springs (marble), Fredericksburg (granite), and Kerrville (limestone). *San Antonio Daily Express*, Dec. 20, 1890.

21. Undated newspaper clipping (ca. late 1892), JRG Collection, box 29.

22. Undated newspaper clipping (ca. late 1892), JRG Collection, box 29.

23. *Victoria Weekly Advocate*, Aug. 13, 1892; and *Houston Daily Post*, Feb. 23, 1893.

24. *Victoria Weekly Advocate*, Dec. 21, 1892; and Sidney R. Weisiger, "Courthouse Construction," *Victoria Advocate*, July 4, 1971.

25. Unidentified newspaper clipping (ca. 1893), JRG Collection, box 29; and *American Architect and Building News* 54 (Oct. 17, 1896): plate.

26. *Victoria Weekly Advocate*, Jan. 21 (third quotation) and Feb. 18, 1893 (first and second quotation).

CHAPTER 7: THE TEXAS STATE BUILDING

1. This chapter is an abridgement, with some additional information, of an earlier treatment of the subject: Chris Meister, "The Texas State Building: J. Riely Gordon's Contribution to the World's Columbian Exposition," *Southwestern Historical Quarterly* 98 (July 1994): 1–24.

2. M. A. Lane, "State Buildings at the Fair," *Harper's Weekly* 36 (Aug. 20, 1892): 813; and Thomas S. Hines, *Burnham of Chicago* (New York: Oxford University Press, 1974), 76–78.

3. *Galveston Daily News*, Dec. 11, 1890; *La Grange Journal*, Dec. 10, 1890, and July 16, 1891; and *Fort Worth Gazette*, Oct. 31, 1891. Dickinson was among a select group that included businessmen, politicians, and noted Civil War veterans from various states appointed to the prestigious National Commission. His selection as its secretary placed him in a powerful position within the upper echelon of the fair's organization. As evidence of their friendship (noted later in this chapter), Gordon attended Dickinson's wedding in Chicago while the Texas State Building was under construction. *San Antonio Daily Express*, Mar. 3, 1890; *Houston Daily Post*, June 9, 1890; *World's Columbian Exposition Illustrated* 1 (Feb. 1891): 4; Hubert Howe Bancroft, *The Book of the Fair* (Chicago: Bancroft Company, 1893; repr., New York: Bounty Books, 1972), 70; unidentified newspaper clipping

(ca. 1893), JRG Collection, box 29; and R. Reid Badger, *The Great American Fair: The World's Columbian Exposition and American Culture* (Chicago: Nelson Hall, 1979), 55.

4. *Fort Worth Gazette*, July 30, 1891, Sept. 6, 1891 (quotation), and Oct. 31, 1891; and *Galveston Daily News*, Oct. 30, 1891.

5. *American Architect and Building News* 31(Mar. 21, 1891): 189; and Hines, *Burnham of Chicago*, 83–86.

6. *San Antonio Daily Express*, Dec. 20, 1891.

7. Correspondence, JRG to Dankmar Adler, Oct. 21, 1891, repr. in Smith, *Since 1886*, 7 (the original is in the AIA archives).

8. Hines, *Burnham of Chicago*, 92.

9. *San Antonio Daily Express*, Dec. 20, 1891.

10. *Fort Worth Gazette*, Oct. 31, 1891; *San Antonio Daily Express*, Nov. 4 and Dec. 20, 1891; and *Houston Daily Post*, Sept. 17, 1893.

11. Correspondence, D. H. Burnham and George R. Davis to P. D. Bryan, secretary, Texas World's Fair Exhibit Association, Waco, TX, Dec. 8, 1891, Burnham Collection, The Reyerson and Burnham Libraries, The Art Institute of Chicago. See Appendix I for the other competitors.

12. Unidentified newspaper clippings, JRG Collection, box 29.

13. *Austin Daily Statesman*, Feb. 19, 1892; and *Galveston Daily News*, Feb. 21, 1892.

14. *Fort Worth Gazette*, Feb. 6, 1893.

15. *San Antonio Daily Express*, July 10, 1892; *Fort Worth Gazette*, Oct. 21, 1892; and *Houston Daily Post*, Sept. 17, 1893.

16. *Corpus Christi Caller*, Sept. 9, 1892; *Fort Worth Gazette*, Sept. 13 and Sept. 16, 1892.

17. *Houston Daily Post*, Oct. 2, 1892, 1; and *Fort Worth Gazette*, Feb. 6, 1893. The contractor was William Harley and Son of Chicago, who also built the state buildings for Colorado, Illinois, and Ohio.

18. *Houston Daily Post*, Sept. 17, 1893 (quotation); *San Antonio Daily Express*, Nov. 5, 1893; and Daniel H. Burnham, *The Final Official Report of the Director of Works of the World's Columbian Exposition, Facsimile Edition* (New York: Garland Publishing, 1989), 1: 94.

19. Unidentified newspaper clipping, JRG Collection, box 29 (second quotation); and Montgomery Schuyler, "Last Words about the World's Fair," *Architectural Record* 3 (Jan.–Mar. 1894), 301 (first quotation).

20. *San Antonio Daily Express*, July 9 and Sept. 17, 1893.

21. *San Antonio Daily Express*, Sept. 17, 1893; and *The Dream City, World's Fair Art Series*, vol. 1, bk. 14 (St. Louis: N. D. Thompson Publishing Company, 1894), not paginated.

22. Montgomery Schuyler, "State Buildings at the World's Fair," *Architectural Record* 3 (July–Sept. 1893), 69. It should be noted that the editors of the *Architectural Record* solicited descriptions of the state buildings from their designers. Gordon surely obliged and information he supplied may have been utilized in Schuyler's critique. Correspondence, editors of the *Architectural Record* to J. Reilly Gordon [*sic*], Feb. 13, 1893, JRG Collection, box 1, folder 2.

23. *Fort Worth Gazette*, Oct. 25, 1892, and Feb. 6, 1893 (first and second quotations); Trumbull White and William Igleheart, *The World's Columbian Exposition, Chicago, 1893* (Philadelphia: World Publishing Company, 1893), 503 (third quotation); and certificate in JRG Collection (fourth quotation). While the text of this certificate provides another contemporary stylistic appraisal of the Texas State Building, its value as a recognition of merit is diluted by a report that the "committee on awards of the World's Columbian Exposition . . . granted an award to each architect who designed buildings at Jackson Park. The judge found that almost every structure had some point of superior excellence." "Award of Medals to World's Fair Architects," *Inland Architect and News Record* 22 (Oct. 1893): 26.

24. *Chicago Tribune*, July 2, 1893; and *San Antonio Daily Express*, July 6, 1893. References to Ney's statues may be found in *Houston Daily Post*, Sept. 17, 1893; *The Dream City*, not paginated; and Emily F. Cutrer, *The Art of the Woman: The Life and Work of Elisabet Ney* (Lincoln: University of Nebraska Press, 1988), 137, 142. Cutrer makes a strong argument that *Stephen F. Austin* was not completed in time for the fair, suggesting *The Dream City* (among others) account of it may have been based upon plans that were not realized—a common source of confusion about Texas's participation in the fair. The *Houston Post* merely notes Ney's statues in the plural, so it is possible that other examples of the artist's work were displayed.

25. *Chicago Tribune*, July 2 and Sept. 17, 1893; *Galveston Daily News*, Sept. 17, 1893; and *San Antonio Daily Express*, Sept. 17, 1893.

26. Unidentified newspaper clipping, July 2, 1893, JRG Collection, box 29.

CHAPTER 8: GORDON'S SIGNATURE PLAN

1. *Galveston Daily News*, Aug. 21, 1895.

2. *San Antonio City Directory for 1889–90*, 179; *San Antonio City Directory for 1892–93*, 332; and interview with Virginia Gordon Ralston at Pelham Manor, NY, Nov. 25, 2000.

3. Roscoe Martin, *The People's Party in Texas* (Austin: University of Texas Press, 1970), 40–41, 58–59, 267.

4. *The National Cyclopaedia of American Biography*, s.v. "Gordon, J. Riely," 28: 312; and Martin, *The People's Party in Texas*, 69.

5. Unidentified newspaper clipping, JRG collection, box 29. Nicholas Clayton was the Southern Chapter's only member from Texas at its February 17, 1892, organizational meeting at Atlanta, Georgia. Smith, *Since 1886*, 6.

6. *Fort Worth Gazette*, Jan. 30, Apr. 16, and Apr. 22 (quotation), 1893. See Appendix I for a list of the competitors.

7. "Romanesque Design for Tarrant County Courthouse, J. Riely Gordon, Architect, San Antonio, Texas," *American Architect and Building News* 42 (Dec. 30, 1893): plate.

8. *Fort Worth Gazette*, Apr. 16 and Apr. 22, 1893.

9. Brazoria County Commissioners' Court *Records*, vol. F, p. 16 (Nov. 27, 1893) (quotation); unidentified newspaper clipping, dateline Mar. 27, 1894, JRG Collection, box 29; and James A. Creighton, *A Narrative History of Brazoria County* (Brazoria, TX: Brazoria County Historical Commission, 1974), 297, 299.

10. Brazoria County Commissioners' Court *Records*, vol. F, p. 349 (Dec. 11, 1893), pp. 350, 352 (Dec. 19, 1893), and p. 366 (Feb. 15, 1894) (quotation).

11. Brazoria County Commissioners' Court *Records*, vol. F, p. 366 (Feb. 15, 1894) (quotation); and Gordon's Affidavit, see Appendix II.

12. The description of the Brazoria County Courthouse that follows is based on plan and building fragments in the collection of the Brazoria County Historical Museum; drawings in the JRG Collection; *Galveston Daily News*, Nov. 2, 1895; and archival photographs.

13. Brazoria County Commissioners' Court *Records*, vol. F, p. 366 (Feb. 15, 1894).

14. Henry Hobson Richardson, "Description of the Church," in *Trinity Church in the City of Boston, Massachusetts, 1733–1933*, ed. Wardens and Vestry of Trinity Church (Boston: Merrymount Press, 1933), 196–97. First published as *Consecration Services of Trinity Church, Boston* in 1877.

15. Henry-Russell Hitchcock, *Richardson as a Victorian Architect* (Northampton, MA: Smith College, 1966), 11, 41–47.

16. Gordon's Affidavit, see Appendix II.

17. Unidentified newspaper clipping, dateline Mar. 27, 1894, JRG Collection, box 29; Brazoria County Commissioners' Court *Records*, vol. F, p. 534 (Jan. 8, 1895); and *Galveston Daily News*, Nov. 2, 1895.

18. Creighton, *A Narrative History of Brazoria County*, 299.

19. Karnes County Commissioners' Court *Minutes*, vol. 2, p. 243 (Feb. 26, 1894).

20. Paul Goeldner, "Our Architectural Ancestors," *Texas Architect* 24 (July/Aug. 1974): 7.

21. Unidentified newspaper clipping, dateline Mar. 17, [1894], JRG Collection, box 29; Hopkins County Commissioners' Court *Records*, bk. F, p. 356 (Mar. 24) and pp. 362–63 (May 12, 1894); G. G. Orren, "The History of Hopkins County" (master's thesis, East Texas State Teachers College, 1938), 71; and *Hopkins County Pictorial History* (Sulphur Springs, TX: Hopkins County Historical Society, 1987), 246, 247.

22. This description is based on personal observation.

23. Hopkins County Commissioners' Court *Records*, bk. F, p. 404 (Oct. 24, 1894) and pp. 418–19 (Nov. 23, 1894).

24. Hopkins County Commissioners' Court *Records*, bk. F, pp. 445–47 (Mar. 22, 1895).

25. Some have viewed Watson's report as an indictment of Gordon, incorrectly attributing additional construction costs to correcting problems identified in the report. As seen, much of the additional cost was due to enhancements before Watson's report. Orren writes that Watson "reported that water was seeping in through the basement. The county accepted the building as it was. A year or so later a great deal of work had to be done in the basement because of water seepage." Orren, "The History of Hopkins County," 74. A review of Commissioners' Court records from the date of Watson's report through June 1898 yielded mostly references to routine work. Exceptions were the employment of persons to "put in drainage in a good workman like manner for basement" and to "properly drain the balconies by grading." Both of these were considered one-man jobs and hardly a great deal of work. Hopkins County Commissioners' Court *Records*, bk. F, p. 544 (Dec. 20, 1895).

26. Hopkins County Commissioners' Court *Records*, bk. F, p. 487 (July 17, 1895) and p. 511 (Aug. 22, 1895).

27. Gonzales County Commissioners' Court *Records*, vol. 4, p. 359 (Feb. 17, 1894); and *The History of Gonzales County, Texas* (Gonzales, TX: Gonzales County Historical Commission, 1986), 4.

28. Gonzales County Commissioners' Court *Records*, vol. 4, p. 372 (Mar. 30 and Apr. 30, 1894). See Appendix I for the list of competitors.

29. *Gonzales Inquirer*, Apr. 5, 1894 (quotations); and Mavis P. Kelsey, Sr., and Donald H. Dyal, *The Courthouses of Texas* (College Station: Texas A&M University Press, 1993), 259.

30. Gonzales County Commissioners' Court *Records*, vol. 4, p. 384 (May 17, 1894) and p. 385 (May 18, 1894); and *The History of Gonzales County*, 4.

31. Martin, *The People's Party in Texas*, 224; and *The History of Gonzales County*, 5.

32. This description is drawn from *Gonzales Inquirer*, Apr. 23, 1896, as transcribed by Murray Montgomery, Jr. (including quotation), and personal observation. Following my inquiry, Mr. Montgomery, a columnist for the *Inquirer*, sought out a 102-year-old clipping in the newspaper's files. Age had taken its toll and the paper was literally crumbling away. Mr. Montgomery transcribed the article, preserving a valuable firsthand account of the Gonzales County Courthouse from the time of its completion.

33. *San Antonio Daily Express*, Dec. 31, 1892.

34. San Patricio Commissioners' Court *Minutes*, vol. 2, p. 76 (July 14, 1894), p. 78 (July 21, 1894), and p. 84 (Aug. 7, 1894) (quotation); and *San Antonio Daily Express*, July 27, 1894.

35. San Patricio Commissioners' Court *Minutes*, vol. 2, pp. 91–92 (Sept. 21, 1894).

36. San Patricio Commissioners' Court *Minutes*, vol. 2, pp. 95–96 (Oct. 13, 1894), p. 105 (Feb. 11, 1894), p. 125 (Aug. 13, 1894) (quotation), and p. 130 (Oct. 18, 1895).

37. *Canton Telephone*, Jan. 31 and Mar. 14 (quotation), 1890; and Van Zandt County Commissioners' Court *Minutes*, vol. 4, p. 434 (Aug. 14, 1894).

38. Van Zandt County Commissioners' Court *Minutes*, vol. 4, p. 383 (Dec. 21, 1893) and p. 434 (Aug. 14, 1894).

39. Van Zandt County Commissioners' Court *Minutes*, vol. 4, pp. 448, 450 (Sept. 4, 1894).

40. Van Zandt County Commissioners' Court *Minutes*, vol. 4, p. 451 (Sept. 5, 1894); *Wills Point Chronicle*, Jan. 31, 1895; and W. S. Mills, *History of Van Zandt County* (Canton, TX: privately published, 1950), 230.

41. *Wills Point Chronicle*, Jan. 10, 1895.

42. Van Zandt County Commissioners' Court *Minutes*, vol. 4, pp. 450–65 (Sept. 5, 1894).

43. *Canton Telephone*, Oct. 25 and Nov. 16, 1894; and *The History of Van Zandt County, Texas* (Wills Point, TX: Van Zandt County History Book Committee, 1984), 45.

44. Undated *Dallas News* clipping (ca. 1936), Texas Room scrapbook, Houston Public Library; and *The History of Van Zandt County, Texas*, 45.

45. Creighton, *A Narrative History of Brazoria County*, 299; and John Toth, "Courthouse Never Saw County Service," *Houston Chronicle*, Oct. 31, 1983.

46. Keith Guthrie, *The History of San Patricio County* (Austin, TX: Nortex Press, 1986), 26.

CHAPTER 9: ELLIS AND WISE

1. *San Antonio Daily Express*, Aug. 8, 1894. At this date, the following courthouses were under construction: Bexar (reported cost $511,000), Brazoria ($57,000), Hopkins ($52,410), Gonzales ($64,450), and Van Zandt ($50,000). Gordon had already submitted a design for San Patricio, for which the commissioners set a budget of $25,000. These total $759,860. Around this time Gordon submitted designs for K (later Kay) and Q (Pawnee) Counties in the Oklahoma Territory (*San Antonio Daily Express*, July 27 and Aug. 19, 1894). Including the estimated costs for these, possibly along with the $110,000 Bexar property costs and perhaps various courthouse furnishing costs, the total might reach a million dollars, but it appears the advertising claim could not really be justified until Kroeger secured Van Zandt and Ellis.

2. *San Antonio Daily Express*, Aug. 19, 1894.

3. *Fort Worth Gazette*, Nov. 18, 1894; and *Waxahachie Enterprise*, Oct. 5 and Dec. 7, 1894.

4. *Waxahachie Enterprise*, Dec. 7, 1894. Commissioner J. T. Johnston consistently voted with Finley against the new courthouse project, but, having already lost in the Democratic primary, was not reelected in November.

5. Ellis County Commissioners' Court *Minutes*, vol. M, p. 56 (Sept. 28, 1894); and *Dallas Morning News*, Sept. 29, 1894 (quotation).

6. *Waxahachie Enterprise*, Dec. 7, 1894.

7. *Dallas Morning News*, Sept. 29, 1894; *Waxahachie Enterprise*, Oct. 5, 1894; and Ellis County Commissioners' Court *Minutes*, vol. M, p. 57 (Oct. 5, 1894).

8. Correspondence, D. F. Singleton, Waxahachie, to JRG, San Antonio, Nov. 1, 1894, JRG Collection, box 6, folder 18; and Ellis County Commissioners' Court *Minutes*, vol. M, p. 59 (Nov. 3, 1894).

9. *Fort Worth Gazette*, Nov. 18 and 28 (quotation), 1894; and Ellis County Commissioners' Court *Minutes*, vol. M, p. 84 (Nov. 19, 1894).

10. *Waxahachie Daily Light*, Sept. 29, 1977.

11. Ellis County Commissioners' Court *Minutes*, vol. M, p. 101 (Dec. 15, 1894) and p. 102 (Dec. 18, 1894).

12. *Fort Worth Gazette*, Dec. 21, 1894.

13. *Fort Worth Gazette*, Oct. 31, 1894; Ellis County Commissioners' Court *Minutes*, vol. M, p. 102 (Dec. 22, 1894); and *Waxahachie Enterprise*, Jan. 4, 1895.

14. *Waxahachie Enterprise*, Jan. 4, 1895.

15. Ellis County Commissioners' Court *Minutes*, vol. M, p. 101 (Dec. 15, 1894), p. 105 (Jan. 11, 1895) (first and second quotations), and pp. 106–7 (Jan. 17, 1895) (third quotation); and *Waxahachie Enterprise*, Jan. 18, 1895. While the spelling of Sanguinet's first name varies, "Marshal," as printed on a 1902 payment voucher, is used here.

16. *Waxahachie Enterprise*, July 12, 1895 (vertical file, Nicholas P. Sims Library, Waxahachie, TX).

17. Unidentified newspaper clipping (ca. 1895) (vertical file, Nicholas P. Sims Library, Waxahachie, TX); *Sketches from the Portfolio of James Riely Gordon, Architect* (St. Louis, MO: A. B. Benesch, 1896), advertisement, not paginated; and Fred Weldon, *Carved Ornament of the Ellis County Courthouse* (Waxahachie, TX: Ellis County History Museum, 1995), 8.

18. *Waxahachie Enterprise*, Nov. 9, 1894. Measurements are drawn from this source. The description that follows is largely based upon personal observation, including structural features exposed during the restoration in 2000, and examination of archival photographs. The JRG Collection contains office renderings of alternate, Provençal versions of some earlier courthouse commissions, notably Fayette. Their exact role in the design process is uncertain.

19. Mariana Griswold Van Rensselaer, *Henry Hobson Richardson and His Works* (Boston: Houghton Mifflin and Company, 1888; New York: Dover Publications, 1969), plate opposite p. 62; Edward Hale, "H. H. Richardson and His Work," *New England Magazine* 17 (Dec. 1894): 517 (quotation); Hitchcock, *Richardson as a Victorian Architect*, 46; and Theodore E. Stebbins, Jr., "Richardson and Trinity Church: The Evolution of a Building," *Journal of the Society of Architectural Historians* 27 (Dec. 1968): 283–90.

20. The listed architects are Burnham & Root and Henry Ives Cobb of Chicago, Peabody & Stearns, and Shepley, Rutan & Coolidge of Boston, Isaac Taylor of St. Louis, and Messer, Sanguinet & Messer. I would like to thank Fred Weldon for bringing my attention to a copy of this card in the collection of the Ellis County Historical Museum.

21. *Sketches from the Portfolio of James Riely Gordon*, advertisement, not paginated. Messer, Sanguinet & Messer's report recommends using structural iron instead of timber for the district courtroom balcony. Presumably the original specifications defined other fireproofing features found in Ellis but not mentioned in the report. *Waxahachie Enterprise*, Jan. 4, 1894.

22. *Waxahachie Enterprise*, June 21, 1895 (vertical file, Nicholas P. Sims Library, Waxahachie, TX).

23. Ellis County Commissioners' Court *Minutes*, vol. M, p. 442 (Jan. 8, 1897) and p. 487 (Apr. 9, 1897) (quotation).

24. Ellis County Commissioners' Court *Minutes*, vol. M, p. 96 (Nov. 30, 1894).

25. Correspondence, JRG to Nicholas Joseph Clayton, June 3, 1897, Nicholas J. Clayton Papers, Mss# 74–0004, box 1, folder 1, Rosenberg Library, Galveston, TX.

26. Rosalie Gregg, ed., *Wise County History, a Link with the Past* (Austin, TX: Nortex Press, 1975), 3–5.

27. Wise County Commissioners' Court *Minutes*, bk. 3, p. 44 (Feb. 13, 1895); *Decatur News*, Jan. 17 1895 (quotation); and *Wise County Messenger* (Decatur), Mar. 1, 1895.

28. Wise County Commissioners' Court *Minutes*, bk. 3, p. 49 (Mar. 4, 1895), pp. 59–60 (May 9 and 10, 1895), and p. 70 (May 18, 1895). See Appendix I for a list of the competitors.

29. *Decatur News*, Mar. 14, 1895 (quotation); and Gregg, *Wise County History*, 4.

30. Wise County Commissioners' Court *Minutes*, bk. 3, pp. 225–26 (Jan. 5, 1897); and Gregg, *Wise County History*, pp. 5, 6.

31. This description is drawn from personal observation. I would like to thank J. Brantley Hightower for drawing my attention to the size difference between the Ellis and Wise courthouses.

32. *Sketches from the Portfolio of James Riely Gordon*, advertisement, not paginated.

CHAPTER 10: COMMISSIONS LOST

1. Lamar County Commissioners' Court *Minutes*, vol. 6, p. 3 (Feb. 19, 1895); and A. W. Neville, *The History of Lamar County* (Paris: North Texas Publishing Company, 1937), 210.

2. See Appendix II.

3. Lamar County Commissioners' Court *Minutes*, vol. 6, p. 10 (Apr. 8, 1895), p. 51 (June 18, 1895), p. 54 (July 17, 1895), p. 69 (Aug. 20, 1895), and p. 10 (Aug. 30, 1895); A. O. Watson v. Lamar County et al., 14, no. 6075 (Lamar County District Court, fall, 1895); and an unidentified newspaper clipping (ca. 1895, Carthage, MO), copy courtesy Daisy Harville, Paris Junior College (quotation).

4. *Some Work from the Office of Sanguinet and Staats, Successors to Messer, Sanguinet and Messer, Architects, Fort Worth, Texas* (1896) (xerographic copy in the collection of the Amon Carter Museum, Fort Worth), not paginated; and Neville, *The History of Lamar County*, 211 (quotation).

5. Lamar County Commissioners' Court *Minutes*, vol. 6, p. 280 (Oct. 15, 1897); *Galveston Daily News*, Aug. 18, 1897; and Neville, *The History of Lamar County*, 211, 223–24.

6. *Dallas Morning News*, Sept. 6, 1894; and Denton County Commissioners' Court *Minutes*, vol. C, p. 453 (May 6, 1895), pp. 454–55 (May 10, 1895), p. 478 (May 18, 1895), and (July 2, 1895) (quotation).

7. Denton County Commissioners' Court *Minutes*, vol. C, p. 502 (July 3, 1895).

8. Denton County Commissioners' Court *Minutes*, vol. C, p. 509 (July 25, 1895); and Gordon v. Denton County, 48 S.W. 738, 739 (Tex. Ct. App. 1899) (quotation).

9. Denton County Commissioners' Court *Minutes*, vol. C, p. 512 (Aug. 6, 1895); and David Strother, "Introduction" in *Building the Denton County Courthouse 1895–1897*, ed. Bullitt Lowry (Denton, TX: Denton County Historical Commission, 1987), 5–6.

10. Denton County Commissioners' Court *Minutes*, vol. C, p. 513 (Aug. 9, 1895); and Strother, "Introduction," 6, 9.

11. Gordon v. Denton County, 741.

12. *Southern Architect* 7 (Mar. 1896): 69; "The Mississippi Capitol," *Southern Architect* 7 (Mar. 1896): 72 (quotations); and *Mississippi House Journal*, extr. sess., Apr. 27, 1897 (Jackson, TX: Clarion-Ledger Printing, 1897), 195.

13. *Inland Architect and News Record* 27 (June 1896): 41; and *Mississippi House Journal*, extr. sess., Apr. 27, 1897, 195–96.

14. *Mississippi House Journal*, extr. sess., Apr. 27, 1897, 197, 198. See Appendix I for the competitors.

15. *Jackson Daily Clarion-Ledger*, May 19, 1897.

16. *Jackson Daily Clarion-Ledger*, May 25, 1897; and *Mississippi House Journal*, extr. sess., Apr. 27, 1897, 195–229.

17. Correspondence, JRG to Ramsey Wharton, June 1897,

subject file "James Riely Gordon," Mississippi Department of Archives and History, Archives and Library Division.

18. *Jackson Daily News*, Mar. 22, 1900.

19. *Jackson Daily Clarion-Ledger*, May 20, 1897, for example.

20. This is based on the specifications as transcribed from McLaurin's veto message. Notable indicators are the references to expanded metal construction (p. 214), which places the document contemporaneous with Ellis (late 1894) or later, and a fourth story (p. 212). The only documentation of four-story courthouse designs by Gordon during this time frame are his account of his redesign for Lamar and an illustration titled "Preliminary Competition, Court-House, Galveston County, Texas" in *Sketches from the Portfolio of James Riely Gordon*. It is doubtful he designed any other four-story, Romanesque courthouses in this period.

21. See, for example, Henry-Russell Hitchcock and William Seale, *Temples of Democracy, the State Capitols of the USA* (New York: Harcourt Brace Jovanovich, 1976), 236. This source also claims that the competing architects' petition for the committee to select a single entry further stipulated that only AIA members be considered. The AIA reference is not supported by McLaurin's veto message or any other primary source reviewed in the research for this volume and it is doubtful that Gordon would be a party to such a restriction since he was not yet a member of the organization.

22. Woods, *From Craft to Profession*, 47–50.

23. Galveston County Commissioners' Court *Minutes*, vol. 4, p. 304 (Oct. 14, 1895), p. 309 (Oct. 24, 1895), and p. 312 (Nov. 14, 1895); and *Galveston Daily News*, Dec. 17, 1896.

24. *Galveston Daily News*, Dec. 17, 18, and 19, 1896.

25. *Galveston Daily News*, Dec. 19, 1896, Feb. 25 and Mar. 7, 1897; and unidentified newspaper clipping, JRG Collection, box 29. See Appendix I for a list of competitors.

26. *Galveston Daily News*, Feb. 26 (quotation) and Feb. 27, 1897.

27. *Galveston Daily News*, Mar. 7, 1897.

28. Barrie Scardino and Drexel Turner, *Clayton's Galveston: The Architecture of Nicholas J. Clayton and His Contemporaries* (College Station: Texas A&M University Press, 2000), 128.

29. Correspondence, JRG to Messers N. J. Clayton & Company, May 23, 1897. Rosenberg Library, Nicholas J. Clayton Papers (1874–1915), Mss# 74–0004, box 1, folder 1.

30. *Galveston Daily News*, May 30 and June 2, 1897; correspondence, JRG to Messers N. J. Clayton & Company, June 3, 1897, Rosenberg Library, Nicholas J. Clayton Papers (1874–1915), Mss# 74–0004, box 1, folder 1; Clayton et al. v. Galveston County, 50 S.W. 738 (Tex. Ct. App. 1899); and Scardino and Turner, *Clayton's Galveston*, 127–28.

31. *Galveston Daily News*, June 2, 1897; and Scardino and Turner, *Clayton's Galveston*, 128. Commissioner Johnson claimed the

check was made out to County Judge Mann, but he seems to have never explained the purpose of $5,000 in earnest money when the second competition already stipulated the winning architect put up a $25,000 bond.

32. Correspondence, JRG to Messers N. J. Clayton & Company, June 3, 1897.

33. *Galveston Daily News*, June 8 and July 13, 1897; and Scardino and Turner, *Clayton's Galveston*, 128.

34. Both F. B. and W. S. Hull disappear from the Dallas rolls by 1898 but are listed as Jackson, Mississippi, agents for the Pauly Jail Building and Manufacturing Company on its letterhead in 1899. While still in Jackson, they later billed themselves as "Hull & Hull." *Dallas City Directory 1894–95*, 177; *Dallas City Directory 1896*, 268; *Dallas City Directory 1897*, 262; and correspondence, D. F. Youngblood, for Pauly Jail Building and Manufacturing Company to Geo. Zoeller, Aug. 5, 1899, collection of the author.

35. *San Antonio Daily Express*, June 4, 1886; *Victoria Advocate*, Jan. 14, 1893; and *Corpus Christi Caller*, July 27, 1892.

CHAPTER II: COMAL AND LEE

1. Such reports are numerous, but Alfred Giles's comments on the "depression" of the previous two years are recorded in the *San Antonio Daily Express*, Mar. 2, 1898.

2. "Texas State Association of Architects," *American Architect and Building News* 45 (Sept. 8, 1894): 95; "Texas State Association of Architects," *American Architect and Building News* 53 (Sept. 26, 1896): 103; Henry H. Saylor, *The A.I.A.'s First Hundred Years* (Washington, DC: American Institute of Architects, 1957), 36; and Smith, *Since 1886*, 8 (quotation).

3. Comal County Commissioners' Court *Minutes*, vol. H, p. 265 (Nov. 11, 1897), p. 267 (Nov. 23, 1897) (quotation), and p. 268 (Nov. 30, 1897).

4. Comal County Commissioners' Court *Minutes*, vol. H, p. 268 (Dec. 7, 1897), p. 269 (Dec. 10, 1897) (quotation), and p. 269 (Dec. 17, 1897).

5. Comal County Commissioners' Court *Minutes*, vol. H, p. 271 (Dec. 21, 1897) and p. 274 (Jan. 19, 1898) (quotation); see Appendix I for a list of the competitors.

6. *San Antonio Daily Express*, Mar. 22, July 3, and July 8, 1890; Mar. 10 and 15, 1891; and *Zeitung* (New Braunfels), Mar. 24, 1898, typescript translation by Bob Govier, vertical files, Sophienburg Archives.

7. *Zeitung* (New Braunfels), Apr. 14, 1898, typescript translation by Bob Govier, vertical files, Sophienburg Archives.

8. Comal County Commissioners' Court *Minutes*, vol. H, p. 274 (Jan. 19, 1898).

9. Comal County Commissioners' Court *Minutes*, vol. H, pp. 286–87 (Feb. 16, 1898) and p. 390 (Dec. 6, 1898); and *San Antonio Daily Express*, Jan. 23, 1899.

10. The description that follows is drawn from a typescript document, apparently prepared by Gordon for submission to a Comal County newspaper, JRG Collection, box 11, folder 3; an unidentified newspaper clipping, JRG Collection, box 29; an inspection of the architects' original plans at the Sophienburg Archives, New Braunfels; and personal observation.

11. Typescript document, apparently prepared by Gordon for submission to a Comal County newspaper, JRG Collection, box 11, folder 3.

12. Unidentified newspaper clipping, JRG Collection, box 29.

13. Comal County Commissioners' Court *Minutes*, vol. H, p. 268 (Nov. 30, 1897); and Robert A. Veselka, *The Courthouse Square in Texas* (Austin: University of Texas Press, 2000), 133–34, 137–38.

14. Lee County Commissioners' Court *Minutes*, vol. D, p. 89 (Feb. 18, 1898) and p. 98 (Feb. 25, 1898) (quotation); and Lee County Historical Survey Committee, Mrs. James C. Killen, ed., *A History of Lee County, Texas* (Quanah, TX: Nortex Press, 1974), 47–49.

15. Lee County Commissioners' Court *Minutes*, vol. D, p. 99 (Mar. 17, 1898), p. 105 (Apr. 22, 1898), and p. 185 (Dec. 19, 1898); Lee County Historical Survey Committee, *A History of Lee County*, 49; and Martha Boethel, "A History of the Lee County Courthouse," undated typescript, courtesy of the Lee County Clerk's Office, 9.

16. Boethel, "A History of the Lee County Courthouse," 9, 17. Other aspects of this description are drawn from archival photos, measured drawings by the Historic American Buildings Survey, and personal observation.

17. Lee County Commissioners' Court *Minutes*, vol. D, p. 185 (Dec. 19, 1898), p. 250 (June 2, 1899), and p. 251 (June 3, 1899).

18. Boethel, "A History of the Lee County Courthouse," 12, 17–19; and Eileen Schartz, "Law and Mortar: Texas Takes the Stand for Historic Preservation," *Texas Construction*, Feb. 2004, http://texas.construction.com/features/archive/0402_cover.asp.

CHAPTER 12: THE ARIZONA TERRITORIAL CAPITOL

1. Michael D. Carman, *Under the Copper Dome: The Arizona Capitol, 1898–1974* (Phoenix: Arizona Capitol Museum, 2001), 2–8.

2. *Arizona Gazette*, Feb. 8, 1898; unidentified clipping (hand identified as *Builder & Contractor*), Nov. 23, 1898, JRG Collection, box 29; and Carman, *Under the Copper Dome*, 9.

3. *Arizona Daily Gazette*, May 20, 1898; and James M. Barney, "Planning for First Capitol Started Heated Disputes," *Phoenix Gazette*, May 25, 1957.

4. *Arizona Republican*, July 21, Aug. 20, and Nov. 2, 1898; and *Prospectus of the Requirements for the Territorial Capitol Building*

to Be Erected in Phoenix, Arizona (Phoenix: Capitol Grounds and Building Commission, n.d.), JRG Collection, box 11, folder 1 (quotation). See Appendix I for a list of the other competitors.

5. *Arizona Republican*, Nov. 18, 1898.

6. Unidentified clipping (hand identified as *Builder & Contractor*), Nov. 23, 1898, JRG Collection, box 29; and unidentified clipping, JRG Collection, box 29 (quotation).

7. This description is based upon a review of a photographic copy of these plans, courtesy Virginia Gordon Ralston.

8. *Arizona Republican*, Nov. 19, 1898; *Arizona Gazette*, Jan. 13 and 14, 1899.

9. *Arizona Republican*, Jan. 13, 1899.

10. *Arizona Gazette*, Jan. 14, 1899.

11. Carman, *Under the Copper Dome*, 2–8.

12. This description is drawn from the *Arizona Daily Gazette*, Mar. 23, 1900; *Arizona Gazette*, Aug. 5, 1900; a review of Gordon's drawings; and personal observation.

13. *Arizona Republican*, Nov. 18, 1898.

14. *Report of the Capitol Commission* (Phoenix: Capitol Grounds and Building Commission, Jan. 1, 1901), 5, Arizona Capitol Restoration Collection, Arizona State Archives, Department of Library, Archives and Public Records (hereafter cited as ASA); and Carman, *Under the Copper Dome*, 20.

15. A photograph of the rendering for Gordon's proposed Arizona Capitol in ASA matches the Mississippi rendering exactly. Carman, *Under the Copper Dome*, 11–12; and *Jackson Daily News*, Mar. 22, 1900.

16. *San Francisco Chronicle*, Feb. 26, 1901.

17. J. Avery Jones writing for the *Jackson Clarion-Ledger*, as reprinted in the *Vicksburg Evening Post*, Mar. 5, 1901.

18. *San Francisco Chronicle*, Feb. 13 and 14 (quotation), 1912.

19. Carman, *Under the Copper Dome*, 30–32; and personal observation.

20. Charlotte Buchen, "Ornate Copper Dome Sparks Capitol Plan," *Arizona Republic*, Mar. 17, 1957.

21. *A Guide to the Architecture of Metro Phoenix* (Phoenix: Central Arizona Chapter of the American Institute of Architects, 1983), 46; and Carman, *Under the Copper Dome*, 33.

22. *Arizona Republic*, Feb. 2, 1975; and Carman, *Under the Copper Dome*, 1.

CHAPTER 13: HARRISON, CALLAHAN, AND MISSISSIPPI REDUX

1. *Marshall Messenger*, July 7, July 27, and July 28, 1899; Harrison County Commissioners' Court *Minutes*, vol. C, p. 5 (Aug. 29, 1899); and Gail K. Biel, "Cornelius Grandbery Lancaster," in Ron Tyler, Douglas E. Barnett, Roy R. Barkley, Penelope C. Anderson, and Mark F. Odintz, eds., *The New Handbook of Texas* (Austin: The Texas State Historical Association, 1996), 4:52.

2. Harrison County Commissioners' Court *Minutes*, vol. C, p. 6 (Sept. 26, 1899), p. 90 (Nov. 12, 1900), and p. 129 (May 13, 1901); and *Marshall Messenger*, Oct. 27, 1899.

3. For a discussion of Richardson's education at the Ecole des Beaux-Arts, see James F. O'Gorman, *Three American Architects: Richardson, Sullivan, and Wright, 1865–1915* (Chicago: University of Chicago Press, 1991), especially Chap. 1. The description of the Harrison County Courthouse that follows is based upon personal observation.

4. *Harrison County Courthouse Historic Structures Report* (Architexas, 1999), 22–25.

5. Bexar County Commissioners' Court *Minutes*, vol. G, p. 166 (Oct. 25, 1892).

6. *Dallas City Directory for 1896*, 492; *Dallas City Directory for 1898*, 209; unidentified newspaper clippings, JRG Collection, box 29; Ellis A. Davis and Edwin H. Grobe, eds., *The Encyclopedia of Texas* (Dallas: Texas Development Bureau, 1926), 1:308; and Carol Morris Little, *Historic Harrison County as Preserved Through Official Texas Historical Markers* (Longview, TX: Carol Morris Little, 1984), 60.

7. Philip Lindsey, *A History of Greater Dallas and Vicinity* (Chicago: Lewis Publishing Company, 1909), 35, 44–45, 189, 224.

8. Unidentified newspaper clipping, JRG Collection, box 29.

9. *Dallas City Directory for 1900*, 217 (quotation) and 342; *Dallas City Directory for 1901*, 259. George Muir Gordon died in Washington, DC, March 21, 1918. Sarah Virginia (Riely) Gordon died the following year. Alice Norris Parran, *The Evolution of Patriotic Ancestry from Year 1 B.C. to Year 1939 A.D., Series II of the "Register of Maryland's Heraldic Families"* (Baltimore: Alice Norris Parran, 1938), chart following 264.

10. Callahan County Commissioners' Court *Minutes*, vol. C, p. 416 (Feb. 15, 1900); and Christopher Long, "Callahan County," in Tyler et al., eds., *The New Handbook of Texas*, 1:906–7.

11. Callahan County Commissioners' Court *Minutes*, vol. C, p. 416 (Feb. 15, 1900) (quotation) and p. 440 (Apr. 14, 1900).

12. Callahan County Commissioners' Court *Minutes*, vol. C, p. 499 (Dec. 11, 1900); and correspondence, B. L. Russell to whom this may concern, Aug. 10, 1901, JRG Collection, box 1, folder 3 (quotation).

13. *Jackson Daily Clarion-Ledger*, Mar. 6, 1900.

14. *Jackson Daily Clarion-Ledger*, Mar. 12, 1900; and *Mississippi House Journal*, reg. sess., Jan., Feb., and Mar. 1900, 538–39 (quotation).

15. *Jackson Daily Clarion-Ledger*, Mar. 6 and Mar. 12, 1900.

16. *Jackson Daily News*, Mar. 22, 1900.

17. *Jackson Daily Clarion-Ledger*, Mar. 19, 1900.

18. *Jackson Daily Clarion-Ledger*, Mar. 19 and Mar. 22, 1900.

19. *Jackson Daily Clarion-Ledger*, Apr. 5, Apr. 12, Apr. 19, and Apr. 20, 1900.

20. *Jackson Daily Clarion-Ledger*, Apr. 18 (quotation) and Apr. 21, 1900.

21. *Jackson Daily Clarion-Ledger*, Apr. 18, Apr. 19, and Apr. 21, 1900; and correspondence, J. G. Carrol to the Mississippi Capitol Commission, May 10, 1900, JRG Collection, box 6, folder 18 (quotation). See Appendix I for a list of the competitors.

22. *Jackson Daily Clarion-Ledger*, Apr. 25, Apr. 27, and May 14, 1900.

23. Correspondence, R. H. Thompson to Dear Sir, May 5, 1900, JRG Collection, box 1, folder 3. The "Governor's Message" regarding the State House Commission is recorded in *Mississippi House Journal*, sp. sess., Jan., Feb., and Mar. 1902, 42–46 (quotation). Thompson, the governor-selected commissioner, was appointed to replace J. C. Hardy on April 7, although his swearing in may have been later (*Jackson Daily Clarion-Ledger*, Apr. 7, 1900). A correspondence in the JRG Collection seems to be in response to an inquiry similar to Thompson's, but is addressed to "Mr. H. K. [*sic*] Hardy, Jackson, Miss." It refers to a letter from Hardy dated April 27. If this was part of the secret State House Commission investigation, it may have begun the day the commission adjourned. There is no mention of the investigation in the official minutes for the period of the pertinent dates. Mississippi State House Commission *Minutes*, 1900, Mississippi State Archives, series 637, box 703.

24. Correspondence, various typescripts, JRG Collection, box 1, folder 3.

25. Correspondence, I. D. Ferguson to R. H. Thompson, May 9, 1900, typescript, JRG Collection, box 1, folder 3.

26. *Fort Worth City Directory for 1899–1900*, 166, 196, 239.

27. Correspondence, Howard Messer to R. H. Thompson, May 9, 1900, JRG Collection, box 1, folder 3. In this reply Messer also notes "the late firm Messer, Sanguinet and Messer competed for your capitol." It is not clear whether he was referring to the 1896 or the 1900 competition when he later states that he "was asked to compete for your building" but declined, but it seems Sanguinet's pursuit of the 1896 Mississippi contest was without Howard Messer's direct involvement.

28. *Jackson Daily Clarion-Ledger*, May 14, May 16, May 18, June 6, and June 7, 1900.

29. *Jackson Daily Clarion-Ledger*, June 14, 1900; and *Mississippi House Journal*, sp. sess., Jan., Feb., and Mar. 1902, 43 (quotations).

30. Mississippi State House Commission *Minutes*, Mississippi State Archives, series 637, box 703, pp. 19–28 (June 12, 1900); and *Jackson Daily Clarion-Ledger*, June 15, 1900 (quotation). As recorded in the minutes, Green indeed recommended four entries, each with its own advantages but

one, design 5, is noted as superior. The minutes provide no indication of who authored which design, but the newspaper notes one was Gordon's.

CHAPTER 14: MCLENNAN AND THE VICKSBURG CITY HALL

1. McLennan County Commissioners' Court *Minutes*, vol. F, p. 116 (Feb. 17, 1900); and W. R. (Bob) Poage, *McLennan County—Before 1980* (Waco, TX: Texian Press, 1981), 143 (quotation) and 200.

2. McLennan County Commissioners' Court *Minutes*, vol. F, pp. 227–28 (June 30, 1900) and p. 254 (Sept. 6, 1900).

3. McLennan County Commissioners' Court *Minutes*, vol. F, pp. 254–60 (Sept. 6. 1900).

4. McLennan County Commissioners' Court *Minutes*, vol. F, pp. 265–67 (Sept. 15, 1900).

5. McLennan County Commissioners' Court *Minutes*, vol. F, p. 316 (Nov. 20, 1900) and p. 333 (Dec. 11, 1900); *Waco Times-Herald*, Dec. 5 and Dec. 13, 1900.

6. McLennan County Commissioners' Court *Minutes*, vol. F, p. 227 (June 30, 1900) (quotation) and vol. G, p. 31 (Oct. 3, 1902).

7. The following description of the McLennan County Courthouse is drawn from a review of the plans; Lovell's contract as recorded in the McLennan County Commissioners' Court *Minutes*, vol. F, pp. 333–37 (June 30, 1900); Courthouse vertical file in the Waco-McLennan County Library; and personal observation.

8. City of Vicksburg *Minute Book*, vol. H, p. 546 (Oct. 29, 1900) and p. 562 (Dec. 17, 1900).

9. City of Vicksburg *Minute Book*, vol. H, pp. 594–95 (Feb. 18, 1901); and *Vicksburg Daily Herald*, Feb. 20, 1901 (quotation). See Appendix I for the competitors.

10. City of Vicksburg *Minute Book*, vol. H, p. 597 (Feb. 21, 1901); *Vicksburg Daily Herald*, Feb. 22, 1901; and *Vicksburg Evening Post*, Feb. 23, 1901 (quotation).

11. *Vicksburg Evening Post*, Feb. 27, 1901.

12. City of Vicksburg *Minute Book*, vol. H, p. 657 (May 27, 1901), p. 698 (Aug. 6, 1901), and vol. I, p. 147 (Feb. 19, 1903); and *Vicksburg Evening Post*, Apr. 8, 1903.

13. The following description is based upon City of Vicksburg *Minute Book*, vol. H, p. 698 (Aug. 6, 1901); *Vicksburg Evening Post*, Apr. 2, 1902, JRG Collection, box 29; and personal observation.

CHAPTER 15: THE J. RIELY GORDON COMPANY

1. Copiah County Board of Supervisors *Minutes*, vol. H, pp. 435–42 (Mar. 8, 1901).

2. *Copiah County Courier*, Courthouse Anniversary Edition, May 1, 2002. The two quotations from this source are from Carolyn Diamond's transcriptions of the Copiah County Board of Supervisors *Minutes*. I wish to thank Paul Cartwright, director of the Copiah-Jefferson Regional Library System, for providing this helpful resource.

3. This description is based on personal observation, comparison with the similar Wilkinson County Courthouse, and a review of archival photographs.

4. Glen R. Conrad, "The Origin and Development of Local Administration in Louisiana," in Carl A. Brasseaux, Glen R. Conrad, and R. Warren Robinson, eds., *The Courthouses of Louisiana*, 2nd ed. (Lafayette: University of Southwestern Louisiana, 1997), vii–x.

5. *Lake Charles Weekly American*, May 11, 1901, and June 7, 1902; and Brasseaux et al., *The Courthouses of Louisiana*, 32.

6. *Lake Charles Weekly American*, Sept. 14 and Oct. 4, 1901, Jan. 4 and Feb. 8, 1902.

7. *Lake Charles Weekly American*, Sept. 14, 1901 (quotation); and *Lake Charles American-Press*, Sept. 14, 1911. The description of Gordon's addition in the text is drawn from this article, others from the same newspaper, Nov. 8, 1902, and Jan. 17, 1903, and the photographic record.

8. *Lake Charles Weekly American*, Dec. 27, 1902.

9. *Lake Charles Weekly American*, Sept. 14, 1901, Nov. 15, 1902, and Jan. 17, 1903.

10. Angelina County Commissioners' Court *Minutes*, vol. G, p. 591 (Sept. 16, 1901), p. 615 (Nov. 13, 1901), and p. 617 (Dec. 2, 1901).

11. Angelina County Commissioners' Court *Minutes*, vol. G, p. 626 (Jan. 16, 1902); *Lufkin News*, Mar. 23, 1915; and unidentified newspaper clipping, JRG Collection, box 29.

12. Angelina County Commissioners' Court *Minutes*, vol. H, p. 31; and unidentified newspaper clipping, JRG Collection, box 29.

13. Kiowa County Board of Commissioners *Record*, vol. 1, p. 35 (Jan. 28, 1902), p. 74 (Aug. 2, 1902), pp. 84–85 (July 9, 1902), p. 116 (Oct. 23, 1902), and p. 122 (Nov. 1, 1902).

14. *Hobart Republican*, Feb. 20, 1903.

15. Kiowa County Board of Commissioners *Record*, vol. 1, p. 210 (July 7, 1903) and loose certificate dated Apr. 23, 1906; and *Hobart Democrat-Chief*, Aug. 4, 1925.

16. *Alexandria Town Talk*, Feb. 27, 1902.

17. *Alexandria Town Talk*, Mar. 12, 1902; and unidentified newspaper clipping, JRG Collection, box 29.

18. *Alexandria Town Talk*, Apr. 9 and Apr. 21, 1902.

19. *Alexandria Town Talk*, July 23, 1902.

20. *Alexandria Town Talk*, July 23, 1902 (quotation); and Brasseaux et al., *The Courthouses of Louisiana*, 131.

21. *Transcriptions of the Parish Records of Louisiana, No. 31 Lincoln Parish (Ruston), Series I. Police Jury Minutes*, vol. II, 1891–1908, Works Projects Administration, Statewide Records Project, Professional and Service Division, Feb. 27 and Apr. 11, 1902,

not paginated. Hereafter cited as *Lincoln Parish Police Jury Minutes*.

22. *Lincoln Parish Police Jury Minutes*, June 23 and July 8, 1902.

23. *Lincoln Parish Police Jury Minutes*, Sept. 12 and Sept. 15, 1902, and Jan. 5, 1903.

24. *Lincoln Parish Police Jury Minutes*, June 24, 1903; and Brasseaux et al., *The Courthouses of Louisiana*, 103.

25. *Woodville Republican*, Mar. 8 (second quotation) and Mar. 22 (first quotation), 1902.

26. Wilkinson County Board of Supervisors *Minutes*, bk. D, pp. 295–96 (Mar. 3, 1902), p. 313 (Apr. 17, 1902), p. 332 (July 7, 1902), and p. 415 (May 2, 1903).

27. This description is drawn from personal observation.

28. *Crowley Signal*, Apr. 19, 1902; *Lake Charles Daily American*, Dec. 27, 1902; and Velma Lea Hair, "The History of Crowley, Louisiana," Reprint from *Louisiana Historical Quarterly* 27 (Oct. 1944): 11.

29. "Our Court House," typescript, George W. Covington Memorial Library, Hazelhurst.

30. *Lake Charles American-Press*, Apr. 24, 1910; Carolyn Moffett, "Long Life Still Happy Claims 92-year Old," *Lake Charles American Press*, May 11, 1975; and Ed Alderman, "Great Lake Charles Fire Was 75 Years Ago," *Lake Charles American Press*, Apr. 21, 1985.

31. A vague accusation of collusion between Gordon and contractor Abright during the Calcasieu project is repeated in Brasseaux et al., *The Courthouses of Louisiana*, 32. The nature and consequences of this alleged collusion are not explained, however, and my attempts to find the original source of the charge were unsuccessful.

32. *Lake Charles American Press*, Sept. 14, 1911.

33. Harrison County, Mississippi, Board of Supervisors *Minutes*, vol. 6, p. 151 (Oct. 30, 1902); and *Midland Reporter-Telegram*, Sept. 10, 1974. See Appendix I for contests in which Gordon and A. J. Bryan (also as Bryan & Gilbert) both participated.

CHAPTER 16: SOMERSET AND GARRETT

1. Correspondence, Lucy Virginia Gordon Ralston to the author, June 8, 2000.

2. Randall Blacksaw, "The New New York," *Century* 64 (Aug. 1902): 493, 513.

3. See Max Page, *The Creative Destruction of Manhattan, 1900–1940* (Chicago: University of Chicago Press, 1999). Spanning about the same years as Gordon's career in New York, this study presents the entire period as one of continual demolition and rebuilding within the city.

4. Joy M. Kestenbaum, "Alfred Zucker," in Adolf K. Placzek, ed., *Macmillan Encyclopedia of Architects* (New York: The Free Press, 1982), 4:476.

5. *San Antonio Daily Express*, Sept. 7 and Sept. 11, 1887, Jan. 20 and Jan. 29, 1888, and Feb. 9, 1888.

6. JRG Collection, ser. I2, bk. 2 (this volume, which contains illustrations of Gordon's final design of the Texas State Building and Tarrant County Courthouse competitive design, was apparently part of Zucker's office collection that he later abandoned to Gordon); *A History of Real Estate, Building and Architecture in New York City During the Last Quarter Century* (New York: The Real Estate Record Association, 1898; repr., New York: Arno Press, 1967), 691–92; partnership agreement between Alfred Zucker and J. Riely Gordon, JRG Collection, box 8, folder 7; and *Inland Architect and News Record* 39 (June 1902): 44.

7. *New York World*, Mar. 30, 1904; and *New York Herald*, Mar. 31, 1904 (quotation), both JRG Collection, box 29; and response to The Mercantile Agency, R. G. Dunn & Co., JRG Collection, box 1, folder 4.

8. Correspondence, Virginia Gordon Ralston to the author, June 8, 2000.

9. *New York Herald Tribune*, Mar. 17, 1937; and *Pelham Sun*, Sept. 14, 1978.

10. Response to The Mercantile Agency, R. G. Dunn & Co., JRG Collection, box 1, folder 4; *New York Times*, Feb. 2, 1922; Egerton Swartwout, "Evarts Tracy," *Journal of the American Institute of Architects* 10 (Mar. 1922): 94; "Egerton Swartwout," in Frank R. Holmes, ed., *Who's Who in New York (City and State), 1924* (New York: Who's Who Publications, 1924), 1217; William Francklyn Paris, *Personalities in American Art* (1930; repr., Freeport, NY: Books for Libraries Press, 1970), 35–46; correspondence, JRG to the Board of Capitol Commissioners, State of North Dakota, June 12, 1931, typescript, JRG Collection, box 17, folder 20 (quotation); and Leland M. Roth, *McKim, Mead & White, Architects* (New York: Harper & Row, 1983), 380, n22. The office was at 224 Fifth Avenue.

11. Arthur P. Sutphen, *Souvenir of the Opening of the Somerset County Courthouse, March, 1909*, not paginated. Vertical file, Somerville Public Library.

12. Sutphen, *Souvenir of the Opening of the Somerset County Courthouse*; and William H. Hinners, James C. Agnew, John J. Bracken, Charles M. Egan, and Thomas R. Layden, *Report of Bergen County Investigating Committee, Hackensack, N.J., Thursday, October 5th, 1911* (hereafter *Hinners Report*), 263–64 (quotation). While most Somerset County sources describe the appointed body as a committee, the term *commission*, as designated by the 1901 law, is used here to be consistent with the discussion of Bergen.

13. Somerset County Board of Chosen Freeholders *Minutes*, vol. 8, p. 47 (Mar. 14, 1905), p. 75 (July 20, 1905), and pp. 86–89 (Sept. 7, 1905); *New York Herald*, Jan. 24, 1909, JRG Collection, box 29.

14. Somerset County Board of Chosen Freeholders *Minutes*, vol. 8, p. 112 (Nov. 28, 1905), p. 130 (Mar. 13, 1906), and p. 152 (May 31, 1906).

15. This description is drawn from *New York Herald*, Jan. 24, 1909, and an unidentified newspaper clipping (both JRG Collection, box 29); an unidentified newspaper clipping, courtesy Virginia Gordon Ralston; and personal observation.

16. Unidentified newspaper clipping, JRG Collection, box 29.

17. Garrett County Courthouse Commission *Minutes* (microfilm, Maryland State Archives, MSA no. CM537), p. 5 (resolution on the formation of the Garrett County Court House Commission); and "John W. Garrett" and "Present County Buildings," both in *The Glades Star* 1 (June 30, 1949), 352–53.

18. Garrett County Courthouse Commission *Minutes*, pp. 8, 9 (Dec. 17, 1906) and p. 11 (Feb. 1, 1907). See Appendix I for a complete list of participants.

19. Garrett County Courthouse Commission *Minutes*, p. 12 (Feb. 2, 1907) and p. 193 (correspondence, JRG to Hon. W. McCulloh Brown, secretary, Courthouse Commission, Garrett County, Oakland, MD, Feb. 21, 1907).

20. Garrett County Courthouse Commission *Minutes*, p. 16 (Mar. 20, 1907) and p. 20 (May 13, 1907).

21. This description is drawn from copies of plans, courtesy the Garrett County General Services Department; and personal observation.

22. *The Republican* (Oakland, MD), Dec. 10, 1908.

23. Garrett County Courthouse Commission *Minutes*, p. 35 (Sept. 28, 1908); and "History of Garrett Co. Courthouses: New Complex to Answer Growth," *The Glades Star* 5 (Mar. 1981), 310.

24. "History of Garrett Co. Courthouses," 313–15.

CHAPTER 17: BERGEN AND MADISON

1. *Historic Structures Report: Bergen County Justice Complex, Hackensack, New Jersey*, prepared by Ford Farewell Mills and Gatsch, Architects, Princeton, NJ, for the County of Bergen, Department of Public Works, Dec. 1993, 3.11–3.12.

2. *Historic Structures Report: Bergen County Justice Complex*, 3.13–3.15.

3. Newspaper clipping hand identified as the *Evening Record*, May 16, 1907, JRG Collection, box 29; Fred Bogert, "Background on Bergen County Courthouse," typescript A-0109(1) 3TB, Fred Bogert Collection, Bergen County Historical Archives; and *Historic Structures Report: Bergen County Justice Complex*, 3.14.

4. In a response to a credit inquiry, probably authored by Gordon, the dissolution is dated as December 1906. Response to The Mercantile Agency, R. G. Dunn & Co., JRG Collection, box 1, folder 4.

5. *Hinners Report*, 205.

6. Correspondence, JRG to the Board of Capitol Commissioners, State of North Dakota, June 21, 1931, typescript, JRG Collection, box 17, folder 20; and Sharon Irish, "Cass Gilbert in Practice, 1882–1934," in Margaret Heilbrun, ed., *Inventing the Skyline: The Architecture of Cass Gilbert* (New York: Columbia University Press, 2000), 22–24.

    Tracy and Swartwout remained together over the next few years, partnering with Electus D. Litchfield from 1908 to 1913. They enjoyed success with the United States Courthouse and Post Office, Denver, Colorado (1909), and the Missouri State Capitol (Jefferson City, 1912). At the onset of the First World War, Evarts Tracy acted on his lifelong interest in the military and joined the army. Commissioned major of engineers, he served at home and abroad as a camouflage specialist, rose to lieutenant colonel, and was awarded the Distinguished Service Cross. Tracy returned to France after the war to help in the rebuilding effort. He died there in 1922, at age fifty-three, of heart disease complicated by a war wound. Egerton Swartwout stayed active with his own architectural practice, involvement with the AIA, and writing about his art until forced to cut back for his health about 1933. He died in New York on February 18, 1943, at age seventy-three. *New York Times*, Jan. 31 and Feb. 2, 1922, and Feb. 19, 1943; and Swartwout, "Evarts Tracy," 94.

7. Unidentified newspaper clipping (hand identified as the *Evening Record*, May 16, 1907), JRG Collection, box 29; *Hinners Report*, 206; Bogert, "Background on Bergen County Courthouse"; and *Historic Structures Report: Bergen County Justice Complex*, 3.14–3.15.

8. *Oneida Dispatch*, Jan. 7, 1910; and Peg Hogan, "Madison County Courthouses," *Historic CNY* 9 (2001): 9–10.

9. *The Journal of the Proceedings of the Board of Supervisors of Madison County, New York, at Their Special and Annual Sessions, 1908*, pp. 8–9 (Jan. 21, 1908) and p. 15 (Apr. 2, 1908); and *Oneida Dispatch*, Mar. 28, 1908.

10. *Oneida Dispatch*, Apr. 3, 1908.

11. *Oneida Dispatch*, May 29, 1908; *The Journal of the Proceedings of the Board of Supervisors of Madison County, New York, at Their Special and Annual Sessions, 1908*, p. 21 (June 12, 1908); and *Oneida Democratic Union*, June 13, 1908, JRG Collection, box 29.

12. *Oneida Dispatch*, July 31, 1908 (quotation), and May 14, 1909; and Hogan, "Madison County Courthouses," 10–11.

13. This description is drawn from personal observation and information from the *Oneida Dispatch*, Dec. 31, 1909, and Jan. 7, 1910, as well as identified newspaper clippings, JRG Collection, box 29.

14. *Oneida Dispatch*, Dec. 31, 1909.

15. *Oneida Dispatch*, Oct. 8 and Dec. 31, 1909 (quotation), and June 1, 1912.

16. *Hinners Report,* 266–67; and *Historic Structures Report: Bergen County Justice Complex,* 3.16–3.19.

17. *Hinners Report,* 267–70.

18. *Hinners Report,* 206, 270–71, 276; and "The Court House Award," *Architectural Record* 33 (May 1913), 469.

19. *Hinners Report,* 271–73, 278–82.

20. James Riely Gordon, *Description of Courthouse* [Bergen], n.d., ca. 1909, p. 22, JRG collection, ser. E, box 18, folder 4. The following description is drawn from an unidentified clipping in the Bergen County Courts vertical file, Johnson Free Public Library, Hackensack, NJ; *Bergen County Historic Sites Survey, Volume One: City of Hackensack* (Hackensack, NJ: Bergen County Board of Chosen Freeholders, 1980–81); *Historic Structures Report: Bergen County Justice Complex;* and personal observation.

21. Correspondence, JRG to Alexander Harvey, Jan. 22, 1937, JRG Collection, ser. E, box 18, folder 7 (quotation); *Historic Structures Report: Bergen County Justice Complex,* 3.92–3.93; and Mary Beth Betts, "Cass Gilbert: Twelve Projects" in Heilbrun, *Inventing the Skyline,* 112.

22. Gordon, *Description of Courthouse* [Bergen], 12–13.

23. *Hinners Report,* 261–62.

24. *Hinners Report,* 197–242, 297.

25. *Hinners Report,* 267–81, 296–301; and *New York Times,* Feb. 22, 1912.

26. *New York Times,* Feb. 22, 1912; *Evening Record and Bergen County Herald,* Sept. 10, 1912; and *Bergen News,* Sept. 10, 1912, JRG Collection, box 29.

27. *Hackensack Republican,* Sept. 19, 1912. Gordon traveled to Europe at least twice. Receipts and other ephemera establish he toured the continent with his wife and daughter, departing July 14 and returning in early October 1906. JRG Collection, box 2, folder 10.

28. Correspondence, JRG to the New York Society of Architects, Oct. 15, 1912, JRG Collection, box 18, folder 4 (quotation); and unidentified newspaper clipping (Oct. 25, 1912), JRG Collection, box 29.

29. Unidentified newspaper clippings, JRG Collection, box 29; and Writers' Program of the Work Projects Administration, *Bergen County Panorama: American Guide Series* (Hackensack, NJ: The Bergen County Board of Chosen Freeholders, 1941), 37.

CHAPTER 18: THE NEW YORK COMPETITION

1. *New York Times,* Feb. 27, 1910. According to the same source, the largest courthouse at the time was in Brussels, with thirty-six courtrooms.

2. Montgomery Schuyler, "New York's City Hall Park Problem," *The Outlook* 95 (July 23, 1910): 654 (quotation); and

Montgomery Schuyler, "The New York Courthouse and Its Site," *Architectural Record* 36 (July 1914): 1–7.

3. *New York Times,* Mar. 13, 1910; and "New York Courthouse Story in Brief," *Architectural Record* 36 (July 1914): 77. For more on the efforts to preserve City Hall Park, see Page, *The Creative Destruction of Manhattan,* 121–42.

4. *New York American,* May 1, 1910. It appears that Gordon's proposal and description for the New York County Courthouse was first published on April 30, 1910. In the following months, images of a model of the design appeared along with excerpts of Gordon's description in many eastern newspapers and journals, as evidenced in the JRG Collection, box 29.

5. *New York American,* May 1, 1910.

6. Lila Stilson, "James Riely Gordon and the Skycolumn: It Is as Logical Today as the Skyscraper Was 20 Years Ago," *Center* 2 (1986): 15.

7. Application numbers 70111–124, James Reily (*sic*) Gordon, San Antonio, TX, Dec. 1, 1898, Indexes and Catalogues of the US Copyright Office, Library of Congress.

8. Correspondence, Lucy Virginia Gordon Ralston to the author, June 8, 2000.

9. *New York Times,* Jan. 5, Jan. 19, and Jan. 20, 1912; and "New York Courthouse Story in Brief," 77–78.

10. *New York Times,* Feb. 2, May 28, June 1, Aug. 2, and Oct. 29, 1912; and *Programme of the Final Competition for the Selection of an Architect for the Court House in the City of New York,* The Court House Board, New York County, Dec. 18, 1912. JRG Collection, box 17, folder 13.

11. *New York Times,* May 11, 1913; and an unidentified newspaper clipping (ca. 1913), JRG Collection, box 29. See Appendix I for a list of participants.

12. *New York Times,* Apr. 14 (quotation) and May 19, 1913.

13. This description is drawn from an examination of drawings in the JRG Collection.

14. *New York Times,* May 11, 1913; and an unidentified newspaper clipping (ca. 1913), JRG Collection, box 29.

15. *New York Times,* Apr. 11 and Apr. 12 (first quotation), and May 11 (third quotation), 1913; and an unidentified newspaper clipping (ca. 1913), JRG Collection, box 29 (second quotation).

16. *New York Times,* Apr. 14, 1913.

17. Chester Holmes Aldrich, "Guy Lowell, 1870–1927," *Architecture* 55 (Apr. 1927): 190.

18. *Boston Post,* Aug. 28, 1910, JRG Collection, box 29.

CHAPTER 19: CAMBRIA

1. Cambria County Commissioners' *Minutes,* no. 4, pp. 369–70 (Apr. 21, 1914).

2. *Brief History, Cambria County*, n.d., vertical file, Cambria County Historical Society; and Wayne Slippy, "County Courthouse—Past and Present," *Barnesboro Star*, July 7, 1982, 9.

3. *Ebensburg Mountaineer-Herald*, Nov. 5, 1915; and Oliver P. Williams, *County Courthouses of Pennsylvania, a Guide* (Mechanicsburg, PA: Stackpole Books, 2001), 6.

4. Cambria County Commissioners' *Minutes*, no. 4, p. 380 (May 12, 1914) (first quotation); *Johnstown Tribune*, May 13, 1914 (second quotation); and Gordon v. County of Cambria, transcript, 18–24 and 48, JRG Collection, box 11, folder 9.

5. *Johnstown Tribune*, June 5, 1914; *Ebensburg Mountaineer-Herald*, Sept. 11, 1914; unidentified newspaper clippings [June and July 1914?], JRG Collection, box 29; and Cambria County Commissioners' *Minutes*, no. 4, p. 396 (Aug. 5, 1914) and p. 397 (Aug. 14, 1914).

6. Unidentified newspaper clipping (July 9, 1914), JRG Collection, box 29; and *Ebensburg Mountaineer-Herald*, Sept. 11, 1914.

7. *Ebensburg Mountaineer-Herald*, Nov. 10, Nov. 11, Nov. 17, and Nov. 27, 1914; and *Johnstown Tribune*, Dec. 10, 1915.

8. *Ebensburg Mountaineer-Herald*, Jan. 19 and Feb. 12, 1915.

9. *Ebensburg Mountaineer-Herald*, Apr. 9, 1915 (quotation); and Hitchcock and Seale, *Temples of Democracy*, 245–49.

10. *Ebensburg Mountaineer-Herald*, Sept. 17 and Nov. 5, 1915; and *Johnstown Tribune*, Dec. 10, 1915.

11. *Johnstown Tribune*, Dec. 10, 1915; and *Ebensburg Mountaineer-Herald*, Mar. 2, 1916.

12. *Johnstown Tribune*, Dec. 28, Dec. 30, 1915, and Apr. 26, 1916; and *Ebensburg Mountaineer-Herald*, Jan. 5, 1916.

13. *Johnstown Tribune*, Jan. 5, 1916.

14. *Johnstown Tribune*, Feb. 25 and Feb. 26 (second quotation), 1916; and *Ebensburg Mountaineer-Herald*, Mar. 2, 1916 (first quotation).

15. Cambria County Commissioners' *Minutes*, no. 4, p. 523 (Mar. 7, 1916) and pp. 525–29 (Mar. 8, 1916); *Ebensburg Mountaineer-Herald*, June 8 and June 15, 1916; and *Johnstown Tribune*, June 16, 1916.

16. *Johnstown Tribune*, June 22 and June 23, 1916.

17. Correspondence, JRG to Cambria County Board of Commissioners (hand dated Jan. 12, 1919), JRG Collection, box 18, folder 7.

18. Cambria County Commissioners' *Minutes*, no. 6, pp. 238–40 (June 19, 1922); and Gordon v. County of Cambria, transcript, 219.

19. Cambria County Commissioners *Minutes*, no. 6, p. 88 (Jan. 3, 1922) and p. 108 (Feb. 8, 1922); and Gordon v. County of Cambria, transcript, 74.

20. Cambria County Commissioners' *Minutes*, no. 6, pp. 504–7; *Johnstown Tribune*, Oct. 2, 1924; *Ebensburg Mountaineer-Herald*, Oct. 23, 1924 (quotation), and Aug. 6, 1925; and Gordon v. County of Cambria, transcript, 10.

21. This description is based on personal observation and Slippy, "County Courthouse—Past and Present," 9.

22. *Ebensburg Mountaineer-Herald*, Aug. 6, 1925; Cambria County Commissioners' *Minutes*, no. 6, p. 519 (June 11, 1926); and Gordon v. County of Cambria, transcript, 175.

23. Statement of Claim, James Riely Gordon v. County of Cambria, no. 5919, 1929, JRG Collection box 18, folder 8; and correspondence, L. S. Jones, Cambria County Solicitor, to Walter Lyson, May 19, 1930, JRG Collection, box 18, folder 7.

24. Unidentified newspaper clipping (ca. 1914), JRG Collection, box 29.

CHAPTER 20: PROFESSIONAL ORGANIZATIONS, CORTLAND, AND THE WORLD OF TOMORROW

1. Gordon-Ralston wedding invitation, JRG Collection, box 29; Carol Lyn Davis, "The Life and Career of James Riely Gordon, Architect, with an Analysis of Three Specific Texas County Courthouses" (master's thesis, Texas Christian University, 1975), 20; and interview with Lucy Virginia Gordon Ralston, Nov. 25, 2000.

2. *The Official Year Book of the New York Society of Architects* (New York: A. M. Madigan, 1911), 11–12.

3. *Official Year Book of the New York Society of Architects* (New York: A. M. Madigan, 1913), 5; and *Bulletin of the New York Society of Architects*, June 1926 (quotations, including *American Architect* excerpt).

4. Unidentified newspaper clipping (after 1913), JRG Collection, box 29.

5. Unidentified newspaper clipping (ca. 1914), JRG Collection, box 29; and *The Official Year Book of the New York Society of Architects* (New York: A. M. Madigan, 1922), 8–9.

6. *Supervisors' Journal, Cortland County. 1921*, p. 71 (Oct. 6, 1921); *Supervisors' Journal, Cortland County. 1922*, p. 15 (Mar. 15, 1922); and unidentified newspaper clipping, Cortland County Historical Society, courthouse vertical file.

7. *Supervisors' Journal, Cortland County. 1922*, pp. 33, 41–42 (June 7, 1922); *Cortland Standard*, Apr. 27 (quotation) and June 8, 1922; and unidentified newspaper clippings, Cortland County Historical Society, courthouse vertical file.

8. This description is drawn from the *Cortland Standard*, Apr. 27 and June 8, 1922; and personal observation.

9. Cortland County officials sold $800,000 worth of bonds to finance this project and some accounts erroneously attach that amount to the courthouse alone. As noted, the courthouse and jail bids totaled $578,112. Contracts for the plumbing, heating, electrical, and other work were let sepa-

rately and totaled $59,322. By the time the courthouse was completed, the county had purchased property at $19,550, with options to buy more. Furnishings, additional property purchases, fees (such as Gordon's commission), finance costs, and other incidentals likely cut into the $143,016 balance, leaving relatively little to be attributed to possible construction overruns. Unidentified newspaper clippings, Cortland County Historical Society, courthouse vertical file.

10. Correspondence, JRG to Arthur A. Seeligson, Jan. 17, 1925, JRG Collection, box 1, folder 4; and correspondence, unknown Cortland County official to John H. Black, Dec. 13, 1928, regarding Gordon's qualifications for a Franklin County, New York, courthouse. Also, a few years earlier, correspondence, Claude A. Swanson to W. E. Chilton, letter of introduction indicating Gordon's interest in the West Virginia Capitol project. Both in JRG Collection, box 1, folder 4.

11. *San Antonio Express*, Feb. 10, 1927.

12. Documents related to the New York City Building Code, 1929–1935, JRG Collection, box 5, folders 10 and 11; *New York Times*, June 21, 1936; and *New York Herald-Tribune*, Apr. 4, 1937.

13. *Bulletin of the New York Society of Architects*, June 1926 and Jan. 15 (second quotation) and Feb. 14 (first quotation), 1930; the New York Society of Architects Web site, http://www.nysarch.com/images/Past Presidents.pdf; and interview with Lucy Virginia Gordon Ralston, Oct. 29, 2003.

14. Application, James Riely Gordon, Feb. 27, 1930, American Institute of Architects Library and Archives; and correspondence, Egerton Swartwout to D. E. Waid, Mar. 14, 1930, JRG Collection, box 1, folder 4.

15. Davis, "The Life and Career of James Riely Gordon," 20; James Ward, *Architects in Practice, New York City, 1900–1940* (Union, NJ: Committee for the Preservation of Architectural Records, 1989), 30 (note: this source places Gordon's last office address as East 14th, but this seems to be a typo, as evidenced by the 1936–37, *New York City Telephone Directory*, 381); and interview with Lucy Virginia Gordon Ralston, Nov. 25, 2000 (quotation).

16. Correspondence, Maxwell A. Cantor to JRG, Feb. 14, 1936, JRG Collection, box 5, folder 1.

17. Ed Tyng, *Making a World's Fair* (New York: Vantage Press, 1958), 15–16, 25–26; and Eugene A. Santomasso, "The 1939 New York World's Fair Three Years Before: Controversy and Architectural Competition," *Arts Magazine* 52 (Nov. 1977): 112, n. 8. Voorhees was the AIA president at the time and a partner in Voorhees, Gmelin and Walker.

18. Correspondence, John T. Briggs, secretary, New York Society of Architects, to JRG, Jan. 16, 1936; correspondence, William W. Del Gaudio, president, New York Society of Architects to "Dear Member," Jan. 29, 1937, both JRG Collection, box 17, folder 13; and Santomasso, "The 1939 New York World's Fair Three Years Before," 108.

19. Correspondence, JRG to Stephen F. Voorhees, Chairman, Board of Design, World's Fair, Jan. 27, 1937, JRG Collection, box 17, folder 13. Some architects competed for fair work and some were directly selected. Judging from the content of this correspondence, it appears Gordon did not pursue this commission aggressively, which leads me to assume that it was a reward.

20. Interview with Lucy Virginia Gordon Ralston, Nov. 25, 2000.

21. *Pelham Sun*, Mar. 26, 1937; and *New York Herald-Tribune*, Apr. 4, 1937 (quotation).

CHAPTER 21: SUMMATION

1. *New York Times*, Mar. 17, 1937; and Henry F. Withey and Elsie Rathurn Withey, *Biographical Dictionary of American Architects* (1956; repr. Los Angeles: Hennessy & Ingalls, 1970; repr. Detroit: Omnigraphics, 1996), 241–42.

2. *Cortland Standard*, Apr. 27, 1922.

3. *Hinners Report*, 242.

4. *Cortland Standard*, Apr. 27, 1922.

5. An example of the latter is the Bandera County Courthouse. B. F. Trester, Jr., was its designer, and the contract was let in July 1890. It was likely still under construction in February 1891, when the forty-five-year-old architect died suddenly of pneumonia and Trester's widow arranged to have Gordon & Laub complete his unfinished work. Gordon may have included the construction in his tally of "over seventy." *San Antonio Daily Express*, June 15, 1890, and Feb. 15 and Mar. 10, 1891.

6. Vitae for James Riely Gordon (New York Society of Architects), Nov. 10, 1932, typescript, JRG Collection, box 4, folder 5.

7. See Appendix IV.

8. Interview with Lucy Virginia Gordon Ralston, Oct. 29, 2003. A program for the April 1931 AIA Annual Convention in San Antonio that is among his office papers suggests he may have returned to the city for another visit. JRG Collection, box 4, folder 5.

9. In addition, Carol Lyn Davis tells of work done by Willard E. Gwilliam, a Phoenix architect, and Glenn Patton of Trinity University, San Antonio. In my travels I have come across letters and other documents by them to indicate at least parts of my path had been tread before. Patton penned the worthy entry on Gordon in *The New Handbook of Texas*, which appears to be the only work by either to see publication. Davis, "The Life and Career of James Riely Gordon," 2–3; and Glenn N. Patton, "James Riely Gordon," in Tyler et al., eds., *The New Handbook of Texas*, 3:248–49.

Bibliography

Government meeting minutes, city directories, and information in archival files are identified in the notes but not enumerated below. Likewise, journal, magazine, and newspaper sources are cited in the notes but only included here if an author is identified.

BOOKS

Aransas County, a Glimpse at Our Past. Rockport, TX: Aransas County–Rockport Centennial, Inc., 1970.

Bancroft, Hubert Howe. *The Book of the Fair.* Chicago: Bancroft Company, 1893; repr., New York: Bounty Books, 1972.

Beaulieu, Jill, and Mary Roberts, eds. *Orientalism's Interlocutors: Painting, Architecture, Photography.* Durham, NC: Duke University Press, 2002.

Betts, Mary Beth. "Cass Gilbert: Twelve Projects." In *Inventing the Skyline: The Architecture of Cass Gilbert*, edited by Margaret Heilbrun, 83–175. New York: Columbia University Press, 2000.

Biel, Gail K. "Cornelius Grandbery Lancaster." In *The New Handbook of Texas*, edited by Ron Tyler, Douglas E. Barnett, Roy R. Barkley, Penelope C. Anderson, and Mark F. Odintz, 4:52. Austin: The Texas State Historical Association, 1996.

Booth, John A., and David R. Johnson. "Power and Progress in San Antonio Politics, 1836–1970." In *The Politics of San Antonio: Community, Progress and Power*, edited by David R. Johnson, John A. Booth, and Richard J. Harris, 3–27. Lincoln: University of Nebraska Press, 1983.

Brasseaux, Carl A., Glen R. Conrad, and R. Warren Robinson. *The Courthouses of Louisiana*, 2nd ed. Lafayette: University of Southwestern Louisiana, 1997.

Breisch, Kenneth L. "The Richardsonian Interlude in Texas: A Quest for Meaning and Order at the End of the Nineteenth Century." In *The Spirit of H. H. Richardson on the Midland Prairies: Regional Transformations of an American Style*, edited by Paul C. Larson and Susan M. Brown, 86–105. Ames: Iowa State University Press, 1988.

Brooks, David B. *Texas Practice Series.* Vol. 35, *County and Special District Law*, 2nd ed. St. Paul, MN: West-Thompson Publishing Company, 2002.

Brooks, Michael W. *John Ruskin and American Architecture.* New Brunswick, NJ: Rutgers University Press, 1987.

Burnham, Daniel H. *The Final Official Report of the Director of Works of the World's Columbian Exposition, Facsimile Edition.* New York: Garland Publishing, 1989.

Carman, Michael D. *Under the Copper Dome: The Arizona Capitol, 1898–1974.* Phoenix: The Arizona Capitol Museum, 2001.

Carson, Chris, and William McDonald, eds. *A Guide to San Antonio Architecture.* San Antonio, TX: San Antonio Chapter of the American Institute of Architects, 1986.

Conrad, Glen R. "The Origin and Development of Local Administration in Louisiana." In *The Courthouses of Louisiana*, 2nd ed., edited by Carl A. Brasseaux, Glen R. Conrad, and R. Warren Robinson, vii–x. Lafayette: University of Southwestern Louisiana, 1997.

Corner, William, ed. *San Antonio de Bexar.* San Antonio, TX: Bainbridge and Corner, 1890; repr., San Antonio, TX: Graphic Arts, 1977.

Creighton, James A. *A Narrative History of Brazoria County.* Brazoria, TX: Brazoria County Historical Commission, 1974.

Crouch, Dora P., Daniel J. Garr, and Axel I. Mundingo. *Spanish City Planning in North America.* Cambridge, MA: MIT Press, 1982.

Cruz, Gilbert R. *Let There Be Towns: Spanish Municipal Origins in the American Southwest, 1610–1810.* College Station: Texas A&M University Press, 1988.

Cutrer, Emily F. *The Art of the Woman: The Life and Work of Elisabet Ney.* Lincoln: University of Nebraska Press, 1988.

Davis, Ellis A., and Edwin H. Grobe, eds. *The Encyclopedia of Texas.* Dallas: Texas Development Bureau, 1926.

The Dream City, World's Fair Art Series. Vol. 1, no. 14. St. Louis, MO: N. D. Thompson Publishing Company, 1894.

Edwards, Holly, ed. *Nobel Dreams, Wicked Pleasures: Orientalism in America, 1870–1930.* Princeton, NJ: Princeton University Press, 2000.

"Egerton Swartwout." In *Who's Who in New York (City and State), 1924*, edited by Frank R. Holmes, 1217. New York: Who's Who Publications, 1924.

Francis, Dennis Steadman. *Architects in Practice, New York City, 1840–1900*. New York: Committee for the Preservation of Architectural Records, Inc., 1979.

Gregg, Rosalie, ed. *Wise County History, a Link with the Past*. N.p.: Nortex Press, 1975.

A Guide to the Architecture of Metro Phoenix. Phoenix: Central Arizona Chapter of the American Institute of Architects, 1983.

Guthrie, Keith. *The History of San Patricio County*. Austin, TX: Nortex Press, 1986.

Hafertepe, Kenneth. *Abner Cook: Master Builder on the Texas Frontier*. Austin: Texas State Historical Association, 1992.

Handbook of the World's Columbian Exposition. Chicago: Rand, McNally and Company, 1893.

Heilbrun, Margaret, ed. *Inventing the Skyline: The Architecture of Cass Gilbert*. New York: Columbia University Press, 2000.

Heusinger, Edward W. *A Chronology of Events in San Antonio*. San Antonio, TX: Standard Printing Company, 1951.

Hines, Thomas S. *Burnham of Chicago*. New York: Oxford University Press, 1974.

The History of Gonzales County, Texas. Gonzales, TX: Gonzales County Historical Commission, 1986.

A History of Real Estate, Building and Architecture in New York City During the Last Quarter Century. New York: The Real Estate Record Association, 1898; repr., New York: Arno Press, 1967.

The History of Van Zandt County, Texas. Wills Point, TX: Van Zandt County History Book Committee, 1984.

Hitchcock, Henry-Russell. *Richardson as Victorian Architect*. Northampton, MA: Smith College, 1966.

Hitchcock, Henry-Russell, and William Seale. *Temples of Democracy, the State Capitols of the USA*. New York: Harcourt Brace Jovanovich, 1976.

Holliday, Kathryn E. *Leopold Eidlitz: Architecture and Idealism in the Gilded Age*. New York: W. W. Norton, 2008.

Holmes, Frank R., ed. *Who's Who in New York (City and State), 1924*. New York: Who's Who Publications, 1924.

Hopkins County Pictorial History. Sulphur Springs, TX: Hopkins County Historical Society, 1987.

Irish, Sharon. "Cass Gilbert in Practice, 1882–1934." In *Inventing the Skyline: The Architecture of Cass Gilbert*, edited by Margaret Heilbrun, 1–34. New York: Columbia University Press, 2000.

James, Herman G. *County Government in Texas*. University of Texas Bulletin, no. 1732, Municipal Research Series, no. 15. Austin: University Publications, University of Texas–Austin, 1917.

Jutson, Mary Carolyn Hollers. *Alfred Giles: An English Architect in Texas and Mexico*. San Antonio, TX: Trinity University Press, 1972.

Kansas City: Its Resources and Their Development. Kansas City, MO: Kansas City Times, 1890.

Kelsey, Mavis P., Sr., and Donald H. Dyal. *The Courthouses of Texas*. College Station: Texas A&M University Press, 1993.

Kestenbaum, Joy M. "Alfred Zucker." In *Macmillan Encyclopedia of Architects*, edited by Adolf K. Placzek, 4:476. New York: The Free Press, 1982.

Larson, Paul C., and Susan M. Brown, eds. *The Spirit of H. H. Richardson on the Midland Prairies: Regional Transformations of an American Style*. Ames: Iowa State University Press, 1988.

Lee, Antoinette J. *Architects to the Nation: The Rise and Decline of the Supervising Architect's Office*. New York: Oxford University Press, 2000.

Lehman, Donald J. *Lucky Landmark: A Study of a Design and Its Survival, The Galveston Custom House, Post Office and Courthouse of 1861*. Washington, DC: General Services Administration Public Building Service, 1973.

Lessoff, Alan. *The Nation and Its City: Politics, "Corruption," and Progress in Washington, D.C., 1861–1902*. Baltimore, MD: Johns Hopkins University Press, 1994.

Lindsey, Philip. *A History of Greater Dallas and Vicinity*. Chicago: Lewis Publishing Company, 1909.

Little, Carol Morris. *Historic Harrison County as Preserved Through Official Texas Historical Markers*. Longview, TX: Carol Morris Little, 1984.

Lotto, F. *Fayette County, Her History and Her People*. Schulenburg, TX: Sticker Steam Press, 1902.

Lowry, Bullitt, ed. *Building the Denton County Courthouse 1895–1897*. Denton, TX: Denton County Historical Commission, 1987.

Martin, Roscoe. *The People's Party in Texas*. Austin: University of Texas Press, 1970.

Meister, Maureen, ed. *H. H. Richardson: The Architect, His Peers, and Their Era*. Cambridge, MA: MIT Press, 1999.

Mills, W. S. *History of Van Zandt County*. Canton, TX: privately published, 1950.

Morrison, Andrew. *The City of San Antonio*. St. Louis, MO: George W. Engelhardt, n.d.; repr., San Antonio: Norman Brock, 1977.

The National Cyclopedia of American Biography. Vol. 28. New York: James T. White & Company, 1940.

Neville, A. W. *The History of Lamar County*. Paris: North Texas Publishing Company, 1937.

O'Gorman, James F. *Three American Architects: Richardson, Sullivan, and Wright, 1865–1915*. Chicago: University of Chicago Press, 1991.

The Official Year Book of the New York Society of Architects. New York: A. M. Madigan, 1911, 1913, 1922.

Page, Max. *The Creative Destruction of Manhattan, 1900–1940.* Chicago: University of Chicago Press, 1999.

Paris, William Francklyn. *Personalities in American Art.* 1930; repr., Freeport, NY: Books for Libraries Press, 1970.

Parran, Alice Norris. *The Evolution of Patriotic Ancestry from Year 1 B.C. to Year 1939 A.D., Series II of the "Register of Maryland's Heraldic Families."* Baltimore, MD: Alice Norris Parran, 1938.

Patton, Glenn N. "James Riely Gordon." In *The New Handbook of Texas,* edited by Ron Tyler, Douglass E. Barnett, Roy R. Barkley, Penelope C. Anderson, and Mark F. Odintz, 3:248–49. Austin: The Texas State Historical Association, 1996.

Poage, W. R. (Bob). *McLennan County—Before 1980.* Waco, TX: Texian Press, 1981.

Quirarte, Jacinto. *The Art and Architecture of the Texas Missions.* Austin: University of Texas Press, 2002.

Ramsdell, Charles. *San Antonio: A Historical and Pictorial Guide,* rev. ed. Austin: University of Texas Press, 1979.

Ransome, Ernest L., and Saurbrey, Alexis. *Reinforced Concrete Buildings.* New York: McGraw-Hill Book Company, 1912.

Richardson, Henry Hobson. "Description of the Church." In *Consecration Services of Trinity Church, Boston, 1877,* repr. in *Trinity Church in the City of Boston, Massachusetts, 1733–1933,* ed. Wardens and Vestry of Trinity Church, 185–98. Boston: Merrymount Press, 1933.

Robinson, Willard B. *The People's Architecture: Texas Courthouses, Jails, and Municipal Buildings.* Austin: Texas State Historical Association, 1983.

Roth, Leland M. *McKim, Mead & White, Architects.* New York: Harper & Row, 1983.

Saylor, Henry H. *The A.I.A.'s First Hundred Years.* Washington, DC: American Institute of Architects, 1957.

Scardino, Barrie, and Turner, Drexel. *Clayton's Galveston: The Architecture of Nicholas J. Clayton and His Contemporaries.* College Station: Texas A&M University Press, 2000.

Sketches from the Portfolio of James Riely Gordon, Architect. St. Louis, MO: A. B. Benesch, 1896.

Smith, Darrell Hevenor. *The Office of the Supervising Architect of the United States Treasury: Its History, Activities and Organization.* Baltimore, MD: Johns Hopkins Press, 1923; repr., New York: AMS Press, 1974.

Smith, Hank Todd, ed. *Austin: Its Architects and Architecture (1836–1986).* Austin, TX: American Institute of Architects, Austin Chapter, 1986.

———. *Since 1886: A History of the Texas Society of Architects.* Austin: Texas Society of Architects, 1983.

Some Work from the Office of Sanguinet and Staats, Successors to Messer, Sanguinet and Messer, Architects, Fort Worth, Texas. Xerographic copy in the collection of the Amon Carter Museum, Fort Worth, 1896.

Staff of the Handbook of Texas. *Handbook of Victoria County.* Austin: Texas State Historical Association, 1990.

Strother, David. "Introduction." In *Building the Denton County Courthouse,* edited by Bullitt Lowry, 3–10. Denton, TX: Denton County Historical Commission, 1987.

Tyng, Ed. *Making a World's Fair.* New York: Vantage Press, 1958.

Van Rensselaer, Marianna Griswold. *Henry Hobson Richardson and His Works.* Boston: Houghton Mifflin and Company, 1888; facsimile edition with a new introduction by William Morgan, New York: Dover Publications, 1969.

Veselka, Robert A. *The Courthouse Square in Texas.* Austin: University of Texas Press, 2000.

Ward, James. *Architects in Practice, New York City, 1900–1940.* Union, NJ: Committee for the Preservation of Architectural Records, 1989.

Weldon, Fred. *Carved Ornament of the Ellis County Courthouse.* Waxahachie, TX: Ellis County History Museum, 1995.

Wermiel, Sara E. *The Fireproof Building.* Baltimore, MD: Johns Hopkins University Press, 2000.

White, Trumbull, and William Igleheart. *The World's Columbian Exposition, Chicago, 1893.* Philadelphia: World Publishing Company, 1893.

Whitehead Memorial Museum. *La Hacienda.* Norman: University of Oklahoma Press, 1976.

Williams, Oliver P. *County Courthouses of Pennsylvania, a Guide.* Mechanicsburg, PA: Stackpole Books, 2001.

Withey, Henry F., and Elsie Rathurn Withey. *Biographical Dictionary of American Architects.* 1956; repr., Los Angeles: Hennessy & Ingalls, 1970; repr., Detroit: Omnigraphics, 1996.

Woods, Mary N. *From Craft to Profession: The Practice of Architecture in Nineteenth-Century America.* Berkeley: University of California Press, 1999.

Writers' Program of the Work Projects Administration, *Bergen County Panorama: American Guide Series.* Hackensack, NJ: The Bergen County Board of Chosen Freeholders, 1941.

ARTICLES

Alderman, Ed. "Great Lake Charles Fire Was 75 Years Ago." *Lake Charles American Press,* Apr. 21, 1985.

Aldrich, Chester Holmes. "Guy Lowell, 1870–1927." *Architecture* 55 (Apr. 1927): 189–92.

Barney, James M. "Planning for First Capitol Started Heated Disputes." *Phoenix Gazette,* May 25, 1957.

Barrett, Eleanor. "Renovation of County Courthouse Cleans Up in Awards Department." *Star-Ledger* (Newark), Oct. 5, 1997, sec. 1, 39.

Blacksaw, Randall. "The New New York." *Century* 64 (Aug. 1902): 493–513.

Blackwell, James E. "United States Government Building Practice." *The American Architect and Building News* 21 (Feb. 5, 1887): 65.

Brinkman, Bob, and Dan K. Utley. "A Name on the Cornerstone: The Landmark Texas Architecture of Jasper Newton Preston." *Southwestern Historical Quarterly* 110 (July 2006): 1–36.

Bryant, Claude W. "Historic Erath County Courthouse Stands Test." *Stephenville Empire-Tribune*, Dec. 15, 1961.

Buchen, Charlotte. "Ornate Copper Dome Sparks Capitol Plan." *Arizona Republic*, Mar. 17, 1957.

Clark, Percy. "New Federal Buildings." *Harper's Weekly*, May 19, 1888, 368.

Connor, Seymour V. "Evolution of County Government in the Republic of Texas." *Southwestern Historical Quarterly* 55 (Oct. 1951): 163–200.

"The Court House Award," *Architectural Record* 33 (May 1913): 469.

Goeldner, Paul. "Our Architectural Ancestors." *Texas Architect* 24 (July/Aug. 1974): 5–8.

Green, William Elton. "'A Question of Great Delicacy': The Texas State Capitol Competition, 1881." *Southwestern Historical Quarterly* 92 (Oct. 1988): 247–70.

Grossman, Elizabeth Greenwell. "H. H. Richardson: Lessons from Paris." *Journal of the Society of Architectural Historians* 67 (Sept. 2008): 388–411.

Hair, Velma Lea. "The History of Crowley, Louisiana." *Louisiana Historical Quarterly* 27 (Oct. 1944): 1119–225.

"History of Garrett Co. Courthouses: New Complex to Answer Growth." *The Glades Star* 5 (Mar. 1981): 310–15.

Hale, Edward. "H. H. Richardson and His Work." *New England Magazine* 17 (Dec. 1894): 513–32.

Hogan, Peg. "Madison County Courthouses." *Historic CNY* 9 (2001): 7–12.

"John W. Garrett." *The Glades Star* 1 (June 30, 1949): 352–53.

King, Edward. "Glimpses of Texas—I: A Visit to San Antonio." *Scribner's Monthly* 7 (Jan. 1874): 302–30.

Lancaster, Clay. "Oriental Forms in American Architecture." *The Art Bulletin* 24 (Sept. 1947): 183–91.

Lane, M. A. "State Buildings at the Fair." *Harper's Weekly*, Aug. 20, 1892, 813.

Longstreth, Richard W. "Academic Eclecticism in American Architecture." *Winterthur Portfolio* 17 (Spring 1982): 55–82.

Meeks, Carroll L. V. "Picturesque Eclecticism." *The Art Bulletin* 32 (Sept. 1950): 226–35.

———. "Romanesque Before Richardson in the United States." *The Art Bulletin* 35 (Mar. 1953): 17–33.

Meister, Chris. "Alfred Giles vs. El Paso County: An Architect Defends His Reputation on the Texas Frontier." *Southwestern Historical Quarterly* 108 (Oct. 2004): 181–209.

———. "The Texas State Building: J. Riely Gordon's Contribution to the World's Columbian Exposition." *Southwestern Historical Quarterly* 98 (July 1994): 1–24.

Moffett, Carolyn. "Long Life Still Happy Claims 92-Year Old." *Lake Charles American Press*, May 11, 1975.

"New York Courthouse Story in Brief." *Architectural Record* 36 (July 1914): 77–78.

"Present County Buildings." *The Glades Star* 1 (June 30, 1949): 353.

Price, Edward T. "The Central Courthouse Square in the American County Seat." *Geographical Review* 58 (Jan. 1968): 29–60.

Robinson, Willard B. "The Public Square as a Determinant of Courthouse Form in Texas." *Southwestern Historical Quarterly* 75 (Jan. 1972): 339–72.

Santomasso, Eugene A. "The 1939 New York World's Fair Three Years Before: Controversy and Architectural Competition." *Arts Magazine* 52 (Nov. 1977): 108–12.

Schuyler, Montgomery. "Last Words about the World's Fair." *Architectural Record* 3 (Jan.–Mar. 1894): 291–301.

———. "The New York Courthouse and Its Site." *Architectural Record* 36 (July 1914): 1–11.

———. "New York's City Hall Park Problem." *The Outlook* 95 (July 23, 1910): 647–56.

———. "State Buildings at the World's Fair." *Architectural Record* 3 (July–Sept. 1893): 55–71.

Slippy, Wayne. "County Courthouse—Past and Present." *Barnesboro Star*, July 7, 1982, 9.

Stebbins, Theodore E., Jr. "Richardson and Trinity Church: The Evolution of a Building." *Journal of the Society of Architectural Historians* 27 (Dec. 1968): 281–98.

Stilson, Lila. "James Riely Gordon and the Skycolumn: It Is as Logical Today as the Skyscraper Was 20 Years Ago." *Center* 2 (1986): 13–17.

Swartwout, Egerton. "Evarts Tracy." *Journal of the American Institute of Architects* 10 (Mar. 1922): 94.

Toth, John. "Courthouse Never Saw County Service." *Houston Chronicle*, Oct. 31, 1983.

Tyrrell, Joe. "State Asked to Help Preserve Old Somerset Jail." *Star-Ledger* (Newark, NJ), Jan. 12, 1992, sec. 1, 39.

Weisiger, Sidney R. "Courthouse Construction." *Victoria Advocate*, July 4, 1971.

INTERNET SOURCES

Schartz, Eileen. "Law and Mortar: Texas Takes the Stand for Historic Preservation." *Texas Construction*. Feb. 2004. http://texas.construction.com/features/archive/0402_cover.asp.

New York Society of Architects. Accessed May 29, 2004. http://www.nysarch.com/images/Past Presidents.pdf.

UNPUBLISHED SOURCES

Boethel, Martha. "A History of the Lee County Courthouse." Undated typescript. Courtesy of the Lee County Clerk's Office.

Bogert, Fred. "Background on Bergen County Courthouse." Typescript A-0109(1) 3TB. Fred Bogert Collection, Bergen County Historical Archives.

Davis, Carol Lyn. "The Life and Career of James Riely Gordon, Architect, with an Analysis of Three Specific Texas County Courthouses." Master's thesis, Texas Christian University, 1975.

Killen, Mrs. James C., ed., and Lee County Historical Survey Committee. *A History of Lee County, Texas.* Nortex Press, 1974.

Orren, G. G. "The History of Hopkins County." Master's thesis, East Texas State Teachers College, 1938.

"Our Court House." Undated typescript, George W. Covington Memorial Library, Hazelhurst, TX.

GOVERNMENT DOCUMENTS

Bergen County Historic Sites Survey, Volume One: City of Hackensack. Hackensack, NJ: Bergen County Board of Chosen Freeholders, 1980–81.

Department of the Interior, Census Division. *Abstract of the Eleventh Census: 1890,* 2nd ed. Washington, DC: Government Printing Office, 1896.

Hinners, William H., James C. Agnew, John J. Bracken, Charles M. Egan, and Thomas R. Layden. *Report of Bergen County Investigating Committee, Hackensack, N.J., Thursday, October 5th, 1911.*

Mississippi House Journal. extr. sess., Apr. 27, 1897.

Mississippi House Journal. reg. sess., Jan., Feb., and Mar. 1900.

Mississippi House Journal. sp. sess., Jan., Feb., and Mar. 1902.

Programme of the Final Competition for the Selection of an Architect for the Court House in the City of New York. The Court House Board, New York County, Dec. 18, 1912.

Prospectus of the Requirements for the Territorial Capitol Building to Be Erected in Phoenix, Arizona. Phoenix: Capitol Grounds and Building Commission, n.d.

Report of the Capitol Commission. Phoenix: Capitol Grounds and Building Commission, Jan. 1, 1901.

Transcriptions of the Parish Records of Louisiana, No. 31 Lincoln Parish (Ruston), Series I. Police Jury Minutes. Vol. II, 1891–1908. Works Projects Administration, Statewide Records Project, Professional and Service Division.

US Congress, House. *Public Building at San Antonio, Tex.* Rep. No. 459 to Accompany H. 4465, 47th Cong., 1st sess., 1882.

US Congress, House. *Public Building, San Antonio, Tex.* Rep. No. 1280 to Accompany H. 3441, 48th Cong., 1st sess., 1884.

US Congress, House. *Public Building at San Antonio, Tex.* Rep. No. 614 to Accompany S. 44, 49th Cong., 1st sess., 1886.

COURT DECISIONS

Callaghan, County Judge v. Salliway. 23 S.W. 837–839 (Tex. Ct. App. 1893).

Clayton et al. v. Galveston County. 50 S.W. 737–740 (Tex. Ct. App. 1899).

Gordon v. County of Cambria. Transcript. JRG Collection, box 11, folder 9.

Gordon v. Denton County. 48 S.W. 737–741 (Tex. Ct. App. 1899).

REPORTS AND EPHEMERA

Harrison County (Texas) Courthouse Historic Structures Report. Architexas, 1999.

Historic Structures Report: Bergen County Justice Complex, Hackensack, New Jersey. Prepared by Ford Farewell Mills and Gatsch, Architects, Princeton, NJ, for the County of Bergen, Department of Public Works, Dec. 1993.

Sutphen, Arthur P. *Souvenir of the Opening of the Somerset County Courthouse, March, 1909.*

Index

Quinby, Frank H., **267**

Rabitt, Patrick S., 92, 152, 284
Ralston, Byron Brown (son-in-law of JRG), 265, **273**
Ralston, Lucy Virginia (née Gordon, daughter of JRG), 102, 216, **273**, 278
  marriage, 265
Ralston, Lucy Virginia Gordon (granddaughter of JRG), 172, 265, **273**, 274, 278
Ransome twisted iron method, 290, 291
Rapides Parish, Louisiana, Courthouse (Hull & Hull), 203
  award to Hull & Hull, 205
  Gordon's design, 203–5, **204**, 288, 295
Raritan, New Jersey, 217
Republican Party
  on Bexar "County Ticket," 59
  influence on San Antonio Federal Building, 16, 26
Richardson, Henry Hobson, 20, 42–43, 175
  "Auvergnat solution," 108, 131, 139
Richardsonian Romanesque, 42–45, 100, 174
  Gordon's exposure to, 20, 43
Richter & Lieber, 285
Rockport, Texas, 27, 30–32, 36, 39–40, **39**
Ruskin, John, 32, 123, 175
Ruston, Louisiana, 205

Sacrey, George F., 28, 45–46
Salliway, Henry B., 60, 64–65, 73
San Antonio, Texas
  Gordon family's move to, 3
  Gordon's return visits to, 270, 315n8
  Main Plaza, 4, 54, 57, 64, 66, **74**, 300n3
  Military Plaza, 4, **5**, 24, **25**, 54
  most expensive buildings ca. 1891, 298n42
  town plan of, 3–4
  state in 1873, 4
San Antonio Central High School (W. K. Dobson), **10**
San Antonio City Hall (Otto Kramer), 24, **25**, 54, 55, 56, 64, 283
San Antonio City Hall (unrealized 1887 joint city-county building project), 23, 24
San Antonio Rifles, 17
San Patricio, Texas, 119–20
San Patricio County, Texas, Courthouse (J. R. Gordon), 119–20, **121**, 124, 285, 292, 294
San Patricio County, Texas, Jail (J. R. Gordon), 120, **121**, 124
Sanguinet, Marshal L. See also Messer, Sanguinet & Messer; Sanguinet & Messer

collusion with Martin and Hull (the Jail Man), 151–55, 183, 309n27
  superintends Ellis courthouse construction, 129, 133–34
Sanguinet & Messer, 151–53, 286. See also Messer, Sanguinet & Messer
Schultze, August, Jr., 157–58
Schutte, E. J., 286
Schuyler, Montgomery, 94–95, 98, 238, 303n22
Shelton, Frederick B., 11, 17. See also Gordon & Shelton
Shepley, Rutan & Coolidge, 306n20
Shire & Kaufmann, 289
Shreveport, Louisiana, 177
Signature Plan, 37, 100–101, 106–8, **107**, 141–42, 290–91, **292**
Singleton, D. F, 125–27
Sinton, Texas, 120
Sioux County, Iowa, Courthouse, possible Gordon design for, 295
Sketches from the Portfolio of James Riely Gordon, Architect, San Antonio, Texas, 148–49
Smith (Mississippi State Representative), 180
Smith, J. W., 205
Smith, Sidney, 284
Snider and Churchill, 288
Snook, T. E., **267**
Somerset County, New Jersey, Courthouse (Gordon, Tracy and Swartwout), 217–20, **218**, **219**, 289, 293, 295, **C-18**, **C-19**
Somerset County, New Jersey, Jail (Gordon, Tracy and Swartwout), 217, **218**, 220
Somerset plan, **293**
Somerville, New Jersey, 217
Sonnefield & Emmins, 112, 116, 135, 173, 178
Sonnefield, Emmins & Albright, 160
Southern Architect, 103
Spanish Colonial. See also Law of the Indies
  architecture in Texas, 4, 30, 34–35
  Gordon's appropriation of motifs, **67**, 68, 70, **93**, 98, **99**, **118**, **119**
  town planning in Texas, 3–4
Sprigg, James Cresap (JRG's father-in-law), 43
Staacke Brothers Building (J. R. Gordon), 270
Stephenville, Texas, 76–77
Stevens, W. L., 207, 211
Stevens Building (Gordon & Laub), 270
Stewart, George W., 92, 284
Stokes, J. W., 202–3
Stone Brothers Company, 288
Stowe, George B., 286, 287
Stuckert, A. Morris, 284
Sullivan, Louis H., 91

Sulphur Springs, Texas, 112
superintendence, defined, 7
Supervising Architect of the United States Treasury, Office of, 15, 34, 40, 53
  regarding the US Courthouse and Post office, San Antonio, 16–28
supervision, defined, 7
Sutcliffe, John, 284
Swartwout, Egerton, 216–17, 271, 275, 312n6. See also Gordon, Tracy and Swartwout; Tracy, Swartwout & Litchfield

Tarrant County, Texas, Courthouse (Gunn & Curtiss), 104–5, **105**
  competition, 103–4, 284
  Gordon's design for, 103–4, **104**, 294
Taylor, Isaac, 306n20
Teich, Frank, 62, 86, 302n20
Texas Historic Courthouse Preservation Program, 279
Texas State Association of Architects (TSAA), 31, 44–45, 88, 90, 103, 118, 135, 272
  disbands, 156
  formation 13–14
  Gordon's involvement in, 31, 103, 156
Texas State Building (J. R. Gordon), 89–101, **92**, **93**, **95**, **97**, **99**, 106, 284, 303n23
Texas World's Fair Exhibit Association, 90–92, 94
36 Gramercy Park East Apartments (J. R. Gordon), 265
T. H. Maddox & Son, 287
Thomas, Andrew J., **267**
Thomas, S. Seymour, 99
Thompson, R. H., 182, 184, 309n23
Tobin, Benedette, 94, 99, 100
Todd, Hugh, 286
Tomlinson, S.A., 77
Torgerson, Guissart and Ginder, 284
town squares in urban planning, 38, 299n14
Tracy, Evarts, 216, 309n27. See also Gordon, Tracy and Swartwout; Tracy, Swartwout & Litchfield
Tracy, Swartwout & Litchfield, 245, 289, 309n27
Trester, Benjamin F., Jr., 315n5
Trinity Church, Boston (H. H. Richardson), **42**, 106, 108, **110**, 131, **132**, 139
Trowbridge & Livingston, 289
Tweed, William Marcy ("Boss"), 238
Tweed Courthouse, 238, **239**, 240, 243, 245, 247, **251**, 252
Tyler County, Texas, Courthouse (T. S. Hodges), 117

The author and Texas Tech University Press are deeply grateful for the generosity of The Summerlee Foundation, whose support has made publication of this work possible.